# When Left Moves Right

# When Left Moves Right

## *The Decline of the Left and the Rise of the Populist Right in Postcommunist Europe*

### MARIA SNEGOVAYA

OXFORD
UNIVERSITY PRESS

# OXFORD
## UNIVERSITY PRESS

Oxford University Press is a department of the University of Oxford. It furthers
the University's objective of excellence in research, scholarship, and education
by publishing worldwide. Oxford is a registered trade mark of Oxford University
Press in the UK and certain other countries.

Published in the United States of America by Oxford University Press
198 Madison Avenue, New York, NY 10016, United States of America.

Library of Congress Control Number: 2023945792

ISBN 978-0-19-769903-4 (pbk.)
ISBN 978-0-19-769902-7 (hbk.)

DOI: 10.1093/oso/9780197699027.001.0001

Paperback printed by Marquis Book Printing, Canada
Hardback printed by Bridgeport National Bindery, Inc., United States of America

# Contents

# What Happens when Left Moves Right?

## The Puzzle

When historians look back on Europe in the early twenty-first century, they will look first at the seemingly miraculous rise of the populist right. Over the past two decades the number of right-wing parties in Europe almost doubled, while support for them more than tripled. Populist right parties gained enough votes to put their leaders into government positions in eleven European countries (Eiermann, Mounk, and Gultchin 2017; Lewis et al. 2018). Right-wing populism is particularly strong and pervasive in Eastern Europe. Populist right parties often outcompete mainstream parties there and have come to power in Hungary and Poland. Since 2000, when Eastern European populist parties took an average of 9.2% of the national vote, their vote share has tripled, reaching 31.6% in 2017 (Eiermann, Mounk, and Gultchin 2017). In some Eastern European countries, right-wing populism has become so pervasive that the main competitors to populist governments are themselves right-wing populists. (For example, in Hungary the populist right Jobbik Magyarországért Mozgalom, Jobbik) party grew to become the main challenger of the populist right Fidesz – Magyar Polgári Szövetség (Fidesz) party. Right-wing populist leaders often embrace and promote xenophobic stances and socially conservative values and when in power implement illiberal reforms, which undermine institutional checks and dismantle the key cornerstones of democracy (Bustikova and Guasti 2017; Bugarič 2019; Grzymala-Busse 2019c). The implications of this phenomenon for the resilience of democracy in the region are therefore tremendous. What explains the dramatic rise of such parties? My book offers a new theory.

The story of communist successor parties in postcommunist Europe presents an interesting conundrum. Throughout the 1990s many leftist parties in Central and Eastern Europe defied predictions that they would sink into oblivion after democratic transition by winning elections all over the region. One popular explanation of leftist parties' electoral success in the

*When Left Moves Right.* Maria Snegovaya, Oxford University Press. © Oxford University Press 2024.
DOI: 10.1093/oso/9780197699027.003.0001

early 1990s focused on their ability to rebrand, embrace social-democratic platforms, and actively promote accession to the European Union in their countries (Grzymala-Busse 2002b). But if this were the case, what explains their sudden change of fate a decade later, when the left's popularity plummeted all over the region, even though most of these parties had not changed their politics since the rebranding took place? Starting in the mid-2000s left-wing parties began to suffer major electoral defeats in the very countries that had so enthusiastically supported them just a decade before. And there were no newly reconstituted left-wing parties to replace them. They simply disappeared. Meanwhile, right-wing populist parties gained traction, particularly with the working class—a traditional constituency of the left. Electoral politics in the region had flipped. What happened? And were these two political dynamics connected?

These processes in postcommunist countries also had direct parallels in Western Europe. In recent years, socialist and social democratic parties on the left have declined dramatically in many Western European countries as well (Manwaring and Kennedy 2017). In France and the Netherlands, they have disappeared almost entirely from the political scene. Even in former social democratic strongholds such as Germany and Scandinavia the left's vote shares saw a striking drop in the twenty-first century. By the mid-2010s, the share of votes for social democratic and socialist parties in Western Europe was at its lowest in seventy years (*The Economist* 2016). And the situation closely resembled that of postcommunist Europe: as left-wing parties declined, the populist right came to power (Figure I.1). Meanwhile, over the past two decades, right-wing populist parties made important inroads across Italy, Germany, Spain, Sweden, and Belgium and have dominated the polls in

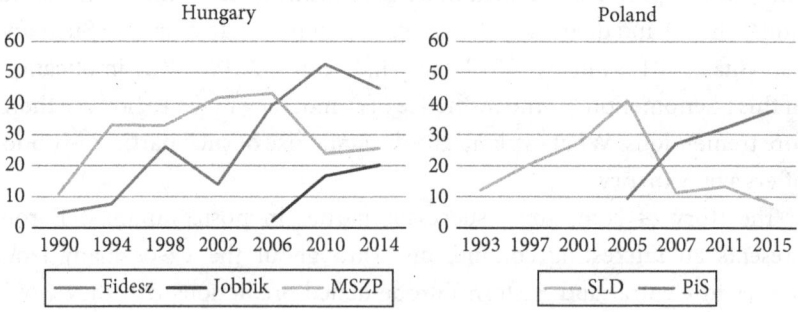

**Figure I.1** Electoral Fortunes of Left and Populist Right Parties in Hungary and Poland (rightist parties in red/orange color, leftist parties in blue).

countries such as France and the United Kingdom. The number of Europeans voting for populist parties in national elections has surged from an average of 7% in 1998 to more than 25% in 2018. In the 2019 European Parliament election, the populist right received 161 seats (23%), compared to 118 (17%) back in 2014 (Lewis et al. 2018).

Given the region-wide nature of this phenomenon, rather than theorizing postcommunist polities as a unique postcommunist anomaly, this book offers a coherent theoretical framework that explains the dynamism of right-wing populism in postcommunist countries by drawing from the literature on Western Europe and by demonstrating parallels in party system dynamics across Europe.

My book merges the studies of left-wing and populist-right parties to demonstrate that the decay of the left and the rise of the populist right are indeed interconnected. Existing scholarship has tended to explore these two phenomena separately. But this book demonstrates that specific policy choices made by parties on the left created opportunities for right-wing populist parties to appeal to the socioeconomic groups that had previously supported the left.

First, I argue that the embrace of pro-market policies and the implementation of painful and unpopular reforms contributed to the electoral demise of left-wing parties in the region. At the time of implementation, these programmatic transformations seemed like the only way for left-wing parties to sway the democratic electorate after losing the support of communist-era patronage networks and the influence of populist leaders. Instead, they ended up containing the seeds for the decay of these parties (Grzymala-Busse 2002a, b). By accepting and promoting pro-market, neoliberal policies at the beginning of the transition, leftist parties gradually pushed away their traditional electorates. By embracing reforms, the ex-communist left ended up discrediting themselves in the eyes of the very constituencies whose interests they had pledged to defend.

Second, I argue that populist parties on the right turned out to be unlikely beneficiaries of the left's policy miscalculations. In the aftermath of EU accession, the reforms-induced frustration with the pro-market left created a political opening for populist parties. Former electorates of left parties, at that point apathetic, frustrated, or abstaining from voting for the left, became available for mobilization by right-wing parties. These parties appealed to the economically vulnerable voters from working-class backgrounds who had made up the bulk of the left's electorate. They did so by adopting traditionally left-wing positions on economic issues while maintaining their nativist stances on cultural issues (Vachudova 2008b; Varga 2014). As result of this dynamic, the pro-market successor leftist parties lost substantive swaths of their core electorates, who were disappointed by the left's inability to represent their interests.

My book traces these dynamics within the party systems of select postcommunist countries. I demonstrate that the decline of the center left and the rise of right-wing populism ultimately resulted from the same process: economically vulnerable voters shifting away from the left to embrace the populist right.

While the availability of large swaths of former electorates of left parties, particularly working classes, created a precondition for the rise of populist parties, much depended on populists' own strategies. Populism and its rise across Europe remains a multicausal phenomenon. Beyond economically redistributionist positions, populist parties also exploited socially conservative issues such as anti-immigration sentiments, fears of sexual minorities, and other forms of cultural revanchism spreading across the region to attract support (Gidron and Bonikowski 2013; Kenny 2017). Yet why did the messages spread by populist right-wing parties work in some contexts but failed in others? This book helps answer that question.

## The Unintended Consequences

After communism collapsed, ex-communist parties all over Central and Eastern Europe had to choose between two possible strategies as they navigated the challenges of their countries' emerging market economies. They could either preserve their ideological Marxist orthodoxy and the redistributionist economic platform, or shift to the center of the ideological spectrum by implementing pro-market reforms. Communist successor parties overwhelmingly viewed the latter strategy as more electorally advantageous. Implementing pro-market reforms allowed them to demonstrate their disassociation from communism while expressing their commitment to the principles and ideals of democracy and the market economy (Grzymala-Busse 2002a ,b; Tavits and Letki 2009).

Embracing pro-market reforms seemed like a great idea. Many observers assumed that left-wing parties were "in relatively good position to implement harsh austerity measures and privatize state-owned enterprises—since they would not be so hurt by the political consequences of such measures" (Fidrmuc 2000: 216). By this logic, the cases of Poland and Hungary, whose ex-communist parties turned out to be more effective reformers than their right-wing predecessors, seemed exemplary. They were touted by politicians and scholars alike as models to be emulated by other countries in the region. For instance, in 2002 Gyzmala-Busse wrote that the Hungarian Socialist Party and the Social Democracy Party of Poland "have not only dramatically turned around their appeals, but have done so with remarkable success—both have successfully pursued broad electorates with their appeals for a continuation of reform, but with greater sensitivity and competence" (52).

Such statements were primarily based on the expectation of voter loyalty. Scholars did not expect policy reversals to constitute a major threat to the stability of left-wing parties' electoral base, for three reasons (Tavits and Letki 2009). First, left-wing parties in the region were able to build considerably stronger and more extensive organizations than their right-wing competitors partly as a legacy of the communist period. This allowed them to insulate supporters from the appeals of opponents and maintain voters during major policy reversals (Grzymala-Busse 2002a, b; Kostelecký 2002; van Biezen 2003). Strong organization, such as widespread local presence, sizable membership that helped reach and appeal to voters on a personal level, and professional management provided leftist parties with an advantage over their rightist competitors in grassroots campaigns, which was crucial for maintaining the support of old adherents (Curry 2003; Morlang 2003; Tavits and Letki 2009: 557).[1] Early on, those left-wing parties that would prove to be successful in the long term managed to forge strong institutionalized links with the trade unions of the communist era. These ties further reinforced their support bases (Orenstein 1998).

Second, the traditional pro-welfare image of leftist parties was expected to provide a safeguard against voter punishment because budget cuts introduced by left-wing parties, unlike those introduced by right-wing parties, could be interpreted as being absolutely essential rather than ideologically motivated (Cukierman and Tommasi 1998: 181; Fidrmuc 2000: 216). At the time, this perspective seemed to find empirical backing: studies of Western Europe had

---

[1] Strong party organization often turned out to be a consequence rather than a reason for ex-communist parties' electoral success. Empirical indicators of parties' organizational decline (such as changes in party membership) tended to follow rather than precede the popularity decline of the ex-communist left parties. Therefore, in statistical terms, the decline in organizational strength appears to be a symptom of ex-communist leftist party failure rather than its cause (Grzymala-Busse 2019b: 575).

discovered that economic policy reversals, such as dismantling the welfare state, were better accepted by the public if pursued by left-wing parties (Ross 2000; Cukierman and Tommasi 1998).

Third, scholars expected that the existence of lingering social constituencies (older people, former members of communist parties, etc.) would facilitate the programmatic turnaround of successor parties (Bozoki and Ishiyama 2002:4). Because of hostility toward anyone associated with the previous regime in the early posttransition years, voters of ex-communist leftist parties often viewed them as the only potential protectors of their interests and were therefore willing to tolerate major policy shifts for the sake of their survival and electoral success (Grzymala-Busse 2002a, b; Tavits and Letki 2009).

Two decades later it has become clear that experts overestimated the level of loyalty for the reformist left. This book argues that the electoral gains made in the 1990s ultimately came at the expense of the left's electoral success in the subsequent decade. Shifting to the center of the economic policy dimension watered down the left's distinctive historical profile and eventually rendered the left unable to take advantage of the widespread discontent over the fallout from neoliberal reforms. After tolerating pro-market rebranding by successor parties for several electoral rounds, supporters abandoned these parties, which led to their subsequent decay.

## Linking Supply and Demand

There are generally two types of explanations for party system dynamics: demand-side and supply-side.

Demand-side explanations focus on individual-level reasons why people choose to support specific parties (Vines and Marsh 2018). For example, popular sentiments like anti-Romanyism and levels of nationalism or nativism exacerbated by external triggers such as immigration and globalization are demand-side explanations for why some voters may support right-wing populist parties (Golder 2016; Inglehart and Norris 2016; Halikiopoulou 2019: 36). Studies have shown a positive correlation between anti-immigrant attitudes and populist right support (Ivarsflaten 2008; Lubbers, Gijsberts, and Scheepers, 2002; Norris 2005; Rydgren 2008; van der Brug and Fennema 2007). Demand-side studies also explain the rise of populism through macro-level economic variables, such as high unemployment (Golder 2003;

Arzheimer 2009), exogenous variation in import flows (Autor et al. 2016; Colantone and Stanig 2016, 2018; Jensen, Quinn, and Weymouth 2016), or a lack of social compensation against market volatility and economic globalization (Swank and Betz 2003; Becker, Fetzer and Novy 2016).

But demand-side approaches have a fundamental problem when it comes to explaining the popularity of populist parties in Europe: while the average levels of nationalism and xenophobia have tended to remain stable in these countries, the vote shares for these parties have fluctuated dramatically. To take one example, perceived threats from Roma minorities have commonly been used as explanations for the growth of populist right parties in the postcommunist region (Bustikova and Kitschelt 2009; Minkenberg 2017a, 2017b). But throughout the observed period average levels of the anti-Roma sentiment were much lower in both Poland and Hungary, countries where right-wing populist parties came to power, than in the Czech Republic and Slovakia, countries where right-wing populist parties had relatively low success (Snegovaya 2018b). In other words, the dynamic was the opposite of what demand-side explanations would predict.

Similarly, the cross-national correlation between levels of racist or anti-immigrant sentiment and the success of right-wing populists is inconclusive (Stockemer, Halikiopoulou, and Vlandas 2020; Diamant and Starr 2018; Roberts 2017c; Berman 2019b; Bartels 2017). For example, despite extremely low levels of racism and anti-immigrant views in Sweden, the right-wing Sweden Democrats became the country's third-largest party. Anti-immigration attitudes and immigration levels are, generally speaking, not a necessary condition of voting for the populist right. Thus Vadlamannati and Kelly (2017: 30), using panel data on twenty-seven OECD countries from 1990 to 2014, found "no direct effect of refugee flows in explaining electoral support for populist-right parties." Roberts (2017c: 18) found a statistically significant negative relationship between the level of immigration and the right-wing populist vote share. And while the popularity of populist-right parties grew in recent decades, racist and anti-immigrant sentiments have actually decreased in Europe and the United States over the same period (Berman 2019b; Bartels 2017). Therefore, one can conclude that "immigration 'objectives' figures are not by themselves sufficient to grasp the impact of the phenomenon on (populist) voters' reaction" (Caiani and Graziano 2019: 1150).

This, as well as further evidence presented in this book, suggests that demand-side explanations alone are not sufficient to account for the phenomenon in question. Any attempts to explain the decay of the left and the rise of the populist right should incorporate an analysis of the supply side, that is, the opportunity structures that parties use.

Supply-side explanations focus on ways in which parties change their rhetoric and programmatic agendas to capitalize on demand-side opportunities and entrench themselves in their respective systems (Carter 2005; Art 2011; Talbot 2015). Under this logic, increasing the salience (or higher relevance to citizens' voting decisions) of xenophobic, racist, and/or anti-immigrant feelings, rather than their absolute levels in a given society, may be what influences growing support for populists (Bonikowski et al. 2019). Politicians and parties are a common factor shaping the growth of salience of specific issues. "Successful politicians . . . structure the world so they can win" by emphasizing the issues that benefit them and their party and sidelining those which do not" (Riker 1986: ix).

However, even when populist parties use platforms politicizing immigration, identity, and/or religion, their successes can vary tremendously depending on the political context. What explains this variation? Whether or not populist right parties succeed is highly dependent on the strategic choices of mainstream parties, as they open up the political space for populist appeals (Kenny 2017). Mainstream parties' failures to respond to the concerns and grievances of the electorate and to articulate clear and convincing policy alternatives made populists an attractive option for many voters (Berman 2019a; Grzymala-Busse 2019b). With regard to this book's argument, the coalescence of mainstream parties around neoliberal reforms driven by leftist parties' rebranding allowed populist parties an opportunity to credibly claim that these projects have ignored the needs of the people, while simultaneously impoverishing and exploiting them (Roberts 2019b). As such, populism may be viewed as a distinctive vehicle "by which wider disenfranchised populations are laboring to make sense of their experiences and discontents about the post-political neoliberal globalized environment" (Kalb and Halmai 2011: 6). In addition, the convergence of mainstream parties around the neoliberal consensus opened up more opportunities for right-wing populists to place a stronger emphasis on the cultural grievances of their electorates. This increased the salience of the sociocultural dimension (Vachudova 2019; Berman and Snegovaya 2019; Berman and Kundnani 2021).

This book connects the supply- and demand-side explanations. By analyzing reasons and consequences for specific economic policy choices adopted by center-left parties, it tracks how the choices on the supply side interacted with voter behavior on the demand side. Specifically, by adopting policies that differed from the preferences of their traditional working-class electorates, reformist left parties opened up new opportunities for right-wing populist parties.

## Terms and Definitions

Several terms in this book warrant additional attention to ensure their meanings are accurately interpreted.

For the purpose of my argument, I introduce the concept of *party competition* and describe the political space in which parties operate. Party competition is a strategic contest among parties as political actors to gain political power by positioning themselves on different policy dimensions (Downs 1957a; Franzmann and Spies 2011). Policy dimensions refer to a particular type of conflict in democratic systems that is created by social structural transformations, such as nation-building, industrialization, marketization, and postindustrialization (Bornschier 2009).

Studies have demonstrated that party competition in Western Europe unfolded primarily along two dimensions: an *economic* axis and a *sociocultural* axis (Lipset and Rokkan 1967; Kitschelt 1994; Kriesi et al. 2008; van der Brug and van Spanje 2009). The economic dimension refers to a conflict about levels of economic regulation and redistribution that occurs between supporters of more stringent socialist and capitalist policies (Kitschelt 1994). The sociocultural dimension usually describes a conflict that occurs between supporters of more traditional and more multicultural, postmaterialist values and issues (Inglehart 1977; van Deth and Scarbrough 1995; Dalton 2002). This conflict emerges when social groups, often older and less educated, feel threatened by the increasing cultural diversity in their countries and seek to defend their traditional ways of life from other ethnic or racial groups (Häusermann and Kriesi 2015; Norris and Inglehart 2019; Vegetti 2019). Conventional left-wing parties stand for stronger market regulation and wealth redistribution on the economic axis, but generally oppose nationalist projects on the sociocultural axis.

*Dealignment* is when a large swath of voters leaves their party without switching to another. *Realignment* is when a large swath of voters switches to another party. These processes typically occur when voter preferences on one of these two dimensions change, or when voters perceive that their political party no longer represents their preferred policies.

Following the collapse of communism, countries underwent the process of a triple *transition* (Offe and Adler 1991). *Political transition* refers to democratization (transitioning from autocratic to democratic political systems). The process of *national transition* led to defining the territorial and cultural boundaries of the nation-state in respective societies (Offe and Adler 1991: 869). Ultimately, *economic transition* refers to marketization, a transition away from the command economies of the communist era to the market economies of postcommunist Europe (Tucker 2006).

Marketization in postcommunist Europe launched the formation of a socioeconomic cleavage between the economic reform *winners* and *losers*. The concept of *cleavage* implies the existence of a common set of values and attitudes among various social groups that are converted into their voting choices (Bartolini and Mair 1990: 199; Oesch 2012: 54). The reforms-induced radical disruption of voters' incomes, lifestyles, and futures provided the impetus for the conversion of divisions in political preferences along socioeconomic lines (Evans 1997, 2000 Eyal, Szelényi, & Townsley, 1998). Across the groups that found themselves on winning and losing sides of the transition, economic liberalization launched the struggle surrounding differences over the economy, distribution of resources, state versus private property, collective versus individualist strategies for economic advancement, the role of the state in redistributing income, merit- versus need-based conceptions of justice, and so on (Evans and Whitefield 2001).

For party competition at the elite level, the positioning of reform winners against losers was often divided along party lines (Evans and Whitefield 1998). The group of winners usually includes highly educated employees who took on a growing number of specialized service jobs requiring expertise (Oesch 2012: 33), as well as the young and those employed by the private sector (Tucker, Pacek, and Berinsky 2002). By contrast, reform losers refer to a broader group of individuals who have been harmed by the unprecedented economic transition and global market integration across the former communist states (Tucker, Pacek, and Berinsky 2002: 557; Margalit 2013: 6). They include various groups, disadvantaged in terms of income and upward mobility (Oesch 2006a). These are the individuals who are unemployed or disproportionately exposed to income cuts, older and less educated, retirees, rural residents, and state workers (Fidrmuc 2000; Tucker, Pacek, and Berinsky 2002; Margalit 2013; Mudge 2018: 44; Bornschier 2010a; Inglehart and Norris 2016).

Different social classes found themselves on winning and losing sides of transition. For the purposes of this book *social class* is conceptualized as an interrelated set of occupational characteristics, which give rise to differentiated economic strategies and link workers from various sectors of the economy (Erikson and Goldthorpe 1992; Evans 1992; Evans and Mills 1999; Oesch and Rennwald 2018).[2] Following the market transition, working-class groups or blue-collar workers, employed as the *clerks*, and *service* and *production workers* (Mudge 2018: 44),[3] were among the groups badly hit by the transition-induced erosion of communist factory-based jobs and were at a greater disadvantage in terms of income and upward mobility (Oesch 2006a). These divisions were further exacerbated by structural changes associated with the integration of postcommunist economies into international markets (Kitschelt 2007: 1181; Kriesi et al. 2008: 4; Oesch 2012: 34). It was often difficult for these social groups to articulate their dissatisfaction along anticapitalist lines, making them easy targets for populist appeals and more likely to join the electorates of populist parties (Linden 2018; Ost 2018).

The bulk of this book focuses on the process of economic transition in postcommunist Europe and the effects of this process on the institutionalization of postcommunist party systems. I use the terms *neoliberalism, neoliberal policies,* and *pro-market reforms* interchangeably to refer to the embrace of three elements: economic privatization, deregulation and liberalization, and work-centric welfare reforms (Mudge 2018: 44). The term *neoliberal* is often poorly understood, particularly in the American context where the center-left Democratic Party has traditionally been considered "liberal." Conversely, this book's focus is primarily on economic liberalism/neoliberalism derived from the continental European conception of liberalism, that is, "nineteenth-century" or "classical" liberalism (Cerny 2008: 9). By the 1990s, *neoliberal* had come to refer to a set of policies designed to promote market

---

[2] Those characteristics are contingently related to others, such as social status or income, but are not defined by them (Evans and Whitefield 2006). Defined as such, class positions are allocated using occupational titles and an established algorithm for popular class schemas like Goldthorpe, Erikson/Goldthorpe classes or Oesch classification schema (Erikson and Goldthorpe 1992; Oesch and Rennwald 2018). See Chapter 2 for more details on specific operationalization.

[3] In this book, I use the terms *production workers, working class, blue-collar worker,* and *manual worker* as interchangeable to denote a working-class person performing nonagricultural manual labor. Bain and Prince (1972) enumerate the characteristics pertaining to white-collar as opposed to blue-collar work, such as intellectual as opposed to manual activities; differing functions (administration, design, analysis and planning, etc. vs. actual production) as opposed to routine; proximity to authority.

competition viewed as the best solution for all kinds of economic problems, and as both the means and the ends of good government (Mudge 2018: 59). *Neoliberalism* came to be translated into a specific reforms package that included the liberalization of trade in goods and capital, the privatization of state institutions and industries, the depoliticization of decision-making on economic and monetary policies, and the separation of regulatory authorities from the executive branch (Bugaric 2016; Mudge 2018: 59). The first stage of reforms included the Washington Consensus policies of "structural adjustment." The second stage of reforms included pension privatization, the flat tax, and the slashing of corporate tax rates (Appel and Orenstein 2018: 26). During the 1990s and 2000s postcommunist countries became global leaders in the adoption of neoliberal ideas and policies "at a dramatic rate." They also became some of the most open economies in Europe (Orenstein 2013a: 375; 2013b).[4]

However, the policies proved to be quite unpopular socially. A particularly painful one was *austerity*. Austerity (fiscal adjustment) packages are a government's deficit-reduction policies involving a combination of spending cuts and/or tax increases. Austerity policies tend to cut household disposable income and reduce consumption (Grittersova et al. 2016). Economically vulnerable social groups, such as working-class voters and those in precarious economic situations, are disproportionally affected by such cuts, since their incomes are already low and they suffer the burden when social benefits are reduced. Because austerity measures involve fundamental decisions about the role of the state in the economy, they tend to frame political discourse along the economic dimension (Grittersova et al. 2016).

The embrace of neoliberalism by mainstream parties opened up space for their opponents to adopt the (*economically*) *protectionist* agenda aimed at compensating those segments of society which bore most of the adjustment costs for reforms and economic openness (Ausserladscheider 2019). While *welfare chauvinism* refers to protecting the welfare state from the external threat of immigrants by restricting specific benefits to citizens or natives only (Schumacher and Kersbergen 2016), economic protectionism focuses on protecting the country from the external threat of unregulated free trade (Van der Waal and De Koster 2017). The belief is that "the economy should

---

[4] In the postcommunist context the terms *neoliberalism* and *pro-market reforms* are often used as synonyms, as they were part of the same overall policies of neoliberal marketization. Many countries of the region adopted avant-garde, radical, and often experimental neoliberal reforms during the periods of market transition and European accession (Appel and Orenstein 2018: 26).

serve the nation and should be controlled by it" (Mudde 2007: 186–187). Parties with such positions oppose economic globalization and view trade in the short term as a zero-sum game whereby the production of goods can employ people either in their own countries or abroad (Otjes et al. 2018). A combination of support for domestic free-market policies with strong anti-free-trade positions and welfare chauvinism is often referred to as *economic nationalism* (Colantone and Stanig 2018: 2).

In this book, I define ex-communist leftist parties as *pro-market* or *reformist* according to the following criteria. First, I outline the various parties that succeeded the communist parties in each country after transition. Typically, this implies identifying the descendants and splinter groups from the initial roundtable negotiations. I also identify the parties that attracted members of the former communist elite. Second, I analyze whether a given party has attempted to reject its communist ideology and platform and reinvent itself as a pro-democratic and a pro-market party. Often this change is combined with a modification of the party's name from "Communist" to "Socialist" or a rejection of incorporating the term "worker." For example, the reformist Hungarian Socialist Party emerged as a reform wing of the Hungarian Socialist Workers' Party. In Poland, after the collapse of the Polish United Workers' Party, some of its former activists established the Social Democracy of the Republic of Poland party, which later became part of the Democratic Left Alliance (Sojusz Lewicy Demokratycznej, SLD). In Slovakia, the main successor of the Czechoslovak Communist Party became the Communist Party of Slovakia, which changed its name to the Party of the Democratic Left in 1991 as part of its efforts to adopt a more reformist approach (Tucker 2006).

I define parties as the *traditional left* if they constituted the part of the unreformed communist party that refused to break away with its communist past and largely preserved its Marxist agenda. Among the countries studied, only one electorally successful party represents such a clear-cut case: the Czech Communist Party of Bohemia and Moravia (Komunisticka strana Čech a Moravy, KSČM), the successor to the Czechoslovak Communist Party in the Czech Republic.

A substantial degree of confusion surrounds the term *right-wing populist party*. A number of terms serve to describe more or less the same concept: "radical right," "authoritarian," "antiestablishment," "anti-immigrant," "nationalist," "antisystem," or "populist." Historically, these parties have demonstrated a high degree of fluctuation in terms of their positioning on key issues, such as antisystemness, immigration, and economic policies (Rovny 2014). Most authors define populist parties as parties that portray their respective societies as being in a constant state of Manichaean struggle between two homogeneous and antagonistic groups, "the pure people" versus "the corrupt elite," while arguing that politics should be an expression of the general will of the people (Mudde 2004; Rooduijn et al. 2019). This book uses the terms *nationalist-populist, right-wing populist,* and *populist right* parties interchangeably. In addition to adopting the Manichaean discourse, populist right parties "emphasize a [socio]cultural cleavage, the national, ethnic, religious, or cultural identity of the 'people' against outside groups who allegedly pose a threat to the popular will" (Rodrik 2018: 22–23).

## The Broader Trends

In explaining how these dramatic transformations unraveled across the postcommunist region, this book contributes to the existing scholarship in several respects.

## Eastern European Distinctiveness[5]

When explaining the left's decay, scholarship of the postcommunist region has tended to emphasize factors more idiosyncratic and specific to this region's unique experience.

One popular explanation has focused on the *anti-incumbent bias* implicit in the nature of these new and volatile party systems. In this view, postcommunist voters have developed "a taste for newness" experimenting with one set of incumbents after another and pushing out all of the incumbents subsequently (Haughton 2001: 18; Pop-Eleches 2010; Sikk 2012; Haughton and Deegan-Krause 2020; Haughton, Rybar, and Deegan-Krause 2021). New parties coming to power typically reflected dissatisfaction with the old parties and old politics (Haughton and Deegan-Krause 2020). The relative novelty and instability of the postcommunist party systems might have led to a power rotation of slow and fast reformers, which roughly corresponds to a rotation in power of the reformed ex-communist

---

[5] A more conventional term for the countries, which constitute the main focus of this book, is "Central Europe" or "East-Central Europe". In this book the term "Eastern Europe" is used for simplicity and for a more explicit rhetorical contrast between the "West" and the "East.

left and the center right. However, while these accounts contribute to our understanding of the complexity of the phenomenon, they do not fully explain the timing of the center-left decline. For instance, it remains unclear why the left's supporters waited many years to punish leftist parties. Despite voters' alleged "taste for newness," many center-left parties across the region managed to win multiple elections before their collapse. For example, the Hungarian Socialist Party won three elections, the Social Democracy of Poland won two, and the Czech Social Democratic Party, four. Nor does the preference for newness explain the other side of the story: why populist incumbents tend to survive in power for so long. The Fidesz, PiS, and Smer parties, for example, have been able to stay in power for several electoral cycles in their respective countries.

Yet another set of prominent explanations stresses the role of *corruption scandals* and *internal conflicts* within ex-communist parties, which, as the argument goes, tended to undermine these parties' claims of responsiveness and integrity (Haughton and Deegan-Krause 2020). Corruption is a much more salient issue in the postcommunist context than in Western Europe; between 2000 and 2010 corruption and related scandals were a major issue in twenty-eight elections—or 70% of the elections in Central and Eastern European region. Indeed, perceptions of political corruption may have mobilized supporters to vote against the elites they viewed as corrupt (Kostadinova 2009; Agerberg 2017, 2019). They may have also contributed to the support of anti-incumbents, including populist parties (Bagenholm 2013a, 2013b; Hanley and Sikk 2016; Abedi 2004; Engler, Pytlas, and Deegan-Krause 2019; Engler 2020; Snegovaya 2020b). The established parties' inability to maintain a clean image may have paved the way for new parties to emerge and attract voters while claiming that they were cleaner and stricter in fighting corruption (De Vries and Hobolt 2020; Haughton, Rybář, and Deegan-Krause 2021). This argument may be particularly applicable to the decay of the left-wing parties in the region. The very same factors that allowed the left-wing Polish and Hungarian parties to gain widespread electoral support in the short term, in the long term contributed to the left's demise: "Their mercenary behavior launched some of the scandals that destroyed these parties' credibility, and then belied the parties' attempts to reassert competence and integrity" (Grzymala-Busse 2019b: 570). This holds particularly true for the volatile party systems of Eastern Europe, where protest voting to punish unpopular incumbents has been a widespread practice (Pop-Eleches 2010):

While it is hard to deny the impact of corruption on postcommunist parties' fortunes, this set of arguments does not explain why such scandals appear to be particularly catastrophic for the left's electoral fortunes and not those of the populist right. First, corruption scandals do not always cause electoral decline. While they tend to damage the image of an incumbent party, they rarely lead to complete collapse (Kenny 2017: 12). Second, this argument also does not explain why the left seemingly gets punished more dramatically for corruption than does the populist right, even though the populist right has inherited many of the left's former constituents.

As this book shows, leftist parties' policy choices often appear to be conditioning the impact of factors such as punishment for corruption. Watering down the left's economic profile was often a prerequisite for the left's decline. That is, weak party organization, scandals, and internal conflicts tended to seal the left's fortunes primarily when combined with an additional element: leftist parties embarking on unpopular economic reforms. When voters suffer from difficult economic conditions, such as the ones created by the left's embracing pro-market platforms, they may be particularly susceptible to the negative effects of corruption. They may also be more likely to punish politicians who they feel abandoned them and who they now see as stealing from the state (Kostadinova 2009). This is consistent with studies that have shown that corruption decreases trust in national governments, particularly in countries where austerity was present (Melios 2020), and that corruption is often treated as a source of the problem of public discontent in cases where austerity was actually the trigger (Gubernat and Rammelt 2012). In other words, corruption scandals may be at least partly endogenous to the overall popularity of ruling parties (Kenny 2017: 12). That is, scandals and political divisions often tend to exacerbate what is already a negative public view of the left-wing parties' policies.[6] Along these lines, in Chapter 4 I demonstrate that while Hungary's "Öszöd speech" scandal contributed to the dramatic erosion of support for the Hungarian Socialist Party, it was in fact merely the last straw: the party's approval ratings had already been declining due to unpopular austerity measures. Similarly, in the Polish case, corruption scandals (such as the "Rywin affair") further undermined support for the Social Democracy of Poland party after its approval had already been halved

---

[6] In addition, case studies in Chapters 4 and 5 demonstrate that internal scandals and splits were often due to internal policy disagreements among members of a reformist left party. These disagreements tended to divide the party into factions of traditionalists (who wanted to continue more traditional party policies) and modernizers (who wanted to pursue a reformist track).

in the aftermath of unpopular reforms. In other words, without taking into consideration their pro-market policy choices, it is hard to explain the specific timing of the leftist parties' demise across the region. Overall, this book contributes to the discussion about the way various factors often raised to explain the left's demise interact with these parties' unpopular policy choices.

## Learning from Western Europe

While scholarship of the postcommunist region often resorts to more idiosyncratic factors in explaining the decay of its leftist parties, the fact is that Western Europe has experienced the same trends. Thus, the account of the left's decline must involve something broader than region-specific developments (Berman and Snegovaya 2019; Bagashka, Bodea, and Han 2022; Binev, 2022a, 2022b). Despite the legacy of communism, there is some correspondence between postcommunist and Western European party families (Hloušek and Kopeček 2016), and this correspondence can provide broader lessons (Pytlas 2018). Establishing cross-regional parallels seems particularly warranted given that, as Chapter 1 discusses, postcommunist leftist parties tended to rebrand themselves directly after their Western European counterparts. The pro-market rebranding of the postcommunist left originally unfolded in a fashion similar to the Third Way patterns of Western Europe (Ishiyama 1997). And subsequently these parties across both regions suffered similar destinies.

Scholarship on Western European politics also offers some clues as to why the left in Eastern Europe has experienced difficulties. Much of the research on this topic has explained the rise of populism across Western Europe as a reaction to failures of traditional parties to adequately respond to existing societal problems and public opinion in the eyes of their electorates (Van Kessel 2015; Albertazzi and McDonnell 2015; de Jonge 2021). Among these arguments, one that is particularly relevant for this book is that Western European social democrats have failed to present an attractive political alternative to their electorates (Amable 2011; Manwaring and Holloway 2022; Mudge 2018; Bandau 2022). And this is largely due to the fact that, since the 1980s, they have incorporated neoliberal ideas in their platforms (Hall 2003; Mudge 2018; Nachtwey 2013). Such policy shifts have loosened or severed the programmatic linkages that connected particular social constituencies to a party (Roberts 2017b). Voters may have interpreted such policy deviations from electoral commitments as a betrayal by traditional constituents, which diluted these parties' image in their minds and weakened their attachment to these parties (Lupu 2014, 2016; Bagashka, Bodea, and Han 2022). As voters realized that they had little to gain from established parties, they tended to turn to more active populist parties on the left and the right (Mouffe 2005, 2019; Blyth 2013: 132–177; Hopkin and Blyth 2019). For example, studies have found an association between mainstream parties' ideological prox- imity and the electoral success of the populist right (Kitschelt and McGann 1997; Carter 2005; Nissan and Carter 2005; Brug and Fennema 2007; Norris 2005; Arzheimer and Carter 2006; Rooduijn 2015; Lynch 2019; Berman and Kundnani 2021). These arguments are broadly consistent with the dynamic observed in the postcommunist region, which is analyzed in this book.

## Bringing Class Back

Western European literature also helps bring class back into the conversa- tion on postcommunist Europe. While Western European scholarship has actively relied on this approach (Karreth, Polak, and Allen 2013; Polk and Karreth 2020; Evans and Tilley 2012, 2017; Rennwald and Evans 2014), studies of the postcommunist region tended to be more skeptical about class-based explanations, for several reasons. Scholars of the region were often averse to class-based approaches that had been imposed by Marxist in- doctrination during communism. So in the aftermath of the postcommunist transition, the class analysis frequently became marginalized (Szelenyi, Fodor, and Hanley 1996; Ost 2015; Doolan and Cepić 2022). To cite Ost (2015: 546), "Class was the key concept of the toppled nemesis" and there- fore was rejected decisively in postcommunist contexts. The class argu- ment also often went under the radar given that the adoption of pro-market policies by the political mainstream tended to diffuse the class-based voting structure for the reasons explained in this book. However, recent years witnessed the tentative reemergence of "class talk" in many postsocialist settings.

This book argues that class also matters in the postcommunist context. Due to the industrial imbalances in the postcommunist states and global- ization that accelerated the export of low-skilled jobs outside of Europe (Chapter 2), working-class groups were hit particularly hard by the tran- sition (Fidrmuc 2000). Pro-market reforms tended to undermine worker sodalities and dramatically shrink their power, prestige, and opportunities (Kalb 2009: 17). These problems were sharpened by the fact that many workers believed their situation would improve under capitalism after the transition and were especially disillusioned with the results. These electorates therefore have been prone to switch their partisan loyalties from the pro-market left to the populist right. The sheer size of working-class electorates also mattered: in postcommunist economies these groups have comprised a more significant share of the electorates than in postindustrial Western economies (see Chapter 2 for details), which might have contributed to more detrimental long-term consequences for the ex-communist left.

This working-class focus helps to elucidate parallels between Western and postcommunist Europe. Much of the scholarship on Western Europe has discussed the phenomenon of the "proletarization" of the populist right (the increasing representation of blue-collar voters among these parties' constituencies). This trend is also quite noticeable in postcommunist Europe (see Chapter 1). Across both regions, it is associated with a double process of the working classes abandoning leftist parties and switching their allegiances to the populist right (Bale et al. 2010; De Lange 2007; Van Spanje and Van der Brug 2007; Arzheimer 2009, 2013). In an effort to attract voters dissatisfied with the left's policies, right-wing challengers commonly adopted more left-leaning economic platforms than other parties in their respective political systems (Allen 2015; Bustikova and Kitschelt 2009). They emphasized protection against market volatility; offered more social spending and state control over the economy; and called for price regulations, increased taxation for the wealthy, renationalization of privatized property, and protections against job loss (Bustikova 2018).

While arguing that the class-based vote matters, I am careful not to offer a one-sided reductionist class explanation of politics. The argument developed in this book goes beyond working classes only. It can be applied to broader groups usually described as transition or reform losers. Individuals who belong to this group tend to have manual occupations and less-qualified jobs. Alternatively, they may be older and less educated, unemployed, or disproportionately exposed to income cuts (Bornschier 2010a, 2010b; Inglehart and Norris 2016). These groups often reside in rural areas or former industrial strongholds that were deindustrialized in the aftermath of the postcommunist transition; they are also often stricken with extremely high unemployment and low wages (Fidrmuc 2000; Scheiring 2020a). These electorates may have been harmed or threatened by the forces of economic liberalization, feel neglected by traditional (political) elites, and share the animosity expressed by populist parties toward those elites (Oesch 2008; Roberts 2017a, 2017b; Szczerbiak 2003; Vanhuysse 2009; Becker 2010). Indeed, as demonstrated in Chapter 4, the sudden rise of the populist right Jobbik party in 2010 was partly due to the support of less economically well-off counties in northeastern Hungary that failed to successfully integrate into the new economy following the market transition of the 1990s. In Poland in 2015, the right-wing populist PiS party attracted not only working-class electorates but also those Poles who had lost as a result of Polish modernization, in particular the poorer part of the population, from the east and rural areas. Similarly, Chapter 5 shows that along with working-class electorates, left-wing parties like KSČM and Smer also attracted many rural and older voters, thus becoming dominant forces in the countryside (Hanley 2001; Hanley and House 2004; Krivý 2006).

However, the working-class focus is particularly important as these are precisely the groups that used to be the strongholds of traditional left-wing parties, and because of the sheer size of these groups (Kitschelt 1994; Bornschier and Kriesi 2012). Even in the postcommunist region the rebranded left often started off positioning itself as a defender of workers' interests. In Chapters 2, 4, and 5, I demonstrate that in presenting themselves as reasonable legitimate social democrats in the early to mid-1990s, many rebranded ex-communist parties have successfully mobilized blue-collar electorates in much the same way the Western European left did at the onset of the Third Way rebranding (Szelenyi, Fodor, and Hanley 1996; Mateju, Rehakova, and Evans 1999; Evans 1997, 2000).

## Economy vs. Culture

The main focus of this book is the competition between the left and the populist right parties along the economic policy dimension. This is not a typical approach; the bulk of the literature on postcommunist Europe has argued that competition along the sociocultural dimension plays a bigger role in support for the populist right than does the economic policy dimension. Research explaining the contemporary rise of populism has offered a number of important insights and has provided deep exploration of the dynamics of European politics. Yet such studies do not fully explain the variation in populist parties' fortunes (Gidron and Bonikowski 2013; Kenny 2017; Eiermann, Mounk, and Gultchin 2017). This book complements such accounts by arguing that the decline of the left is often an important pre-condition for the success of populist-nationalist parties. The role of the competition along the economic dimension can complement the sociocultural accounts.

Most scholarship on the rise of populism in contemporary Europe has stressed the role of minorities and the backlash against diversity and inclusiveness in the electoral success of these parties (Spies 2013; Golder 2016; Bustikova 2018; Norris and Inglehart 2019; Krastev and Holmes 2018). The cultural backlash theories link the success of right-wing populist parties to their ability to politicize issues on the sociocultural dimension (Bornschier 2010b; Norris and Inglehart 2019). As this argument goes, the "silent revolution" in Western societies (an intergenerational shift bringing greater emphasis on freedom of expression, environmental protection, gender equality, tolerance of LGBTQIA people and foreigners) provoked a negative reaction on the right side of the political spectrum. This reaction against the erosion of familiar values, sometimes described as the "silent counterrevolution," contributed to the rise of right-wing populist parties that took stronger stances on traditional values, nationalism, law and order, and opposition to multiculturalism (Ignazi 2003; Inglehart and Norris 2017; Pytlas 2018). The inflow of working migrants and refugees into Europe further exacerbated a cultural backlash among the populations of these countries, which in turn led to an upsurge in the popularity of the populist right (Mudde 2016; Inglehart and Norris 2019; Betz 2018).

In the postcommunist context, a related argument has been made about the crisis of values and authority that followed the collapse of the communist bloc and opened the door for its own distinctive variant of populist right ideology (Pirro 2015). From the onset of the transition, the political conflict was shaped by intense "value wars" (Pytlas 2018). In light of their nativist and authoritarian profile across the region, nationalist-populist parties have politicized issues such as clericalism and irredentism (precommunist issues), identity, treatment of ethnic minorities, and the role of the EU (Pirro 2015; Snegovaya 2022a). For example, the Polish PiS party's emphasis on a return to the nation and the values of the Church, as well as presenting itself as the persecuted last bastion of traditional Polishness (Pytlas et al. 2018), contributed to its electoral success (Rupnik 2018).

This book does not reject the importance of such accounts. Rather, it argues that the populist phenomenon needs to be understood in combination with leftist parties' policy choices on the economic dimension. Focusing on the sociocultural dimension alone does not fully explain the variation in right-wing populist parties' fortunes because it ignores the role of political opportunities available to them. For example, while many right-wing populist parties discussed in this book tended to use similar nativist and anti-immigration appeals, their electoral fortunes varied dramatically (Pirro 2015; Eiermann, Mounk, and Gultchin 2017). Thus, while insightful, the sociocultural explanations fail to fully explain why similar platforms adopted by populist movements in some European countries brought electoral breakthrough, while in others they did not. Reintroducing the competition along the economic axis helps explain this conundrum; it shows that as long as left-wing parties preserved party alignments more consistent with traditional left/right divides, populist-right parties had limited electorates available for mobilization. The Czech case is particularly telling; as Chapter 5 demonstrates, throughout the 1990s and 2000s the presence of viable left-wing alternatives in the party system has consistently limited electoral opportunities available for populist-right parties. By contrast, as shown in Chapter 4, where left-wing parties rebranded and dealigned their traditional electorates, populist-right parties grew in popularity. Populist parties then appealed to such voters by integrating redistributive appeals with their sociocultural conservative nativist stances on the sociocultural dimension. Chapter 2 shows that this combination was particularly appealing to working-class electorates and contributed to a large populist swing in the countries with reformist left parties. Hence, rather than rejecting the importance of sociocultural accounts, my argument helps integrate them with economic explanations and more convincingly explain the success of the populist right.

In the context of the competition between the center left and populist right, some scholars have argued that center-left parties declined while populist-right parties grew because the latter adopted anti-migrant stances while the former ignored or took overly progressive positions on sociocultural issues. As this argument goes, because working-class and less-educated voters on average prefer more culturally conservative, authoritarian, and nationalist positions (Kitschelt and Rehm 2014), more-progressive positions on sociocultural issues usually presented social democratic parties with a strategic challenge—they pushed away traditional supporters of the left (Kitschelt 1994).

However, available empirical evidence does not back the claim that party competition in European party systems occurs primarily along the sociocultural dimension (Norris and Inglehart 2019). Positions on the sociocultural dimension by the left-wing and populist-right parties do not satisfactorily account for the variation in their electoral fortunes (Snegovaya 2018b; Stockemer, Halikiopoulou, and Vlandas 2020; Angelucci and Vittori 2021). Studies have shown that leftist parties' liberal turn on sociocultural issues does not necessarily lead to their losing votes (Abou-Chadi and Wagner 2020; Bandau 2022). Empirical evidence for the postcommunist region presented in this book also does not corroborate the assumption about the importance of the sociocultural dimension for support of the left. To test the argument that competition in postcommunist countries occurs predominantly over noneconomic issues (Kitschelt et al. 1999) Chapter 3 features an empirical model that includes party-level positions on the sociocultural dimension, as well as individual-level controls for religiosity and immigration. However, controlling for noneconomic issues did not alter the main conclusions—the independent effect of leftist parties' positions on the economic dimension remained significant. These findings contradict the assumption that competition in postcommunist countries occurs primarily over noneconomic issues. Had that assumption been correct, the positioning of left-wing parties on economic issues should have become irrelevant when controlling for noneconomic issues. Instead, it remains significant. In the experimental section, which appears in Chapter 6, I test the assumption that populist parties compete with leftist parties primarily along the sociocultural dimension. In surveys stipulating that parties on the left embraced pro-market policies, working-class voters said that they would choose the populist party in the next election as long as it promised them greater social protection. Without such promises, the anti-immigrant appeals were not enough to cause these voters to shift support to the populist right.

There are two more reasons why sociocultural explanations need to be complemented with a focus on the competition along the economic axis.

First, one popular explanation of the populist right's electoral successes in postcommunist regions emphasizes these parties' ability to mobilize anti-Roma sentiments. Karácsony and Róna (2011) and Nagy and Róna (2013) argue that antiestablishment attitudes, nationalism, and anti-Roma sentiments are the main explanatory factors behind the Jobbik vote in Hungary. However, separating this explanation from economic arguments is tricky. In Hungary the anti-Roma sentiment led to anti-Roma mobilization in economically distressed regions reeling from neoliberal globalization (Szombati 2018). While the rise of the Jobbik party to power coincided with violent clashes between ethnic Hungarians and the Roma population, tensions between Hungarian and Roma populations were at least partly driven by underlying economic problems. The transition-induced decline of heavy industry exacerbated unemployment among the Romani people, previously employed in low-skilled manufacturing jobs (Kalb 2018: 315). By the early 2000s, exclusion from the labor market had become a permanent feature of Roma lives across many villages of the northeastern periphery (Ladányi and Szelényi 2006; Feischmidt and Szombati 2017). This reinforced the stereotype of the "work-shy, lazy Gypsies" preying on hardworking taxpayers (Feischmidt and Szombati 2017; Scheiring and Szombati 2020) and fostered an uptick in racism.

Hungary's political elites were slow to address the issue, not wanting to alienate their existing voters (ethnic Hungarians) while not attracting new ones (the electoral participation of Roma populations is low in Hungary). Policies introduced in an effort to integrate these social groups mostly failed. The economic crisis that started in Hungary in mid-2006 contributed to the further deprivation of Romani people and resulted in a series of clashes between ethnic Romani and ethnic Hungarians (see, e.g., the 2006 murder in Olaszliszka and the murder case in Veszprem). Rising levels of unemployment and the increasing relevance of redistribution issues provided populist-right parties with opportunities to mobilize their electoral support using anti-Roma rhetoric (Krekó and Juhasz 2017: 155). Szombati (2018), who ran an in-depth ethnographic study of eastern Hungary, showed that the anti-Romanyism was primarily fueled by rural Hungarians' disenchantment with their place and trajectory in the new democratic regime and was exacerbated by what they saw as the left liberal elite's "undeserved attention and support" for the Romani minority. Therefore the loss of social security and the increasing reliance of downwardly mobile rural citizens' livelihoods on the state had a strong impact on the eruption of anti-Roma passions. Hence, while anti-Roma sentiment contributed to these parties' electoral breakthrough, the underlying grievances were also significantly influenced by economic causes.

Another popular explanation for the success of the populist right—the role of the migrant crisis and anti-immigration sentiment—is less applicable in the postcommunist context, where the electoral breakthrough of the populist right often predated the immigration crisis. The wave of Middle Eastern refugees that entered Europe in 2015 has indeed catalyzed the rise of the populist right parties in Western Europe (see the discussion of the Czech case in Chapter 5; Grzymala-Busse 2019a), for many of which immigration has become a singularly dominant issue (Allen 2015; Arzheimer and Berning 2019). However, in postcommunist Europe this explanation fails to account for the performance of right-wing populist parties before 2015. In terms of the timing of their electoral breakthrough, many populist parties, such as Fidesz, Jobbik, and PiS, became electorally successful before the refugee crisis erupted in Europe (Rovny 2014; Bustikova 2018, see also Chapters 4 and 5).

After 2015, postcommunist populist right-wing parties, such as the Estonian Conservative People's Party and Action of Dissatisfied Citizens (ANO 2011) and Freedom and Direct Democracy (SPD) in the Czech Republic (see Chapter 5), definitely exploited anti-immigration sentiment and benefited from it (Stefanovic and Evans 2019: 1445). Hungary's Fidesz in particular gained a reputation for its hostile position toward international immigration. The emblematic events widely covered in the international press included the weeks-long stand-off between the Hungarian police and thousands of migrants at the Keleti railway station in Budapest, the construction of the barbed-wire fence along the Hungarian-Serbian border, and the clashes at the Röszke border-crossing at the same fence (Bocskor 2018). Similarly, both ANO and SPD in the Czech Republic quite successfully framed the refugee crisis as a security threat and attracted substantial swaths of the left's former electorates using such rhetoric (see Chapter 5). However, when doing so, all of these parties tended to combine nativist cultural positions with more redistributionist positions on economy.

In addition, the immigration issue has historically been less relevant in a postcommunist European context than in Western Europe. Postcommunist societies suffered less from the 2015 refugee crisis and tended to supply rather than receive migrants (Bustikova and Kitschelt 2009; Rovny 2014). Due to the lack of a sizable migrant population, until the 2015 refugee crisis immigration was not as salient in postcommunist Europe and played a secondary role in the different threat scenarios formulated by reactionary groups (Allen 2015; Bluhm and Varga 2019). As Scheiring and Szombati (2020: 731) point out, "Immigrants did not matter at all in Hungary until 2015, only well after the establishment of the illiberal state. Thus, a reference to immigration and xenophobia is not enough to explain the success of illiberal populism."

Instead of making reductionist claims that socioeconomic conflict is the only kind that matters, this book offers to bring back into the scholarly discourse the analysis of economic divisions. The formula for success of the populist right is clear, and it tends to follow the preferences of the working-class electorates (as seen in Chapter 2): combining nativism on the sociocultural dimension with redistributionist positions on the economic dimension. This combo seems to have worked particularly well for populists electorally. Watering down the left's distinctive historical economic profile provided an important precondition for populist-right parties to achieve electoral dominance over the left.

## The Structure of the Book

### Why Postcommunist Europe?

This book's main argument draws from the experience of Western Europe and is applicable to both Western and Eastern Europe. There are substantive similarities between the two regions. However, in the postcommunist context, the consequences of the adoption of pro-market policies should have been arguably even more pronounced than in Western Europe for four major reasons.

First, postcommunist countries embraced pro-market economic policies more strongly than any other developing world region after 1989. The simultaneous emergence of twenty-seven newly ex-communist societies, along with international competitors like India and China, provided postcommunist countries particularly strong incentives to win the competition for foreign investment in order to revive their economies. To make this competition even more challenging, international organizations, such as the International Monetary Fund, the World Bank, and the European Commission—all of which embraced neoliberalism in the 1990s and early 2000s—continuously rated postcommunist countries against one another, putting them under intense pressure to compete in adopting neoliberal reforms and to avoid backtracking (Appel and Orenstein 2016: 317; Myant and Drahokoupil 2012). In an effort to become attractive for international investors and minimize perceptions of a communist legacy, they adopted a range of avant-garde reforms that made them a testing ground for neoliberal ideas. These reforms, known as "shock therapy" or the

Washington Consensus, included the immediate liberalization of prices (with a few exceptions, such as housing, energy, and transport), the liberalization of trade, the introduction of convertible currencies, the lifting of capital controls, the elimination of state subsidies to firms, the privatization of pensions, and the introduction of the flat tax (Appel and Orenstein 2016: 316–318). As result, in the aftermath of EU accession "new Europe [was] significantly more neoliberal than old Europe" (Beblavý 2014: 55–56). Not only were there major differences in social-protection expenditures, with the Western European average being above postcommunist country levels, but all of the postcommunist new member states, with the exception of Slovenia, introduced at least one of the flagship neoliberal reforms— large-scale pension privatization or flat income tax reforms (and, often, both)—that were largely absent in Western Europe.

Second, while in Western Europe the economic shocks were more evenly distributed over time, the postcommunist region experienced the painful effect of rapid economic liberalization. The economic liberalization in the region launched a struggle over differences about the distribution of resources, state versus private property, collective versus individualist strategies for economic advancement, the role of the state in redistributing income, merit- versus need-based conceptions of justice, and so on (Evans and Whitefield 2000). Clashing positions on socioeconomic issues among different social groups, which were shaped primarily during market reforms, split those societies across *reform winners* and *reform losers*.

These divisions deepened after the "fourth revolution," globalization, as the opening of national borders exacerbated the pain inflicted by domestic economic reforms (Kriesi et al. 2008, 2012). The structural economic changes that followed, including the automation of manufacturing, lean production, and the outsourcing of routine activities, further deepened these divisions between reform winners and losers (Saarts 2015: 30). The evolution toward a more skill-intensive, rational, and competitive service economy additionally worsened reform losers' job prospects and reduced demand for their skill sets (Kitschelt 2007: 1181; Oesch 2012: 34). The losers of transition became the losers of globalization. The winners, a group which included highly educated people with more specialized skills, were much more supportive of opening up borders than those who were far less educated or skilled (Kriesi et al. 2012: 73).

Third, in the postcommunist context the impact of the left's centrist shift was much more pronounced in scale. The communist legacy created enduring mass support for a state-funded provision of social welfare, which contributed to a stronger backlash against pro-market policies in the long run (Orenstein and Bugarič 2019; Mason et al. 2000). The Leninist legacy created significant potential for economic populist measures at the mass level (Pop-Eleches and Tucker, 2017). Having systematically suppressed private enterprise while heavily relying on central planning, communist regimes developed a very different economic logic and a series of typically communist pathologies in their respective societies (Kornai 1992). Namely, since they were "[s]ocialized under communism, which claimed to take care of the people from the cradle to the grave, East Europeans have become accustomed to the idea of a protective welfare state" (Mudde 2000: 43). Indeed, during the early postcommunist years, driven partly by memories of better social welfare provisions under communism and partly by a growing demand for a safety net in an uncertain context, postcommunist citizens tended to express higher levels of support for social welfare. For example, Pop-Eleches and Tucker (2017: 188) found that citizens of postcommunist countries were substantially more likely to agree that it is the state's responsibility to provide for the social welfare of its citizens, as compared to the citizens of other European countries. Accordingly, the backlash against welfare retrenchment in this region was more pronounced than in Western Europe, which lacked such a legacy.

Fourth, in postcommunist countries the market transition took place during a relatively condensed period in the 1990s. Because of this, it is easier to identify and compare the effects of transition on the various countries involved than it would be had the process occurred over a longer period of time, as it had in Western Europe. The fact that these countries had to comply with EU conditionality also helps to address endogeneity concerns related to leftist-party policy choices, which were often driven by international pressure.

While focusing on postcommunist regions more broadly, this book pays particular attention to the experiences of four countries, also known as the Visegrád Four, namely Hungary, Poland, the Czech Republic, and Slovakia. Located in East Central Europe, these countries have multiple historical and geographic similarities. However, the electoral outcomes and timing of the emergence of populist-right parties in these countries varied dramatically. While Hungarian and Polish right-wing populist parties steadily attracted voter support throughout the 2000s and consistently made it into these countries' national parliaments, in the Czech Republic and Slovakia the success of such parties remained limited at best. This variation represents a particularly interesting puzzle, which this book tries to solve. To analyze these dynamics in more detail, I trace working-class preferences on the economic and socio-cultural dimension, as well as associated party choices in each of the Visegrád Four countries in subsequent chapters.

Economic and sociocultural explanations of complex social phenomena are often intertwined. Methodologically separating the economic policy positions from the cultural is tricky. Periods of economic distress or decline in one's individual well-being may fuel xenophobic sentiment, racism, and anger against other cultural groups (Sniderman, Hagendoorn and Prior 2004; Mayda 2006; Sides and Citrin 2007).[7] Therefore, in the cross-country data set and case studies, I wanted to focus on the period preceding the 2015 refugee crisis in Europe, since the crisis gave an extra boost to the populist right and further weakened left-wing parties by increasing the salience of a sociocultural dimension, which might conflate the analyzed dynamics (primarily focused on the left/right competition on the economic dimension).[8]

Because it was the events prior to 2015 that actually helped reveal the dynamics discussed in this book, I have had to rely on surveys and other data collected beforehand. To account for possible biases in source materials in

[7] Economic misfortunes may trigger a sense of insecurity, which often manifests in cultural grievances. Indeed, studies have shown that economic losers are more prone than economic winners to feel culturally threatened (McLaren 2005; Hooghe, Huo, and Marks 2007). Lower-skilled socioeconomic groups may be more likely to perceive immigrant workers as an economic threat and therefore demonstrate higher levels of anti-immigration sentiment than voters from wealthier socioeconomic groups who benefit from the additional supply of cheap labor (Arzheimer 2013). For example, Svitych (2021) shows that Hungarian voters from the working and lower-middle classes made insecure by socioeconomic transitions have resorted to the neonationalist solution as an alternative system of identification and as a coping strategy. Because of this, they were more likely to support the populist right-wing party Jobbik.

[8] The dynamic of right-wing populism is strongly affected by immigration crises. In Europe, the 2015 refugee crisis, one of the most serious crises in the EU's history (Freedom House 2019), allowed right-wing populists to shift the focus of the party competition to the sociocultural dimension and raise support around the alleged cultural threat posed by immigration (Zumbrunnen and Gangl 2008: 201; Pop-Eleches 2010; Bustikova 2014; Schwartz 1999: 27). While before 2015, in the postcommunist context immigration-related concerns played a secondary role in party mobilization (Allen 2015; Bluhm and Varga 2019; Kovář 2022), afterward the salience of the sociocultural dimension soared, further spreading national populism across the region (Guiso et al. 2017; Roberts 2017c; Krastev 2018; Stefanovic and Evans 2019). In contrast, leftist parties, which have engaged on the immigration issue, have generally seen mixed electoral fortunes (Downes and Loveless 2018). Due to their more socially liberal and cosmopolitan positions on the sociocultural dimension, left parties tended to be constrained on immigration. They were further constrained in their positions by concerns of alienating immigrant and ethnic minority electorates, which constitute a large and growing source of support for this party family (Bale et al. 2010; Ford and Goodwin 2014a; Van Heerden et al. 2014). In postcommunist Europe, in the aftermath of the 2015 immigration crisis, left parties, such as Smer-SD in Slovakia (Rybář 2020) and ČSSD and KSČM in the Czech Republic (Chapter 5), experienced electoral losses.

my case studies, I relied on different types of evidence, including historical polling data as well as primary and secondary sources: scholarly and journalistic work, policymakers' memoirs, and my own open-ended interviews with political elites and observers from this period. Furthermore, in my own data collection conducted after 2015, I used survey experiments in which I had a far higher degree of control over exogenous variation and could thereby minimize the impact of timing.

## Plan of the Book

The book is organized as follows.

The first two chapters introduce the key arguments and review supporting literature drawing on comparative evidence from the different parties, elections, and countries.

Chapter 1 outlines the book's key theoretical argument. This chapter also introduces the comparison between processes in Western and postcommunist party systems. It reviews the literature on the interplay between the policy choices of left-wing parties and the electoral successes of populist-right parties. In Western Europe, the rebranding of center-left parties as pro-market entities and their participation in neoliberal reforms became known as the Third Way. This Third Way contributed to the recent rise of populist-right parties in countries such as the United Kingdom, Germany, and Sweden. Chapter 1 goes on to review the pro-market rebranding of ex-communist leftist parties in the Eastern European context, traces the subsequent decline of these parties, and explains how and why populist-right parties became the primary beneficiaries of antiestablishment sentiment in the region. This chapter also reviews the roles of international institutions. While in the 1990s international institutions such as the IMF and the World Bank helped push the Washington Consensus agenda, the EU subsequently helped seal the deal. EU conditionality helped deepen reforms and make them more uniform. Across the postcommunist region mainstream parties on both sides of the spectrum tended to embrace these policies to ensure their countries' EU accession. The chapter concludes by arguing that the observed trends in postcommunist Europe constitute part of a broader process also occurring in other polities.

In the postcommunist context the effects of left rebranding were particularly pronounced due to the role played by the working-class electorates.

Chapter 2 introduces the role of class in the postcommunist region. It discusses the challenging posttransition experiences for working-class electorates in postcommunist Europe who faced not only the disappearance of communist-era factory jobs and the erosion of safety net protections but also the fallout from the 2008 financial crisis. This chapter also explains why, unlike in Western Europe, working-class populations still constitute an electoral majority in the postcommunist European context. It also examines the individual attitudes of workers on issues of redistribution and immigration in the Visegrád Four countries. Postcommunist workers display a particular set of political attitudes that combine pro-redistributive preferences on economic policies with anti-immigration preferences on the sociocultural dimension. This is consistent with trends discussed in scholarly literature on Western Europe. This chapter also reviews the literature on class-based support to discuss how these preferences converted into party choices.

Subsequent chapters engage more directly with empirical evidence that supports the key argument. Rather than using a "silver bullet" test on which the main argument rises or falls, this book tests its argument on various levels of analysis using a number of qualitative and quantitative methods, including cross-country regression, case study, and experimental survey analysis. Each chapter discusses the strengths and weaknesses of a respective method, as well as how the strengths of some approaches may compensate for the weaknesses of others.

The first method involves a comparative quantitative analysis of how pro-market positions of left-wing parties in the region influenced support for them across various socioeconomic groups. Chapter 3 presents the results of a cross-country analysis of postcommunist European countries using data from the European Social Survey and the Chapel Hill Expert Survey, in which I link leftist parties' positions on the economy to their electoral support. Consistent with my expectations, the findings demonstrate that the increasingly pro-market positions of leftist parties are associated with a decrease in electoral support. These effects are more pronounced among economically vulnerable voters, particularly working-class electorates. In countries with reform-oriented left-wing parties, such groups are more likely to be incorporated by right-wing (conservative and radical) parties. Contrary to many studies arguing that positions on the *sociocultural* dimension largely determine the electoral fortunes of left-wing parties, this chapter presents empirical evidence that the *economic* axis has a stronger impact.

However, a downside of comparative analysis of this nature is that it provides evidence of correlation, not causation, and skimps on the specifics of how economic policies adopted by the left and the populist right affected the vote for any one individual party or election. Therefore, the cross-country comparative analysis is supplemented with a more in-depth exploration of this dynamic across paired case studies, presented in Chapters 4 and 5.

Chapter 4 explores this book's hypothesis as seen in the cases of Hungary and Poland. In both countries the ex-communist left rebranded itself to become more centrist and introduced pro-market reforms, which created more opportunities for a populist swing. Left parties followed the examples of Western social democratic parties, alienating working-class supporters and creating opportunities for the populist right to pander to the left's dissatisfied constituents. This chapter traces how these policies led to the demise of left-wing parties and explores how populist-right parties—Fidesz, Jobbik, and PiS—enjoyed extraordinary success in part because they managed to attract voters who had traditionally voted for the ex-communist leftist parties by adopting an increasingly antimarket, redistributionist agenda. Chapter 5 focuses on the experiences of two other Visegrád countries—the Czech Republic and Slovakia—where some leftist parties remained more faithful to their more traditional economic positions and thus retained the support of their traditional constituencies. It demonstrates how for a while the left's faithfulness to its traditional platform curtailed the rise of populist-right parties.

While the results of cross-country analysis and case studies support my main argument, they allow me little control over sources of variation other than leftist parties' policy choices. Experimental designs allow me to do just that by making conditions as similar as possible for all treatment groups. Thus, Chapter 6 supplements the evidence presented in previous chapters by more systematically tackling the issue of causality. It relies on an experimental survey to analyze the impact of leftist parties' centrist shifts on party alignment dynamics in Hungary. During the experimental surveys conducted in Hungary some respondents were told that left-wing parties embraced pro-market policies. These respondents said that they would choose the populist right in the next election, as long as these parties promised greater social protection. Those effects were more pronounced among working-class respondents. Without these economic promises, the anti-immigrant, nativist appeals from the populist right were not enough to cause these voters to shift their support to the populist right. These findings are then interpreted through the book's central hypothesis: that the embrace of neoliberal policies helps populist-right parties incorporate former electorates of left parties using a redistributionist platform.

The conclusion offers a summary of the book's main findings and discusses their scholarly contribution and implications. This chapter also deepens the comparison between Western and Eastern Europe. It explains how higher volatility and the fluidity of postcommunist systems in addition to the larger size of working-class electorates available for incorporation into right-wing populist parties have reinforced the party realignment dynamic in the region. It also discusses how center-left parties could adjust their economic policies and programs; adopt more distinctly leftist policy stances; address the demands of frustrated and economically vulnerable voters who currently find their economic needs best represented on the right side of the political spectrum; and reduce the rightward drift of party systems. This chapter also analyzes the limitations of such policy adjustments; the endorsement of redistributionist-leaning policy stances seems to work for the left when their policies are not constrained by the requirements of the European Union, and when a political opening (sizable shares of electorates of other parties available for mobilization) exists in a given political system.

# 1

# How the Left Moved Right

Embracing neoliberalism might have seemed like a highly improbable choice for ex-communist left parties. After all, these choices meant a complete rejection of their historical track. Not just because newly adopted policies were, in fact, quite opposite to the ideals of communism and Marxism these parties espoused for decades, but also because during communist rule these parties "became the stereotype of unchanging behemoths, the progenitors of the stolid homo sovieticus and political organizations unable to change their bureaucratic and plodding ways" (Grzymala-Busse 2002b: 19). How, then, can one explain the process that unraveled following the transition? Which factors prompted these rigid ex-communist structures to undergo an almost revolutionary change, and how did their supporters respond to it? This chapter tells this story.

To understand the rebranding of left-wing parties in Eastern Europe, we first have to step back and look at the history of what was happening to the left in Western Europe. Finally free of communist rule, postcommunist societies were inspired and motivated by the desire to join Europe more broadly, and the EU project more specifically. To do so, they were actively and sometimes almost religiously embracing policy prescriptions coming from the West. Krastev and Holmes (2018) describe the motto of the time as "Imitate the West!" Beyond broader societal agreement in favor of reforms, further pressure came from international institutions, such as the IMF, the World Bank, and the EU, which put additional constraints on the policy options of Eastern European governments (Pop-Eleches 2010; Appel and Orenstein 2018).

The consensus around market transition through neoliberal policies at the time of the transition in the West radically impacted the positions of most political actors across the region. Thus, following the Third Way rebranding of leftist parties in countries such as the United Kingdom, Germany, and Sweden, their Eastern European counterparts tended to copy this behavior and adopt similar platforms. This chapter traces this dynamic in detail. I first explain how the Western European left came to embrace neoliberal ideals and then describe related choices faced by the ex-communist left following

*When Left Moves Right.* Maria Snegovaya, Oxford University Press. © Oxford University Press 2024.
DOI: 10.1093/oso/9780197699027.003.0002

the transition. I complement this analysis with a review of existing scholarship on Western and Eastern Europe to demonstrate notable parallels across both regions.

Little did these parties know that their embrace of neoliberalism had long-term strings attached. Pro-market reforms in postcommunist Europe launched a socioeconomic cleavage between the economic "winners" and "losers" of the transition. While initially they attracted support and won elections, in both regions reformist left parties ended up losing their key support groups, particularly groups that missed out on the transition and, among them, significant chunks of working-class electorates. In both regions there was a delayed reaction due to the dynamic of electorates' realignment. As this chapter explains, in the postcommunist context the backlash against the reformist left was both further delayed and exacerbated by EU conditionality.

Ultimately, the watering down of the left's distinctive historical profile rendered reformist left parties unable to take advantage of widespread discontent over the fallout from neoliberal reforms, EU accession, and the 2008 financial crisis (Berman and Snegovaya 2019). It further opened the door for populist right parties to incorporate large swaths of former left parties' electorates. Those "left behind" by the reforms could no longer look to traditional leftist parties to address their grievances and thus turned to right-wing populist parties instead (Berman and Snegovaya 2019; Roberts 2015: 22).

This chapter traces this dynamic. Rather than presenting the postcommunist story as unique and idiosyncratic, it demonstrates the pronounced parallels across both regions.

## Is There a Third Way?

> We thought we could find a third way,
> but it turned out there isn't one.
> —Pierre Mauroy, prime minister of France's
> first majority socialist government, 1990
> (quoted in Lewis 1990)

Historically, Western European left party positions unfolded along two axes that structure electoral competition: the economic axis, where left parties stand for stronger market regulation, economic equality, and wealth redistribution; and the sociocultural axis, where left parties generally oppose nationalist projects (Lipset and Rokkan 1967; Bartolini and Mair 1990). The traditional economic policies offered by left parties aligned with the preferences of economically vulnerable social groups, commonly found among classes with access to fewer socioeconomic resources, such as working classes and lower-level white-collar workers. At the time, these groups constituted the left parties' primary support base (Berman 2006; Arzheimer 2013; Kitschelt 2013; Mudge 2018; Rennwald 2020). The essential goals of social democracy focused on minimizing "the cost of capitalism" for these groups through employment and welfare policies and reducing inequalities within the confines of a democracy and market economy (Hirst 1999: 87; Berman 2006; Bremer 2018). The long interdependence between left parties, trade unions, and socialist societies also differentiated the social democratic left from other political parties. While these ties reinforced the salience of class identity for left parties, they also constrained the extent to which ideology could be strategically expanded, creating the "dilemma of electoral socialism" (Przeworski and Sprague 1986). In comparison to other parties, left parties were less likely to shift ideological positions because of changes in public opinion (Karreth, Polk, and Allen 2013). Yet by the end of the twentieth century, a series of dramatic events led to a radical change within these patterns of party competition.

Since the 1950s, the Western left had come to be dominated by Keynesian economic policies, which included a focus on public spending and income redistribution, an interventionist role of the state in the economy, and stronger regulation. Left parties combined these policies with promises to temper or even eliminate capitalism's dangerous consequences and promote greater equality. The three decades that followed the Second World War saw an extraordinarily high level of economic growth, which fostered social policy expansion. However, by the late 1970s, the structural context of social policy had changed dramatically. The welfare state was strained by slowing economic growth and deindustrialization, rising structural unemployment, demographic aging, and declining birth rates. All of this undermined the egalitarian achievements of the postwar era (Häusermann 2018: 11; Meyerson 2020). Ongoing globalization further undermined left parties' capacity to sustain these policies; to remain competitive in the global economy, countries increasingly needed to reform their welfare state systems and make labor markets flexible (Blyth 2003). It was uncertain whether expansionist social policy could continue or if globalization would radically erode social policy programs (Kuhnle 2000).

Doubts about the long-term viability of interventionist policies coincided with a transformation of left party electorates during the late twentieth century. The expansion of higher education access contributed to the emancipation of the working class, which weakened its dependence on left-wing subcultures and organizations and transformed it into a more heterogeneous group (Oesch 2006a, 2006b; Rovny 2018). The workforce has become more individualized, fragmenting the organized electoral basis of the left parties (Mann 1995; Eley 2002; Clark 2003; Azmanova 2004). During this period, unions and other social groups that supported working-class allegiance to left parties were on the decline (Poguntke 2002). Meanwhile, the share of blue-collar workers that made up the voter population was halved. (For example, in the 1970s production workers represented almost 33% of the population and were by far the largest group in Western Europe; by the 2010s they formed about 16% of the population, a proportion equivalent to that of managers and slightly smaller than that of service workers [Rennwald 2020: 27].) As the traditional working class shrank, a new economically vulnerable occupational group emerged, the precariat, a social class defined by its irregular employment and lack of occupational identity (Standing 2014). In the context of these changing dynamics, the left had an incentive to appeal to new electorates, such as middle-class professionals, with pro-market-oriented economic platforms (Rovny 2018).

In response to mounting doubts about the economic viability of the redistributive state, the overuse of economic interventionist policies, and changing voter profiles, an alternative consensus started to take shape among left parties during the 1980s. Many parties started searching for an intermediary approach between social democracy and neoliberalism. The underlying idea, the catch-all thesis, presumed that moderating their ideological positions would help the left cast a wider net and catch more floating voters located nearer to the center of the political spectrum (Kirchheimer 1966; Safran 2009; Allen 2009). Tony Blair (1997: 1), for example, argued that the rebranded "New Labour is neither old left nor new right. . . . Instead we offer a new way ahead, that leads from the centre but is profoundly radical in the change it promises." In an effort to expand their electorates, left parties in the Netherlands, Belgium, France, Germany, Great Britain, Austria, Sweden, and elsewhere started changing their platforms to globalize and deregulate their economies (Glyn 2001; Moschonas 2002; Bonoli and Powell 2004). Simultaneously, the background of key leaders in economic policy changed dramatically: the Keynesians gave way to transnational-finance-oriented economists and technocrats, unassociated with unions and instead closely connected to financial institutions (Berman 2010; Mudge 2018; O'Grady 2019). The consensus that emerged from a reevaluation of economic policies among various center-left movements and parties came to be defined as a "Third Way" (Lewis & Rebecca 2004: 3–4; Keman 2011). In several countries, Third Way policies were associated with specific political leaders; for example, in Britain this shift was led by Blair's New Labour, in the United States by Bill Clinton's New Democrats, in Germany by Gerhard Schroeder's Social Democratic Party (Die Neue Mitte), and in Sweden by Olof Palme's Swedish Social Democratic Party.

This shift toward increasingly centrist, pro-market, neoliberal policies was extraordinary and unprecedented for the historic trajectory of left parties. Many of them abandoned such traditional tools of social democracy as industrial policy, active fiscal policy, and the expansion of social policies (Mudge 2018; Bremer and McDaniel 2020; Bremer and Rennwald 2022). Contrary to state interventionism, rigid welfare entitlements, and the state regulation of the market economy, Third Way parties promoted market-friendliness, the decentralization of government power, and a shift away from spending to maintaining balanced budgets. Such parties accepted and often pioneered policies like partial privatization of the welfare state and government-run services and enterprises, taxation reforms, and heavy restrictions on trade tariffs that, in an earlier era, would have been unthinkable (Berman and Snegovaya 2019). Instead of redistributing incomes, they emphasized equal opportunities (Giddens 1998; Rosenau 2003). Governments treated supporting the market as their primary responsibility and allowed educational self-investment, work, and law and order to take precedence over protective welfarism, decommodification, and regulation (Mudge 2018: 63).[1]

At first, the Third Way looked like a roaring success. The embrace of pro-market policies allowed left parties to expand their voter bases by including more centrist moderate voters. While social democratic parties previously appealed primarily to production workers and lower-middle-class workers,

---

[1] Even the underlying notion of traditional left-wing concepts started to change. For example, in the 1950s the former leader of Swedish Social Democratic Party Tage Erlander understood *security* to mean the abolition of poverty and insecurity through extended societal responsibilities (Andersson 2006). But under Third Way rebranding in the party's platform, *security* came to imply individual "freedom of choice." As the updated party's program stated in 1984, "Now, when a major expansion of the public sector has taken place, greater weight can be attached to another dimension of the social democratic concept of freedom. Now our efforts should be focused on allowing citizens greater choice in how to take advantage of the resources of the public sector" (Andersson 2013 : 119).

this centrist move further expanded their reach to other constituencies. They transformed from hybrid working-class parties into "catch-all" parties (Allen 2009; Rennwald 2020: 91). As a result, these parties often won elections throughout the mid-1990s. Blair's New Labour in 1997, Gerhard Schröder's Neue Mitte in 1998, and the Italian Olive Tree coalition in 1996 all won their elections by adopting a moderation strategy (Kitschelt 1994; Karreth, Polk, and Allen 2013).

Despite their initial successes, however, these parties tended to lose subsequent elections (Arndt 2013). To give a sense of the scale: in the late 1990s, left parties or coalitions with left participation governed twelve of the then-fifteen EU countries, but by 2011 social democratic parties had suffered across most of the EU. They experienced substantial defeats in traditional strongholds of social democracy such as Germany, France, Britain, and Finland (Karreth, Polk, and Allen 2013; see Figure 1.1).

While the centrist shift was first rewarded with electoral victories, it transformed left parties' long-standing profile in a way that weakened their

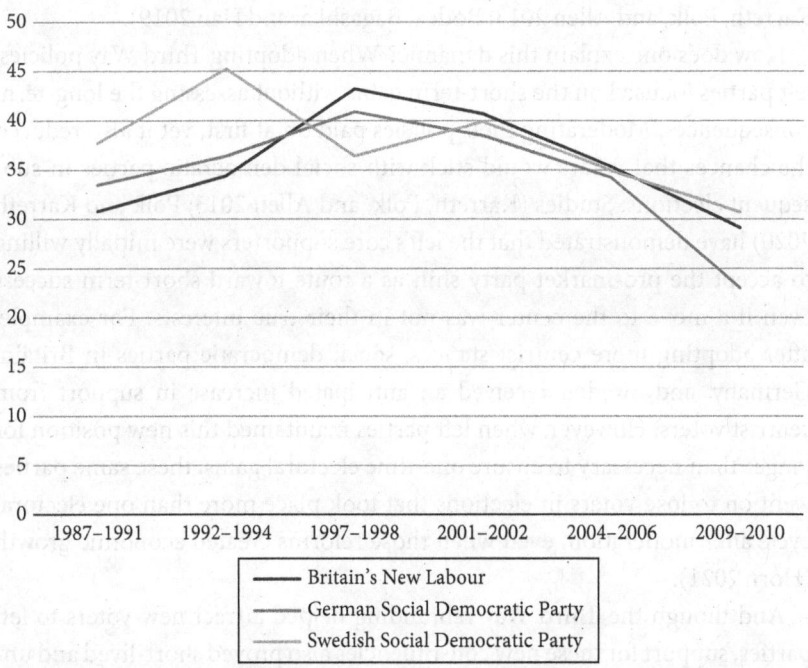

**Figure 1.1** Electoral Fortunes of Social Democratic Parties in Britain, Germany, and Sweden in 1992–2010.

ability to capture the support of economically vulnerable social groups (Berman and Snegovaya 2019). The success of Western European left parties in the postwar era relied on the assertion that the democratic state could temper the market's dangerous consequences. Left-wing parties typically aligned a core constituency comprising manual workers and lower-level white-collar employees. Given their, on average, below-median income, these classes benefited more from income redistribution and therefore favored generous and universal social security schemes and redistribution-oriented policies.

When social democrats reformed welfare state systems, their former voters either increasingly abstained from voting or (in the presence of viable competitors) switched to other parties, consequently launching a realignment process (Arndt 2013). Reformist left parties were poorly positioned to capture the resentment that followed the weakening of the postwar social democratic order and its fallout: the sharp increase in economic inequality and insecurity (Berman and Snegovaya 2019: 9). As a result, following the adoption of new policies, many social democratic parties in Europe saw their electoral support decline within several electoral rounds (Arndt 2013; Karreth, Polk, and Allen 2013; Bodea, Bagashka, and Han 2019).

How does one explain this dynamic? When adopting Third Way policies, left parties focused on the short-term gains without assessing the long-term consequences. Moderating their policies paid off at first, yet it also reduced the chances that voters would stick with social democratic parties in subsequent elections. Studies (Karreth, Polk, and Allen 2013; Polk and Karreth 2020) have demonstrated that the left's core supporters were initially willing to accept the pro-market party shift as a route toward short-term success even if a move to the center was not in their true interests. For example, after adopting more centrist stances, social democratic parties in Britain, Germany, and Sweden received an anticipated increase in support from centrist voters. However, when left parties maintained this new position for longer than necessary to ensure one-time electoral gains, these same parties went on to lose voters in elections that took place more than one electoral cycle after moderation, even when those reforms created economic growth (Horn 2021).

And though the Third Way rebranding helped attract new voters to left parties, support for these new constituencies also proved short-lived and unsustainable. The influx of centrist support receded because these new voters were less attached to social democrats and just as willing to vote for other parties or abstain from voting altogether (Padgett 2001; Polk and Karreth 2020: 4). In the long run, moderating strategies cost left parties their traditional electorates and did not attract enough new voters to compensate for the loss of their former constituencies (Karreth, Polk, and Allen 2013). As a result, left parties' centrist moves in the 1990s, "while initially successful, contributed to their losing power by the early to mid-2000s" (Allen 2009: 636).

The adoption of pro-market policies by left parties had other unintended consequences. The centrist move by left parties diminished political polarization between left and right in traditional economic terms, which resulted in fewer class-related options available for voters (Evans and de Graaf 2013; Jansen, Evans, and De Graaf 2013). Studies of Austria's, the United Kingdom's, and Sweden's political systems demonstrate that such moves led to an ideological convergence between major parties, which in turn resulted in a reduction in class voting (Evans and Tilley 2012, 2017; Rennwald and Evans 2014; Oskarson and Demker 2015).

Importantly, the transformation of the left's relationship to the working class was not purely a function of structural change, that is, of workers representing a smaller share of the electorate as a whole (Benedetto, Hix, and Mastrorocco 2020). The disassociation of working-class interests from center-left parties has become a chief feature of social democratic parties since the 1990s (Meyerson 2020). While in the 1970s working-class electorates voted for social democratic parties more often than average and represented a large share of their electorates, by the 2010s they had become much less distinctive in their support for center-left parties and represented a smaller share of these parties' constituencies (Bürgisser and Kurer 2021; Gingrich and Häusermann 2015; Bremer and Rennwald 2022).

Working-class electorates (primarily production and service workers) are more pro-redistribution and anti-immigration than average, and their preferences have remained stable over time (although they have become more distinctively opposed to immigration) (Rennwald 2020: 83, see also Chapter 2). However, while left parties' positions on immigration have remained relatively unchanged over the period under review (they have always been more liberal on the sociocultural dimension than most parties), their economic positions changed considerably when they adopted positions more friendly toward the market. Therefore, the social democratic parties' programmatic shift on economic policy accounts for a significant portion of the observed changes in voting patterns.

For example, after Britain's Labour Party shifted to the center on the economic policy dimension in the mid-1990s, the main parties converged ideologically. This shift can explain the decline in class voting (Evans and Tilley 2017). The pattern of economic policy convergence within the Austrian Social Democratic Party was associated with a reduction in class voting during the 1990s (Rennwald and Evans 2014). The financial collapse of 2008 and the unequal recovery that followed have further accelerated the working-class's abandonment of social democratic parties (Meyerson 2020).

The rebranding of left parties launched an in-depth party realignment process in these countries. The centrist shift of left parties dealigned their traditional support groups and created opportunities for parties on the opposite side of the political spectrum to attract former left parties' electorates to their cause. When mainstream parties cut popular social policies, right-wing populist parties transformed into zealous defenders of the welfare state. These new positions mixed nicely with the populist right parties' vision that immigrants make excessive use of the welfare state, which makes it unaffordable (Schumacher and Van Kersbergen 2016). Combining their nativist stances with a newly adopted redistributionist economic platform, right-wing parties appealed primarily to economically vulnerable social groups. In doing so, they attracted former left party supporters (Harteveld 2016; Arndt 2013). Subsequently, electorates that previously voted for left parties were gradually incorporated by many conservative and radical right parties (Kriesi 1999; Bornschier 2010a; Arzheimer 2013).

Since the 1990s, working-class constituencies that had supported left parties gradually became the core support groups of many populist right parties. For example, in Sweden former supporters of the Social Democratic Party who switched to the populist right Swedish Democrats were more likely to belong to the working class, to have lower socioeconomic status and more left-leaning socioeconomic preferences, and to express welfare chauvinism than other voters (Jylhä, Rydgren, and Strimling 2019). In Britain, some former supporters of the Labour Party were incorporated into populist right parties—the British National Party and the United Kingdom Independent Party (Kite 2006; Bale at al. 2012; Evans and Mellon 2016). And many former supporters of the Social Democratic Party of Germany shifted their support to the nationalist-populist Alternative for Germany (Wurthmann et al. 2020; Hansen and Olsen 2019; see the book's conclusion for more details).

Scholarship described this increasing representation of working-class voters among populist right constituencies as the "proletarianization" of the populist right in Western Europe (Kriesi 1999; Gougou and Mayer 2013; Harteveld 2016). Blue-collar workers have become the core constituency of the Austrian Freedom Party, the Belgian Flemish Block, the Danish People's Party, the French National Front (Front National, pronounced, FN), and the Norwegian Progress Party (Bornschier 2010b; Arzheimer 2013). More recent studies expand this observation beyond working-class electorates to include lower-middle-class non-manual workers like clerical, sales, and service workers. For example, Harteveld (2016) argues that voters with more precarious occupations tend to be deterred by parties' neoliberal policies and instead support radical right parties that embrace redistributionist economic positions.

Below I illustrate this dynamic in the cases of Britain, Germany, and Sweden, whose left parties were at the forefront of the Third Way rebranding.

## Britain

Britain's Labour Party was originally established by the trade union movement to fight for working-class interests and became one of the most conventionally Keynesian center-left parties in Europe (Clasen and Clegg 2004: 94). By the early 1990s, long-term social changes were eroding the electoral support of the Labour Party, which created the need to expand its social base by wooing middle-class voters (Evans and Tilley 2012; Heath, Jowell, and Curtice 2001). After his accession to the party leadership in 1994, Tony Blair and some of his close advisors introduced the Third Way rebranding of the party. To demonstrate an affinity with professional and middle-class voters, Blair's "New Labour" Party replaced the party's traditional left-wing ideology with more economically centrist and socially liberal positions (Ford and Godwin 2014b: 281; O'Grady 2019). The party also adopted welfare reforms, which, among other policies, substantially reduced welfare generosity and made social payments more temporary, means-tested, and subject to greater conditions (Clasen 2005; Lupton et al. 2013). Simultaneously the Labour Party scaled down its previous working-class focus. While it had once "regularly referred to the working class in both speeches and policy documents," by century's end "there [was] little recognition of class" in its platform (Evans and Tilley 2017: 192; Berman and Kundnani 2021).

This rebranding strategy resulted in the gradual loss of Labour's traditional working-class supporters during the 2000s. Studies show that during the 1980s and 1990s, a large majority of blue-collar voters and low-skilled employees most often identified with the Labour Party (Ford and Godwin 2014b: 281). However, in 2005 and 2010, the rebranding of Labour was followed by a huge drop in electoral participation from the areas of the country that were typically full of Labour supporters (Ford and Goodwin 2014a).

In subsequent years, some former Labour supporters were incorporated by populist right parties. The British National Party drew disproportionally high support from older, less-educated working-class men living in the declining industrial towns in the mid-2000s (Ford and Goodwin 2010), so that some observers suggested the party had become a "home for many disgruntled former Labour voters" (Kite 2006) and was establishing "itself as a rival to Labour" in many of its traditional strongholds (Bale, Hough, and Van Kessel 2012: 97). The United Kingdom Independent Party (UKIP) also drew significantly on working-class support. Its agenda resonated with working-class Britons, many of whom sought greater unionization and expansion of social services, while also opposing immigration and backing EU dissolution (Gest 2016). Among these electorates, UKIP attracted significant shares of disaffected former Labour voters (Evans and Mellon 2016). Subsequent studies have shown that UKIP has had the largest working-class following in British politics since Michael Foot led the Labour Party into the 1983 general election (Ford and Goodwin 2014b: 282). Some observers even described UKIP as "the most working-class party" in British politics (Goodwin and Ford 2014).

To win back some of the working-class electorates, the Labour Party attempted some rebranding, by appointing far-left socialist Jeremy Corbyn in 2015. Studies show that many alienated voters joined Labour for the first time when Corbyn appeared on the leadership ballot, particularly those with anticapitalist and left-wing values (Whiteley et al. 2019).

## Germany

The Social Democratic Party of Germany (SPD) historically drew support from workers and lower-middle-class voters. During the 1990s, under the leadership of former chancellor Gerhard Schröder, the party subscribed to the Third Way. It adopted a new label, Neue Mitte (the New Center), that emphasized the party's shift to the center. Along with this rebranding, the SPD significantly moderated its platform on economic matters and during the mid-2000s implemented a series of reforms of the welfare state and labor markets, making it easier to lay off employees and slash benefits. From 2003 to 2005 the SPD engaged in further welfare state retrenchment and labor market deregulation during the "Hartz reforms." These policies undermined the social contract to defend high standards of employment rights and welfare entitlements for core workers that underpinned the long-standing alliance between the SPD and the trade unions. The effect was especially deleterious for working-class constituencies in declining economic sectors and socially disadvantaged groups (Dostal 2017).

The rebranding drew working-class constituencies from the SPD and opened opportunities for other parties to incorporate these electorates (Adorf 2018: 37–38). Subsequently the SPD lost up to half of its former electoral coalition, namely blue-collar voters and socially disadvantaged groups, while efforts to gain access to centrist and middle-class voters failed to produce compensating gains (Dostal 2017). By the late 2000s, former SPD voters had flown in multiple directions, many of them abstaining from voting, others joining other centrist parties. A significant share of former SPD voters also turned away from the center-left electoral camp and moved to the right—initially to the center-right but more recently (since its founding in 2013), to the new Alternative for Germany (Alternative für Deutschland, AfD) party (Dostal 2017).

Founded in 2012, the AfD started as a Euroskeptic and market-liberal party that focused on attracting primarily middle-class voters. However, by 2017 the AfD had transformed into a right-wing nationalist party combining anti-immigration positions with a welfare chauvinist agenda, that is, social protection "for Germans" (Bennhold 2018).[2] As it veered further to the right, the AfD also made inroads into the working-class electorate. In the 2017 German federal election, the AfD received 11.5% of votes, with particular success in eastern Germany. There, it attracted electorates dissatisfied with the political establishment (Olsen 2018), economically insecure voters (Bergmann 2017), and workers in the manufacturing sector (Berning 2017; Franz, Fratzscher, and Kritikos 2018; Rennwald 2020: 59). AfD drew significant shares of its support from former SPD voters, at a rate of about 10% (Wurthmann et al. 2020; Hansen and Olsen 2019). Some observers believe

---

[2] In this sense, its trajectory was close to that of Fidesz in Hungary, which also started as a center-right party in the 1990s but increasingly adopted more nationalist-populist themes (Krekó and Mayer 2015).

the AfD is on its way to becoming the preferred party of working-class voters (Adorf 2018).

## Sweden

In the postwar era, the Swedish Social Democratic Party (SAP) has consistently attracted large shares of working-class and lower-middle-class electorates. Throughout this time Sweden's party system was structured around the economic dimension based on class cleavage (Knutsen 2006; Oskarson 2005). During the 1990s, however, the SAP adopted more neoliberal ideas and implemented several pro-market reforms (Andersson 2013). Since the 1990s, under the leadership of Hans Göran Persson, the SAP has abandoned its earlier commitment to full employment, reduced social insurance replacement rates, introduced wholesale pension reform, and adopted price stability as a key point of reference in wage bargaining (Belfrage and Ryner 2009: 126). Welfare cuts and tax increases introduced under the SAP government decreased the country's budget deficit and placed Sweden in a position to qualify for the European Economic and Monetary Union.

This programmatic shift blurred the SAP's identity and ended up eroding its support among working-class and lower-middle-class voters. It especially alienated those public service workers and civil servants maintaining the welfare state (Andersson and Östberg 2020: 327). This led to dealignment between the working class and the SAP in subsequent years (Oskarson and Demker 2015) and a massive electoral decline of the SAP. Notably, in the 2018 elections it performed worse than it ever had in its hundred-year history (Andersson and Ostberg 2020: 323).

These developments provided political openings for other parties. Since 2010, the nationalist-populist Sweden Democrats party (SD) has rapidly emerged from obscurity, becoming the country's third-largest party. It did so by combining nostalgia for a substantial welfare state with a nativist platform that blames immigration for the decline of the social safety net. SD members portrayed themselves as the true defenders of the welfare state and criticized mainstream parties for betraying it (Bergmann 2017). These ideas strongly resonated with many former SAP voters (Belfrage and Ryner 2009: 127), while the presence of significant working-class electorates dealigned from the SAP has given the SD an opportunity to mobilize their support (Oskarson and Demker 2015).

Subsequent studies have shown that SD voters typically belong to the working class, have lower socioeconomic status as well as left-leaning socio-economic preferences, face lower relative income and higher job insecurity, and have more readily expressed welfare chauvinism than other voters (Dal Bó et al. 2018; Jylhä, Rydgren, and Strimling 2019). Oskarson and Demker (2013) show that by the late 2000s the majority of support for the SD came from lower-skilled technical workers: the SD was the second-largest party in the sympathies of skilled blue-collar (lower-level technical) workers, outnumbered only by the SAP. Slightly over 50% of SD sympathizers had occupations in lower-level sales and service or low-skilled technical occupations. This means that the SD received its strongest support from what used to be the core supporters of SAP (Oskarson and Demker 2013: 177).

## The Eastern European Story

In the Eastern European context this dynamic unraveled in a similar fashion under the influence of several factors including the international and domestic ones.

## International Pressure

An important consequence of the acceptance of pro-market policies by the Western European left was that it critically shaped and determined the trajectories of the postcommunist left as well. The consensus that formed around the rapid market transition through neoliberal policies in the West influenced the positions of most mainstream political actors and reformers across postcommunist Europe, from Czechoslovakia to Russia (Roháč 2013; Orenstein 2009). Citing Krastev and Holmes (2018: 118), at the time "the political philosophy of postcommunist Central and Eastern Europe could be summarized in a single imperative: Imitate the West! The process was called by different names—democratization, liberalization, enlargement, convergence, integration, Europeanization—but the goal pursued by postcommunist reformers was the same. They wished their countries to become 'normal,' which meant like the West." Across the region, people wanted to experience the dividends of growth in an elevation of living standards and wages, converging with Western European levels. In Hungary the key phrase in the public debate during the institutional and legal standardization with EU requirements was *real harmonization* (Tóth, László, and Hosszú 2012). This process implied importing liberal-democratic institutions, applying Western political and economic recipes, and endorsing Western values. Postcommunist countries widely viewed borrowing Western institutions as the shortest pathway to freedom and prosperity (Krastev and Holmes 2018: 118).[3]

Beyond a simple desire to imitate the West, the pressure of international institutions gave postcommunist politicians additional incentives to engage in competitive signaling to foster economic reforms (Appel and Orenstein 2018). The first stage of reforms was greatly assisted by the IMF and the World Bank, which helped push the Washington Consensus agenda. The adoption of pro-market policies by reformed left parties was partly a function of the need for Western economic assistance in light of the failure of previous administrative economic systems. Financial and institutional constraints reduced the range of policy options available to the regional governments. The early postcommunist governments in countries like Hungary and Poland were in debt from the communist period and thus dependent on the IMF's continuous debt restructuring and aid. This provided the IMF with the leverage to push the parties in power to implement painful pro-market reforms by making access to debt refinancing and international credit markets conditional on the adoption of austerity measures and market-based structural adjustment policies (Stone 2002; Blyth 2013; De la Porte and Heins 2015).

In Poland, for example, the IMF provided a strong impetus for neoliberal reforms. While Polish governments were generally ideologically committed to reforms (see Chapter 4), the IMF imposed additional incentives to ensure their strict adherence to reform plans (Stone 2002: 114). In particular, Bönker (2006: 119) shows that the reforms by the ex-communist government led by the Democratic Left Alliance (Sojusz Lewicy Demokratycznej, SLD)

---

[3] The desire to join NATO was less straightforward in this regard. Most of the former communist countries have applied for membership in both NATO (or its precursor Partnership for Peace initiative) and the EU. Yet when it comes to the ex-communist governments, the positions on NATO among leaders who had previously advocated orientation toward the Soviet Union were mixed. While most of them accepted the idea of European integration, many, like the Bulgarian Socialist Party, continued to reject participation in a military alliance with the United States (Lunak 1994; Kostadinova 2010). Even in Poland, the electoral victory of the left-wing coalition of the SLD and the Polish Peasant Party in 1993 originally led to a setback in Polish ambitions to join NATO, but the Polish left changed their stance on NATO in subsequent years (Piotrowski and Rachwald 2001). In other cases, such as the Hungarian Socialist Party, the left actively advocated for integration into NATO and the EU from the start (Ziblatt 1998; Rizova 2014).

were greatly assisted by the IMF's insistence on fiscal constraints.[4] Similarly, in Hungary the collaboration between the Hungarian Socialist Party (Magyar Szocialista Párt, MSZP) the reformed ex-communist party and the IMF, which was established in the late 1970s, continued after the transition. The strong indebtedness of the Hungarian economy made the left MSZP government consistently dependent upon IMF support.[5] The downfall of the MSZP in the 2010 parliamentary election followed another round of implementation of austerity measures, which had been introduced in 2008 under the IMF loan agreement (Csaba 2013; Chapter 4).

While international institutions like the IMF and the World Bank helped push reforms in the 1990s, the EU subsequently helped complete the job (Lendvai 2009: 26; Appel and Orenstein 2018: 87). As a result, postcommunist governments were often pressured "to make unpalatable and politically unpopular policy choices that broke with established policy baselines and charted new trajectories of economic development" (Roberts 2017b: 223).

## Domestic Pressure

Along with international pressure came a domestic push to reform. In light of the collapse of communism and existing pro-market consensus in their respective societies, rebranding strategies helped ex-communist parties regain democratic access to governmental power by winning elections and entering democratic governments. Programmatic transformations were often the only way for these parties to sway the democratic electorate without their

[4] The new SLD-led government aimed to defy critics and demonstrate its respectability by not losing the support of the IMF. The reliance on the IMF-imposed standards strengthened the position of the Polish finance minister Marek Borowski in the negotiations on the 1994 budget and helped him to fend off the demands for further spending increases. The SLD's desire not to risk IMF support also became visible after Borowski's resignation in February 1994. While the minister of finance's position remained vacant for three months, the government managed to prevent budget renegotiation throughout this period (Bönker 2007).

[5] Ziblatt (1998) illustrates the Hungarian left government's adherence to the IMF-imposed constraints with the following episode. In 1995, the MSZP government under Bokros and Horn pursued an extensive austerity program that aimed to receive a special "stand-by" three-year loan from the IMF as a reward for its efforts at budget cuts, socialist state reduction, and inflation control. But while the IMF commended the MSZP's austerity efforts, it demanded further cuts in social security and accelerated privatization (Szilagyi 1995: 64). This pushed Bokros and Horn into announcing an even deeper budget deficit reduction in January 1996, finally winning the IMF loan in February 1996. Therefore, the pro-reformist orientation of Hungary's left MSZP was further reinforced by an external factor: dependence upon the IMF loans.

old patronage networks and populist leaders (Grzymała-Busse 2002b). As Marcin Piatkowski points out, "The only way for these parties to recover from their tainted communist past was 'to become holier than the Pope.' It meant becoming more pro-democratic, more pro-market and more technocratic than their right-wing competitors" (in discussion with the author, July 2022).[6] The increasingly professional approach these parties used to win elections was reminiscent of variants of the catch-all and electoral professional party of Western European type (Lewis, 2002).

As a result, many ex-communist parties in postcommunist Europe became avowedly socially democratic and engaged in reforms in an effort to credibly signal that they were economically pro-market and culturally modern (Kitschelt et al. 1999; Grzymala-Busse 2002a, b; March and Mudde 2005). Reformed ex-communist left parties often directly modeled themselves after mainstream left parties in Western Europe by distancing themselves from "dogmatic Marxism," renouncing the label "communism," and redefining themselves as "European" social democratic parties consisting of "experts," "technocrats," and "pragmatists" (Bozoki and Ishiyama 2002). Competition over who was the better manager and the more efficient administrator gave transformed ex-communist parties a competitive advantage (Grzymala-Busse and Innes 2003). They were able to create a credible image as a party capable of providing more economic security during the transition to a market economy (Mahr and Nagle 1995: 398). Consequently, successor parties in postcommunist Europe effectively filled the sociopolitical niche occupied by social democratic parties in Western Europe (Mahr and Nagle 1995: 397). This is what Hungary's MSZP and Poland's SLD did. They became proponents of privatization and integration into the European Union.

For example, in Poland, the SLD viewed its collaboration with social democratic international organizations, such as the Party of European Socialists, as an important way to signal a clear break from its communist past and legitimate itself as a "normal" European social democratic party (Szczerbiak and Bil 2009). The SLD claimed to have particularly close bilateral ties with reformist left parties such as the Swedish Social Democrats, the Italian Democratic Left, and the British Labour Party. In its early electoral program SLD made multiple references to programmatic themes embraced by the European social democratic parties, including the need for a "social Europe"

---

[6] Marcin Piatkowski served as an advisor to Poland's deputy premier and minister of finance Grzegorz W. Kolodko in 2002–2003 and contributed to the fiscal reform program.

and defending the rights of women and sexual minorities (Szczerbiak and Bil 2009). Similarly, the MSZP combined promises of a rapid improvement in living standards for all segments of the population and economic growth with social protection for pensioners, parents, young people, and the unemployed (Oltay 1994a, 1994b). The MSZP leaders, activists, and supporters frequently traveled to the West and studied and worked there. Thus, since the early transition years, the MSZP strongly embraced Europeanization and Westernization and was the pioneer in creating the left party of European type in the postcommunist region (Agh 1995: 493, 495). Similarly, the rebranding of the Slovak ex-communist Party of the Democratic Left (SDĽ) was largely driven by the desire to join the Socialist International (Haughton 2002: 1321). The party openly professed its support for "political orientations manifested in the Socialist International"[7] (Handl and Leška 2005: 112). Other ex-communist parties, such as the Bulgarian Socialist Party and the Socialist Party of Albania, also professed their "social democratization," albeit relying more heavily on political nostalgia to mobilize electoral support (Ishiyama 1995, 1997; Bozoki and Ishiyama 2002).

Newly reformed ex-communist parties ardently sought to prove their capitalist bona fides by outpacing the right in advocating for neoliberal market reforms (Innes 2017; Orenstein and Bugaric 2020). The latter typically included tax incentives and continuously lowered corporate tax rates, deregulation, flexible labor standards, and low wages for a relatively well-educated labor force. Between 1990 and 2010 the reformist left parties led the most pronounced wave of neoliberalism (Orenstein 2013a, 2013b), which included the privatization of pensions (Appel and Orenstein 2018) as well as energy and water utilities (Boda and Scheiring 2006), and decreasing the value and duration of unemployment insurance (Scheiring and Szombati 2020: 4). There was also a failed attempt to liberalize health insurance (Korkut and Buzogány 2015). The austerity policies proved to be particularly painful for economically vulnerable groups dependent on state safety nets (Grittersova et al. 2016; Hugrée, Penissat, and Spire 2020). Throughout this period left parties embraced such ardently pro-market policies that whether they could still be considered leftist was a matter of debate. Statistically, they were more likely to adhere to fiscal austerity and tighter budgets than the rightist parties of the region (March and Mudde 2005; Tavits and Letki 2009).

---

[7] The Socialist International is a worldwide organization of parties seeking to establish democratic socialism.

At the same time, in the early 1990s reformist left parties retained the support of reform losers in a way consistent with the traditional left-right divide. As Chapter 2 demonstrates, once the reforms began in the Czech Republic, Hungary, Poland, and Slovakia, the patterns of voting behavior reflected voter experience with economic reforms and were consistent with social class-based preferences: those voters who benefited from the reforms (the private entrepreneurs, urban residents, white-collar workers, and highly educated voters) voted for the right-wing pro-reform parties, whereas those who became worse off (the unemployed, retirees, blue-collar workers, and rural residents) voted for the left-wing parties (Fidrmuc 2000: 215; Mateju, Rehakova, and Evans 1999). The working-class vote in support of the ex-communist parties was the most important factor explaining why these parties won the elections only four years after the fall of communism (Szelenyi, Fodor, and Hanley 1996: 216). To attract reform losers, left parties promised to provide these groups with social security and protection from market volatility. For example, during the 1994 electoral campaign, Hungary's reformist left MSZP portrayed itself as the only representative of worker interests in Parliament and collaborated with Hungarian unions to oppose new legislation by the then-ruling right coalition, which it presented as a direct threat to worker interests. Similarly, the Polish pro-market left SLD collaborated with Polish trade unions and combined pledges for further marketization with promises to defend the interests of labor, increase social spending, and continue "central intervention" in the economy to reduce the costs of transition.

Thus, the pro-market rebranding of left parties in Central and Eastern Europe originally unfolded in a similar fashion to the Third Way patterns of Western Europe; at first, it seemed like a great electoral success (Ishiyama 1997). At the beginning of the transition, reformist left parties maintained their previous substantial support and significantly broadened their electoral base (Grzymala-Busse 2002a, b). First, given the pro-reform orientation and fragmentation of many right-wing parties in these countries, reform losers often had no other choice but to stick with left parties, which at least rhetorically claimed to represent their best interests (Tavits and Letki 2009: 557). Second, the pro-market rebranding of successor parties helped attract new supporters. As a result, the rebranded left made net electoral gains by attracting new voters without losing their old supporters (Bodea 2010; Bagashka and Stone 2013).

For example, Polish and Hungarian left-wing parties maintained 80% to 90% of their previous voters throughout the 1990s (Tavits and Letki 2009: 557;

Chapter 4). By combining appeals for reforms continuation with promises of greater sensitivity to the needs of economically vulnerable groups, by 1994 MSZP had gained a broad support base and won the election with 33% of the vote. Its Polish counterpart, SLD, became the most popular party in that country, more than doubling its support between 1991 and 1997 and winning the elections of 1993 and 2001. In other words, in the first several elections that followed their rebranding, the dynamic was very similar to the one described for social democratic parties in Western Europe (Karreth, Polk, and Allen 2013; Polk and Karreth 2020): left parties attracted new centrist voters while simultaneously retaining more traditionalist supporters who favored redistributionist policies.

But the seemingly successful rebranding strategy would eventually destroy them. As left parties transitioned from their traditional platforms toward pro-market ones, and the traditional dividing lines between left and right became blurred (Shields 2007: 173), they lost increasing numbers of supporters. These effects were particularly pronounced among working-class occupations. These social groups were especially severely hit in areas where state-owned enterprises were shut down, such as in steel towns and agricultural areas (Scheiring and Szombati 2020: 6). Being left to the mercy of uncontrollable forces and abandoned by their political representatives, these groups experienced increasing alienation from and anger toward political elites. The preexisting links between left parties and their traditional constituencies weakened, and the voters who suffered most from pro-market reforms became vulnerable to the mobilization efforts of new actors (Bornschier 2009: 4), particularly the populist right. This "neoliberal disembedding" (Scheiring and Szombati 2020) led to the deepest electoral slump that the social democratic movement in Europe has experienced since the Second World War (Bremer and McDaniel 2020) and contributed strongly to the ability of populist right forces in the region to win over these social groups and their subsequent triumphant rise to power.

## EU Conditionality: The Road to Hell Is Paved with Good Intentions

For postcommunist countries, an additional push to reform came from the EU (Grabbe 2006; Kelley 2006; Pridham 2005; Vachudova 2005). Qualifying for EU membership at that time served as the single most salient *external* influence on party politics (Benoit and Baturo 2005: 7). The rebranding strategy of the ex-communist left worked as long as EU conditionality ensured the ideological convergence of the political mainstream in favor of a liberal democracy and comprehensive economic reform in candidate states.

The pre-accession processes required candidate countries to satisfy the Copenhagen Requirements[8] and adopt the EU's *acquis communautaire*[9], with substantial implications for policies ranging from state regulation of the economy to ethnic minority rights (Kelley 2004; Schimmelfennig and Sedelmeier 2005; Vachudova 2005). On the economic dimension, the EU enlargement was associated with the second wave of neoliberalization in the region, which helped deepen and reinforce the first wave of reforms; while in the 1990s international institutions like the IMF and the World Bank helped push the Washington Consensus agenda, the EU subsequently helped finish the job by institutionalizing a "disciplinary neoliberalism" (Lendvai 2009: 26; Appel and Orenstein 2018: 87; Gill 2003: 65–67; Bailey 2009; Ryner 2012: 34; Bremer and McDaniel 2020). In Grabbe's (2002: 252) words, the thrust of the EU's economic agenda for postcommunist Europe was "neoliberal, emphasizing privatization of the means of production, a reduction in state involvement in the economy (particularly industry), and further liberalization of the means of exchange. Considering the variety of models of capitalism to be found among EU member states, the accession policy documents . . . promote[d] a remarkably uniform view of what a 'market economy' should look like."

Candidate states were willing to undertake these reforms. Carrots of EU membership (such as access to the internal market, EU funds and subsidies, transfers of technology and managerial experience, stronger administrative capacities, and increased investor confidence), reinforced by the sticks of falling behind other candidate states, constituted a powerful magnet shaping the agendas of parties across the region (Havlik 2001; Vachudova and Hooghe 2009; Vachudova 2008b; Appel and Orenstein 2018: 66).

The impact of EU leverage on parties' positions throughout this period was threefold.

First, it helped the transformation and adaptation of the reformist ex-communist parties, which could sell their technocratic expertise and a newly gained pro-Western orientation as an asset in preparing the country for EU membership. Beginning in the early 1990s, these parties actively embraced

---

[8] The Copenhagen criteria are the rules defining whether a country is eligible to join the EU based on the quality of its political and economic institutions, as well as acceptance of all EU legislation.

[9] Body of legal rights and obligations that bind all member states within the EU.

European integration, among other reasons, to demonstrate their repudiation of the past (Pienkos 2003). The active engagement with reforms often meant shifting from their earlier policies or electoral promises. For example, when in power during the pre-accession process the Romanian Social Democratic Party and the Bulgarian Coalition for Bulgaria, both left wing, implemented dramatically different policies than during their respective tenures in government prior to 1996 (Vachudova and Hooghe 2009).

Second, because the impact of EU leverage constrained the choice of coalition partners and moderated parties' policies (Vachudova 2018b), it helped sustain the "neoliberal momentum" delaying the backlash against socially costly reforms. Once the countries committed to accession, the mechanisms of the EU conditionality limited national policymaking from hampering reform (Vachudova 2008b). The EU's pre-accession process demanded economic discipline and helped exclude parties with more extreme economic positions and EU hostility. Despite the pain of implementing EU legislation, the predominant belief was that the medium- and long-term advantages of EU membership far outweighed the short-term costs associated with reforms (Appel and Orenstein 2018: 66–67). A consensus emerged; postcommunist parties passing the necessary laws, creating the institutions, and adopting policies mandated by the EU led to a convergence of mainstream party platforms prior to EU accession (Vachudova 2008b; Appel and Orenstein 2018).[10] In the run-up to negotiations for EU membership, this meant that no mainstream political party in the EU wanted to be viewed as hindering the accession process, and most responded to EU leverage by adopting agendas consistent with EU requirements (Vachudova 2008b). There was almost no variation in left and right parties' economic platforms in late 1990s and early 2000s (Grzymala-Busse and Innes 2003; Appel and Orenstein 2018: 87). Thus, the momentum of neoliberal policymaking "a decade after Communism was sustained by the all-important goal of attaining EU membership" (Appel and Orenstein 2018: 67).

Third, once the EU accession was achieved, compliance often endured (Sedelmeier 2008; Epstein 2008; Johnson 2008; Orenstein 2008), partly

---

[10] The EU's conditionality proved particularly effective in locking in reforms in the countries where societies and the ruling elites were more divided regarding the transformation trajectory, such as Romania, Bulgaria, Slovakia, and Croatia (Ekiert et al. 2005). Thus in Bulgaria and Romania, the EU conditionality worked by lifting the supply-side constraints of structural reforms and restraining the governing elites from rent-seeking behavior to make sure that even nonliberal governments remained on the reform track (Vachudova 2005; Ahrens and Zweynert 2012). For example, two successive center-right governments in Bulgaria (1997–2001, 2001–2005) implemented austerity programs to prepare the country for EU membership, even though these reforms reduced their chances of reelection.

because parties continued to be subject to further EU discipline (Lendvai 2009). Specifically, application to the Eurozone by severely indebted states endowed the EU with further leverage over their domestic fiscal policies, placing it in the position of institutional enforcer of orthodox market discipline, similar to that of the IMF (Roberts 2017a, b). The Maastricht convergence criteria needed to join the Eurozone proved particularly consequential. It aimed to foster the economic and monetary union, forcing countries to achieve macroeconomic stability by reducing inflation, interest rates, exchange rate volatility, government deficits, and public debts. Within this agenda, the sustainability of public finances came to the forefront of attention in all new member states (Lendvai 2009). As such, the European Commission often pressured governments to make unpalatable and politically unpopular policy choices that broke with established policy baselines and charted new trajectories of economic development (Blyth 2013). This is most visible in the case of the Hungarian MSZP, where the pressure of the European Commission to comply with Maastricht criteria led to the adoption of austerity in the post-2006 election cycle, causing a sharp drop in the party's popularity (see Chapter 4).

The need to satisfy the EU's Maastricht criteria greatly limited the capacity of postcommunist governments to spend on social welfare (Varga 2014). Convergence to a single European model tended to impose a deadweight cost on diverse national welfare systems (Hooghe and Marks 2009). In the Visegrád Four countries, such measures proved to be especially difficult to maintain. The politicians who led their countries through the process of neoliberal reform knew that this would generate social discontent. To weather the costs imposed on the population by transition-era economic reforms, they spent generously on pensions, healthcare, education, and industrial subsidies and preserved more permissive labor-market policies. In the 1990s, they introduced unemployment benefits and pension schemes to counterbalance the most corrosive effects of deindustrialization (Bohle and Greskovits 2006, 2007, 2012; Bruszt 2002, 2006; Cernat 2002, 2006; King and Sznajder 2006). This allowed many redundant workers to leave the labor market legally by making use of liberalized early old-age or disability retirement, easier access to higher education, and unemployment benefits. Beyond the law they resorted to subsistence farming, illegal work, and tax evasion (Greskovits 2007: 41). Initially such opportunities kept disruptive social protest and political radicalism at bay.

However, in the long run, the coexistence of generous welfare provisions and a large informal economy put excessive burdens on Visegrád economies. Complying with the EU's Maastricht criteria required these countries to decrease their welfare spending and reform the labor market, which further deepened already existing dissatisfactions with the fallout of transition-era economic reforms. For example, as Chapter 4 demonstrates, it was the budget cuts introduced under the EU's Maastricht criteria that proved particularly consequential for the reformist left in Hungary. To comply with the Maastricht criteria, the left-wing MSZP-led government introduced austerity in June 2006, reversing its earlier electoral promises of "reform without austerity." Another round of painful fiscal stabilization to comply with Maastricht requirements followed after the 2008 financial crisis. Both proved extremely unpopular in Hungary and played a major role in the collapse of MSZP approval. Similarly, the Polish SLD suffered electorally from implementing budget cuts in 2001, which were needed to comply with the European Commission's demand to ensure macroeconomic stability. The unpopular budget cuts led to a sharp downturn in the SLD's approval ratings and contributed to the party's electoral demise. In Slovakia, the radical austerity measures introduced by the ruling coalition paved the way toward fulfilling the Maastricht criteria for Eurozone entry. While SDL' finance minister Brigita Schmögnerová stood behind many of the economic and financial reforms undertaken during this period, the unpopularity of these measures contributed to the dramatic decline in electoral support and eventual decay of the left-wing SDL' (Pechova 2012; see also Chapter 5).

The EU leverage helps explain why backlash against neoliberal reforms did not spread in many countries of the region until the mid-2000s. Anti-EU parties and actors had little success across the region in the late 1990s and early 2000s, before the EU accession. Moreover, parties that criticized reforms during their campaigns had to continue with the reforms track once in power. Most notably, the opposition right-wing party Fidesz in Hungary criticized austerity measures introduced by the ruling MSZP in the mid-1990s. Yet, once it won the subsequent election in 1998, the Fidesz-led coalition maintained a basic pro-membership policy from 1998 until 2002, and continued fiscal reforms and other policies to satisfy the EU demands (Bönker 2006: 129). Similarly, while the Polish left-wing SLD was critical of the reforms (and associated decline in living standards) by the right-wing Solidarity Electoral Action (Akcja Wyborcza Solidarność, AWS) (1997–2001), once elected to power in 2001 it had to comply with EU conditionality to ensure EU accession and continue with the reforms track, which included painful expenditure cuts (see Chapter 4). The same was true of the Czech Social Democratic Party (Česká strana sociálně demokratická, ČSSD) party, which, upon winning the 1998 election, reached an agreement with the second-largest center-right party and implemented an extensive program of reforms and legislative acts to ensure EU accession. In Slovakia, after the country was not included in the 1997 Luxembourg group of EU candidates, many segments of civil society mobilized to bring to power reformist parties from both sides of the political spectrum. Once elected, joining the EU gave an extra powerful incentive for reformist forces to coalesce and to keep the ideologically broad-based 1998–2002 government together (see Chapter 5).

The Post-Accession Backlash

However, the socially costly reforms made inevitable a backlash against reformist parties and created opportunities for the emergence of political actors capable of capturing the frustration unleashed by these changes (Ost 2006; Vanhuysse 2007). This backlash took time to unravel. The timing of EU accession explains why serious backlash to reforms in many cases began only in the mid-2000s. As accession neared, EU leverage on the party system weakened, and once countries gained EU membership, it declined more dramatically (Levitz and Pop-Eleches 2010). This occurred for several reasons.

First, the EU threat to suspend accession became less credible closer to the accession date. EU demands were tied directly to membership prospects. Once membership became more of a certainty, EU influence over candidate states waned (Vachudova and Hooghe 2009). At the 1997 Luxembourg European Council, the EU began accession negotiations with five postcommunist states—Hungary, Poland, Estonia, the Czech Republic, and Slovenia—while stressing that the door was open for other countries to join in the future. The EU's willingness to open negotiations with those deemed to have met the criteria demonstrated that its offer of membership was genuine and provided a clear signal for the countries left out of the process (Bulgaria, Latvia, Lithuania, Romania, and Slovakia) that by enacting the required changes the sought-after reward could be obtained (Haughton 2007).

As the countries progressed through the negotiations, the threat of exclusion lessened, and the attitudes changed (Vachudova and Hooghe 2009; Moravcsik and Vachudova 2003). Growing opposition to the implementation of EU requirements provided politicians with reason to start resisting and delaying the required measures (as happened with the SLD and the

MSZP with the implementation of the Maastricht criteria in the early 2000s; see Chapter 4). As Rupnik (2007: 22) has observed, it was "striking that most of the pro-European coalitions that dominated CEE politics over the last decade or so fell apart as soon as they had accomplished the 'historic task' of achieving EU membership." The overwhelming support for EU integration was replaced with criticism of EU requirements (Taggart and Szczerbiak 2004).

Second, further down the road, the perceived costs associated with implementing accession requirements became increasingly obvious by the societies that would be affected. By the end of the accession process, the neglected social demands contributed to a "representation crisis"—an outburst of public dissatisfaction in postcommunist states, expressing the loss of patience of the greater part of the population after an extended period of systemic change (Agh 2010). Szczerbiak (2002: 29–30) describes the Polish case: "Support [for EU accession] was bound to fall once it became apparent that conforming to EU norms would involve negative economic and social consequences as well as benefits." Those who found themselves on the losing side of reforms increasingly embraced the belief that EU accession was an elite-driven process from which only a narrow, wealthy section of the population could benefit (Szczerbiak 2002: 29–30; Tucker, Pacek and Berinsky 2002). They started to enter the national debate in an effort to block further reform. These groups were more likely to oppose European integration and to support Euroskeptic parties (Chicowski 2000; Tucker, Pacek, and Berinsky 2002; Marks et al. 2006).

Inflated expectations concerning EU membership and fatigue from long-lasting austerity measures along with an emerging perception that mainstream parties were being overly compliant with an "exploitative" EU created political openings for parties that took nativist stances on sociocultural issues and redistributionist stances on economic ones (Grzymala-Busse and Innes 2003; Varga 2014). This boosted the resurgence of the populist radical right, which adopted a Euroskeptic agenda to attract new electorates (Smilov and Krastev 2008: 9). In this sense, albeit inadvertently, the EU accession catalyzed the rise of populism across the region (Grzymala-Busse 2019a).

As Chapters 4 and 5 demonstrate, closer to the accession the resurgence of populist parties became very pronounced across countries. By 2002, more citizens were voting for Euroskeptic and Euroneutral parties in Poland and Hungary than in Romania and Bulgaria (the two countries which were not part of the 2004 accession wave) (Vachudova 2011). For example, once Hungary attained EU accession, Fidesz (in opposition at the time), which when it was in power in 1998–2002 had implemented many reforms needed to bring Hungary into the EU, adopted increasingly more Euroskeptic rhetoric. The party even initiated a referendum to prevent EU-driven liberalization of the land market in Hungary and warned that EU membership might put thousands of Hungarian farmers out of business (Batory 2002: 5). Similarly, in Poland, Prawo i Sprawiedliwość (PiS) adopted more Euroskeptic stances during the 2005 election, after the EU accession was achieved. In the Czech Republic, the left-wing Communist Party of Bohemia and Moravia (Komunistická strana Čech a Moravy, KSČM) party's criticism of the consequences of joining the EU for prices and wages, employment, and the position of industrial and agricultural producers was one of the reasons behind the party's electoral bump in the 2002 election (Hanley 2008; Taggart and Szczerbiak 2004; Kopecky and Mudde 2002). Starting in 2004 Euroskepticism occupied an even greater space in Czech parties' platforms (Havlík and Hloušek 2017). Euroskeptic parties also spread by the end of Bulgaria's and Romania's accession preparation (Andreev 2008; Stoyanov and Kostadinova 2021).

A further paradox was that in the aftermath of EU accession reformist ex-communist left-wing governments often continued pushing for more reforms needed for speedy Eurozone entry and implementing more euro-friendly policies (Tavits and Letki 2009). Dandashly and Verdun (2018) show that whenever a country had social democrats or liberals in power, the enthusiasm toward the euro tended to increase. (Chapter 4 describes that dynamic using the examples of attempts by the ruling left-wing governments in Poland and Hungary to satisfy convergence criteria.) By contrast, conservative and right-wing nationalist ruling elites (like Fidesz and PiS) tended to postpone euro adoption (Dandashly and Verdun 2018). Reformist left parties eagerness' to demonstrate their commitment to the markets and to Europeanization contributed to their failure to respond to the changing societal mood and eventually led to their demise.

Hence, in the postcommunist region EU conditionality was an important contributing factor that reinforced the depth and strength of reforms, but also inadvertently contributed to a stronger populist backlash in the long run. The timing of the EU accession provided a focal point for the electoral breakthrough of parties adopting populist and Euroskeptic agendas. Paradoxically, as Krastev (2007: 58) puts it, these consequences were "an outcome not of the failures but of the successes of postcommunist liberalism."

In recent years Western Europe also saw the growth of peripheral political actors adopting a "losers" program combined with a Euroskeptic agenda
(Taggart 1998). The logic of support and opposition to European integration
was similar across both regions (Marks et al. 2006). Losers of globalization
and European integration tended to flock to parties that promised protectionist measures against external competition, while winners sought out
parties advocating for international integration (Kriesi et al. 2006). However,
in the West this process unraveled more smoothly, as part of a long-term
transformation of national party systems (Kriesi et al. 2006; Kriesi 2016).
While several developments, such as the adoption of the Maastricht Accord
or the Eurozone crisis,[11] had a strong impact on Western European party
competition as well (Marks 1997; Benoit and Laver 2008: 160, 176; Edwards
2008; Kriesi et al. 2006; Hoogheand Marks 2009), the long-term rise of the
populist right dated at least as far back as the early 1980s, when the French
Front National achieved its first electoral success (Kriesi 2016). Thus in the
Western European context this trend was more dispersed over time and less
driven by EU conditionality, as compared to Eastern Europe.

## The 2008 Crisis: The Irony of Fate

The 2008 financial crisis further accelerated these trends by deepening
accumulated disappointment in neoliberalism (Bohle and Greskovits
2009).[12] The "Great Recession" originated in Western economies and led to
declining gross domestic products, increasing public debts, and rising borrowing costs across Europe. Following the crisis, the economic success of
many postcommunist countries was brought to a halt and in most cases even
reversed. Orenstein (2013b: 236) shows that by 2009 every EU-10 country[13]
but Poland entered into recession. The Baltic states experienced double-digit
negative growth, and Slovenia experienced close to −10% negative growth.
On the individual level the crisis resulted in dramatic job losses, reduced

[11] The Euro crisis had much less of an impact on postcommunist economies, many of which were
either less affected economically or recovered rather quickly (Coffey 2013; Kriesi 2016; Grzymala-
Busse 2019a). Several of these countries even decided to enter the Eurozone during the euro crisis
(Slovakia 2009, Estonia 2011, Latvia 2014, Lithuania 2014).

[12] Appel and Orenstein (2018) point out three ways in which the 2008 crisis influenced the depar-
ture from neoliberalism: reform backsliding, the reversal of neoliberal policies such as pension privatization and flat taxes, and the rise of statist development paradigms.

[13] EU-10 refers to the ten countries that joined the EU in 2004: Cyprus, the Czech Republic,
Estonia, Hungary, Latvia, Lithuania, Malta, Poland, Slovakia, and Slovenia.

salaries, plummeting home values, and widespread financial insecurity (Awan 2015: 4).

By some irony of fate, the countries hit hardest by the crisis were often those that had reformed most deeply and were more dependent on the volatility of international markets. Many such countries were found in the postcommunist region. After communism fell, these countries wanted to seem competitive to foreign investors and liberalized their economies at a pace unparalleled by any other region in the world (with the exception of Eurasia). They sold substantive shares in their banking systems to foreign, mostly Western European conglomerates (Appel and Orenstein 2016: 325; Orenstein and Bugarič 2020: 8).

Foreign direct investment (FDI) was an important condition for EU membership. The EU promoted privatization via foreign ownership in strategic sectors and sponsored national investment promotion agencies' efforts to attract FDI (Bohle and Greskovits 2019: 1074). However, these reforms had unintended consequences. Strong dependence on Western capital made the sudden stop of capital flows in the aftermath of the 2008 crisis all the more painful. In these countries the radical openness, extreme dependence on foreign credit, and lack of domestic development policies and social safety net further exacerbated the effects of the crisis (Bugaric 2016). Thus, the suspension of foreign investment inflows led to deeper recessions and sharper output declines in postcommunist Europe than in most other developing regions (Appel and Orenstein 2016: 325).

The crisis hurt Hungary particularly badly. Formerly a point of pride, Hungary's financial and trade openness and its international integration appeared to have made it exceptionally vulnerable to the 2008 crisis as both FDI and exports to Western markets (in particular Germany) came to a standstill (Connolly 2012; Johnson and Barnes 2015: 544). Subsequently exports plummeted by 18.7% in 2009, and industrial production by 17.7%—the sharpest decline since 1991. The manufacturing sector fell by 18.4% on an annual basis, with automobile production decreasing by nearly 30% (Fabry 2019: 112–113). Furthermore, in the 2000s, Hungarian governments sought to offset the lack of wage growth by helping families acquire homes and by boosting private consumption. They relied on Western banks to offer citizens relatively cheap mortgages and consumer loans. The 2008 financial crisis led to the depreciation of the national currency, which made interest (which had been borrowed in Swiss francs and euros) on both public debt and private mortgages skyrocket. As a result, hundreds of thousands of Hungarian families descended into debt spirals (Scheiring and Szombati 2020: 5). This contributed to diminishing confidence in neoliberal reforms, which had already been spreading across the region before the crisis.

The crisis had heterogeneous impacts across Europe. It led to electoral punishment of incumbents and opened up an opportunity for new parties to enter parliaments (Bartels 2014; Bellucci 2014; Hernandez and Kriesi 2016; Magalhaes 2014; Marsh and Mikhaylov 2012; Funke and Trebesch 2017). It also contributed to the electoral successes of populist right parties (Hopkin and Blyth 2020). The average vote share of right-wing populists across Europe, which was about 5% prior to the crisis, climbed to double-digit levels two elections after the crisis (between 10% and 20%) (Funke and Trebesch 2017: 8). Also in the aftermath of the crisis many new populist right parties emerged, like the People's Party in Belgium (after the 2010 election), the Independent Greeks (2012 election), Brothers of Italy (2013 election), Dawn in the Czech Republic (2013 election), Team Stronach in Austria (2013 election), Kukiz'15 in Poland (2015 election), and the Alternative for Germany (2017 election) (Funke and Trebesch 2017: 8). The crisis also allowed established populist right-wing parties like Freedom Party of Austria and Norwegian Progress Party to advance to significantly higher levels of their parliamentary representation. In postcommunist Europe, Hungary's Fidesz reentered government in 2010 on promises to end austerity, while the Polish PiS party's vote share grew from 32.1% in 2007 to 37.6% in 2015, when it formed a majority government.

However, the impact of the crisis on populist right fortunes was not consistent across Europe. For example, Grzymala-Busse (2019a) argues that the 2008 crisis is neither necessary nor sufficient to explain the surge in populist support. Populist parties succeeded in countries where the global financial crisis brought about a near-collapse of the national economy (Greece) and in countries relatively untouched by this crisis (Poland and Finland). By contrast, no populist parties arose in Ireland or Portugal, where the crisis was severe. In some countries, including Belgium, Denmark, and Norway, populist parties even lost electoral support in the aftermath of the financial crisis. So while the economic crisis tended to exacerbate popular grievances, it did not, by itself, translate into a consistent surge of support for populists (Grzymala-Busse 2019a). This conclusion is echoed by Hutter and Kriesi (2019), who show that the crisis might have had a stronger impact on Southern Europe, where it came in the wake of an economic boom, than on Eastern Europe, where the Great Recession followed a preceding deep transition crisis, which had arguably better prepared Eastern Europeans for the experience of the economic downturn. They argue that the economic crisis, although (with the exception of Poland) very severe, had only a limited impact on the restructuring of postcommunist party systems (Hutter and Kriesi 2019: 20, 38; Innes 2014). Polls have shown that among postcommunist societies the deep-seated dissatisfaction with the way their politics worked did not change much following the Great Recession (Kriesi 2016).

In line with this book's argument, the impact of the 2008 crisis on populist right fortunes may have been conditioned by the types of parties implementing structural adjustment policies (Bojar et al. 2022). In response to the crisis, the EU government body and international institutions like the IMF required incumbent parties to adopt unpopular austerity policies specifically targeting pensions and other social expenditures (Freudenberg, Berki, and Reiff 2016). The EU, in particular, emerged as an advocate of even more contractionary or pro-cyclical measures in return for loans (Lütz and Kranke 2014; Jacoby and Hopkin 2020). The painful social impact of austerity led to significant social resistance. For example, in the Czech Republic, Latvia, Lithuania, Romania, and Poland in 2009–2010 trade unions organized large anti-austerity protests (Dale and Hardy 2011: 261; Fabry 2019: 111).

Roberts (2013) shows that structural adjustments during economic crises have a way of aligning or dealigning party systems programmatically (see also Morgan 2012; Lupu 2014). Where conservative parties are in power during economic crises, their reforms generally tend to stabilize party competition and channel societal resistance toward institutionalized leftist parties. This is consistent with the Czech case, where in the aftermath of the 2008 financial crisis left-wing parties won elections to replace the fiscally conservative right-wing ruling coalition. Specifically, ČSSD won the 2013 elections with 20.5% of votes, and KSČM received its best result since 2002, with 14.8% and thirty-three seats, to become the country's third-strongest political party (Havlík 2014). By contrast, where center-left parties in power during the economic crisis implemented structural adjustment policies, they tended to dealign party systems programmatically, which led to these parties' decay and to the surge of populist parties (Hutter and Kriesi 2019: 24). Indeed, this logic is consistent with the case of Hungary, where in the aftermath of the crisis the ruling center-left MSZP party was required by the EU and the IMF to implement a set of austerity measures as a condition for the country's bailout loan. These austerity measures delivered the coup de grâce to the MSZP party (already quite unpopular at that time), because "many blamed the Socialists for the severe impact of the global economic crisis in the first place" (Batory

2010; Johnson and Barnes 2015). This further deepened societal dissatisfaction, challenged the validity of pro-market policies, and provided populist forces an opportunity to challenge incumbent parties. Pro-cyclical austerity policies enforced by the IMF and EU not only did not improve the economic situation in the short term but "made matters worse politically as [Viktor] Orbán and other opposition leaders blamed the Socialists, austerity-oriented international conditionality, and foreign-owned banks for the economic struggles of ordinary Hungarians" (Johnson and Barnes 2015: 544). This is in contrast with the approach adopted by Slovakia's ruling Direction – Social Democracy (Smer – sociálna demokracia, Smer-SD), which chose to avoid substantial cuts in public spending and restrictions on welfare-state policies during the 2008 crisis. Increased deficit spending (by 2012 the government debt-to-GDP ratio exceeded 50%) helped mute the social impact of the economic downturn and its perception by citizens (Malová and Dolný 2016). Although the party lost the 2010 election, Smer-SD returned to power in the 2012 election, following a major financial crash in August 2011 (Grzymala-Busse 2019a, d).

Where the crisis did make a particularly notable difference was in the modification of the populist right's electoral platforms. As skepticism about the neoliberal orthodoxy imposed by international institutions spread across Europe, the salience of the economic issues increased (Singer 2013), and the 2008 financial crisis gave an additional incentive to populist right parties to adjust their economic programs (Hanley and Sikk 2016; Judis 2016: 103; Otjes et al. 2018; McManus 2019, 2022). Because their constituencies of economic losers had been particularly hard hit by the Great Recession, the populist right started adopting more social-democratic positions on the economic dimension (Hutter and Kriesi 2019: 22). Politicizing austerity-induced societal frustration, right-wing parties adopted platforms that placed more emphasis on socioeconomic issues. They offered alternatives to neoliberalism and bolstered skepticism about international institutions. As an alternative to marketization, they started offering economic nationalist policies designed to bolster and protect national economies against the volatility and unpredictability of world markets, as well as the influence of banks, multinationals and international institutions (Johnson and Barnes 2015; Mikecz 2019; Bohle and Greskovits 2019). To decrease their countries' economic dependence on international investors, these parties shifted their policy focus increasingly toward state-run capitalist models, using China and Russia for inspiration (Kurlantzick 2016; Orenstein and Bugarič 2020: 9). This strategy was often electorally successful.

## The Right Moves Left

With left parties no longer able to capture the imagination of a growing constituency discontented with neoliberalism, a golden opportunity arose for
an enterprising political force on the opposite side of the political spectrum.
Once EU accession was guaranteed in the early 2000s, new parties emerged
and old parties adopted new platform positions that challenged incumbents
on antireform and Euroskeptic agendas (Vachudova 2008b). Attacking the
reformist left from the right side proved to be particularly advantageous.

For opposition challengers it was more beneficial to attack the discredited
incumbents from the opposite side of the political spectrum. Due to the
legacy of the left-wing communist regimes, not only ex-communist parties
but even some new left parties across the region "had to stay away from
strong socialist policy positions to avoid being associated with the former
regime" (Tavits and Letki 2009: 556; Ost 2018).[14] These parties embraced neoliberal reforms and adopted pro-European positions.

Despite the salience of economic issues in the region (Rohrschneider and
Whitefield 2009; Pop-Eleches and Tucker 2010), the convergence of mainstream left and right on economic policy often made parties turn to sociocultural issues to appeal to voters (Evans and Tilley 2012, 2017; Rennwald and
Evans 2014; Oskarson and Demker 2015). Subsequently, the competition
in postcommunist regions tended to shift to the sociocultural dimension,
giving further advantage to right-wing parties (Bornschier 2018: 226; Kriesi
et al. 2006). These parties mobilized supporters using nationalist frames, offering a defense against enemies both internal (e.g., Roma and Jewish ethnic
minorities) and external (foreign corporations, the EU imposing undesired
policy measures, and immigrants) (Hutter and Kriesi 2019: 22). Their ability
to capitalize on these issues was reinforced by voters' more culturally conservative orientations in postcommunist region where the experience of
political and economic transitions came to be associated with the erosion
of traditional social structures (Pirro 2015; Pytlas 2015, 2018; Minkenberg
2017a).

While doing so, right-wing populists conflated nationalist with economic
frames, packaging economic messages in nationalist terms and capitalizing
on feelings of injustice and disillusionment with respect to the economic

---

[14] Hutter and Kriesi (2019: 10) point out that the opposite effect was seen in Southern Europe,
where the legacy of authoritarian right-wing regimes gave an advantage to the rise of populist left
parties.

transformation. For example, while presenting "the people" as morally decent, economically struggling, hard-working, and family-oriented, right-wing populists contrasted them to "the elite," which was seen as living in a different world, playing by different rules, insulated from economic hardships, corrupt, out of touch with the concerns and problems of ordinary people, and condescending toward ordinary people's values, habits, and lifestyles (Brubaker 2020: 54). They described the "ordinary people" as the primary victims of a multicultural society, living in poor areas with high immigration rates or "Roma crime" (Cleen 2017: 11) and (specific to the postcommunist region) the prime sufferers of the social injustices of the transition period. They portrayed these "ordinary people" as losing their jobs to immigrants or having their already low pensions threatened by the cost of helping refugees and other minority groups. Hence while the economic dimension plays a crucial role here, it is subordinate to and used in the service of nationalism (Cleen 2017: 11; Hilmar 2022; Waterbury 2020).

Moreover, since many of the party elites in the region were drawn from the nomenklatura (former elite) structures of the left communist regime, the opposition commonly held these parties responsible for corruption related to the privatization of national assets (Hanley 2004: 17–18). Across the region, the sense of injustice associated with the transition period was fueled by the notion that while the transformation brought substantial economic growth and material progress, the fruits of this growth were distributed unfairly (Hilmar 2022). Communists were "often blamed not so much for what they did in the 1970s and 1980s but for the offhandedness with which they remade themselves into heartless capitalists in the 1990s" (Krastev and Holmes 2018: 63). Anders Aslund, who at the time served as an economic advisor to several reformist governments in the region, points out, "Old nomenklatura links allowed many of the ex-communist elite members to hold on to control of state institutions. Across postcommunist societies perceptions of corruption were reinforcing the belief that apart from enriching themselves while in power these parties did little for either the working class or the emerging bourgeoisie" (in discussion with the author, June 2022).[15]

As a result, challenger parties that used this agenda primarily emerged on the right side of the political spectrum.

---

[15] Anders Aslund worked as an advisor on economic policy for Polish and Latvian governments throughout the reform period.

The "New Winning Formula"

It was after the populist right altered their economic policy stances that they became particularly successful in incorporating former left parties' electorates.

Populist right parties' positions on economic issues have evolved over recent decades. In the 1990s, they tended to hold classical pro-market positions on the economic dimension (Betz 1994). Scholars explained this choice by the fact that while these parties used nativist and conservative sociocultural agendas to attract working-class voters, they needed a free-market economic platform to draw support from small domestic producers and businessmen (Kitschelt and McGann 1997). By this argument, the resulting "winning formula" contained pledges that appealed to both of these groups. It combined authoritarian and nationalistic appeals with extreme economic neoliberalism, calling for the dismantling of public bureaucracies and the welfare state and for a strong and authoritarian state (Kitschelt 1995b; Kitschelt and McGann 1997; McGann and Kitschelt 2005). At the time, the "market-liberal appeal" of the populist right parties was viewed as "a necessary, albeit not a sufficient condition" of their electoral success Kitschelt 2007: 1183).

By the mid-2000s, and particularly following the 2008 crisis, scholars noticed that populist right parties increasingly shifted away from pro-market policies toward more centrist economic policies, thus abandoning their "winning formula." De Lange (2007) was one of the first to conclude that established populist right parties tended to shift their economic policy positions to the center after analyzing three cases: the French National Rally (Front National, FN), the Flemish Vlaams Blok, and the Dutch List Pim Fortuyn. When in Parliament, such parties supported quite heterogeneous economic policies (Cavallaro, Flacher, and Zanetti 2018), and when in office, they tended to mix general liberalizing policies with targeted redistributionist measures for selected groups (Heinisch 2003: 103; Afonso 2015). Scholars reasoned that populist right parties may have deliberately adopted blurred, "vague, contradictory or ambiguous" economic policy stances (Rovny 2014: 5; Afonso 2015; Cavallaro, Flacher, and Zanetti 2018; Rovny and Polk 2020) or downplayed their economic policy programs altogether (Spies and Franzmann 2011) to attract broader support (Mudde 2007: 119).

However, many recent studies suggest that populist right parties eventually shifted further to the left on the economic dimension, away from centrist or blurred economic positions toward more decidedly protectionist economic positions (Mudde 2007). For example, in France, Italy, and Austria, radical right parties have become more supportive of welfare spending, with limitations as to who should access the funds (Afonso and Rennwald 2018). Combining more left-wing economic policies with their nativist claims that immigrants make excessive use of the welfare state, populist right parties increasingly adopted welfare chauvinism, calling to restrict welfare access to the "deserving" natives (Schumacher and van Kersbergen 2016; de Koster, Achterberg, and van der Waal 2013; Van der Waal, Achterberg, and Houtman 2010). This "new winning formula" also included economic protectionism and opposition to austerity on the economic dimension (de Koster, Achterberg, and van der Waal 2013; Bustikova 2018; Fenger 2018). As part of ruling governments, populist parties refrained from welfare state retrenchment and were less inclined to engage in deregulation compared with right-wing governments without their participation (Malka, Lelkes, and Soto 2019; Röth, Afonso, and Spies 2018).

Figure 1.2 provides a stylized representation of the respective trajectories of social democratic left (SD) and populist right (PR) parties in a two-dimensional political space that summarizes domestic political competition—an economic, left/right dimension and a noneconomic, sociocultural dimension axis (Kitschelt 1992, 1995a, b; Marks et al. 2006; Arzheimer 2013). The horizontal economic dimension reflects positions on redistribution, welfare, and government regulation. While the left side

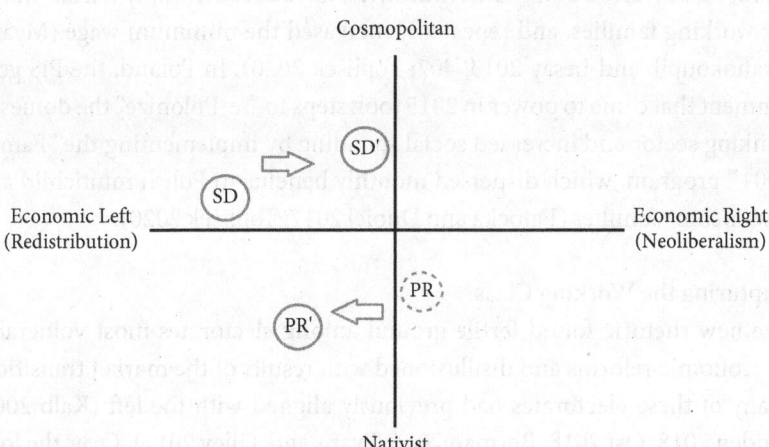

**Figure 1.2** European Party Systems, Left Parties Providing a Political Opening for the Populist Right.

Source: Arzheimer (2013), Kitschelt (1995a), Hutter and Kriesi (2019).

prioritizes economic equality, the right prioritizes individual economic freedom and less market regulation. The vertical sociocultural dimension captures conflict about traditional values rooted in a secular/religious divide, as well as immigration and defense of the national community (Inglehart 1977; van Deth and Scarbrough 1995; Dalton 2002; Marks et al. 2006). Figure 1.2 shows that the rebranding of the social democratic parties has opened up the space for populist right parties to move to the lower-left quadrant by adding more redistributionist positions on the economic dimension to their existing nativist positions on the sociocultural dimension.

This trend was also pronounced in the postcommunist context. For example, In Hungary and Poland, populist right parties Fidesz and PiS, respectively, adopted economic nationalism—a set of protectionist and heterodox economic policies associated with the idea of subordinating national economies to national interests and protecting them in the context of world markets (Szanyi 2016; Miszerak and Rohac 2017; Toplišek 2020). When in power these parties resisted pressure from international institutions to impose austerity on public spending and combined left-wing economic policies (in the case of Poland) and market-constraining state interventionism (in both cases) with conservative ideology and calls to protect national identity (Johnson and Barnes 2015; Krastev and Holmes 2018; Bluhm and Varga 2019; Dandashly and Verdun 2018). In Hungary, the Fidesz government took steps to renationalize strategic sectors of the economy, imposed taxes on foreign investor-dominated industries, introduced a family tax allowance for working families, and repeatedly increased the minimum wage (Myant, Drahokoupil, and Lesay 2013: 407; Toplišek 2020). In Poland, the PiS government that came to power in 2015 took steps to "re-Polonize" the domestic banking sector and increased social spending by implementing the "Family 500+" program, which dispersed monthly benefits to Polish multichild and low-income families (Patocka and Dubiel 2017; Toplišek 2020).

## Capturing the Working Class

The new rhetoric found fertile ground among electorates most vulnerable to economic reforms and disillusioned with results of the market transition. Many of these electorates had previously aligned with the left (Kalb 2009; Linden 2018; Ost 2018; Berman 2016; Evans and Tilley 2017). Over the long term, right-wing parties in countries with a pro-market left lured away large shares of working-class electorates, some of whom had originally supported left parties (Bustikova 2018; Ganev 2017). Eventually, many of the former left parties' constituencies ended up being incorporated by the populist right (Ignazi 2003; Kai 2013).

Indeed, scholarship on Western Europe finds that the evolving economic stances of populist right parties tend to correspond to the changing composition of their electorates (Derks 2006). Economic platforms mixing egalitarianism and welfare chauvinism may be better positioned to capture votes of working-class electorates hurt by globalization and facing challenges to the supply of cheaper immigrant labor because these social groups lean to the left in their economic preferences (Engler and Zohlnhöfer 2019; Van Spanje and Van der Brug 2007). For example, Adorf (2018) argues that populist right parties realized that their former preferences for small government policies offered little appeal to blue-collar voters. Once the populist right no longer merely offered a nativist platform but also appealed to their economic and welfare preferences, these parties have become even more attractive for working-class voters (Adorf 2018: 33). Recent studies have discovered that working-class constituencies are indeed either steadily increasing (Betz 2002; Spies 2013; Afonso and Rennwald 2018) or are already overrepresented among populist right electorates (the so-called "proletarization") (Ignazi 2003; Arzheimer 2013).

Case studies conducted across Western Europe confirm these observations. Populist right parties with redistributionist economic platforms tend to attract support from working-class electorates. For example, the UKIP started off as a libertarian, anti-EU party, but over the past decade its economic positions have shifted to the left, corresponding to a growing representation of working-class voters in its electorates (Evans and Mellon 2016; Ford and Goodwin 2014a, 2014b). Similarly, the FN under the leadership of Marine Le Pen significantly modified its economic platform and endorsed statist redistributive economic policies, as demonstrated by the party's motto "Social without socialism." Subsequently, the FN consolidated strong support from the working class, which leans left economically (Ivaldi 2013; Stockemer 2017). In the 2017 presidential election, Le Pen made it to the second round, obtaining a majority among blue-collar voters (56%), being particularly successful in the industrial areas of the French northeast (Adorf 2018: 35; Mondon 2017). In Germany, the AfD emerged against the backdrop of the Eurozone crisis as a middle-class conservative party which advocated a smaller state and took pro-market economic positions. However, by 2017, the AfD had transformed into a right-wing nationalist party combining anti-immigration positions with support for social protection "for Germans." Subsequently, the party made inroads into the working-class electorate, making some observers suggest that the AfD was on its way to becoming the preferred party of Germany's working-class voters (Adorf 2018). In the 2017 German federal election, the AFD received 11.5% of the vote, showing particular success in eastern Germany, where it attracted electorates dissatisfied with the political establishment (Olsen 2018), economically insecure voters (Bergmann 2017), and workers in the manufacturing sector (Berning 2017; Franz, Fratzscher, and Kritikos 2018). In Sweden since 2010, the nationalist-populist SD has rapidly transformed from a marginal political force into the country's third-largest party, combining a nativist platform with nostalgia for a substantial welfare state while blaming immigration for the former's decline (Bergmann 2017). Studies have shown that the SD voters who previously voted for the SAP more commonly belonged to the working class, had lower socioeconomic status and left-leaning socioeconomic preferences, and more often expressed welfare chauvinism than other voters (Jylhä, Rydgren, and Strimling 2019).

This review seems to suggest that a correspondence exists between parties' economic platforms and the composition of their electorates.[16] However, there is no systematic analysis of this kind in the case of Eastern Europe. Based on the parallels across the party dynamic in both regions, this book's argument is that the rebranding of left parties in the postcommunist context led to dealignment of working-class electorates and their subsequent incorporation by the populist right in a way similar to how this process unraveled in the West.

## Summary

This chapter has fleshed out the key parallels in the party system dynamic across Eastern and Western Europe lying at the core of the book's theoretical argument.

It discussed why and how, due to the changing voter profile and compounding doubts about the economic viability of the redistributive state in the 1980s, Western European center-left parties adopted increasingly

---

[16] In 2016, the ethnonationalist Estonian Patriotic Movement merged with the agrarian People's Union (a radical left party) to create the Conservative People's Party of Estonia (EKRE). EKRE combined cultural nationalist and economic socialism and attracted support from rural voters, the elderly, the unemployed, and the self-employed (Lust 2016). Subsequently, EKRE's popularity surged significantly. In the 2019 Estonian parliamentary election, the party gained 17.8% of the vote (compared to 8.1% in 2015) and increased its number of seats to nineteen from seven seats in 2015.

pro-market economic platforms, which came to be known as the Third Way. Subsequently, in the 1990s their Eastern European counterparts followed this example by renouncing Marxist ideology and presenting themselves as social democratic parties composed of experts, technocrats, and pragmatists. They commonly committed to neoliberal market reforms by adopting the monetary and fiscal policies traditionally associated with right-wing parties.

The ex-communist left's rebranding strategy received a strong external push from international institutions. The role of EU conditionality was particularly important, as it provided additional strong incentives for parties in candidate states to implement comprehensive economic reform in light of EU accession. At first, accession to the European Union contributed to the policy convergence of parties and voters in their respective societies, which delayed the emergence of populist right parties. However, in the long run EU conditionality also inadvertently contributed to a stronger populist backlash by fueling dissatisfaction with economic reforms and eventually boosting Euroskeptic sentiment. In the Visegrád Four countries the policies embraced under EU conditionality proved to be especially painful. Complying with the EU's accession requirements forced the candidate states to cut down welfare spending policies adopted early on to weather the costs of economic transition. These reforms further deepened the already existing dissatisfaction with neoliberal reforms and contributed to the rise of populist political actors who criticized the reforms, the political establishment, and the European Union itself. The 2008 crisis deepened these trends by further undermining public confidence in international institutions and mainstream parties' neoliberal policies.

Although their rebranding was at first rewarded with electoral victories, this move by left parties in both Western and Eastern Europe ultimately alienated many of those voters —namely economically vulnerable voters and working-class electorates. By contrast, earlier studies of the region often assumed that left parties' voters tended to stay loyal to rebranded left parties (see introduction; Fidrmuc 2000; Grzymala-Busse 2002a, b; Tavits and Letki 2009). This chapter challenges such assumptions. Instead, it suggests that the consequences of the programmatic convergence of mainstream parties before EU accession often went unnoticed, making it seem as if voters had remained loyal to the left despite its programmatic turnaround. It was primarily after EU accession that other (often conservative and radical right) parties relied on populist appeals to sweep up economically vulnerable voters abandoned by the left's pro-market shift. This suggests that voters in postcommunist countries are consistent and tend to support parties that best represent their interests.

In response to these shifts, right-wing parties in their respective countries adopted more redistributive economic platforms consistent with preferences of these social groups and incorporated sizable shares of these electorates. When in power these parties tended to resist the pressure from international institutions to limit public spending, combining protectionist economic policies with conservative ideology and calls to protect national identities. These platforms allowed populist right parties with redistributionist economic platforms to gradually incorporate large swaths of working-class support.

While this chapter has traced important parallels in party system dynamics across Eastern and Western Europe, in the postcommunist context the effects of left rebranding were even more pronounced. Chapter 2 goes into further detail, highlighting the particular role played by the postcommunist working class in this context.

# 2

# The Class Politics
# in Postcommunist Europe

The previous chapter outlined the main logic of this book's argument by demonstrating that the decline of the center left and the rise of right-wing populism ultimately resulted from the same process: economically vulnerable voters shifting away from the left to embrace the populist right.

The groups that played an important role in this process are working-class electorates, those with manual occupations and jobs requiring fewer qualifications. However, beyond working-class groups the argument outlined in Chapter 1 also applies to broader electorates described as reform losers—the groups hurt by the economic transition, underprivileged and disadvantaged in terms of income and upward mobility (Tucker, Pacek, and Berinsky 2002: 557; Oesch 2006a; Margalit 2013; Mudge 2018: 44), including the unemployed, older and less educated groups, retirees, and rural residents (Bornschier 2010a, 2010b; Inglehart and Norris 2016). Why, then, is this book's focus primarily on working-class electorates?

This chapter helps explain this choice. First, working-class electorates are precisely the groups that are typically associated with traditional left support and the classic alignment of left parties on the left side of the political spectrum along the economic axis (Kitschelt 1994; Bornschier and Kriesi 2012). As this chapter will demonstrate, just as in Western Europe, in the postcommunist region more redistributionist positions along the economic dimension tend to correspond to economic preferences of working-class electorates.

Scholarship on the postcommunist region has generally tended to avoid the concept of class in academic discourse given the general aversion to its overuse by official Marxist ideology during communist times (Ost 2015: 546; Doolan and Cepić 2022). However, the review of the literature on postcommunist voting provided in this chapter helps demonstrate that across the postcommunist region members of different social classes tend to diverge in their economic preferences in a manner similar to that observed

*When Left Moves Right*. Maria Snegovaya, Oxford University Press. © Oxford University Press 2024.
DOI: 10.1093/oso/9780197699027.003.0003

in Western democracies. These patterns are also consistent with left parties' economic policy choices. Where ex-communist left parties look much like traditional left-wing parties, working-class support is more likely to be associated with them. Where these parties adopt more pro-market positions, working-class groups are less likely to vote for them.

Second, in the Eastern European context, working-class groups are particularly important electorally. As this chapter demonstrates, unlike in Western Europe, where structural change in the economy has led to a reduction in the sheer size of working-class groups, in the postcommunist context working-class groups still constitute a disproportionally high share of voters. This fact helps highlight why in Eastern Europe the programmatic rebranding of ex-communist left parties (which followed the Western European model) tended to have such a consequential impact on their fortunes. Dealigning working-class groups made much larger swaths of their electorates than in the West available for mobilization by other (populist right) parties. Eventually this process conditioned the swing of Eastern European polities to the right. This chapter provides evidence that helps explain this dynamic.

This chapter thus helps explain why the main focus of this book is on working-class groups; it also contributes to our understanding of how ex-communist left rebranding ended up being so consequential for corresponding party systems in the region.

## The Working Class after Communism

The working class in Western Europe has been on a path to increasing atomization and invisibility since the 1970s. Because of trends like globalization and mechanization, rising employment in the retail and banking sectors, and the growth of the "precariat" class—workers lacking job stability and occupational identity—the traditional working class has eroded over time (Rovny 2018). With the decline of the manufacturing industry, class structures started to disintegrate and the workforce has become more individualized (Mann 1995; Eley 2002; Azmanova 2004). Today in Western Europe, production workers no longer represent a majority of the population. Not only have service jobs come to overshadow industrial jobs, but more people working in service jobs have come to identify with the middle class (which comprises the largest share of the population) (Hugrée, Penissat, and Spire

2020). Political scientist Line Rennwald (2020: 26) estimates that the share of production workers in the Western European workforce declined from 31% to 16%. Concurrently, other manual workers and low-skilled white-collar workers have increasingly started to describe themselves as belonging to the middle class rather than the working class.[1] All of this has resulted in a smaller share of working-class voters in Western European electorates (Rennwald 2020: 8).

In postcommunist Europe these trends have played out quite differently. To be fair, the postcommunist region also saw the growing "tertiarization" of the economy, with an expanding service sector and the rapid increase of part-time, nonbenefited, and other precarious forms of employment (Ost 2000). Simultaneously, however, in recent decades many companies relocated industrial jobs from Western to Eastern Europe, which has led to the continued domination of industrial jobs in the postcommunist workforce (Hugrée, Penissat, and Spire 2020: 4). Take Poland, for instance, which opened its doors to many Western European electronics and large house-hold appliance manufacturers (such as Dell and the Whirlpool Corporation) after joining the European Union in 2004. Hungary has also been one of the net beneficiaries of industrial jobs relocation, particularly those from the developed EU-15 countries (Sass and Hunya 2014). These trends were con-sistent across postcommunist Europe, where working-class groups, partic-ularly skilled manual workers, continued to form the largest proportion of the population, considerably larger than that of other social classes (Hugrée, Penissat, and Spire 2020: 4, 6).

Figure 2.1 shows the aggregate share of working-class respondents in ten selected postcommunist countries using the European Social Survey and the Oesch classification schema. The Oesch schema is based on the International Standard Classification of Occupations. This schema identifies three classes belonging to the salaried middle class: (1) managers, such as personnel managers, accountants, and administrators; (2) technical specialists, such as engineers, information technology specialists, and technicians; and (3) soci-ocultural professionals and semi-professionals, such as doctors, teachers, and social workers. Located in the twilight zone between the middle and working class are (4) large employers and liberal professionals, such as self-employed

---

[1] The European working class includes predominantly low-skilled and unskilled manual and white-collar workers (40%)—mainly manual workers and domestic cleaners—and skilled workers (38%), most of them in industry. It also includes other, primarily female occupations, such as nursing assistants and childcare workers (Hugrée, Penissat, and Spire 2020: 5).

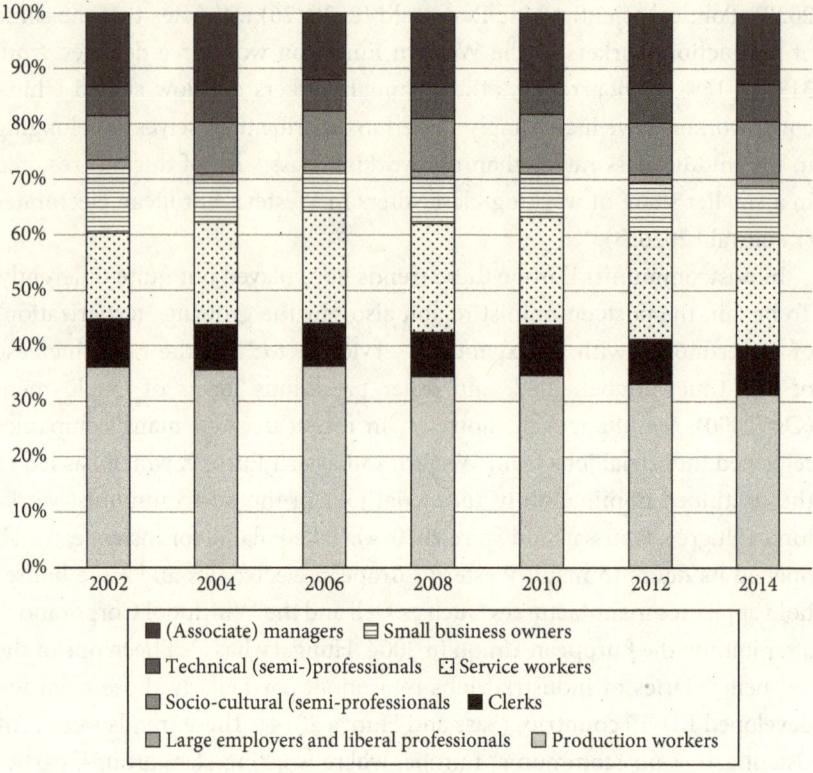

**Figure 2.1** The Share of Different Classes in Ten Postcommunist Countries (Bulgaria, the Czech Republic, Estonia, Hungary, Latvia, Lithuania, Poland, Romania, Slovakia, Slovenia). Oesch classification schema based on the International Standard Classification of Occupations (Oesch and Rennwald 2018).
*Source*: European Social Survey.

lawyers and dentists; (5) small business owners, such as shop owners, independent artisans, and farmers; and (6) clerks, such as secretaries, postal clerks, and receptionists. Ultimately, two other identified subcategories form the working class: (7) service workers, such as waiters, shop assistants, and nursing aides; and (8) production workers, such as mechanics, assemblers, and carpenters (Oesch and Rennwald 2018).

According to Figure 2.1, the share of production workers in postcommunist countries constitutes about 30% to 35% of respondents, with a slight decrease from the mid-2000s to 2014. The share of service-class workers has slightly increased over the same period and comprises about 20% of respondents.

The combined share of production workers, service workers, and clerks has remained stable and constituted around 60% during this period.

The social shifts that took place in the region after the collapse of communism were extremely painful for the working class. The years since 1989–1991 have featured rising unemployment, declining real incomes, and spreading poverty. The dismantling of the communist state, the opening of domestic markets to the global economy, the disruption of protection safety nets, and especially the transition-induced erosion of communist factory-based jobs threw millions of workers' lives into chaos and put them at a greater disadvantage in terms of income and upward mobility (Oesch 2006a; Mudge 2018: 44). Subsequent structural changes associated with the integration of postcommunist economies into international markets, such as occupational upgrading, automation of manufacturing, lean production, and the outsourcing of routine activities, further undermined these groups' positions in the labor market (Kitschelt 2007: 1181; Kriesi et al. 2008: 4; Oesch 2012: 34). These groups were of no strategic importance for employers and thus did not possess any bargaining power. They also faced more direct labor competition from immigrants than did members of other social classes. Hugrée, Penissat, and Spire (2020: 21) argue that in many respects, the working class in postcommunist Europe has occupied "the lowest position in the European social space" and has shown "signs of great financial poverty, combined with working conditions that are harsher than anywhere else."

While the degrees of state protection for economically vulnerable groups varied in different countries (higher in the Czech Republic, lower in Poland and Hungary; see Chapters 4 and 5), entire generations of workers in the postcommunist region commonly found themselves on the losing side of transition reforms. Blue-collar workers with little to no education often experienced a significant loss of social status, survived on small underpaid jobs, and/or were often forced to return to rural areas (which reinforced the economic disparity between urban and rural zones) (Ciobanu 2009; Hugrée, Penissat, and Spire 2020: 23). Scheiring (2020b: 156), for example, demonstrates that a large part of the Hungarian working class was extremely vulnerable financially: in 2005–2010, 40% of Hungarian households lived in material deprivation, while the share of people living in extreme material deprivation was over 20%. For skilled male manual workers, once celebrated by the old system as heroes of socialist labor, the loss of status was most extreme (Kiblitskaya 2000; Kideckel 2004).

These trends were exacerbated by several factors.

First, the postcommunist working class in Eastern Europe has always been weak. This is because communist rulers manipulated trade unions and replaced them with fictitious structures. Eventually, like most other quasi-independent communist institutions, the unions existed only to conduct procommunist policies—often at the expense of workers. As demonstrated by Andras Toth (1994: 88), unions were transformed into subordinate dummy organizations during the communist period. Their goal was to serve as "transmission belts," conveying central economic policy from the decision-making communist bodies to the workers. This detached the unions from their original social functions—collective bargaining and social rights protection. As a result, the interests of Hungarian trade unions and workers diverged. Toth speaks of a double history of the official trade-union hierarchy on the one hand, and of workers' attempts to defend their own rights outside the trade unions on the other. This left workers with a negative impression of unions even after communism collapsed. Rather than being perceived as part of a struggle for social justice, unions were often viewed as part of the system against which people struggled.[2] After the collapse of communism, union membership plummeted across the region (Kubicek 1999; Ost 2009). Most trade unions in the region remained weak and avoided structured political alliances except for several initial alliances with more moderate forces, such as the social democratic successor parties of Poland and Hungary.

Second, where new elites sought to collaborate with unions, their integration into the political process remained largely symbolic. With some exceptions in Slovakia and the Czech Republic, new elites tended to deploy tripartite agreements between the government, employer associations, and labor organizations in a superficial way to win workers over to neoliberalism (Ost 2000).[3] This is because these institutions tended to be copied from the West and created from above, avoiding the social conflicts that gave rise to these institutions in Western democracies in the first place (Scheiring 2020b: 68). While providing unions a forum to negotiate over broad issues and incorporating some working-class demands into politics, postcommunist governments repeatedly tried to use tripartite bodies to legitimate the neoliberal policies they introduced (Ost 2000: 515). This dynamic

---

[2] Even Lech Wałęsa, a leader of the Solidarity trade union, argued against rebuilding it to make it stronger. He stated, "We will not catch up to Europe if we build a strong union" (quoted in Ost 2000: 519).

[3] *Tripartism* refers to an institutionalized system of labor input into policymaking through collaboration among unions, employers, and the government.

is particularly notable in the case of Poland, where throughout the 1990s reformist left and right parties relied on the support of the Ogólnopolskie Porozumienie Związków Zawodowych (OPZZ) and Solidarity unions. Yet rather than strengthening the positions of the Polish working class, collaboration with ruling parties contributed primarily to the subordination of trade union demands to the needs of political coalition-making in reformist governments (Chapter 4; see also Trappmann 2012: 8; Sil 2017: 429).[4]

Third, the 2008 financial crisis further exacerbated social inequality (Piketty 2014; Scheiring and Szombati 2020). Postcommunist working classes were particularly badly hit by the crisis, given the sharp increase in unemployment (except in the Czech Republic) and the rise of insecure jobs (short-term contracts) (Hazans 2011; Orenstein 2019; see also Chapter 1). Furthermore, adjustment to the crisis in this region has often taken the form of austerity policies and a significant wage restraint, and hence has further spread poverty among working-class electorates (Hugrée, Penissat, and Spire 2020: 10). The lingering threat of unemployment additionally exacerbated the sense of insecurity and abandonment among working-class groups (Castel 2003; Scheiring and Szombati 2020).

Scholars of the postcommunist region, with their general aversion to class-based analysis associated with communist times and Marxist dogmas, have long refrained from introducing class analysis into their explanations of the political dynamics in the region (Ost 2015). This is puzzling given that working-class electorates constitute a significantly higher share of the population in the postcommunist region than in Western Europe. This book is one of the few recent attempts (Fabry 2019; Scheiring 2020a, 2020b; Gagyi 2015, Ost 2006, 2015a, 2015b, 2018) to bring class back into the conversation.

---

[4] Hungary is a canonical case for illustrating the trade union situation in the postcommunist world. Hungary's fragmented union structure, with "partial links with political parties," led to partial successes but mostly failures in enacting pro-labor policy (Avdagic 2005; Sil 2017). The independent anticommunist Hungarian unions (particularly LIGA and MOSZ) have never been particularly strong. However, some ties between the unions and political parties developed, as described by Avdagic (2005). MOSZ established links with the Hungarian Democratic Forum (MDF) and its chairman entered the first parliament on the MDF ticket (Bruszt 1995). LIGA developed strong informal links to the Alliance of Free Democrats (SZDSZ). MSZOSZ, one of the descendants of the old official union center SZOT, established a formal alliance based on the common "leftist values" with the Hungarian Socialist Party (MSZP) (Rácz 1993: 662). In the first years of transition, unions often signed tripartite agreements, mostly limited to the income policy. When MSZP won the 1994 elections, the president of MSZOSZ, Sándor Nagy, ran second on the Socialist Party list. The new MSZP-led government started negotiations on a broader social pact, which were soon abandoned. Because of the worsening economic situation and government conflicts, MSZP turned its back on the union and initiated the harsh austerity Bokros package, and Nagy resigned from his union post. This general trend continued under the subsequent right-wing governments.

## Preferences of Working-Class Electorates

Introduction and Chapter 1 have described how pro-market reforms in postcommunist Europe created a socioeconomic cleavage between the economic "winners" and "losers" of the transition. To map the preferences of different socioeconomic groups and their associated party preferences, this section integrates into the analysis the economic and cultural preferences of postcommunist voters by mapping them in a two-dimensional political space (Oesch 2012; Kitschelt 1994; Kriesi et al. 2008).

Studies of Western Europe have demonstrated that working-class voters tend to hold a particular combination of political attitudes, which often distinguishes them from other social classes: they have stronger support for redistribution and more pronounced anti-immigration sentiments.

Workers' preferences in favor of redistribution are linked to their more disadvantaged position on the labor market (Iversen and Soskice 2001; Moene and Wallerstein 2001; Cusack, Iversen, and Rehm 2006). Working-class jobs usually offer lower wages and less secure incomes and positions than middle-class jobs. They do not guarantee sick pay, generous pensions, or established promotion ladders, and they involve less autonomy, more supervised monitoring, more rigid schedules, and less pleasant working conditions (Evans 2017: 179). Because individual redistribution preferences are driven by factors related to labor market risks, economically vulnerable, lower-skilled groups view higher redistribution as a way to insulate themselves from such risks (Evans and De Graaf 2013; Marx and Schumacher 2018). Recent studies confirm that personal experience of economic hardship increases support for redistribution (Margalit 2013; Owens and Pedulla 2014). Exposure to globalization further increases risk perceptions and demands for social protections among low-skilled individuals (Rehm 2009; Walter 2017).

When it comes to positions on the sociocultural dimension, social class also influences attitudes on immigration. First, working-class electorates (particularly lower-skilled workers) are more likely to face tougher labor market competition from immigrants. In crisis periods, this higher competition may lead to more powerful tensions and reactions in these socioeconomic categories (Hugrée, Penissat, and Spire 2020: 11). Therefore, these groups are more inclined to hold anti-immigration views and favor stricter control over immigration (Lubbers, Gijsberts, and Scheepers 2002). Second, lower education levels and a lack of material resources make these lower-income socioeconomic groups more likely to view immigration as a cultural threat (Hainmueller and Hiscox 2007; Rydgren 2013).

In light of this reasoning, working-class respondents are therefore expected to have a combination of pro-redistributive preferences and anti-immigration preferences. A recent study by Rennwald (2020) backs these expectations. She analyzes the positions of working-class electorates on economic and sociocultural issues in six Western European countries (Austria, France, Germany, Great Britain, the Netherlands, and Switzerland) using the European Social Survey (ESS) and the Oesch occupational schema to reveal that individuals belonging to working-class occupations (production and service workers) tend to have greater pro-redistribution preferences and to hold views that are systematically more unfavorable toward immigration than the average respondents in their respective countries (Rennwald 2020: 76–77, 80–84). Importantly, workers' attitudes on these issues have remained remarkably consistent for decades, from the 1970s to the 2000s. The stability of workers' pro-redistributive and anti-immigration preferences (voters' preferences on the demand side) suggests that changes in the ability of parties to reach out to these groups (in other words, changes on the supply side of the political spectrum) may have a stronger impact on workers' evolving voting patterns. Therefore, the ways in which parties present political options to workers may better explain workers' changing voting patterns (Rennwald 2020: 85).

This section explores the preferences of postcommunist working-class electorates on economic and immigration issues using ESS data for the Visegrád Four countries that are of particular interest in this book. To identify respondents' occupational status, the analysis introduces the commonly employed Oesch classification schema explained in the previous section and follows the approach used by Oesch (2012).

Alongside the class variable, I used 2008 ESS data—2008 is the only year in the data set for which all relevant variables were available—to construct two composite indices to locate citizens' preferences on the two-dimensional space (economic-distributive and cultural-identitarian axis). Yet based on Rennwald's (2020) findings, one can also expect a level of continuity in the preferences of working-class electorates on both dimensions for the period under consideration in this book.

The horizontal axis locates respondents' preferences on the economic dimension, going from a redistributionist far-left pole toward a free-market capitalist pole. To construct the horizontal axis (the economic dimension)

I ran a factor analysis on a set of economic attitudes from the ESS using the following four items (Oesch 2012): (1) standard of living for the unemployed is the government's responsibility; (2) standard of living for the old is the government's responsibility; (3) universal employment is the government's responsibility; (4) the government should reduce income inequality. The variables were recorded so that higher values corresponded with less redistributive preferences. This resulting factor provided a measure for an economic axis going from a socialist (redistributionist) to a capitalist pole.

The vertical axis distinguishes respondents on the sociocultural dimension in accordance with their attitudes toward immigration from a libertarian-universalistic to an authoritarian-communitarian pole (Oesch 2012: 45). For the sociocultural dimension, respondents were asked to rank their positions on immigration issues on a scale of 0 to 10, with the highest value corresponding to the most favorable attitudes toward immigration: (1) a country's cultural life is undermined or enriched by immigrants; (2) immigrants make a country a worse or better place to live in; (3) allow few/many immigrants of same race/ethnic group as majority; (4) allow few/many immigrants of different race/ethnic group from majority; (5) allow few/many immigrants from poorer countries outside Europe. These measures allow me to map a cultural axis that spans from an authoritarian-communitarian pole to a libertarian-universalistic pole.

The factor loadings of these two composite indices are shown in Tables A.1 and A.2 in Appendix I. The combination of the attitudes on the two axes allows me to determine voters' position in a two-dimensional political space (Kitschelt 1994: 27). The intersection is located at the midpoint of the minimum and maximum values of each factor variable. Figure 2.2 represents positions of the above socioeconomic groups on these dimensions in the Visegrád Four countries.

Figure 2.2 maps the preferences of various socioeconomic groups on a two-dimensional space. There are several findings that stand out. First, in all Visegrád Four countries, except the Czech Republic, the majority of socioeconomic groups (except for the class of large employers and liberal professionals) tend to place themselves on the left side of the graph, suggesting that the respondents under consideration are largely in favor of redistributional policies regardless of individual socioeconomic status. This is consistent with other studies that have demonstrated that the legacy of communism created enduring mass support for the state-funded provision

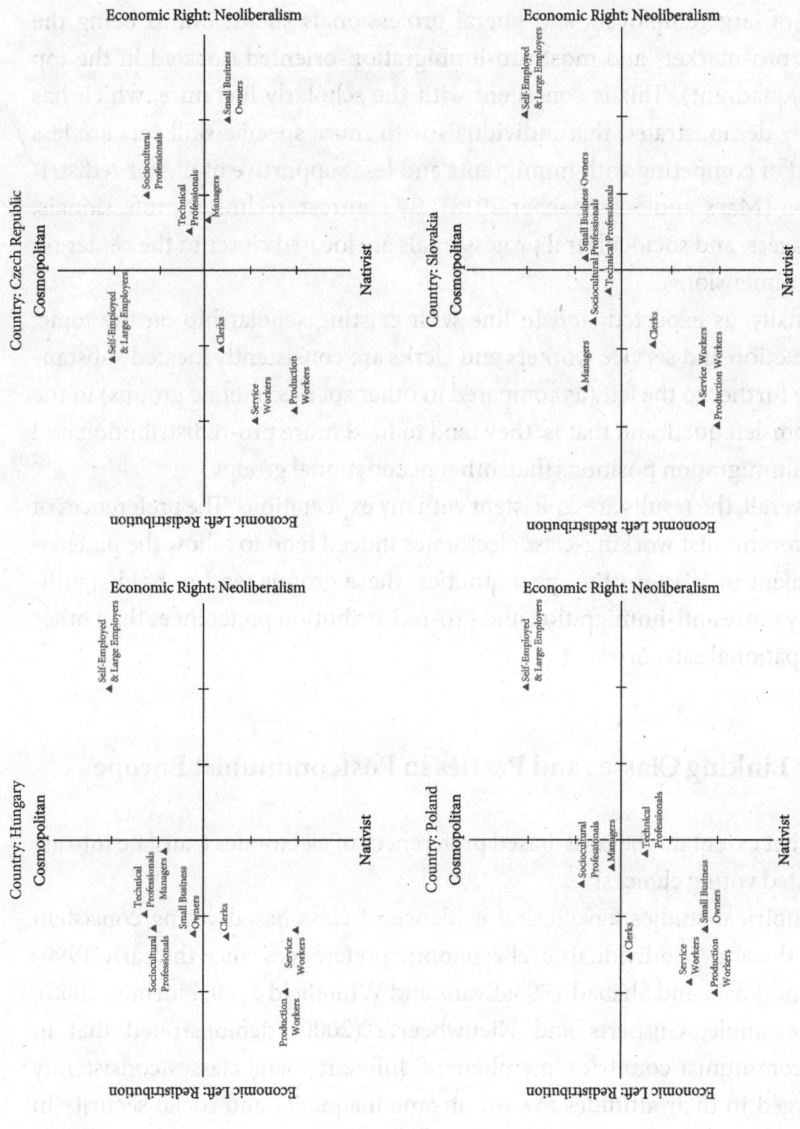

**Figure 2.2** Voters' Mean Position on the Economic (State-Market) and Cultural (Integration-Demarcation) Preference Axis, Aggregated by Class and Party Choice.

*Note:* See Tables A.1 and A.2 in Appendix I for the questions used to build the factors underlying the two axes.

of social welfare among different social groups (Orenstein and Bugarič 2019; Pop-Eleches and Tucker 2014; Mason et al. 2000).

Second, with the exception of respondents from the Czech Republic, the class of large employers and liberal professionals stands out as being the most pro-market- and most pro-immigration-oriented (located in the top right quadrant). This is consistent with the scholarly literature, which has largely demonstrated that individuals with more specific skill sets are less afraid of competing with immigrants and less supportive of higher redistribution (Marx and Schumacher 2018). By contrast, technical professionals, managers, and sociocultural professionals are located closer to the center on both dimensions.

Finally, as expected, and in line with existing scholarship on the topic, production and service workers and clerks are consistently located substantively further to the left (as compared to other socioeconomic groups) in the bottom-left quadrant; that is, they tend to hold more pro-redistribution and anti-immigration positions than other occupational groups.

Overall, the results are consistent with my expectations. The preferences of postcommunist working-class electorates indeed tend to follow the patterns prevalent in Western European polities: these groups tend to hold significantly more anti-immigration and pro-redistribution preferences than other occupational categories.

## Linking Classes and Parties in Postcommunist Europe

To what extent do the class-based preferences of electorates translate into associated voting choices?

Empirical studies have found evidence of class-based voting consistent with the above individual-level economic preferences since the early 1990s (Słomczyński and Shabad 1996; Evans and Whitefield 2000; Fidrmuc 2000). For example, Gijsberts and Nieuwbeerta (2000) demonstrated that in postcommunist countries, members of different social classes consistently diverged in their attitudes toward income inequality and social security in a manner similar to that observed in Western democracies. Working-class groups were among those most committed to "the egalitarian and collectivist values of the 'caring' paternalistic state" (Słomczyński and Shabad 1996: 188).

In the very first free elections in the region there was little effect of class and education, as other issues (such as the struggle of civil society against those in power) tended to dominate the debate (Szelenyi, Fodor, and Hanley 1996). Early on, ex-communist left parties that embraced pro-market positions became instant catch-all parties; their support bases were mixed, with both anti-reform and reform supporters (Innes 2002; Karreth et al. 2013). For example, Hungary's MSZP, which rejected its old Communist Party image and rebranded itself as a social democratic party, combined promises of rapid improvement in living standards for all Hungarians with social protections for lower-income groups (Oltay 1994) and attracted blue-collar workers along with intellectuals and entrepreneurs (Andorka 1999; Szelenyi, Fodor, and Hanley 1997; Racz 1993). Similarly, in early 1990s Poland, the support base of the left-wing SLD included workers and pensioners, but also employers, including private entrepreneurs (Hunter and Ryan 1998; Curry 2003).

Yet once the reforms began, the radical disruption of voters' incomes, lifestyles, and futures during the transition provided the impetus for political divisions along socioeconomic lines, launching the formation of socioeconomic cleavages (Evans 1997; Szelenyi et al. 1997; Evans 2000). As "the almost universal 'pro-market euphoria' of the early stages of the transformation has faded," different social groups and classes began forming their own views of the ideal socioeconomic order (Mateju, Rehakova, and Evans 1999: 235). Election results started to reflect voters' experience with economic reforms: those who benefited from the reforms (private entrepreneurs, white-collar workers, and university-educated voters) voted for right pro-reform parties, whereas those for whom the reforms proved detrimental (the unemployed, retirees, the precariat, blue-collar and agricultural workers) voted for left-wing parties that promised protection against market instability (Fidrmuc 2000).

Over a four-year period throughout which the costs of marketization became increasingly apparent to postcommunist electorates, class voting realigned and polarized to the left-right alignments similar to those observed in the West (Mateju, Rehakova, and Evans 1999; Fidrmuc 2000). Specifically, working-class groups started to align with left parties, which adopted more protectionist economic stances. For example, a study by Szelenyi, Fodor, and Hanley (1996) found that by 1993–1994 in Hungary and Poland, voting patterns aligned with this expectation. Growing support of blue-collar electorates for the ex-communist parties became very pronounced at that time, even if the most important predictor of party choice was religiosity (Jasiewicz 2009). The working-class vote was the main "factor that explains why these parties won the elections just four years after the fall of Communism" (Szelenyi, Fodor, and Hanley 1996: 216). In Poland, in particular, the proportion of those voting for ex-communists increased across all occupations, but this increase (about 80%) was by far the greatest among blue-collar workers. These effects were similar in Hungary, where the proportion of left voters increased especially among blue-collar electorates (Szelenyi, Fodor, and Hanley 1996).[5] A very similar pattern of strengthening of class-based voting behavior and the crystallization of a "traditional" left-right divide was also visible in the case of the Czech Republic in the mid-1990s. Mateju, Rehakova, and Evans (1999) discovered that while there was virtually no difference between professionals and routine nonmanual workers in 1992, by 1996 both classes revealed significantly distinct propensities for left voting. The working class moved toward voting for left-wing parties more than other economically active groups (Mateju, Rehakova, and Evans 1999).

Therefore, in the mid-1990s, based on their electoral appeals and composition of the vote, in these countries left parties looked much like traditional left-wing parties in Western Europe at the onset of the Third Way rebranding. As Chapters 4 and 5 demonstrate, these findings are consistent with more redistributionist stances adopted by the ex-communist left in corresponding elections and targeted at the social groups that missed out as result of reforms.

There are other, more recent empirical studies of the Visegrád Four that show changing party alignments throughout the 2000s that are in line with my argument in this book. For instance, Minkenberg and Pytlas (2013) find that in Slovakia, where the left party Smer-SD adopted a more traditional protectionist platform on the economic dimension (see Chapter 5), manual workers still oriented themselves closer to the leftmost end of the spectrum. Similarly, in the Czech Republic these groups were more likely to associate with left parties (Hlousek and Kopecek 2008; Linek 2015). By contrast, in Poland, where the left SLD adopted more pro-market positions (see Chapter 4), manual workers and farmers were rather evenly distributed on the left-right scale, with a slight overrepresentation at the rightmost end (Szczerbiak 2007; Minkenberg and Pylas 2013; Rae 2017). Similarly, in Hungary, where the MSZP also embraced pro-market reforms, blue-collar constituencies and farmers were underrepresented at the leftmost end of

---

[5] The same trends were noted for agricultural workers.

the scale and tended to lean right (Knutsen 2013; Győri 2015; Bartha and Toth 2017).

While these dynamics of party alignments have been documented, few empirical studies of the region have attempted to explore the support for parties across their positions on the economic policy dimension and among different socioeconomic groups.

## Summary

This chapter focused on the fortunes and preferences of working-class electorates in the postcommunist context.

The chapter began by discussing the experiences of working-class constituencies in postcommunist Europe after the transition and their relative share in these countries' electorates. It demonstrated that, contrary to the situation in Western European postindustrial democracies, where working-class constituencies form a smaller share of the electorates as compared to the middle class, in postcommunist Europe working-class groups still represent a majority (up to 60%) of the electorates. This is partly a consequence of the process of industry relocation that has been unraveling over the past two decades. Many industrial jobs have relocated from Western to Eastern Europe, leading to a continuing domination of industrial jobs in the postcommunist workforce.

The chapter also explored the challenges faced by working-class groups after the transition. Communist-era factory-based jobs disappeared and welfare protections eroded, leaving smaller safety nets and scant insulation from the 2008 financial crisis. These economic misfortunes put postcommunist working classes at a greater disadvantage in terms of their incomes and upward mobility as compared to other socioeconomic groups in the region. And rather than integrating union demands into policymaking, reformist postcommunist governments often used collaboration with trade unions to legitimize neoliberal policies they introduced.

This chapter also examined the political attitudes of workers in the Visegrád Four countries on issues of redistribution and immigration. Consistent with literature on Western Europe, postcommunist workers display a particular set of political attitudes that combine pro-redistributive preferences on the economic policy dimension with anti-immigration preferences on the sociocultural dimension.

In order to illuminate how these preferences of working-class electorates translate into voting choices, this chapter reviewed the literature on class-based support for left-wing and right-wing parties in postcommunist Europe. Overall, the pattern discovered by empirical studies on the region is in line with this book's argument. It reveals that early on after the transition, many postcommunist left parties tended to attract working-class support with a protectionist platform. It also reveals the subsequent tendency of postcommunist working-class groups in countries with a pro-market left to increase support for right-wing parties.

While many empirical studies of the postcommunist region hint at the pattern discussed in this book, few (if any) have tested it empirically. The next chapter provides empirical evidence directly connecting left parties' economic policy positions to voting choices of different socioeconomic groups.

# 3

# How the Postcommunist Left Reformed and Lost

Chapter 1 formulated the theoretical argument of this book about the role of left parties' pro-market positions in their subsequent fortunes. Chapter 2 provided evidence highlighting the importance of working-class electorates in the postcommunist context. Compared to advanced Western economies, working-class groups constituted a larger size of postcommunist electorates, but were also more severely hurt by marketization, which contributed to their dealignment from ruling parties. Since labor interests were not suffi- ciently incorporated in the agenda of postcommunist reformers, a signif- icant segment of the working class became attracted to and influenced by emerging right-wing, conservative, nationalist, or populist trends (Ost 2006; Ciobanu 2009).

In postcommunist Europe, the consequences of the adoption of pro- market policies should have been even more pronounced than in Western Europe. That is because the region had experienced a much more pro- nounced effect of rapid economic liberalization multiplied by the effects of economic globalization. As discussed in the Introduction and Chapter 1, these countries embraced pro-market economic policies more strongly than any other developing world region after 1989 (Appel and Orenstein 2016). The legacy of communism that created enduring mass support for a state- funded provision of social welfare should have contributed to a stronger backlash against pro-market policies in the long run (Orenstein and Bugarič 2019; Pop-Eleches and Tucker 2014; Mason et al. 2000).

However, so far this argument has remained largely qualitative. Few studies of the region have attempted to empirically connect changing patterns of party alignment in postcommunist regions with the economic positions of the left and to analyze the role of working-class electorates in this process. Cross-country analysis testing these assumptions is lacking.

This chapter fills this gap by contributing to existing scholarship on sev- eral dimensions. First, few empirical studies of the region have attempted to

*When Left Moves Right.* Maria Snegovaya, Oxford University Press. © Oxford University Press 2024.
DOI: 10.1093/oso/9780197699027.003.0004

explore the support for left parties across their positions on the economic policy dimension and among different socioeconomic groups—this chapter does just that. Second, the literature, which analyzed the short-term effects of such rebranding, often assumed that the adoption of pro-market positions of the left parties had been largely beneficial to them, primarily due to the loyalty of their supporters (see the Introduction). This chapter aims to empirically analyze whether this has indeed been the case across the postcommunist region. Do left parties' pro-market positions have any effect on their support, particularly among economically vulnerable voters? To explore this question, this chapter empirically tests the association between left parties' economic positions and their support among working-class electorates. Third, studies have often postulated that the competition in these countries occurs primarily over noneconomic issues. This chapter empirically tests this assumption by looking at the role of sociocultural positions in left parties' support and connecting them with their economic stances.

This chapter tests the merits of this book's argument on a cross-country study. Cross-country studies allow us to compare a select number of countries in order to gain a better understanding of the phenomenon in question while controlling for country-specific sociocultural settings (Hantrais and Mangen 1998). This approach makes it possible to test the book's argument on a broader set of cases and thus to extend its external validity.

## The Pro-Market Left and Class-Based Support

This chapter combines individual-level data from the European Social Survey (ESS) with data on party positions from the Chapel Hill Expert Survey (CHES). The data cover forty-one elections in ten Eastern European countries (Bulgaria, the Czech Republic, Estonia, Hungary, Latvia, Lithuania. Poland, Romania, Slovakia, and Slovenia) from 2006 to 2014.

This time interval was selected for several reasons. First, on the lower end, the data availability for the ESS and CHES surveys in the postcommunist context allows a systematic cross-country analysis starting only in 2006. The theoretical framework of this chapter relies on the assumption that left parties abandoned their traditional left-wing policies in the context of market transition and EU accession. Both of these processes started in the early and mid-1990s; one of them, EU accession, culminated later (2004+). By contrast, given the availability of cross-country data sets, the empirical analysis starts in 2006, after most of the causal mechanisms had taken place. These data, however, still allow the study to examine the dynamic of interest. As shown in Chapter 1, the realignment derived from the left parties' centrist policy shift took time to unravel. The electoral gains of the 1990s were short-lived and came at the expense of electoral success in the subsequent decade (typically one or two periods after moderation occurred) (Karreth et al. 2013). In the postcommunist context, in particular, the realignment was further delayed by the timing of EU accession. As discussed in Chapter 1, the serious backlash to reforms began, in many cases, only in the mid-2000s. While these data do not allow this research to capture the starting point in the 1990s, when the ex-communist left was still attracting large swaths of working-class electorates, they illustrate how economic positions relate to party support across various socioeconomic groups.

Second, on the upper end, as explained in the Introduction, the main focus of this book precedes the 2015 immigration crisis, which provided political space for parties to mobilize around less-structured political cleavage, namely immigration, making parties' positions on this issue more salient (Guiso et al. 2017; Roberts 2017a, 2017b). Thus, the 2015 crisis might have altered the reasons why voters chose to shift their support from some parties to others. This explains the main focus of the analysis on the period preceding 2015. In addition, by 2015, the key realignment of interests had already taken place: in many analyzed countries populist parties were strongly established while left parties had declined. Focusing the main analysis on the period preceding the immigration crisis thus allows me to reduce the extra noise in the data and concentrate on this book's main focus: the economic axis of parties' competition.

Table 3.1 presents the overview of the parties used in the empirical analysis. The attribution of most parties to left and right was based on the CHES socialist, conservative, and radical right categories using the Derksen classification triangulated by (a) membership or affiliation with European Parliament party families, (b) Parlgov classifications, and (c) self-identification (Polk et al. 2017).[1] Only the parties mentioned in both the ESS and CHES surveys were included in this analysis.

---

[1] As a slight modification, the Estonian Center Party was recorded as a left party. (It is classified as a liberal party in the CHES.)

**Table 3.1** List of Parties Included in the Empirical Analysis

| Country | Left Party | Conservative | Radical Right |
|---|---|---|---|
| Bulgaria | • Socialist Party, KzB; BSP | • Movement for Rights and Freedoms, DSB<br>• The Union of Democratic Forces, SDS, ODS<br>• Democrats for a Strong Bulgaria<br>• Citizens for European Development of Bulgaria, GERB | • Ataka |
| The Czech Republic | • Czech Social Democratic Party, ČSSD | • Civic Democratic Party, ODS<br>• Top09 | • Dawn of Direct Democracy, Usvit |
| Estonia | • Estonian Social Democratic Party, SDE | • Pro Patria and Res Publica Union | • Estonian Independence Party<br>• Conservative People's Party of Estonia, EKRE |
| Hungary | • Hungarian Socialist Party, MSZP | • Fidesz, Hungarian Civic Union<br>• Hungarian Democratic Forum, MDF | • MIEP<br>• Jobbik |
| Latvia | • Concord Centre, SC; SDPS | • The People's Party<br>• New Era | • For Fatherland and Freedom, LNNK<br>• Party Order and Justice, TT |
| Lithuania | • Lithuanian Social Democratic Party, LSDP | • Homeland Union–Lithuanian Christian Democrats, TS-LKD<br>• National Resurrection Party, TPP<br>• Party Order and Justice, TT | Party "Young Lithuania," JL |
| Poland | • Alliance of Democratic Left, SLD | | • League of Polish Families<br>• Samoobrona<br>• Polish People Party<br>• Law and Justice<br>• Kukiz'15 |
| Romania | • Social Democratic Party, PSD | | • Greater Romania Party |
| Slovakia | • Direction–Social Democracy, Smer, Smer-SD | • Most-Híd<br>• Christian Democratic Movement, KDH | • Slovak National Party |
| Slovenia | Social Democrats, ZLSD, SD | • Slovenian Democratic Party, SDS | • Slovene National Party |

This chapter uses the CHES's "LRECON" variable to account for the economic policy positions of left parties, referring to a single (largest) left party present in both data sets. This is a continuous variable that classifies parties according to their stances on economic issues, with a value of "0" corresponding to parties on the economic left-right side, signifying an active state role in the economy, and a value of "10" corresponding to parties on the extreme pro-market side, signifying a reduced governmental role in the economy. My primary argument here focuses on the centrist economic policy positions of left parties—more specifically, those positions located around the mean of the set of values of the economic variable (between values 4 and 6).

Figure 3.1 shows how left parties are distributed on the economic policy dimension over time. There is a substantial variation in the left parties' economic positions over the years. Although most of the left parties fall between 2 and 5 on the economic policy dimension, the distribution reveals considerable variation from extreme left to centrist positions.

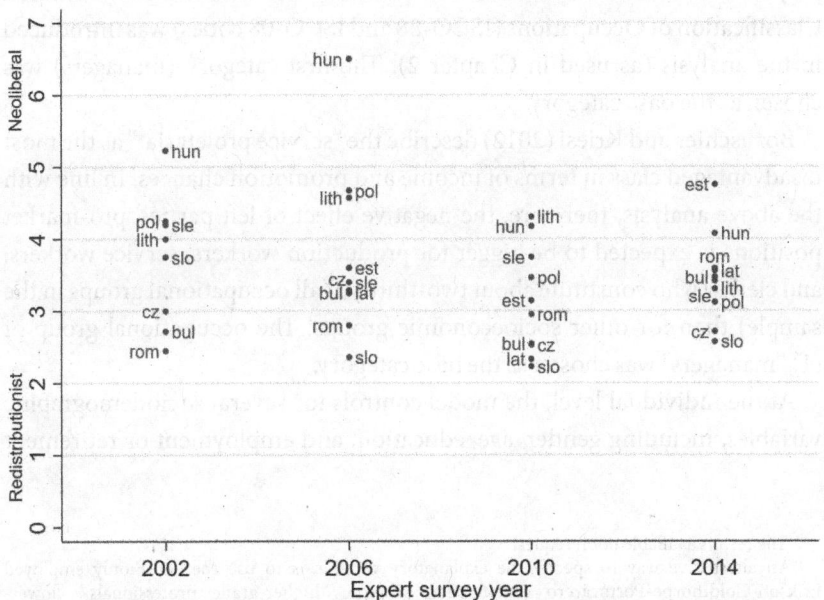

**Figure 3.1** Distribution of Eastern European Left Party Positions on Economic Policy Positions over Time.

*Source*: Chapel Hill Expert Survey.

The dummy dependent variable was coded based on the answer respondents gave to the ESS question "Which party did you vote for in the last election?" It was assigned a value of "1" when respondents named a left party and a value of "0" for other party choices.

The data were combined so that the election year in the ESS data set referenced by the respondent matched a lagged value for the CHES party position. The lagged CHES value was used in the analysis, as previous research on catch-all party literature suggests that parties' positions influence their electoral support with a lag (Erikson, MacKuen, and Stimson 2002; Adams, Ezrow, and Somer-Topcu 2011; Karreth, Polk, and Allen 2013). For example, Adams and Somer-Topcu (2009) argue that the electoral effect is pronounced only in the election after the policy moderation occurred. "Economic dimension" refers to the economic positions of the major left party. Alternative specifications of this variable, using the value on the economic dimension for the most left-leaning party or averaged left party positions, weighted by each respective party's share of the vote in line with Arzheimer (2013), bring very similar results.[2]

To control for the respondents' occupational status, a commonly employed Oesch classification schema based on the International Standard Classification of Occupations (ISCO-88 and ISCO-08 codes) was introduced in the analysis (as used in Chapter 2). The first category (managers) was chosen as the base category.[3]

Bornschier and Kriesi (2012) describe the "service proletariat" as the most disadvantaged class in terms of income and promotion chances. In line with the above analysis, therefore, the negative effect of left parties' pro-market positions is expected to be bigger for production workers, service workers, and clerks (who constitute about two-thirds of all occupational groups in the sample) than for other socioeconomic groups. The occupational group of (1) "managers" was chosen as the base category.

At the individual level, the model controls for several sociodemographic variables, including gender, age, education, and employment or retirement

---

[2] The results available upon request.

[3] An alternative way to specify the explanatory variable is to use the commonly employed Erikson-Goldthorpe-Portocarero classification schema: "higher-grade professionals," "lower-grade professionals," "routine non-manual employees," "small proprietors with employees," "small proprietors without employees," "skilled manual workers and manual supervisors," "semi- and unskilled manual workers," "agricultural workers," "farmers and smallholders" (Erikson et al. 1979; Hendrick 2002). This specification brings very similar results. (The estimates are available upon request.)

status. Some specifications included controls for left party positions on the sociocultural scale measured by the CHES. "Sociocultural dimension" is a continuous variable that classifies parties by their stances on sociocultural issues, with a value of "0" corresponding to parties with extreme traditional/ authoritarian positions, and "10" corresponding to parties that take pronounced libertarian/postmaterialist positions. Since the two dimensions are intrinsically linked, including both of them may artificially increase standard errors. Therefore, it is questionable whether one should control for one dimension while testing the impact of the other (Abou-Chadi and Wagner 2020: 254). The tables demonstrate both specifications: with and without control for left party positions on sociocultural dimension. The analysis employed standardized values of corresponding variables. Table 3.2 presents the descriptive statistics for the data.

Because of the binary nature of the dependent variable, probit models were used in the analysis controlling for the fixed year and national effects to account for time and country-specific effects (such as changes in the national composition of the sample over time). The coefficients can be interpreted as average differences across all country-years. Due to the limited sample size, clustering errors by country could bias estimates; therefore robust standard errors have been used in the analysis (Cameron, Gelbach, and Miller 2008; Esarey and Menger 2018). To account for the different sampling strategies affecting individuals' probability to be included in the survey and varying sample sizes, I used the ESS design weights in the analysis.

Table 3.3 presents the analysis of the effect of left party economic positions on support for these parties after controlling for basic sociodemographic characteristics. The full model is provided in Appendix II.

Column 1 in Table 3.3 explores the effects of the economic positions of left parties on overall support for these parties. Among individual-level controls, age is positively and significantly correlated with the left vote (see the full model in Appendix II). This result is in line with the literature on the region, which demonstrates a stronger correlation between older age and voting for ex-communist parties (Evans 2006). Similarly, the effect of the retirement variable is positive and significant. This result may be driven by age (older people are more likely to be retired and vote for left parties), as well as the weaker socioeconomic positions of older respondents. Compared to other parties, left parties draw significantly less support among the self-employed, technical professionals, and small business owners (at a 99% confidence interval).

Table 3.2 Descriptive Statistics for Cross-Country Analysis

| Variable | Obs | Mean | Std. Dev. | Min | Max |
|---|---|---|---|---|---|
| Oesch schema: | | | | | |
| Self-employed professionals and large employers | 106,249 | 0.0131578 | 0.1139507 | 0 | 1 |
| Small business owners | 106,249 | 0.0850361 | 0.2789367 | 0 | 1 |
| Technical (semi-)professionals | 106,249 | 0.0583253 | 0.2343586 | 0 | 1 |
| Production workers | 106,249 | 0.3424315 | 0.4745253 | 0 | 1 |
| (Associate) managers. | 106,249 | 0.1300812 | 0.3363944 | 0 | 1 |
| Clerks | 106,249 | 0.0826172 | 0.2753041 | 0 | 1 |
| Sociocultural (semi-)professionals | 106,249 | 0.0948338 | 0.2929867 | 0 | 1 |
| Service workers | 106,249 | 0.1935171 | 0.3950566 | 0 | 1 |
| | | | | | |
| Economic policy position | 83,162 | 3.653577 | 1.034987 | 1.67 | 6.5 |
| Sociocultural policy position | 83,162 | 5.807552 | 1.445315 | 3.11 | 8.43 |
| | | | | | |
| Male | 106,108 | 0.4470162 | 0.4971871 | 0 | 1 |
| Age | 105,762 | 49.96934 | 17.12444 | 15 | 102 |
| | | | | | |
| Education: | | | | | |
| Less than lower secondary | 105,879 | 0.0355122 | 0.1850714 | 0 | 1 |
| Lower secondary | 105,879 | 0.1799035 | 0.3841088 | 0 | 1 |
| Upper secondary | 105,879 | 0.5236544 | 0.4994425 | 0 | 1 |
| Postsecondary nontertiary | 105,879 | 0.0485271 | 0.2148782 | 0 | 1 |
| Tertiary | 105,879 | 0.2124028 | 0.4090103 | 0 | 1 |
| | | | | | |
| Retired | 106,249 | 0.3222807 | 0.467352 | 0 | 1 |
| Unemployed | 106,249 | 0.046871 | 0.2113636 | 0 | 1 |

As expected, model 1 demonstrates that when left parties have increasingly pro-market positions on the economic policy dimension, there is a significant negative correlation to the level of political support for those parties. Using average marginal effects based on model 1, a one-unit increase in pro-market policy orientation generates about a 6% decrease in electoral support for left parties while keeping other variables at their means (see Appendix II).

To visualize these findings, Figure 3.2 shows the predicted probability of voting for a left party as dependent on the party's economic positions based

**Table 3.3** Left Parties' Vote as Opposed to Other Parties Conditional on Their Economic Positions

|  | (1) | (2) | (3) | (4) |
|---|---|---|---|---|
| Self-employed professionals and large employers | −0.328*** | −0.323*** | −0.328*** | −0.323*** |
|  | (0.068) | (0.067) | (0.068) | (0.067) |
| Sociocultural (semi-)professionals | −0.035 | −0.037 | −0.035 | −0.037 |
|  | (0.031) | (0.031) | (0.031) | (0.031) |
| Small business owners | −0.297*** | −0.303*** | −0.297*** | −0.303*** |
|  | (0.035) | (0.035) | (0.035) | (0.035) |
| Technical (semi-)professionals | −0.136*** | −0.135*** | −0.136*** | −0.135*** |
|  | (0.037) | (0.037) | (0.037) | (0.037) |
| Clerks | 0.029 | 0.027 | 0.029 | 0.027 |
|  | (0.033) | (0.033) | (0.033) | (0.033) |
| Service workers | −0.012 | −0.010 | −0.012 | −0.010 |
|  | (0.029) | (0.029) | (0.029) | (0.029) |
| Production workers | −0.027 | −0.025 | −0.027 | −0.025 |
|  | (0.027) | (0.027) | (0.027) | (0.027) |
| **Economic policy position** | −0.274*** | −0.212*** | −0.274*** | −0.212*** |
|  | (0.020) | (0.028) | (0.020) | (0.028) |
| **Self-employed professionals# Economic policy position** |  | 0.124* |  | 0.124* |
|  |  | (0.070) |  | (0.070) |
| Sociocultural (semi-)professionals# Economic policy position |  | 0.001 |  | 0.001 |
|  |  | (0.032) |  | (0.032) |
| Small business owners# Economic policy position |  | −0.002 |  | −0.002 |
|  |  | (0.036) |  | (0.036) |
| Technical (semi-)professionals# Economic policy position |  | −0.002 |  | −0.002 |
|  |  | (0.039) |  | (0.039) |
| **Clerks#Economic policy position** |  | −0.059* |  | −0.059* |
|  |  | (0.033) |  | (0.033) |
| **Service workers#Economic policy position** |  | −0.104*** |  | −0.105*** |
|  |  | (0.028) |  | (0.028) |
| **Production workers#Economic policy position** |  | −0.124*** |  | −0.124*** |
|  |  | (0.025) |  | (0.025) |
| Sociocultural policy position |  |  | −0.003 | 0.004 |
|  |  |  | (0.032) | (0.032) |

*(continued)*

**Table 3.3** Continued

|  | (1) | (2) | (3) | (4) |
|---|---|---|---|---|
| Constant | −1.021*** | −1.025*** | −1.025*** | −1.018*** |
|  | (0.090) | (0.090) | (0.104) | (0.104) |
| Observations | 39,448 | 39,448 | 39,448 | 39,448 |
| r2_p | 0.0883 | 0.0897 | 0.0883 | 0.0897 |

* $p < 0.1$, ** $p < 0.05$, *** $p < 0.01$.
*Note:* The table reports effects of probit regressions. Significant coefficients important for the discussion are selected in bold. For the full model and marginal effects, see Appendix II.

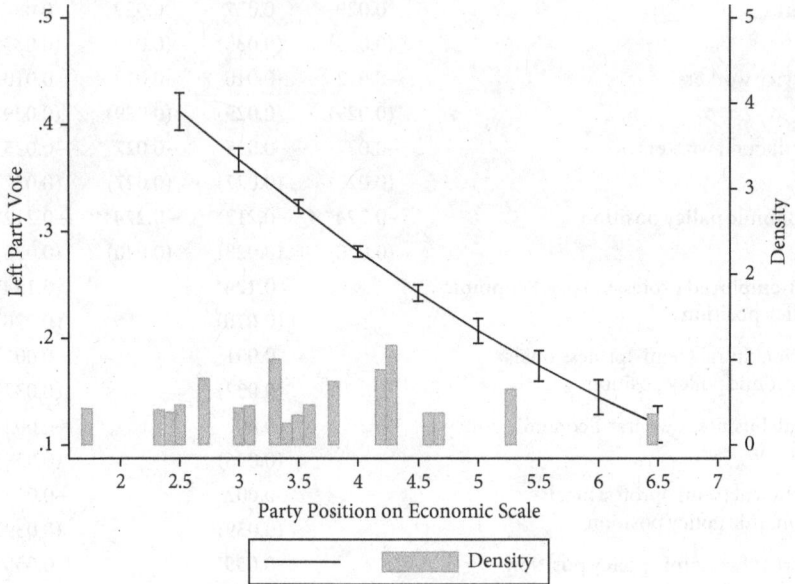

**Figure 3.2** Predicted Marginal Probability of the Left Party Vote Conditional on Left Party Positions on Economic Policy. Other variables held at their observed values. Histogram shows distribution of left parties' positions on economic dimension.

on model 1. Figure 3.2 suggests that left parties that take up more pro-market positions on economic policy tend to receive less support than those that take up more redistributive positions.

These findings are in line with the book's argument. They also contribute to the scholarship relating the electoral difficulties of left parties to their programmatic turns to the ideological right (Berman 1998, 2006; Bremer 2018; Karreth et al. 2013; Kitschelt 1994; Moschonas 2011). These studies have shown that when social democratic parties adopt platforms that contradict their previous left-wing positions, they tend to face significant electoral losses (Berman 1998: 28, 380; Downs 1957a, 1957b: 113). Indeed, case studies of Western European social democratic parties demonstrate that social democrats' turn to the ideological middle/right was subsequently punished at the polls (Amable and Palombarini 2017; Arndt 2013; Berman 2006; Bremer 2018: 35). For example, Karreth, Polk, and Allen (2013) and Schwander and Manow (2017), using the cases of Germany, Sweden, and Great Britain, have shown that the gains social democratic parties derived from the policy shift toward the middle in the 1990s were short-lived and came at the expense of electoral success in subsequent decades.

These findings are also in line with studies that have shown that Third Way policies in general, and fiscal austerity in particular, have indeed driven many traditional voters away from social democrats (Polk and Karreth 2020; Schwander and Manow 2017; Loxbo et al. 2021). In particular, Horn (2021) has demonstrated that neoliberal reforms tended to affect parties on the left and right unequally: while they allowed right parties to reap the economic fruits of their reform, left parties struggled to claim credit even if the positive economic legacy they promised materialized. Polacko (2022) has shown that (under specific conditions like higher levels of income inequality or when combined with a sociocultural shift) rightward economic movements of social democrats significantly reduce their vote share. Similarly, in a postcommunist context Bagashka, Bodea, and Han (2022) have shown that the incumbent left-wing parties were systematically punished at the ballot box for moving to the right on economic policy.

We now turn to testing the relationship between the economic positions of left parties and their support across different occupational groups by adding an interaction between the individual-level class variable and the parties' economic scores. Model 2 in Table 3.3 demonstrates that left party economic positions can partly account for the correlation in the class-party relationship. The interaction coefficients between the occupational categories of clerks, service workers, and production workers and left party positions on the economic dimension are negative and statistically significant. This supports the expectation that groups in precarious jobs are particularly unlikely to back left parties with more pro-market policy stances.

There is also a positive correlation between more pro-market positions of left parties and their support among self-employed professionals and large employers.

Using average marginal effects based on model 2, a one-unit increase in the pro-market position of a left party decreases the likelihood of a vote from production workers, service workers, and clerks by about 6 to 7 percentage points while keeping other variables at their means (see Appendix II). The marginal effects are negative for most occupational groups, which might be explained by the enduring mass support for a state-funded provision of social benefits created by the communist legacy, which contributed to a stronger backlash against pro-market policies (Orenstein and Bugarič 2019; Pop-Eleches and Tucker 2014; Mason et al. 2000; Alesina and Fuchs-Schündeln 2007). This is also consistent with the findings in Chapter 2 showing that the majority of socioeconomic groups in the countries studied were largely in favor of redistributionist policies regardless of individual socioeconomic status.

However, these effects are particularly pronounced among working-class groups. The original probit model interactions with left parties' more pro-market economic positions are negative and significant only for the socioeconomic groups of clerks, service workers, and production workers.

Figure 3.3 displays predictions of left party support (y-axis) from various occupational groups (lines) based on the economic stances of the left party in question (x-axis). The slopes of the lines suggest that a left party's pro-market orientation will negatively impact its electoral support from all socioeconomic groups. However, the effects are particularly pronounced among production workers, service workers, and clerks. As the left moves away from redistributionist stances, these groups tend to reduce their support for left parties more than other socioeconomic groups do. These findings are in line with the scholarship on working classes' redistribution preferences (Evans 2017; Rennwald 2020). These groups' preferences for higher redistribution are explained by their more disadvantaged positions on the labor market; they view redistribution as a way to insulate themselves from higher labor market risks (Iversen and Soskice 2001; Moene and Wallerstein 2001; Cusack, Iversen, and Rehm 2006; Evans and De Graaf 2013; Marx and Schumacher 2018). Hence such groups are more likely to distance themselves from pro-market left parties following their programmatic rebranding.

As my findings show, in contrast to working-class respondents, there is hardly any impact of pro-market left economic positions on support from

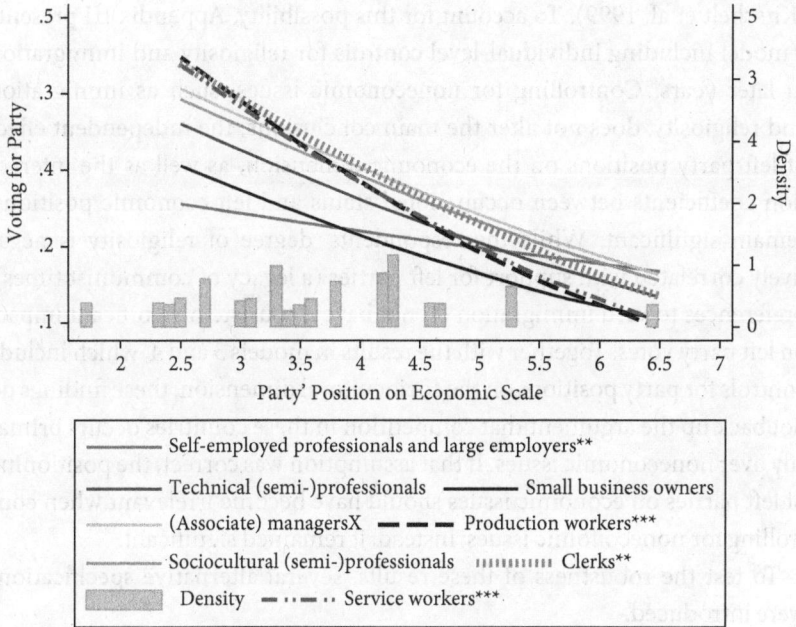

**Figure 3.3** Predicted Marginal Probability of Voting for the Left by Occupational Group Conditional on the Left Party's Economic Policy Position. Other variables held at their observed values. *Note*: The reference category is indicated with an X, and slopes that differ significantly from this reference category at the 10%, 5%, or 1% level are marked with *, ** or ***, respectively.

self-employed professionals and large employers. (In graphs with categorical variables, an asterisk next to a category label indicates a statistically significant interaction between that category and the parties' economic positions when compared to the reference category [associate managers, indicated with an X].)

Last, models 3 and 4 in the Table 3.3 also control for left party positions on both the economic and sociocultural dimensions. The inclusion of a control for the sociocultural dimension does not alter the main conclusion—the independent effect of left party positions on the economic dimension, as well as the interaction coefficients between occupational groups and left party positions on the economic dimension, are still significant and negative. By contrast, the independent coefficient of left parties' positions on the sociocultural dimension variable is insignificant in both model specifications.

The literature on the region has often postulated that competition in postcommunist countries occurs predominantly over noneconomic issues

(Kitschelt et al. 1999). To account for this possibility, Appendix III presents a model including individual-level controls for religiosity and immigration in later years. Controlling for noneconomic issues, such as immigration and religiosity, does not alter the main conclusions; the independent effect of left party positions on the economic dimension, as well as the interaction coefficients between occupational status and left economic positions, remain significant. While the respondents' degree of religiosity is negatively correlated with support for left parties (a legacy of communist times), preferences toward immigration do not have a consistent significant impact on left party votes. Together with the results in models 3 and 4, which include controls for party positions on the sociocultural dimension, these findings do not back up the argument that competition in these countries occurs primarily over noneconomic issues. If that assumption was correct, the positioning of left parties on economic issues should have become irrelevant when controlling for noneconomic issues; instead, it remained significant.

To test the robustness of these results, several alternative specifications were introduced.

First, Appendix V presents an estimated result for a multilevel probit model with random intercepts for each country and country-election (Schmidt-Catran and Fairbrother 2016). The models remain robust to this additional specification.

Second, models presented in Appendix IV also control for the presence of an established radical-right party (with a vote share higher than 3%). The overall conclusions remain unchanged: the effect of the more pro-market positions of left parties on their support is negative and particularly pronounced among respondents in precarious economic situations.

Third, maintaining a high level of matching among analyzed countries is a nontrivial task in observational studies, as the data often vary substantively from one country to another (in terms of timing and outcome variables) (Milliman and Glinow 1998). In particular, in my analysis some country cases and periods of observations were missing due to differences in ensuring correspondence between multiple datasets, the CHES and the ESS. Therefore, for an additional robustness check, I excluded one country at a time from the analysis to ensure that outliers do not drive the results.[4] In all cases, the association between left party positions on the

---

[4] The results are available upon request.

economic dimension and support for left and right parties remained robust for production and service workers. Among the clerk category,
the results were somewhat sensitive to the exclusion of a few countries.
The sign and size of the coefficient to the sociocultural dimension variable was sensitive to excluding particular observations and therefore
should be interpreted with caution. This, however, does not alter the main
conclusions.

The results presented in this section back up this book's theoretical expectations. They also help highlight the parallels in party system dynamics
across the postcommunist and Western European regions.

## Left vs. Right

Studies engaging with the consequences of the Third Way argue that in countries with pro-market left parties, voters in precarious economic situations
are more likely to support populist right-wing (conservative and radical)
parties (Decker 2016; Kurer 2017; Baiocchi 2019).

Do those conclusions apply to the postcommunist context as well? To account for this possibility, following Arzheimer (2013), the sample was restricted to respondents who vote for left or right parties, keeping the vote
for a left party as the baseline category (0). Party coding is based on the ESS
question "Which party did you vote for in the last election?" CHES classification was used to classify parties into "Conservative" and "Radical Right"
party categories. The model also controls for gender, age, education, fixed
country, and year effects, as well as the left's position on the economic scale.
Table 3.4 presents the results of this analysis (see also Appendix VI).

Table 3.4 demonstrates that in countries with pro-market-oriented left
parties, support for right-wing parties is higher among voters in precarious economic situations. These are precisely the occupational groups that
are particularly responsive to the increasingly pro-market positions of left
parties as shown in Table 3.3: clerks and service and production workers.

Using average marginal effects based on Table 3.4 (Appendix VI), a one-
unit increase in the pro-market position of a left party increases the likelihood of a vote for conservative right parties among production, service
workers, and clerks by about 8 to 13 percentage points (0.125, 0.112, and
0.079, respectively). Similarly, a one-unit increase in the pro-market position
of a left party increases the propensity of a radical right party vote among

**Table 3.4** Right Parties' Vote Conditional on Left Parties' Positions on Economic Policy

| | (1) Conservative | (2) Radical Right |
|---|---|---|
| Self-employed professionals and large employers | 0.394*** | −0.019 |
| | (0.075) | (0.174) |
| Sociocultural (semi-)professionals | 0.024 | 0.164** |
| | (0.036) | (0.064) |
| Small business owners | 0.244*** | 0.496*** |
| | (0.041) | (0.066) |
| Technical (semi-)professionals | 0.156*** | 0.153** |
| | (0.042) | (0.074) |
| Clerks | −0.050 | 0.136* |
| | (0.038) | (0.069) |
| Service workers | −0.057* | 0.211*** |
| | (0.034) | (0.058) |
| Production workers | −0.083*** | 0.289*** |
| | (0.032) | (0.054) |
| **Economic policy position** | 0.148*** | 0.460*** |
| | (0.031) | (0.063) |
| **Self-employed professionals#Economic policy position** | −0.133* | 0.048 |
| | (0.081) | (0.190) |
| Sociocultural (semi-)professionals#**Economic policy position** | 0.008 | −0.070 |
| | (0.037) | (0.072) |
| Small business owners#**Economic policy position** | 0.032 | 0.066 |
| | (0.041) | (0.070) |
| Technical (semi-)professionals#**Economic policy position** | 0.007 | 0.049 |
| | (0.045) | (0.082) |
| **Clerks#Economic policy position** | **0.070*** | 0.097 |
| | (0.037) | (0.070) |
| **Service workers#Economic policy position** | 0.168*** | 0.169*** |
| | (0.032) | (0.058) |
| **Production workers#Economic policy position** | 0.207*** | 0.124** |
| | (0.029) | (0.055) |
| Retired | −0.043 | −0.081* |
| | (0.030) | (0.047) |
| Unemployed | −0.024 | −0.086 |
| | (0.043) | (0.067) |

Table 3.4 Continued

|  | (1)<br>Conservative | (2)<br>Radical Right |
|---|---|---|
| Constant | 0.608*** | −0.376** |
|  | (0.104) | (0.162) |
| Observations | 26,596 | 16,041 |
| r2_p | 0.0957 | 0.410 |

Note: Table reports the effects of probit regressions. Left party vote chosen as the base category. Significant coefficients important for the discussion are selected in bold. $p < 0.1$, ** $p < 0.05$, *** $p < 0.01$.

production and service workers and clerks by about 10 to 12 percentage points (0.112, 0.115, and 0.098, respectively). These results were robust to additional model specifications.

Overall, the results of this analysis are in line with the theoretical expectations of this book. In postcommunist Europe, the pro-market positions of left parties are correlated with the higher propensity of respondents to vote for conservative and radical parties, and these effects are stronger among economically vulnerable electorates: clerks, service workers, and production workers.

These results are also consistent with other recent studies on the postcommunist region showing that populist parties have greater vote gains from left incumbent losses than do other parties (Bagashka, Bodea, and Han 2022). Binev (2022a, 2022b) has argued that the embrace of economic liberalization by traditional leftist parties had alienated voters who were most likely to become a resource for antiestablishment illiberal parties. Such parties then strategically adopted economically leftist banners as a viable electoral strategy. This is in line with this book's argument: as left parties vacated redistributionist positions, right-populist parties shifted leftward on the economic axis. This enhanced their appeal to working-class constituencies with preferences located in the lower left quadrant, which traditionally voted for communist or social democratic parties (Roberts 2019b). Such parties then successfully attracted support from working-class electorates, a phenomenon that became known in the Western European context as "proletarization" of the populist right (see Chapter 1; Evans and Mellon 2016; Ford and Goodwin

2014a, 2014b; Ivaldi 2013; Stockemer 2017; Adorf 2017, 2018: 35; Mondon 2017; Bergmann 2017; Berning 2017; Franz, Fratzscher, and Kritikos 2018).

## Summary

This chapter has reported on an empirical analysis on an association between pro-market-oriented positions among postcommunist left parties and their support. It found evidence in favor of several arguments made in this book.

First, a negative correlation exists between left party support and their more pro-market positions. Second, the negative effects of left parties' pro-market positions are particularly pronounced among economically vulnerable occupational groups, in particular, working-class electorates. Third, in postcommunist countries with a pro-market left these groups also have a higher propensity to support right-wing parties.

Overall, these results support the main argument of the book: left parties that adopted pro-market economic positions saw decreased electoral support, particularly from economically vulnerable voters. These findings challenge conventional arguments that left-party voters in postcommunist Europe remained loyal to left parties despite their programmatic turnarounds (Grzymala-Busse 2002a, 2020b; Fidrmuc 2000; Bozoki and Ishiyama 2002; Tavits and Letki 2009). Instead, voters at first remained loyal to left parties due to a lack of viable alternatives. This is because during the period leading up to EU accession, the programs of many mainstream parties converged. But in the long run, this approach deprived left-wing parties of their distinct ideological profile and pushed away economically vulnerable electorates. It was primarily after EU accession that other (often conservative and radical right) parties used populist appeals to sweep up economically vulnerable voters abandoned by the left's pro-market shift (see Chapter 1).

These findings highlight critical parallels between the dynamics of Western and Eastern European party systems (Berman 1998, 2006; Bremer 2018; Karreth et al. 2013; Kitschelt 1994; Moschonas 2011). Studies of Western European social democratic parties have traced the deleterious impact of the watering down of their social democratic profile on their electoral fortunes (Amable and Palombarini 2017; Arndt 2013; Berman 2006; Bremer 2018: 35; Berman and Snegovaya 2019). While the argument regarding the long-term impact of the Third Way has been developed in Western European studies, few studies attempted to apply it to the postcommunist context (Snegovaya

2018b; Berman and Snegovaya 2019; Bagashka, Bodea, and Han 2022; Binev 2022a, 2022b), where the effect of pro-market positions of the left parties should arguably have been even more pronounced (Appel and Orenstein 2016; Myant and Drahokoupil 2012; Beblavý 2014). The empirical evidence presented in this chapter fills in this gap in the literature and suggests that the causes of the electoral backsliding of left parties might have been the same in both regions—the adoption of more pro-market positions by left parties decreased the propensity to vote for them among their core support groups.

Several important limitations of this analysis should be addressed. First, the available data sets limit the empirically observed time period of left-party positions. As presented in the case studies, both the 1990s (posttransition) and the early 2000s (EU accession) were critical periods for left parties and their changing policy positions.

Second, the nature of the data under consideration limits one's ability to make dynamic assessments about party realignments. The increased probability of choosing one party over another depending on economic policy stances does not indicate that voters switch between left and right parties, but rather that they develop a higher or lower propensity to vote for them. Panel data or voters' recall of their previous election vote would be needed to provide a fully dynamic assessment.

In addition, regression analyses of this type offer evidence of correlation, not causation, by failing to eliminate substantive variation present at a high level of aggregation and abstracting away from daily politics in specific political contexts. These limitations can be addressed by turning to case studies, which offer more flexibility in uncovering the evidence of causal mechanisms and in explaining their outcomes. This is what the next chapter addresses.

# 4

# When Left Moves Right, Right Wins

The previous chapter used a cross-country analysis to demonstrate that when left parties in the postcommunist region adopt pro-market positions, their popularity tends to wane, and that this trend increases the propensity of voters, particularly those who are economically vulnerable (like working-class electorates), to support right-wing parties. It found empirical confirmation of these expectations.

However, cross-country studies alone do not suffice to account for party systems dynamics. And it is usually a good idea to complement them with qualitative case studies, which select a small geographical area as the subject of study and trace the key elements of the theoretical argument in greater depth. The case study approach compensates for limitations of quantitative cross-country studies by closely examining the data within a specific context. By focusing on within-country variation, case studies allow us to maintain the constancy of many other potentially causal variables (Culpepper 2005; Gerring 2007; Tarrow 2010) and provide for a more nuanced and complex description of these causal mechanisms than large-N analysis (Collier, Brady, and Seawright 2010; Johns 2013). For example, while the evidence presented in Chapter 3 allowed us to establish a relationship between more pro-market policies of center-left parties and a higher propensity to support right-wing parties among working-class electorates, it could not persuasively identify the causal link between the adoption of those policies by left-wing parties, dealignment of working-class groups, and the subsequent success of the populist right. This chapter does just that by tracing how and when pro-market policies of the left parties opened political opportunities on the right side of the political spectrum. In my case studies, I relied on different types of evidence to account for possible biases in source materials. This evidence includes historical polling data as well as primary and secondary sources such as scholarly and journalistic work, memoirs of policymakers, and my own open-ended interviews with political elites and observers from this period.

*When Left Moves Right*. Maria Snegovaya, Oxford University Press. © Oxford University Press 2024.
DOI: 10.1093/oso/9780197699027.003.0005

These two case studies trace how the party realignment induced by left parties' pro-market rebranding opened opportunities for populist right parties to appeal to the electorates that previously supported left parties. Specifically, this chapter looks at the experiences of two Visegrád Four countries—Hungary and Poland—to explore why the ex-communist left parties in these countries chose to adopt pro-market policy stances. It examines the party realignment process that followed those choices. And it traces the subsequent emergence of populist right parties.

First, this chapter looks at the example of Hungary, where the two populist right parties—Fidesz and Jobbik—enjoyed extraordinary success. Their success was partly the result of the incorporation of large shares of working-class voters who had traditionally voted for the Hungarian Socialist Party (MSZP), the successor to the communist MSZMP (Magyar Szocialista Munkáspárt). Second, this chapter also examines the case of the SLD, a center-left ex-communist party that lost electoral support after it implemented pro-market reforms, when many of its former supporters flocked to the Polish populist right party, PiS. This party had promised more redistributionist policies and to improve conditions for Polish workers.

This book explores how the collapse of the left opened up the opportunities for the populist right. These cases attempt to keep many other potentially causal variables constant. In the European context the immigration crisis that unraveled in 2015 tended to alter voters' calculus by shifting the focus of party competition to the sociocultural dimension (hence giving additional advantage to the populist right while further undermining the left). However, as this chapter demonstrates, by the time the refugee crisis reached its peak, the key dynamic of voter realignment between left and right had already taken place in the countries of interest. Thus, to eliminate the effects of potential confounders (Culpepper 2005), much of my analysis focuses primarily on the period preceding the refugee crisis.

This chapter also offers a quantitative examination of the party dealignment process in these countries. Using survey evidence, it demonstrates that working-class constituencies reduced their support for center-left parties in Hungary and Poland while gradually embracing the populist right. The evidence proves to be consistent with this book's argument: the sharpest decline in working-class support for left-wing parties was associated with the timing of the implementation of pro-market reforms.

# Hungary

Among countries of the communist bloc, Hungary was known as the "happiest barrack" due to a series of pro-market reforms launched by Janos Kadar, the general secretary of the Hungarian Socialist Workers Party (Magyar Szocialista Munkáspárt, MSZMP) after the 1956 Hungarian Revolution. In 1966, the Party's Central Committee approved the New Economic Mechanism, aimed at boosting Hungary's economy. It increased consumer expenditure, reintroduced market mechanisms into the Hungarian market, and encouraged more trade with Western countries. Although these reforms proved quite successful, they also dramatically raised the country's public debt. By the end of the 1970s, Hungary's per capita debt was among the highest in the world. The situation kept deteriorating, and by the 1980s, the country faced serious insolvency issues and was on the brink of a financial and economic collapse (Csizmadia 2008: 11). All these factors, together with growing political dissatisfaction, served to launch the process of democratization in Hungary. A series of roundtable discussions from June to September 1989 between the reformist wing of the MSZMP and a united coalition of opposition parties led to the adoption of an interim constitution, the introduction of a mixed electoral system, and the first competitive elections in over forty years (Benoit 2001; Benoit and Schiemann 2001; Schiemann 2005).

In light of this dynamic, embracing the market and pursuing reforms seemed to provide the MSZMP with the only viable long-term strategy for party development (Grzymala-Busse 2002b; Morlang 2003). Rebranding was all the easier because the reformed wing of the Communist Party already had a legacy of reform implementation and established relations with international economic institutions.

Starting in 1989, Hungary's Socialist Party (Magyar Szocialista Párt, Socialists, MSZP) rejected its old Communist Party image and rebranded itself as a social democratic party that combined promises of a rapid improvement in living standards for all Hungarians with social protection for lower-income groups (Oltay 1994a). MSZP had joined and accepted the ideals of the Socialist International, that is those of a supranationalist Europe concentrated on socioeconomic and welfare issues (Navracsics 1997; Kopecký and Mudde 2002: 308). It attempted to become "a genuine catch-all party embracing left-wing ideals and capable of laying the foundation of a new social consensus" (Grzymała-Busse 2002b: 112). This was reflected in its support base, which represented a cross-class co-alition of former nomenclature elites with intellectuals, entrepreneurs, and blue- and white-collar workers (Evans and Whitefield 1995: 1191; Andorka 1999).

Since the early transition years, party leaders looked to the West as an example to emulate. Its "leaders, activists and supporters were among those who visited the West frequently; many of them studied and/or worked there (with Miklos Nemeth, the prime minister in 1989–90, as a Harvard graduate in Economics) and thus the European model was not one about which they had to be convinced" (Agh 1995: 493). Therefore, since its inception the MSZP had become a strong supporter of Europeanization and Westernization.[1] The MSZP adopted a culturally more liberal image (however modest that was), stressing the importance of European integration and "civil society" as opposed to "the nation." The MSZP also strongly emphasized social tol-erance, human rights, and multiculturalism. This strategy, which echoed the approach of many Western European left-wing parties, aimed to promote the party's image as an organization of left-leaning reformist technocrats (Berman 2016; Tóth 2015).

The MSZP's self-portrayal as the initiator of economic reforms and its subsequent coalition with the liberal Alliance of Free Democrats (Szabad Demokraták Szövetsége – a Magyar Liberális Párt, SZDSZ) further rein-forced its liberal, free-market-oriented image (Tavits and Letki 2009: 559). By contrast, Hungary's right-wing parties were quite nonrightist in their ec-onomic positions. The first postcommunist government in Hungary after the 1990 election—which included three right-wing parties: the Hungarian Democratic Forum (Magyar Demokrata Fórum, MDF), the Independent Party of Smallholders, and the Christian Democratic People's Party (Kereszténydemokrata Néppárt)—was reluctant to undertake difficult eco-nomic reforms despite the country's dire economic conditions. This approach served as the best survival strategy for the newly emerged, fragmented, and poorly organized rightist parties (Bakke and Sitter 2005; Fowler 2004). Having come to power by criticizing the economic reforms implemented by the socialists (Racz 2000), these parties adopted the rhetoric that promised

---

[1] The party also supported NATO membership, suggested first in Hungary by Gyula Horn, then-minister of foreign affairs and subsequently a president of the MSZP.

to protect the "common people" from the "antisocial reforms" pursued by the MSZP (Morlang 2003). While in power in 1990–1994, rather than implementing radical economic reforms, the right government primarily focused on calming public dissatisfaction by increasing government spending (Morlang 2003: 70).

Between the years 1990 and 1994, the economic situation remained dire. Most Hungarian companies were inefficient and unaccountable, and many went bankrupt. The unemployment and inflation levels reached double digits. Some Hungarians with experience of the "second economy," or young, newly qualified professionals, adapted to these new conditions. But the vast majority, particularly the older or retired workers and public-sector employees, suffered (Dingsdale and Kovacs 1996).

In the 1994 election, as an opposition party in the previous Parliament, the MSZP emphasized issues of social concern for workers and the less fortunate (Mahr and Nagle 1995: 403). During the 1994 campaign, the MSZP portrayed itself as the only representative of worker interests in Parliament and collaborated with Hungarian unions to oppose new legislation from the ruling right coalition in power at the time, which it portrayed as a direct threat to workers' interests (Racz 1993). The MSZP established a formal alliance based on common "leftist values" with the National Confederation of Hungarian Trade Unions (MSZOSZ), one of the descendants of the old official communist unions (Rácz 1993: 662). For the 1994 election, the president of MSZOSZ, Sándor Nagy, ran second on the MSZP party list. Laszlo Bekesi, a leader of the social democratic line within the MSZP, advocated for a "social pact" involving government, unions, and employees to set prices, wages, and other policies while the country moved to a full free-market system (Ottaway 1994; Mahr and Nagle 1995).

As a result, working-class representation in the MSZP vote increased, and during the 1994 election, these groups became the main support base for the MSZP (Szelenyi, Fodor and Hanley 1997: 216). Using the Median exit-poll data, Szelenyi, Fodor, and Hanley showed that blue-collar respondents were significantly more likely to vote for the MSZP than professionals or white-collar workers (216; see also Chapter 2). But whereas 71% of socialist voters presumed that they could now expect the advantages of the communist system to return, party leaders appeared divided over whether the "socialist" welfare systems could be sustained during the economic reforms (Bozoki 1997: 79).

## The Realignment Begins

For the 1994 parliamentary election, MSZP won 33% of the vote and 54% of the seats. The MSZP's support coalition demanded the protection of social subsidies, but, during this period, requirements imposed by the EU and the IMF forced the MSZP leadership to commit to the free marketization of Hungary's economy. Bozoki explains that at that time the MSZP was internally divided between two party wings: those who wanted the party to primarily implement modernization/reforms, and the group that wanted to support the "left-behinds." The modernizing wing won (Andras Bozoki in discussion with the author, May 2022).[2] The MSZP entered into a coalition with the liberal SZDSZ and launched far-reaching economic reforms that were needed in light of a possible financial crisis and national bankruptcy due to the country's extensive debt.

While the coalition accelerated the privatization of Hungarian state-owned companies, the key element of the reform was the so-called Bokros Package. Announced in 1995, the Bokros Package included a series of austerity measures, such as the gradual devaluation of the forint and the reduction of social benefits and real wages. Extensive austerity programs pursued by the MSZP government aimed to receive a special "stand-by" three-year loan from the IMF as a reward for its efforts at budget cuts, social state reduction, and inflation control (Ziblatt 1998). In exchange for the loan, the IMF demanded more cuts to social security and accelerated privatization (Szilagyi 1995: 64). This forced the coalition to announce an even deeper budget deficit reduction in January 1996, finally obtaining the IMF loan in February 1996. Designed to avoid national bankruptcy, the Bokros Package devalued the forint to counterbalance the deficit, while decreasing social benefits and real wages.

Although the Bokros Package improved Hungary's economic situation and ensured the resumption of economic growth, the population was reluctant to accept its huge costs. The 1994 electoral coalition of the MSZP relied on an organizational network of trade unions inherited from communist times. These groups disproportionately opposed the reforms. Bálint Magyar,

---

[2] Andras Bozoki was a participant of the Hungarian Roundtable Talks and subsequently a spokesman for Fidesz in 1990. In 2003–2004 he was a political advisor to MSZP's Prime Minister Péter Medgyessy. From February 2005 to June 2006, he was a minister of culture in the first Gyurcsány government.

who was a head of the SZDSZ parliamentary election campaign at that time, said that "the situation created a paradox of a pro-reform government relying on largely anti-reform-oriented constituencies." He compared the MSZP's attempts to push forward reforms under such an electoral coalition to "trying to cross the Sahara desert with an ice cube in one hand" (Bálint Magyar in discussion with the author, April 2022).[3] The reforms resulted in a sharp decline in living standards for the vast majority of Hungarians (Greskovits 2000). The severe cuts in public spending (unemployment benefits, education, pension, and healthcare) and the devaluation of the forint led to an increase in mortality rates and a reduction in fertility (Kando 2001). Accordingly, the reforms were followed by a sharp decline in support for the ruling coalition. The Bokros Package put a strain on the MSZP's relationship with the working-class constituencies and trade unions. Nagy, the president of the MSZOSZ union, who ran on the MSZP party list, had to resign from his union post following these austerity reforms. These policies would end up costing the MSZP the 1998 election.

The Bokros Package brought on strong criticism from right-wing forces that argued for more gradual, stabilizing policies (Köves 1995; Boros-Kazai 2005) and reinforced the divide between Hungary's right and left parties. The left had now been defined based on its more pro-market, conservative austerity measures and as taking advice from international institutions (the IMF and the EU) for structural assistance. On the other hand, the right had more decisively embraced increasingly paternalistic and pro-redistribution policy stances, focusing on the social mechanisms of redistribution and welfare (Fowler 2004).

Right-wing parties succeeded in defeating the MSZP in the 1998 election (while the latter still garnered 32.9% of the list voting).[4] Among them was the Hungarian Justice and Life Party (Magyar Igazság és Élet Pártja, MIÉP), a small radical right party that had entered the 1998 parliament with 5.5% of the votes. The party relied on an anti-Semitic platform and criticized the EU for its harsh accession requirements to applicant states (often using economic arguments).

---

[3] Bálint Magyar was previously a founder of the SZDSZ (1988), a member of the Hungarian Parliament (1990–2010), and the Hungarian minister of education under left-wing governments (1996–1998, 2002–2006).

[4] Hungary Parliamentary Chamber, Elections Held in 1998, http://archive.ipu.org/parline-e/reports/arc/2141_98.htm.

Another party, Fidesz (Magyar Polgári Szövetség), advocated for the defense of Hungary's national interests and domestic employers, state-led economic development, and against foreign influences and the takeover of state companies by foreigners through privatization (Tóth 2015). During the early democratization period, Fidesz campaigned on a liberal agenda, confirmed by its accession to the Liberal International in 1992. In the first two election campaigns in 1990 and 1994, Fidesz emphasized the need to adopt Western European economic and political standards, limit the role of the state and the role of religion in public life, and develop a neutral education system. Kálmán Mizsei (in discussion with the author, July 2022), Fidesz' party leader Viktor Orbán's economic advisor from 1990 to 1994, remembers, "At that time Orbán was totally pro-market. There was not a single reform suggestion that I offered that he would reject."[5] However, this platform put Fidesz in contestation against another liberal party, SZDSZ, splitting the electorate of both parties. In 1993 a group of activists with liberal views headed by Gábor Fodor left the party, and Orbán and the head management team decided to alter the party's ideological profile from one that espoused liberal values to one that embraced conservative, right-wing values. This transformation led to Fidesz signing cooperation agreements with several small right-wing parties and the right wing of MDF, Hungary's center-right political party. The move consolidated the core of the conservative political parties around Fidesz (Herbut 2002: 174–179). By 1998, Fidesz's earlier image of a cosmopolitan pro-market party had fully changed into that of a conservative party which combined Christian morality with protectionist economic stances. When challenging the social-democratic/liberal camp, Fidesz's discursive strategy combined criticism of its economic policies with portrayals of the country as facing challenges from the "cosmopolitan elites" opposed to "the nation" or "the national interests" (Kim 2021). This strategy proved to be a winning one—the support for Fidesz, which had never been in power before, rose from around 9% in 1990 to 26% by 1998, giving the party first place in the parliamentary election. Fidesz's victory came, in part, due to its ability to incorporate former MSZP supporters from the poorer regions of eastern Hungary.

Having won the 1998 election, Fidesz's leader Orbán became Hungary's new prime minister and formed a coalition government with the MDF

[5] Kálmán Mizsei worked as an advisor to the governor of the National Bank of Hungary in 1990–1992. He was also Orbán's economic advisor in formal and informal capacities in 1990–1994.

and the Independent Smallholders (Független Kisgazda-, Földmunkás- és Polgári Párt) parties. While in power, Fidesz continued to criticize the neoliberal policies of the previous MSZP-SZDSZ government, especially those related to industry privatization and welfare cut-offs. For example, in a series of public speeches, Orbán referred to neoliberalism as a Western ideology, which was not to be entirely trusted due to its tendency to prioritize the market over individuals, culture, and society (Wilkin 2016: 61). Yet the need to ensure Hungary's accession to the European Union (and hence to comply with the restrictions imposed by the EU) constrained the choices of the ruling coalition. Thus, despite its rhetoric, Orbán's government undertook a series of reforms aimed at cutting the existing budget deficit and public-sector debt once in power, and largely continued on the MSZP policy track.

A perceived "need" to follow the EU's advice was widespread in pre-accession societies, since at that time all major political actors agreed that they had to get into the EU. This consensus around the need to pursue EU accession-related reforms limited other parties' ability to appeal to reform losers (Vachudova 2008b) and contributed to mainstream parties' economic policy convergence. Fidesz—the party that came to power after MSZP—continued negotiating with the EU and implementing associated reforms. Between 1998 and 2002, the Fidesz-led government achieved considerable progress in the accession negotiations, hoping for a second term in office. By 2002, the main requirements imposed by the EU had been met. Because of its active role in negotiating the deal with the EU, Fidesz was not in a position to adopt a more Euroskeptic rhetoric at the time (Batory 2002; , 2008: 271).

By the early 2000s, the MSZP had managed to preserve about 80% of its voters, including some working-class supporters (Curry 2003; Morlang 2003). About 70% of party members approved and supported the reform policies pursued by the party, and only about 13% favored returning to a more welfarist course (Markus 1999; Curry 2003; Morlang 2003). During the 2002 electoral campaign, both Fidesz and MSZP tried to outbid each other on spending pledges.[6] MSZP won the election by guaranteeing to finance the population's direct consumption through "welfare system change" such as 50% wage increases in the public sector, with a thirteenth-month pension payment to all pensioners; the abolition of income tax for low-paid workers;

---

[6] The parties' turn toward Keynesian-style state-financed economic development by boosting consumption spending was partly a consequence of an economic slowdown in Hungary in the early 2000s (Tóth, Neumann, and Hosszú 2012: 142).

and an ambitious investment program for infrastructure (Tóth, Neumann, and Hosszú 2012: 142; Lehndorff 2014: 236).

When the MSZP-SZDSZ coalition returned to power, its economic policy was subordinated to reelection campaign promises. Bozoki (in discussion with the author, May 2022), who was a political advisor to MSZP's prime minister in 2003–2004, explains, "For example, the public sector wages were increased by 100%. These generous spending policies at the time became known as 'fiscal alcoholism.'" While the expansive spending program gave a boost to Hungary's economy, the increase in public debt had by now become a permanent problem (Batory 2010). In 2003, to comply with the EU requirements to join the Eurozone, Prime Minister Peter Medgyessy attempted to reduce the budget deficit and overall debt level. Such measures initiated in 2003, however, led to a rapid loss of the government's popularity. In the fall of 2004, faced with unfavorable electoral prospects in the upcoming 2006 election, the MSZP appointed a new prime minister, Ferenc Gyurcsány (Tóth, Neumann, and Hosszú 2012: 142–143). While the European Commission repeatedly asked the Hungarian government to sustain a prudent economic policy, Gyurcsány, aiming to win the upcoming election and to live up to the MSZP's reputation as a "caring" party, reverted to debt accumulation to fund the rapid increase in domestic consumption (Enyedi and Róna 2018: 256). The popularity of these policies was evidenced by the MSZP's subsequent reelection in 2006—the first reelection in the history of postcommunist Hungary. But while the MSZP's policies were popular, its reckless spending hugely increased the debt, leaving the country on the brink of bankruptcy. By 2006, the public deficit exceeded 10%; the national debt reached 65.9% of the GDP, and it increased to 79.8% by 2009 (as compared with 52.7% in 2001) (Enyedi and Róna 2018: 256). The huge public deficit and rising debt were repeatedly criticized by the European Commission, which demanded a more prudent economic policy. The European Commission eventually rejected Hungary's 2005 Maastricht convergence program, needed to meet the Maastricht criteria.[7] It insisted that after the autumn 2006 elections, the Hungarian government come up with a new convergence program (Tóth, Neumann, and Hosszú 2012: 143).

Meanwhile, after its 2002 election loss, Fidesz started building a new economic profile that emphasized the need for an active state to protect

---

[7] The euro convergence, or the Maastricht criteria, are the criteria EU member states are required to meet in order to enter the Eurozone.

Hungarian citizens against the instability of the market economy. While its ideological foundations remained unaltered, Fidesz added to its conservative nationalist profile a set of "socialistic" demands, including free education, free healthcare, low utility fees, and high pensions (Enyedi and Róna 2018: 255–256).

In the aftermath of the 2002 elections, the potential contradictions between a de facto pro-EU policy and Euroskeptic rhetoric no longer constrained Fidesz: Hungary was going to enter the EU no matter what, so it could give free rein to its discursive critique of the EU. Therefore, the party started adopting more Euroskeptic stances, consistent with resistance to pro-market, EU-inspired reforms. Fidesz's renewed platform emphasized its prioritization of the interests of the "people" over the interests of the elites and the "rule of institutions" (including the EU). It also appealed to citizens by urging them to organize, sign petitions, and participate in referendums and demonstrations (Enyedi and Róna 2018: 255). Fidesz presented itself as the "one official defender" of the Hungarian nation, highlighting internal and external threats to the survival of the nation and its "ethnic and cultural composition" (Waterbury 2020: 963). For example, Fidesz offered to initiate a referendum to prevent the liberalization of the land market and warned that EU membership may put thousands of Hungarian farmers out of business (Batory 2008: 271).

## The Collapse of the Left

During the 2006 election campaign, the MSZP presented a rosy portrait of the economy, while the Fidesz presented a gloomy one (Stegmaier and Lewis-Beck 2011). MSZP leader Ferenc Gyurcsány ran on a platform of "reform without austerity" and won (Johnson and Barnes 2015: 543). However, the detrimental effects of such expensive policy measures surfaced a few months later, when the MSZP-SZDSZ coalition had to comply with the European Commission's request to curb new debt under the Maastricht stability criteria (Korkut 2007; Sitter and Batory 2006). For Hungary to regain credibility on issues of macroeconomic stability, the convergence program included comprehensive structural reforms of public administration, education, healthcare, and pensions (Greskovits 2008: 289). Accordingly, in June 2006, shortly after winning the election on promises of increased social payouts, the MSZP-SZDSZ government announced a new round of austerity measures. The impending implementation of austerity policies stayed in the "top fifteen" news in Hungary in April and May 2006 (Biró-Nagy and Róna 2012). The first set of measures, the so-called New Balance Program, started on June 9. The key elements of this program included raising gas prices by 30%, raising electricity prices by 10% to 14%, increasing the medium VAT rate from 15% to 20%, and cutting the government deficit to 3% of GDP by 2008.

But the majority of Hungarians were not prepared for a sudden change of course in the direction of public spending cuts (Lehndorff 2014: 236). And while the MSZP succeeded in stopping the debt from growing, the economy stopped growing as well (0.1% in 2007 by Word Bank estimates). Furthermore, these policies reinforced MSZP's reputation as the party of austerity, which formed following the implementation of the Bokros Package back in 1995–1996 (Johnson and Barnes 2015: 543–544). The new proposed economic plan revealed that despite its electoral assurances that the economy was in good shape, the MSZP leadership had been well aware of the deep problems in Hungary's economy (Stegmaier and Lewis-Beck 2011).

Within three months of the announcement, MSZP support within the population at large dropped by 11 percentage points, from 37% in May 2006 to 26% in August 2006, while its relative position vis-à-vis Fidesz fell by 20% below the level seen immediately following the elections (Biró-Nagy and Róna 2012). By August, 72% of Hungarians thought that their country was headed in the wrong direction, compared to 49% of Hungarians who felt this way in June. Over the summer of 2006, the popularity of MSZP experienced its greatest decline in the 2006–2010 term (Biró-Nagy and Róna 2012).

In September 2006, the situation worsened after a private speech delivered by MSZP Prime Minister Gyurcsány in May 2006 was leaked to the press and aired on national radio. In the speech Gyurcsány admitted that his party had hidden the true state of the economy from the public in order to win April's general election. In Gyurcsány's own words: "We have screwed it up. Not a little but a lot. No European country has screwed up as much as we have. It can be explained. We have obviously lied throughout the past 18 to 24 months. It was perfectly clear that what we were saying was not true. . . . And in the meantime, by the way, we did not do anything for four years. Nothing. . . . Instead, we lied, morning, noon, and night."

Hungarian citizens had known about the economic problems since MSZP introduced the austerity measures in June. Yet Gyurcsány's "Őszöd speech" and the accumulated disappointment with the MSZP had the effect of a political explosion. The country was inundated with antigovernment riots and protests. It was a crisis of political legitimacy that created the greatest political unrest since 1989. Irritated Hungarians, among them militant nationalist crowds, supporters of Fidesz and Jobbik, and members of the illegal Hungarian Guard organization (Becker 2010), took to the streets throwing bottles and rocks at the police, who fired tear gas and rubber bullets back at them.

The dramatic collapse in MSZP support is often blamed on the leak of the "Őszöd speech." But in reality, the erosion of Gyurcsány's and the MSZP's approval ratings after the speech was less dramatic than it had been during the events leading up to it. For instance, the party's preceding austerity measures had already done the job of lowering support from 37% to around 28% before the speech was leaked (Snegovaya 2018b). And this was true for Gyurcsány's popularity as well: whereas in May 2006, 55% of respondents said they wished him to play an important role in politics (a regular question to measure a politician's popularity in Hungary), by August this ratio had dropped to 34%, and stayed at the exact same level in the months following the release of the Őszöd speech that September (Nagy and Rona 2012: 10). While the speech was a dramatic moment in Hungarian politics and sealed the demise of Gyurcsány and the MSZP, the major collapse in their popularity had already taken place.

After a wave of riots and protests spread around the country, the right-wing Fidesz, in opposition, accused the MSZP of election fraud and demanded new elections. The MSZP government refused and Gyurcsány did not resign. Instead, the party continued its austerity program. Subsequent criticism ran so high that the public ended up supporting Fidesz's campaign for a referendum on the reforms. The referendum was held in spring 2008 and dramatically reinforced Fidesz's image as the party that promised to defend the welfare state against neoliberal deregulation (Lehndorff 2014: 236).

The economic problems led to further impoverishment of a large part of the population. In 2007, during the span of only one year, real wages and earnings decreased by 5%, while unemployment increased to about 10% and inflation to 7% (Eickhoff 2008: 26; Becker 2010: 32). As if the situation were not dire enough, the global economy unraveled during mid-2008. Forint devaluation followed, pushing up monthly payments for foreign-currency-denominated mortgages and putting a severe burden on many Hungarian households (Batory 2009). As a result, the Hungarian economy stalled, and by mid-2008 Hungary was on the verge of bankruptcy. Things deteriorated to such an extent that the MSZP government was forced to rely on an IMF-led bailout. The loan of 20 billion euros secured by the European Commission, the IMF, and the World Bank helped Hungary to avoid bankruptcy, but it also included a series of bailout-linked austerity policies that severely restricted the Hungarian government's operations (Csaba 2013: 8). These socially un-popular stipulations included raising the retirement age, severing disability benefits, and cutting unemployment benefits, wages, and pensions (Johnson and Barnes 2015: 544).

In March 2009, after his economic plan failed to pass through Parliament and public discontent continued to rise, Prime Minister Gyurcsány announced his resignation. The MSZP scrambled to find a new prime min-ister; a number of candidates refused the offer. Eventually, in April 2009, they appointed Gordon Bajnai. In an attempt to gather cross-party and pop-ular support, Bajnai promptly introduced a comprehensive set of austerity measures designed to reform the tax and benefits systems. A new round of austerity measures introduced in 2009 included a two-year pay freeze for public-sector workers, an increase in the VAT from 20% to 25% (excluding a number of basic consumer goods), excise taxes, pension cuts, a decrease in maternity leave, cuts in paid parental and sick leave and pensions and gov-ernment support for housing, and a decrease in state subsidies for residential heating (Fabry 2019: 114).

By spring 2009, even before the introduction of the Bajnai Package, Hungary's public opinion of the MSZP government was exceptionally neg-ative. In a poll conducted in March 2009 by Median Opinion Ltd., 87% of respondents reported that their household's financial situation had worsened in the previous year (47% thought it got a lot worse), while the vast majority expected it to get even worse in the following year (Snegovaya 2018b). A few weeks after his appointment, the new prime minster was almost as unpopular as his predecessor (Batory 2009). Bajnai's fiscal sta-bilization succeeded in significantly reducing the deficit from 3.7% in 2008 to 2.6% in 2009, going beyond the requirements of the Maastricht criteria (Lengyel 2011: 31). But the austerity measures, together with IMF-imposed conditionalities, gave the MSZP government little room to relax crisis measures—its only hope to recover popular support. In June 2009, MSZP received the smallest share of the vote in European parliamentary elections since the year 1990 (Batory 2010).

Ultimately, a number of noisy corruption scandals, such as a series of revelations about large sums stolen from the (massively subsidized) Budapest public transport company, delivered the final blow to MSZP in the run-up to the 2010 elections (Batory 2010).

Biró-Nagy and Róna (2012) argue that the combined effect of austerity measures and corruption allegations toppled MSZP during 2006–2010 electoral round. They demonstrate that from June 2008 onward, there was not a single month when news favorable to MSZP dominated the media. The party suffered the greatest blow in the early months following the Gyurcsány government's entry into office, when the prime minister announced his austerity package. Subsequent erosion of MSZP popularity continued more gradually over time. The domination of austerity measures, the unsuccessful reform policies, and the corruption scandals within the MSZP between 2006 and 2010 undermined the party's claims of managerial competence and administrative effectiveness, resulting in massive drops in the polls (Biró-Nagy and Róna 2012). A March 2009 public opinion poll found that support for the MSZP was at a record low 16%—the lowest in ten years (Fabry 2019: 115). The April 2010 parliamentary elections turned into a referendum on the MSZP's economic policies (Johnson and Barnes 2015: 553): the MSZP received only 19.3% of the vote (down from the 43.2% in 2006, losing more than 23% of its support) and has continued to lose votes over time. New left parties subsequently emerged in Hungarian politics, but they too were unable to gain substantive levels of popular support.

## The Adaptation of the Right

Studies show that throughout the 2000s Hungarian electorates followed the typical economic voting dynamic: rewarding the MSZP government for the good times and punishing it for the bad (Stegmaier and Lewis-Beck 2011). New rounds of austerity amid crisis set the stage for financial nationalism in Hungary, as right-wing parties in opposition, Fidesz and Jobbik, contested the 2010 parliamentary elections on a nationalist-populist platform (Johnson and Barnes 2015: 544). This period marked a shift: right-wing parties reached out to disaffected population groups, using a platform that combined criticism of austerity policies pursued by the Gyurcsány and Bajnai governments (Fabry 2019: 118) with nativist and economically protectionist slogans. These parties vowed to cut taxes, restore economic growth, and support local business. And Hungarian voters responded to these promises by continually transferring their support to the right.

The radical right party Jobbik (Jobbik Magyarországért Mozgalom) rose on the wave of MSZP frustration and came in third, winning 16% of the vote in the 2010 election. Jobbik embraced a radical nationalist agenda claiming to safeguard Hungarian national identity from perceived "foreign" influences. It presented supranational bodies like international organizations and multinational companies as alien to the national interest (Kim 2016). The newly formed party relied on paramilitary proxy organizations to mobilize workers and peasants against Roma in economically deprived communities where Roma and non-Roma groups were competing over increasingly scarce public goods and services (Scheiring and Szombati 2020).

While the use of nationalist and radical anti-Roma appeals contributed to an increase in Jobbik's popularity (Karácsony and Róna 2010; Kovács 2012; Pirro 2015; Tamás 2011), combining it with a more redistributionist focus on the economy further reinforced its success (Varga 2014). The nativist overtones in the party's platform were strongly intertwined with economic frames—attacks against globalization and the multinational corporations allegedly responsible for the destruction of Hungary's economy and the bankruptcies declared by its businesses (Bartha and Tóth 2017). A significant portion of Jobbik's electoral program blamed MSZP for its overly neoliberal economic policies, for misleading the country, for causing devastating economic conditions during the transition process, and for giving up Hungary's sovereignty to the EU, which it dubbed a "corrupt capitalist organization" (Jobbik Magyarországért Mozgalom 2010; Volford 2012). To correct these ills, Jobbik promised to provide social justice and "honest" jobs and wages, and to defend the interests of "the people" (Batory 2010).

According to multiple polling data, in 2009–2010 Jobbik supporters were most dissatisfied with the household financial situation among Hungarian voters, were more likely to feel that they experienced a decline in their social status in comparison to their father's (in terms of impoverishment, vanishing solidarity, and a loss of prestige), and identified themselves primarily as belonging to the lower-middle and working-class groups (Svitych 2021).

Polls also show that Jobbik has been able to take away significant shares of former MSZP supporters over time. A Budapest polling firm, the Perspective Institute, ran a survey after the 2009 European parliamentary election (when Jobbik won 16.2% of the vote) and found that Jobbik had primarily recruited its supporters from the left's former electorate—voters disappointed with MSZP performance (Phillips 2010). In the 2010 parliamentary election Jobbik became the third-largest party in Parliament, winning 16.7%

of the vote. During its breathtaking rise in 2010, Jobbik won over many counties in northeastern Hungary that were previously considered MSZP strongholds, including Borsod-Abauj-Zemplen, Szabolcs-Szatmar-Bereg, Hajdu-Bihar, Jasz-Nagykun-Szolnnok, Heves, and Nograd (Phillips 2010; Snegovaya 2018a; Scheiring 2020b). Many of these were former communist industrialized strongholds that failed to successfully integrate into the new economy following the market transition of the 1990s. The failure to integrate resulted in a substantive decline in socioeconomic well-being and the loss of social status for many Hungarian peasants and workers. This was exacerbated by the dramatic upsurge in unemployment among ethnic Roma groups, who previously held lower-skilled jobs in communist factories. Combined with spreading unemployment among ethnic Hungarians, this situation fueled ethnic tensions between Roma and Hungarian groups. Szombati (2018) conducted an in-depth ethnographic study of northeastern Hungary which revealed that anti-Roma sentiment was galvanized by large-scale socioeconomic dislocations and political pressures that were acutely felt in these areas.[8]

Together with Jobbik, in the 2010 election Fidesz continued a campaign against the MSZP government. In its platform the populist overtones intertwined with nationalist ones. The party promised to return the state to its rightful owners: hard-working ethnic Hungarians and entrepreneurs who could come to a new compromise in the sharing of national wealth. Attacking the measures demanded by the IMF and the European Commission and presenting itself as the mouthpiece for the general discontent, Fidesz promised to end austerity and to protect the value of pensions, arguing that once it put an end to the neoliberal and corrupt politics of the ex-communist left, a new period of strong growth could finally begin (Lehndorff 2014: 237; Bohle and Greskovits 2019: 1080). Along with Jobbik, Fidesz sought to mobilize working-class constituencies in defense of public services under the banner of more inclusive nationalism (Scheiring and Szombati 2020).This rhetoric combined with a significant effort to politically integrate disaffected

---

[8] Workers often named Jobbik the only party which put trade unions' rights in its program and promised to remove the trade union leaders who aligned with corrupt politicians, make the unions completely politically independent, and fight only for workers' rights (Eszter-Tóth 2015). However, in a private conversation with me in August 2016, Jobbik's politician Márton Gyöngyösi Marton Gyongyosi in conversation with the author, August 2016 argued that trade unions played next to no role in Jobbik's ability to attract working-class constituencies in the unemployed regions of Hungary in the 2010–2014 elections. While subsequently Jobbik attempted to attract the support of smaller trade unions (such as teachers' unions), overall this approach played a marginal role in its electoral success.

constituencies through the creation of locally rooted civic networks and the organization of rituals of resistance and solidarity (Greskovits 2020; Halmai 2011). As a result of a combination of these factors, many Hungarian workers shifted to the right, choosing Fidesz over the MSZP in 2010 (Szombati 2018; Scheiring and Szombati 2020: 7).

The overwhelming economic protest vote against the socialists resulted in the Fidesz parliamentary supermajority (Johnson and Barnes 2015: 553). Fidesz won the 2010 election with a landslide victory of 52.7%, securing a two-thirds majority in Parliament.

Around that time, as a result of the party realignment in Hungarian politics, working-class supporters increasingly aligned with Jobbik and Fidesz rather than the left-wing parties (Győri 2015). In a study of self-reported voting in the 2006–2009 election, Knutsen (2013) discovered that Fidesz had the strongest support among the working class and the petite bourgeoisie and the weakest support among managers. Managers, along with middle-class professionals, gravitated toward the MSZP and made up the largest part of its new base. The realignment was so drastic that in-depth interviews with Hungary's factory workers conducted in 2015 revealed overwhelming support for Fidesz and Jobbik, with only a small margin backing the MSZP (Bartha and Tóth 2017). Many workers were ashamed to admit that they had ever voted for MSZP. In their view, the party had completely discredited itself with its neoliberal economic policies and corruption scandals (Bartha and Tóth 2017). Some interviewees even wondered why workers and trade unions would ever vote for a left party. (These views differed markedly from those presented in interviews conducted in early 2000.)

Many blamed the MSZP for abandoning the working class. Scheiring (2020b: 208) provides a quote from one of his interviews with a Hungarian worker that is particularly revealing:

> I voted for the, what's their name, Socialists, because I thought as a worker, from birth and on a social level, erm, I am left-wing, and they were the so-called workers' party. I went and voted for them. When I saw, and not mentioning, I got this book, about the oil mafia. These so-called socialists got into power, with what, erm, sort of money, well, I, from then . . . Moreover, most of all, in this town, which they destroyed, and what I experienced myself, personally. So, I turned away from them. And I didn't find anybody else to vote for. . . . So, this was the first time I voted for Orbán.

> For Fidesz, not for Orbán, for Fidesz. (Skilled manual worker, Dunaújváros, Steel Works)

Scheiring points out that Fidesz's type of nationalism, which included redistributionist appeals, resonated well with former MSZP voters. It was particularly successful with voters living in deindustrialized areas who felt left behind (Scheiring 2020b: 210).

Since 2010, national themes have been omnipresent in Orbán's public addresses. Following the 2010 election, Orbán presented a populist vision of the unification of the Hungarian people in the System of National Cooperation. On April 25, 2010, the day of the second round of parliamentary elections, he told a crowd of supporters, "Today there was a revolution in the polls" and "Hungarians have overthrown the system and created a new one. The old system of leaders misusing their power was replaced by one of national unity" (quoted in Visnovitz and Jenne 2021: 688). The supermajority two-thirds control of the unicameral Parliament helped him solidify control over the political system and implement its preferred financial nationalist policies.

Because of the party's electoral dominance[9] and the absence of opposition parties that could contest Fidesz policies, international institutions such as the IMF and the EU lost an important source of domestic leverage, allowing the Orbán government to implement unorthodox financial policies (Johnson and Barnes 2015: 553). The ability of the Fidesz government to keep the deficit and debt under control further undermined IMF and EU ability to insist on policy reforms.[10] Fidesz also removed the Constitutional Court's power to adjudicate cases concerning state finances and economic policies (Reuters 2010). These policies, along with the creation of external enemies, ranging from refugees to supranational institutions such as the European Union and individuals such as George Soros, became important for cultivating and maintaining Fidesz's popular support (Scoggins 2022).

---

[9] The country's disproportional electoral system could have further helped sustain electoral domination by incentivizing strategic voting and disadvantaging "third parties" (Nikolenyi 2004; Bánkuti, Halmai, and Scheppele 2012; Tóka 2014; Pap 2017).

[10] Simultaneously Hungary's EU membership helped facilitate Orbán's policies by providing the government with annual billions of euros in direct financial assistance through the EU Cohesion Funds (Johnson and Barnes 2015: 554).

In its economic approach Fidesz pursued the policy of economic nationalism, offering to bring the interventionist nation-state back into
the economy (Bluhm and Varga 2019). The combination of nationalism
and anti-austerity orientation is visible in such Fidesz claims as the
following:

> We have introduced a system in which we distributed the public burden be-
> tween multinational companies and Hungarian people in a more propor-
> tionate way than before. This is why we could complete the restructuring
> without any austerity measures. . . . [T]he grand work of restructuring
> the Hungarian economy could not be prevented by outsiders, either from
> the capitals of other European Union member states or from Brussels.
> (MTIE 2013)

Among its first policies, Fidesz nationalized over $14 billion of private pen-
sion fund assets, shares, and properties and imposed a "crisis tax" on large
businesses in banking, retail, telecommunications, and energy. Special taxes
served to increase public revenues but were also tied to a broader agenda
of renationalization and redistribution of privatized property. The state also
increased its role in the energy market, promoted local retailers at the expense of foreign companies, and fostered new regulations or direct takeovers
(Bohle and Greskovits 2019: 1076). Johnson and Barnes (2015: 545) argue
that while these policies protected the system "insiders" (native Hungarians)
from austerity policies, they de facto imposed austerity on "outsiders" within
Hungary (such as transnational corporations, financial institutions, and
ethnic minorities).

Among other policies, the Orbán government also implemented redistributionist policies through populist programs, such as enforcing utility price
cuts and increasing the minimum wage to compensate low-income workers
(Myant, Drahokoupil, and Lesay 2013: 407).

## Individual-Level Surveys

To illustrate the above dynamic, Figure 4.1 depicts the structure of political competition in Hungary using the Chapel Hill Expert Survey on the
positions of national political parties in 2002–2010 (Polk et al. 2017). The
data set provides the position of each party on two dimensions of political

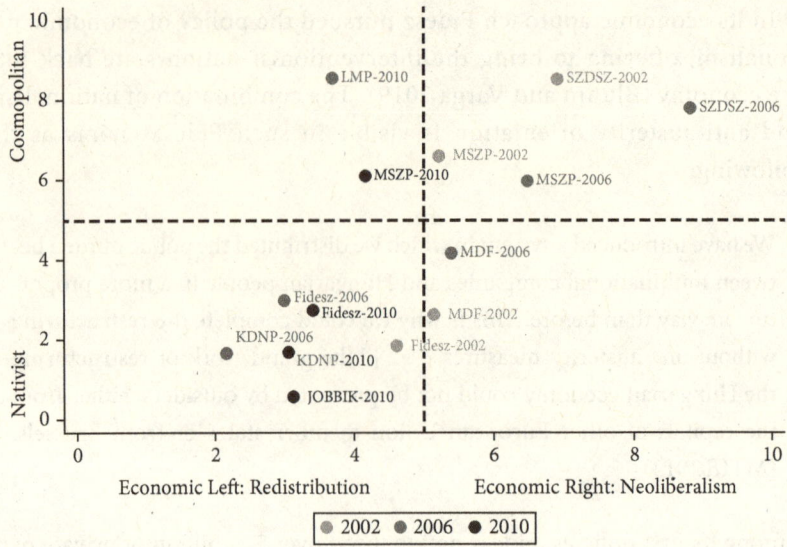

**Figure 4.1** Structure of Party Competition in Hungary in the 2002, 2006, and 2010 elections.

*Source*: Chapel Hill Expert Survey.

competition: the (redistributionist-neoliberal) economic dimension and the (nativist-cosmopolitan) sociocultural dimension.

First, Figure 4.1 demonstrates the convergence of parties around centrist economic positions at the time of EU accession (around 2002). Second, it shows that by 2006 MSZP positions had become increasingly pro-market (shift to the right along the economic dimension in the top right quadrant). Correspondingly, Fidesz adopts more redistributionist positions in 2006–2010 (shift to the left in the bottom left quadrant), and Jobbik emerges in the bottom left quadrant by 2010. Note that the preferences of working-class electorates also tend to appear in the bottom left quadrant, as per Figure 2.2. This dynamic also demonstrates the correspondence between positions of populist right parties and working-class supporters.

How has the association between class and party in Hungary changed over time? To demonstrate the dynamic of class-based support, Figure 4.2 plots the actual proportion of working-class supporters against the actual proportion of professional-class voting for the parties of interest. The resulting Alford Index is a convenient way of plotting the class vote (the working-class

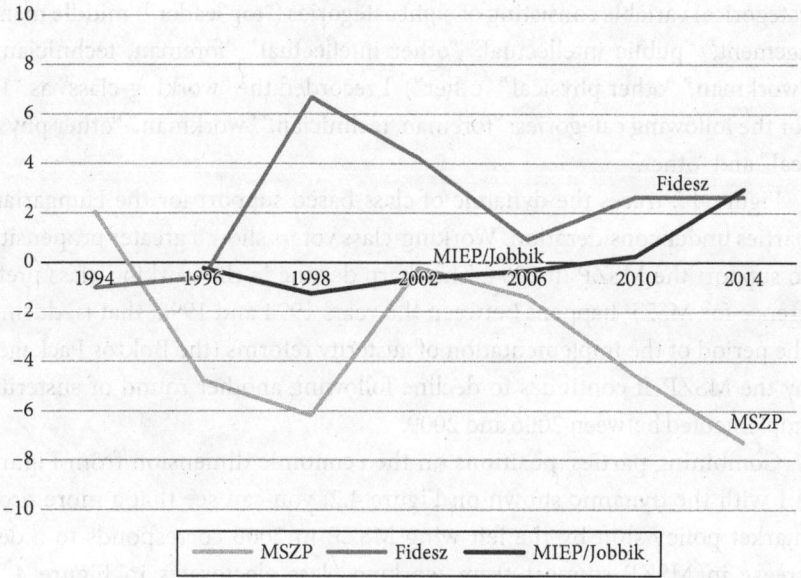

**Figure 4.2** Index (% party vote among working class) – (% party vote among professional class) for the left MSZP, the populist right Fidesz, and Magyar Igazság és Élet Pártja (MIEP)/Jobbik parties.
Source: Medián Opinion and Market Research Ltd. Omnibus Polls, Hungary.

minus the professional-class vote share for a given party).[11] A higher value shows a higher representation of working-class voters in a party's base.

The data used to build the graph were collected in the years 1994–2014 by Median Opinion and Market Research Ltd., a major, well-respected Hungarian polling company. Median's monthly omnibus-type opinion polls (representative surveys for the population 18+, sample size: 1,200 individuals) control for basic party preference questions. Some monthly surveys were missing, so I used seven to twelve surveys per electoral year (1994–1995, 1998, 2002, 2006, 2010, 2014), depending on availability. In each case I coded all variables identically. Belonging to the working-class category was coded based on the variable "fogl" ("the occupation of a respondent"), a

---

[11] Using the Alford Index to explore the class-based relationship across parties is a convenient way of looking at these relationships by plotting raw numbers, and a much simpler and easier way for the reader to see what is going on. The Alford Index is equivalent to the slope in a linear regression equation where the probability of voting for a given party is regressed on a dichotomous measure of class (Evans, Heath, and Payne 1995).

categorical variable consisting of eight categories ("top leader," "middle management," "public intellectual," "other intellectual," "foreman, technician," "workman," "other physical," "other"). I recorded the "working-class" as "1" for the following categories: "foreman, technician," "workman," "other physical," and "other."

Figure 4.2 traces the dynamic of class-based support for the Hungarian parties under consideration. Working-class voters show a greater propensity to support the MSZP in 1994. The sharp decline in the working-class preference for MSZP happens between the years 1994 and 1998, that is, during the period of the implementation of austerity reforms (the Bokros Package) by the MSZP. It continues to decline following another round of austerity implemented between 2006 and 2009.

Combining parties' positions on the economic dimension from Figure 4.1 with the dynamic shown on Figure 4.2, you can see that a more pro-market policy shift by the left-wing MSZP in 2006 corresponds to a decrease in MSZP support from working class electorates in Figure 4.2. Simultaneously, as Fidesz shifts further to the left along the economic policy dimension (Figure 4.1), you can see its increasing association with working-class electorates in Figure 4.2. The same is true for Jobbik in 2010.

## Poland

By 1989 Polish communist authorities faced immense pressure from the broad anticommunist social movement led by the Solidarity trade union to democratize Polish politics. Throughout the 1980s Solidarity remained *the* symbol of all the hopes the communist regime had attempted to crush. Having sustained the constant threat of being wiped away by the regime, Solidarity was able to enter the roundtable talks of 1989 and secure the regime's agreement to a "contract" leading to semi-free parliamentary elections in June 1989 (Jasiewicz 1992). In those elections Solidarity candidates won all but one of the contested seats. And the first free presidential elections in 1990 were won by Lech Wałęsa, the Nobel Prize–winning Solidarity leader. This opened a pathway for the first democratically elected coalition government led by Solidarity. The breakup of the Solidarity movement in 1989–1991 opened the door to the formation of political parties that identified themselves as right-wing or center right (Szczerbiak 2004).

The election held in October 1991 led to the formation of a center-right coalition government. Faced with hyperinflation and an alarming economic decline (legacies of the communist regime), the new government decided to take prompt action. In December 1990, it embarked on a program of economic reform aiming to start the transition to a market-oriented economy. The key components of these reforms, known as *shock therapy*, were implemented in early 1990 by a team of economists headed by Leszek Balcerowicz. The Balcerowicz Plan aimed to curtail hyperinflation, reduce government spending, liberalize trade, and privatize state-owned companies. Solidarity union leadership at that time was tightly connected with emerging political elites pressured by international bodies like the IMF and World Bank (Shields 2012). Thus, the party had to support neoliberal reforms (Kaminski and Rozbicka 2016: 196). Solidarity put "its considerable stock of social movement energy and expertise fully behind the campaign" in favor of pro-market reforms (Ost 2002: 40). The embrace of reforms was not costly for Solidarity at first, as Polish unionists at the beginning of transformation tended to support the shift to capitalism (see Gardawski and Zukowski 1992, 1994).

However, the immediate macroeconomic effects of the reforms were devastating. Between 1990 and early 1992 the country went into a deep recession. Industrial production dropped by more than 30% between 1990 and 1991, and the bankruptcies of state-owned enterprises led to large-scale job losses. Workers' wages fell dramatically, and the GDP plunged by 11.6% in 1990 and by 7% in 1991 (Piętka 2007). The unemployment rate skyrocketed from virtually zero in January 1990 to 6.5% by the end of the year, and then doubled during the subsequent twelve months (Bernaciak 2017). Inequality also increased for certain groups, especially wage earners (Milanovic 1993), inevitably giving rise to perceptions of "winners" and "losers" (Kramer 1995). After 1991 it became clear to voters that the costs of transitioning to a market economy included a sharp fall in real wages and a rise in unemployment. And many in Polish society felt it was the Solidarity-backed political leaders who allowed this to happen (Ost 2006).

In the 1993 election, fatigue from the reforms implemented by the center-right coalition contributed to the success of the left. Former activists of the communist Polish United Workers' Party opted to dissolve it and establish the Social Democracy of the Republic of Poland (Socjaldemokracja Rzeczypospolitej Polskiej, SdRP) in its place. Together with other left-wing groups the party formed an electoral alliance known as the Democratic Left Alliance, which opposed the reformist coalition. Shortly after the postcommunist transition, the SLD's support base included white-collar workers and pensioners, as well as employers, including private entrepreneurs. Such a diverse interest coalition made for a contradictory SLD platform that combined pledges for further marketization with promises to defend the interests of labor, increase social spending, and continue "central intervention" in the economy to reduce the costs of transformation (Hunter and Ryan 1998: 172). Strong support for European integration played a vital role in establishing the SLD's image as a modernized, Western-style social democratic alliance[12] and allowing it to distance itself from its communist past (Szczerbiak 2002: 7).[13]

During its 1993 electoral campaign, SLD endorsed market reforms, but it also demanded more consideration for the interests of labor and continued its intervention in the economy to reduce the costs of transformation. This platform allowed it to adapt to attract support from reform "losers" who demanded reform modification, a greater emphasis on spending, and an increase in social services (Paradowska, Janicki, and Markowski 1993; Gibson and Cielecka 1995: 769). The SLD drew support from skilled and unskilled working-class supporters, farmers, and private business owners from small and midsize towns with high unemployment where state industries had closed (Szelenyi, Fodor, and Hanley 1997; Curry 2003: 31). Many SLD supporters opposed privatization and the closure of factories (Gibson and Cielecka 1995).

The Polish Trade Union Alliance (Ogólnopolskie Porozumienie Związków Zawodowych, OPZZ), an SLD ally, further helped the party attract significant support from working-class groups. The OPZZ was created during communist times as a government-sponsored counterweight to the Solidarity movement.[14] By the early 1990s OPZZ appeared to have become irrelevant as Solidarity activists took control of the labor movement and became part of a new political elite committed to a rapid economic transition (Sil 2017: 429). However, soon its fortunes turned around. Once the pain of the reforms became more pronounced, many workers and local unions started defecting from Solidarity to OPZZ. While Solidarity continued to support the center-right government and distanced itself from the broad and public discontent

[12] The SdRP remained the most powerful part of SLD, a broad electoral coalition until 1999. Then the SdRP formally dissolved itself, and the SLD transformed into an eponymous party (Buras 2005).

[13] In the first 1991 election, the SLD finished second with 12% of the vote (only 0.3% below the winning center-right coalition of five parties, which continued along the reform track).

[14] Since the mid-1980s, the Polish communist regime sought to weaken the oppositional Solidarity-led democratic movement by creating another regime-sponsored trade union apparatus: the Polish Trade Union Alliance (OPZZ). By the early 1990s OPZZ appeared to have become irrelevant as Solidarity activists took control of the labor movement and became part of a new political elite committed to rapid economic transition (Sil 2017: 429). However, its fortunes soon turned around.

of regular workers, the OPZZ, allied with the SLD, expressed rather hostile attitudes toward Balcerowicz's shock therapy (Kaminski and Rozbicka 2016: 197). Eventually, OPZZ became the major postcommunist trade union and helped SLD incorporate a substantive share of working-class support. In the 1993–1997 Parliament about one-third of the SLD deputies were OPZZ people (Orenstein 1998: 491).

In the 1993 election, as frustrations with the reforms grew, the SLD gained 20.4% of the vote, which allowed it to form a ruling coalition with the agrarian Polish Peasant Party (Polskie Stronnictwo Ludowe, PSL). PSL represented the interests of Polish farmers and, as the party of the countryside, drew the support of the Catholic Church and had a large proportion of practicing churchgoers among its voters. After the 1993 election, the SLD and the PSL together controlled nearly two-thirds of the seats.

The division between the OPZZ and Solidarity became a constant feature of Polish politics from the mid-1990s on. While Solidarity unions regularly sided with right-of-center parties, OPZZ, which owed its creation to communist authorities, remained closely associated with the left successor party. The point of contestation was particularly pronounced in the Socio-economic Tripartite Commission, where Solidarity trade unions almost automatically opposed reforms proposed by the "hostile" SLD-led government (Kaminski and Rozbicka 2016: 198). But after Solidarity came to power in the subsequent electoral round, the roles quickly reversed.

Solidarity and OPZZ became such an integral part of the two opposing political sides that up to one-fifth of all MPs were at the same time trade-union members (Gardawski and Meardi 2010; Kaminski and Rozbicka 2016: 198). Alas, the opportunities for labor officials to participate in different governments did not strengthen the position of the Polish working class, because, as discussed below, "there was little to divide the centre of gravity of the Polish centre-right and centre-left in terms of their approach to economic policy" (Szczerbiak 2004: 60). However, government participation contributed to the "subordination of trade union demands to the exigencies of political coalition-making" (Trappmann 2012: 8; Sil 2017: 429).

## The Realignment Begins

Having come to power in 1993, the parties in the left coalition found themselves facing two opposing demands. Their supporters expected them to reduce the costs of transition and increase pensions, unemployment insurance, and wages. They also expected them to protect farmers, limit foreign participation in the economy, and raise taxes. By contrast, the government urgently needed the IMF's approval to qualify Poland for the second stage of a 50% cut in its $33 billion foreign debt. A need for debt restructuring and an inflow of the much-needed greater foreign investment created strong incentives to limit budgetary spending (Gibson and Cielecka 1995: 770). After hesitating for a while, the new government announced that it would "push ahead with a mass privatization scheme" and continued with the Balcerowicz Plan of privatization, deregulation, and sound fiscal policies (Hunter and Ryan 1998: 172). The government passed a relatively tight budget for 1994, with pension and social payment increases well below what was promised during the election campaign (Gibson and Cielecka 1995: 770).

When in 1994 Deputy Premier and Minister of Finance Grzegorz Kołodko announced his Strategy for Poland, which stressed controlling budget deficits, combating inflation, cutting expenditures, and opening the Polish economy to foreign investors, many observers referred to it as the neoliberal turn of the ruling left coalition (Bozóki and Ishiyama 2002: 66). Robinson (1997), for example, argued that Poland's former communists "changed their name to social democrat, adopted the 'Balcerowicz programme' as their own and won the September 1993 general elections by promising to reduce the social costs of reforms. They then proceeded to maintain the budgetary restraint and the macroeconomic stability which had underpinned economic growth and pushed slowly ahead with privatization and other reform[s]." In discussions with the author (June 2022), Kołodko disagreed with this assessment, stressing that along with an embrace of pro-market reforms his Strategy for Poland was considerably more socially oriented than the Balcerowicz Plan and was targeted at combating unemployment and building the institutions of the social market economy.[15] Along with continuation of pro-market reforms, the program emphasized boosting investment in public infrastructure (housing, transport, telecommunications, energy) and labor-intensive industries in regions with high structural unemployment (Buras 2005).[16]

---

[15] Kołodko was a vice president of the Council of Ministers and minister of finance in 1994–1997 and 2002–2003 and the creator of the socioeconomic development programs Strategy for Poland, Package 2000, and the Program for Repairing the Finances of the Republic of Poland.

[16] Buras (2005) points out that Western European social democracy has provided an important source of programmatic inspiration for the SLD. While its leadership often dismissed the Third Way as not being applicable to the Polish context, the language and concepts of the Third Way found a reflection in SLD programs and leadership statements (Buras 2006). This reflection included the

However, others point out substantive overlap in the programs. For example, Marek Siwiec (in discussion with the author, July 2022), who at that time was a member of the SLD in the Polish Sejm, argues that despite declaring himself anti-Balcerowicz, Kołodko and other policymakers in power largely continued what Balcerowicz had begun.[17] Closely dependent on the reformist left-wing government, the trade union OPZZ found itself torn between support for protests and support for government, and eventually resorted to discouraging strike action even at the cost of a disproportional decline in its membership (Robertson 2004: 260).

In its 1997 electoral program, the SLD continued to evolve toward a more neoliberal economic platform and openly advocated support for new and small businesses (Jackson, Klich, and Poznanska 2005: 43). By contrast, its main competitor, the Solidarity Election Action (Akcja Wyborcza Solidarność, AWS), a right-wing coalition of Solidarity trade unions and Catholic parties,[18] campaigned on a less liberal platform than the SLD. The AWS offered to continue with privatization and economic reforms but also emphasized economic interventionism and offered to aid the badly lagging coal and steel sectors, which had not yet been restructured or privatized. This is an important reason why, despite four years of economic growth and decreasing unemployment, the SLD lost the 1997 election to the AWS.

In spite of its electoral promises, the AWS formed a coalition government with the pro-market Freedom Union Party, headed by the reformer Balcerowicz, who became the deputy prime minister and the minister of finance. The new government focused on reforms necessary to ensure EU accession, which included further privatization of services and industries and overhauling the state administration and welfare services (pensions, healthcare, and education) (McKenna 2013: 200). The AWS also initiated a series

emphasis on the need for "the state to conduct the policy of establishing opportunities, especially through education . . . [so that] as few people as possible feel excluded from society" (Celiński 1999). SLD's 1999 programmatic manifesto also emphasized the idea of "inclusion," also central for the Third Way, by highlighting that Poland was "becoming a society of inherited poverty . . . with increasing numbers of people excluded from the benefits of growth and social progress" (Buras 2014: 103).

[17] Marek Siwiec is a member of the SLD; from 1991 to 1997 he was a member of the Polish Sejm from the Kalisz district. In 1993–1996 he was a member of the Parliamentary Assembly of the Council of Europe. From 1996 until 2004 he was an advisor at the Chancellery of the President of the Republic of Poland, Aleksander Kwaśniewski.

[18] The creation of the Solidarity Electoral Action followed the shock of center-right parties' defeat in the 1993 parliamentary election, which was further exacerbated by their defeat in the November 1995 presidential election by the SLD leader at that time, Aleksander Kwaśniewski. It led to the formation of Solidarity Electoral Action in June 1996 by twenty-two parties and other groupings spearheaded by the Solidarity trade union (Szczerbiak 2004).

of measures that weakened union power, especially in healthcare and education, and passed legislation almost completely eliminating the mining sector (Robertson 2004: 261). The ruling coalition was quickly knocked off-balance by a wave of protests and labor disputes. Despite the economic recovery that followed, the unemployment level remained high due to the pro-market policies, and a sense of social and individual dislocation spread in Poland. As a result, support for the AWS declined. The government's flagship reforms (healthcare, pensions, local government) became increasingly unpopular and exacerbated tensions between and within the coalition parties. The economic policy pursued by Balcerowicz provided a particular source of conflict with the more economically interventionist elements within the AWS (Szczerbiak 2004). The coalition finally broke down in June 2000, leaving the AWS at the head of a minority government prior to the 2001 election.

During its 2001 campaign, the SLD promised to reverse the decline in living standards caused by the AWS government's reforms, but simultaneously emphasized its commitment to EU accession. The SLD won the 2001 election with a 41% landslide in a coalition with the Labor Union Party. This time it drew support from all groups: reform winners and losers, old and young, urban and rural dwellers (Domanski 2000). For the first time, opinion polls showed that a majority of Solidarity members had voted for the SLD (Gardawski and Meardi 2008: 5; Kamiński and Rozbicka 2016: 202).

## The Collapse of the Left

Once again in power, the SLD attempted some pro-labor reforms. Minister of Labor Jerzy Hausner, who subsequently became minister of the economy, reached out to trade unions and made considerable efforts to achieve social pacts and revive tripartism (Hausner 2007; Gardawski and Meardi 2008). However, once more the left government was not in any position to cater to social demands—EU conditionality constrained the ruling parties' policy choices, demanding that the government continue with its reform program to achieve macroeconomic stability in order to ensure EU accession. As Marek Siwiec (in discussion with the author, July 2022) remembers, "While the Polish economy was now on a more stable track, a new challenge emerged: guaranteeing Poland's EU membership, which implied passing another large set of reforms."

The key issue in Poland was a large structural budget deficit, which reflected the active use of social transfers to ease the pain of the economic transition (Zubek 2008; Bohle and Greskovits 2012). Social security and welfare consumed the largest share of government expenditure in 2001, at 20% of GDP, which was further exacerbated by high spending on public-sector wages (Zubek 2008). The SLD's economic policy subsequently prioritized the interests of business by introducing a more flexible labor code, expanding entrepreneurship support, and proposing a flat income tax instead of progressive taxation. The first budget of the new government was linked with eighteen budgetary laws that reduced spending by almost 18 million złoty (Holland 2007: 259). To support small and medium-size enterprises, the new government also intended to make the labor market more flexible and more closely in line with EU laws. Its program document, "Entrepreneurship Above All," which was approved at the beginning of 2002, reflected this spirit and sought to liberalize the Polish Labor Code by making hiring and firing easier, cutting sick pay, reducing overtime pay, and limiting union consultation rights (Phelan 2007: 313). While the program intended to decrease the level of unemployment, the already high unemployment rate saw an initial spike that reached 20%.[19]

The voters did not appreciate the new government's policies. Having introduced large tax increases and expenditure cuts in its first budget, the left parties in power immediately noticed an unusually sharp downturn in their approval ratings (Szczerbiak 2002). Between November 2001 (when the cuts were announced) and December 2002, support for the SLD dropped by 20 percentage points, from 45.8% to 25.6% (CBOS data based on author's estimates). Several corruption scandals during the SLD term (such as the "Rywin affair") helped to further weaken support for the party. By the end of 2003, this trend was further exacerbated by the introduction of additional economic austerity measures to prevent the budget deficit from spiraling out of control (Shields 2012; Grzymała-Busse 2019b), as well as Prime Minister Leszek Miller's proposal to introduce a single income-tax rate, or flat tax, for individuals and business, which led to splits within the SLD government (Strzelecki and McQuaid 2003). Marcin Piatkowski (in discussion with the author, July 2022), who at the time served as an advisor to Poland's deputy premier and minister of finance and contributed to the fiscal reform program,

[19] Macrotrends, Poland Unemployment Rate 1991–2003, https://www.macrotrends.net/countr ies/POL/poland/unemployment-rate.

argues that it was "the stark contrast between Miller's postcommunist past and his neoliberal tax proposal that helped convince Polish voters that the party leaders had no ideology, no mission, and that they would do anything to hold on to power."[20]

By 2004 the SLD was trailing with 12% approval (CBOS 2004). Faced with an unfavorable ratings dynamic, in 2004 alone the government had to back away from one-third of the expected reductions in social spending under the new Hausner Plan, a comprehensive fiscal stabilization package aimed at ensuring Eurozone entry by 2009 (Vincensini 2015).[21] The main reason for backing down was a major crisis that had unraveled within the SLD party. Public expenditure cuts, which were likely to be painful for many SLD voters were in stark contrast to the party's election pledges and brought the SLD into conflict with the trade unions. The implementation of the plan was certain to hurt the SLD's electoral prospects. As one regional party leader put it, "The Hausner plan is good for Poland but disastrous for the SLD" (Zubek 2008: 301).

However, the damage was already done. The party lost the 2005 election, gaining only 11% of the vote. For the first time since its establishment, it entered Parliament as the third party, having lost 30% of its 2001 voters (Rae 2017). Since then, the party has remained on the margins of Polish politics.

Partly owing to the split within the Polish trade unions and partly to its pro-market orientation, SLD failed to ensure a sustained working-class backing for several continuous electoral cycles. As a result, it had to negotiate with other groups, including private employers' associations and international financial institutions. Under these conditions, its survival depended

---

[20] Marcin Piatkowski is an associate professor at Kozminski University in Warsaw and a senior economist at the World Bank. Previously, he served as chief economist and managing director of PKO BP, the largest bank in Poland; economist in the European Department of the IMF; and advisor to IMF's executive director. During 2002–2003, he served as an advisor to Poland's Deputy Premier and Minister of Finance Grzegorz W. Kołodko, contributing to the fiscal reform program.

[21] The "Hausner plan" was a second attempt at fulfilling the Maastricht criteria. In mid-2002, the left-wing government joined the National Bank of Poland in pushing for fast-track Eurozone entry. The key force behind the ambitious plan to enter the Eurozone in 2007 was Finance Minister Grzegorz Kołodko. His comprehensive package entailed a sharp lowering of the fiscal deficit in 2004 and 2005 through a combination of restrictive tax policy, spending cuts, and extraordinary revenues (Zubek 2008). But the bid collapsed in mid-2003, when it became obvious that the plan received little support from domestic business associations and trade unions united in calling for lower taxation and higher deficits, even if that meant a delayed Eurozone entry. Kołodko also had disagreements with his government colleagues, who were concerned that spending cuts would hurt the government's already low approval ratings (Zubek 2008).

on being able to act as a catch-all party (Cook and Orenstein 1999), which meant that it did not maintain a recognizable electoral base that could generate stable support for it over successive electoral cycles. This contributed to the party's electoral demise (Sil 2017: 435).

This trend continued in subsequent elections. Despite the fact that several new left parties formed to fill the vacuum of left-wing reformism (i.e., the Greens and Razem, Left-Together, party), none has been able to achieve any substantial success. During the ten consecutive years since the collapse of the SLD, the main contest on the Polish political scene occurred between two right-wing parties: the populist, PiS and the center-right Civic Platform (Platforma Obywatelska, PO).

Overall, for more than a decade every party in Poland that won elections on a more protectionist economic platform continued with a market reform program once in office. In fact, in one of his interviews Balcerowicz openly admitted that at some point the SLD's economic policies and goals were virtually indistinguishable from those of the Balcerowicz-led pro-market Freedom Union Party (Kolodko and Nuti 1997). In other words, Polish voters were consistently left with no party representing a viable pro-redistribution alternative.

> A leading charge against the Polish democratic system has been its lack of responsiveness to real social problems. It is quite possible to argue that the main political debates in Poland in the 1990s and beyond did not reflect some of the serious and genuine issues the country faced. Since the early 1990s, consecutive election results suggested the majority of voters favoured a more "solidary" economic policy over strict monetarism. Such sentiments, however, while vaguely encouraged in the course of electoral campaigns, were routinely ignored by the political establishment when it came to policy making. Importantly, socio-economic issues were accorded little prominence by two actors who could have been expected to act upon them: the political left and the trade unions. (Pankowski 2010: 75)

After the SLD had secured Poland's EU membership, political costs associated with the adoption of alternative economic policies and more Euroskeptic rhetoric declined. Subsequently, opposition parties could seriously begin challenging EU-related reforms without worrying about losing their membership. This explains why serious opposition to the ruling left coalition's neoliberal pro-EU policies did not emerge until the mid-2000s.

## The Adaptation of the Right

In the 2005 election, the decline of electoral support for the SLD was partly due to the abstention of some of its voters, but also because its voters increasingly switched to support right-wing parties, such as Self-Defense (6% of SLD voters) and the PiS party (13% of SLD voters) (Szczerbiak 2007).

PiS was a conservative right-wing party founded by the Kaczyński brothers shortly before the 2001 parliamentary elections in opposition to both the SLD ·and the AWS. PiS was a direct successor of the right-wing Centre Agreement Party,[22] which formed the PiS's core but also incorporated parts of the AWS. PiS adopted a populist platform, combining a critique of economic reforms and European integration with an emphasis on Polish traditions and Catholic religious values. Attitudes toward socioeconomic issues emerged as one of their dominant themes in the 2005 election (Szczerbiak 2007). In its 2005 campaign, the PiS attacked what it dubbed as the "far-too-liberal" policies of the ruling parties. It blamed them for Poland's numerous failures and promised to improve conditions for Polish workers who felt abandoned in the wake of the elites' neoliberal policies (Ost 2018: 114). This emerging populist discourse created an ideological narrative: the virtuous, homogeneous Polish people confronted by a set of self-serving, corrupt politicians (predominantly from left parties), who allegedly conspired to deprive the Polish "people" of what was rightfully theirs in terms of their economic and social standing (Wolchik and Curry 2008: 175).

PiS's Fourth Republic program for the moral and political renewal of the Polish state included a vague pledge to build a "solidaristic" Poland. The party drew a stark contrast between its own platform and that of the center-right PO's economic liberalism. The program emphasized the fate of workers abandoned by postcommunist, neoliberal economic policies, but blamed the identity of new leaders rather than the nature of the new capitalist system for their misfortunes (Ost 2018: 114). As a solution, the PiS argued that the conditions of Polish workers could have been improved if Poland had leaders who had promoted true Polish values. They called for banning abortion, purging former communists, and distributing state property among

---

[22] The Center Agreement (Porozumienie Centrum, PC), a center-right anticommunist party, was the first political project of the Kaczyński brothers; it emerged in 1990, after the Solidarity Citizens' Committee dissolved into competing factions. The PC program emphasized legalism, traditional values, the role of the church, and Catholic social teachings (Pytlas 2015, 2020). PC played a relatively minor role in the 1990s after breaking with Solidarity (Szymański 2014).

all citizens. The PiS's electoral program largely echoed the promises made by AWS leaders during the mid-1990s, who did not oppose capitalism but wanted to offer solutions for the economic problems experienced by their supporters (Ost 2018: 119).[23]

Using such rhetoric, PiS won the 2005 parliamentary election with 27% of the vote, luring away between 13% and 17% of SLD supporters. The SLD came in fourth (Szczerbiak 2007; Rae 2017). PiS rhetoric resonated with particular strength among lower-educated working-class and rural voters who felt excluded by the incumbent party's neoliberal policies. The party became popular in less economically developed Polish regions (Markowski 2006). In October 2005, the PiS leader, Lech Kaczyński, won the presidential election by relying on a socioconservative program and pledging not to renominate the reformer Balcerowicz for another six-year term as president of the National Bank of Poland. In other words, dissatisfaction with the economic reforms was one of the key themes of the 2005 electoral campaign and contributed to pulling the working-class constituencies away from the left and toward the Polish populist right parties.

However, despite having made ambitious verbal promises, during its first tenure between 2005 and 2007, the PiS continued espousing fairly neoliberal economic policies by eliminating the inheritance tax, cutting payroll taxes, and creating a deficit in the social security account, which resulted in pressure to raise the retirement age (Ost 2018: 114). To be sure, the party avoided radical social or economic reforms that could have produced negative short-term electoral consequences (Szczerbiak 2007). In particular, the party decided to delay Eurozone entry. Kaczynski concurred: "Poland is not ready for the euro yet" (quoted in Zubek 2008: 302).[24] This decision resulted from the party's preference for improvements in living standards over politically sensitive fiscal rationalization. The new government also adopted some spending programs, including subsidies for farmers' petrol, birth premiums, pay raises for teachers, and higher disability benefits and pensions (Zubek 2008: 303). Throughout this time Kaczyński was often at odds with Balcerowicz (then president of the National Bank of Poland) over

---

[23] In the local 2006 elections, PiS pushed populist slogans even further, using the motto "Close to the People" and promising "to create a social order in Poland, in which good is good, and bad is bad" (PiS 2006; Wysocka 2009).

[24] In 2015 PiS prime minister Beata Szydlo was even more straightforward, asserting, "We are not going to lead Poland to the Eurozone" (quoted in Dandashly and Verdun 2018).

prioritizing social spending before budgetary discipline (Shields 2007).[25] But despite having announced ambitious plans to legislate "for a more socially sensitive economy," the party failed to undertake such reforms, which even provoked public protests (Stanley 2016: 267–270). Similarly, throughout that period the party introduced "no special proactive initiatives for women . . . or socially disadvantaged people" (Bertelsmann Stiftung 2010: 13). As result, PiS was unable to increase its support the way it would after it implemented dramatically expanded public spending in 2015.

A political crisis resulting from corruption allegations targeting Andrzej Lepper, the leader of the Self-Defense of the Republic of Poland, broke up the ruling coalition and called for an earlier parliamentary election in 2007. The main competition was between the PO and the PiS. This time both parties moved away from economic liberalism by embracing more redistributionist slogans and therefore squeezing the center-left. The PO promised to bring about an "economic miracle" that would pay for improved public services and infrastructure by abandoning excessive regulation. Distancing itself from an open espousal of economic liberalism, the PO targeted the dissatisfaction of public-sector workers with the PiS-led government by promising better salaries for doctors, nurses, and teachers. The party argued that such policies would prevent Poles from being forced to work abroad in order to improve their living standard (Szczerbiak 2007: 5). On this platform the PO won the 2007 election with 41.5% of the vote and 209 (out of 460) seats in the Sejm. In contrast, the Left and Democrats—an electoral alliance of four center-left parties anchored by the SLD—came in third with 13.2% of the vote and 53 seats. This was below the total combined vote of 17.7% these parties received in the 2005 election and below the 55 seats that the SLD had won on its own in the 2001 election.

PiS was able to return to power in the 2015 election. Its electoral success, when compared with the poor results of the left, is at least partly attributed to the fact that, on top of its ideological conservatism, it adopted many elements of traditional left-wing rhetoric and called for vastly expanded public spending (Bernaciak 2017: 177). The party made a number of costly pledges popular among the wider public: new child support benefits (Family 500+

---

[25] This manifested in January 2007 when Kaczynski refused to reappoint Balcerowicz upon termination of his six-year term: "I want to turn to this school of economic thought which does not adhere to the line of Balcerowicz. . . . There are people who have a much better understanding of economic realities but who had no clout. I want to give them that clout. . . . [S]ometimes I get the impression when it comes to Governor Balcerowicz that I'm facing an ideology, not economic science" (Shields 2007).

program), housing subsidies, free prescription drugs for seniors, increased tax-free income thresholds, and a reversal of the previous government's unpopular plan to increase the retirement age (Jaskiernia 2019: 159).

PiS joined forces with a new right populist movement, Kukiz'15, set up by the rock singer Paweł Kukiz. Together they argued that Polish economic development was proceeding more slowly than it should be and that Poland had been left "in ruins" by the mismanagement of previous governments and corrupt elites. While preserving its nationalist focus, PiS presented itself as a protector of those who had not benefited from the transition to capitalism (*The Guardian* 2015). Throughout the 2015 campaign, PiS representatives repeatedly expressed their commitment to social principles. Prior to the May 2015 presidential election, the PiS candidate Andrzej Duda signed an agreement with the Solidarity trade union. In exchange for the union's support, Duda promised to raise the minimum wage to 50% of the average wage, strengthen tripartite social dialogue, and fight the widespread short-term "junk contracts." Referring to Solidarity's heritage, future prime minister Beata Szydło repeatedly promised that the union's demands "concerning work and social issues" would be fulfilled "if the Poles . . . gave power to PiS" (Polskie Radio 2015); she outlined the party's National Employment Plan, which included the creation of 1.2 million jobs for the young and promises to raise wages in the public sector. These political promises corresponded to demands voiced by trade unions and renewed the unions' interest in political alliances. While the Solidarity union officially backed PiS's presidential candidate, after PiS's victory in the parliamentary elections the OPZZ deputy chair Andrej Radzikowski acknowledged that the reforms direction chosen by Kaczyński's party was "congruent with OPZZ demands" (Prokop 2015).

Besides working-class groups, PIS promises attracted broader swaths of Polish society that had lost as a result of Polish modernization, even if that loss was only relative. This included the lower income parts of the population, living mainly in the eastern part of Poland and in rural areas. The strongholds of PiS's support in the 2015 election included industrial workers employed full-time in manufacturing firms (Ost 2018: 121), nonunionized workers from small towns and cities, and residents of the economically depressed rural regions in the south and east of Poland, more broadly those groups whose sense of marginalization had a basis in economic reality (Traub 2016). PiS had unusually high numbers of (a) people with primary (53%) and vocational (56%) education; (b) peasants and farmers (53%); (c) people over fifty years of age (48%); (d) pensioners (49%); Eurozone workers and rural residents (47%) in its electorate. Kukiz'15, too, had a disproportionate representation of working-class supporters (13%) (Markowski 2016: 1317).

PiS mostly appealed to these groups using a combination of nativist and redistributive economic pledges. In addition, nationalism had a concrete economic appeal for these groups. Consider this example of rhetoric the party used to attract voters: "We will build industry at home, we will renovate the places liberalism bypassed, and we will not allow Poles to be treated as neocolonial subjects" (Ost 2018: 122). By positioning itself as a culturally rightist but economically leftist party, PiS attracted voters who in the past may have voted for the left (Jaskiernia 2019: 159).

PiS was also helped by the 2015 migration crisis in Europe together with preexisting anxieties about secularization, "gender ideology," and other threats to traditional values, which PiS addressed in its platform. In Poland the fear of migrants and refugees coming from predominantly Muslim countries prevailed not only among rural and less-educated voters, but also urbanites and the better-educated (Fomina and Kucharczyk 2016). Kaczyński's hard line on refugees helped attract support from people who normally would never have voted for PiS. Indeed, according to opinion polls, those who were less generous in their attitude to refugees tended to support PiS (Sengoku 2018).

Both anti-immigration and pro-redistribution economic platforms contributed to the PiS victory, but which factor proved more decisive? One way to answer this question is to look at the polls run in Poland just before the refugee crisis peaked in Europe. The migrant and refugee arrivals in the EU were growing gradually throughout the first half of 2015, until July, when they skyrocketed, peaking in September–November 2015. However, already in May 2015, when the refugee inflow was still fairly low, PiS presidential candidate Andrzej Duda won the presidential elections with 51.5% of the vote. Immigration-related concerns did not play a key role in Duda's platform. Instead, he emphasized unsatisfactory living standards, high unemployment, and low wages and signed an agreement with the Solidarity trade union. Subsequently, according to CBOS polls collected in Poland, support for PiS exceeded that for PO (Sengoku 2018) quite consistently from that point on until the October elections.[26] It was not until fall 2015 that immigration became an issue featuring prominently in the parties' electoral platforms

[26] Politico, "Poll of Polls," accessed June 2, 2023, https://www.politico.eu/europe-poll-of-polls/poland/.

(Janczak 2019). Hence while it helped PiS expand its outreach to broader segments of society, the immigration crisis itself was likely not a decisive factor in the party's victory.

In October 2015, PiS won the election with 37.6% of the vote and gained an absolute majority of the seats. For the first time in democratic Poland, a winning party was able to create a government without having to negotiate with coalition partners. But the more striking difference between the 2015 election and elections of the previous twenty-five years was the complete absence of parliamentary representation for left parties. This was in part because the two main left parties (United Left, the alliance formed by the SLD with other left parties and Left Together) split the vote, leaving each of them with just under the electoral threshold. And it only intensified the realignment process unraveling in Polish politics.

Having learned from its 2005–2007 experience, PiS proceeded to deliver on its electoral promises once in power. It embraced an economic nationalist program and introduced a range of welfare measures. PiS reversed the previous government's increase in the retirement age, offered new drug benefits for the elderly, and promised a broad program for the construction of new affordable housing (Ost 2018: 115). The most universally popular and identifiable policy introduced by PiS was the flagship "500+" program, offering families monthly payments of 500 złoty ($130) for every child (after the first) up to age eighteen (Goraus-Tańska 2017). PiS also imposed limits on the use of insecure short-term "junk contracts," raised the guaranteed hourly minimum to 13 złoty, and introduced a surcharge tax on foreign-owned banks and insurance companies (Orenstein 2019). Finally, as Fidesz had done in Hungary, PiS aimed to "re-polonize" the economy and significantly increased government control over the banking sector by buying shares in private banks (Miszerak and Rohac 2017; Bluhm and Varga 2019). Kołodko (in discussion with the author, July 2022), the minister of finance in left-wing governments in 1994–1997 and 2002–2003, points out that such policies played a significant role in PiS popularity: "They adopted many social policies, which delivered what people wanted, while—for now—having managed to avoid the economic catastrophe."[27]

---

[27] Redistributive policies boosted support for PiS, allowing the party to stay in power in consecutive terms. Gromadzki, Sałach, and Brzezinski (2022), for example, show that a cash transfer amount of $100 per capita translated into a sizable increase in the vote share for the ruling party, allowing it to stay in power in subsequent elections.

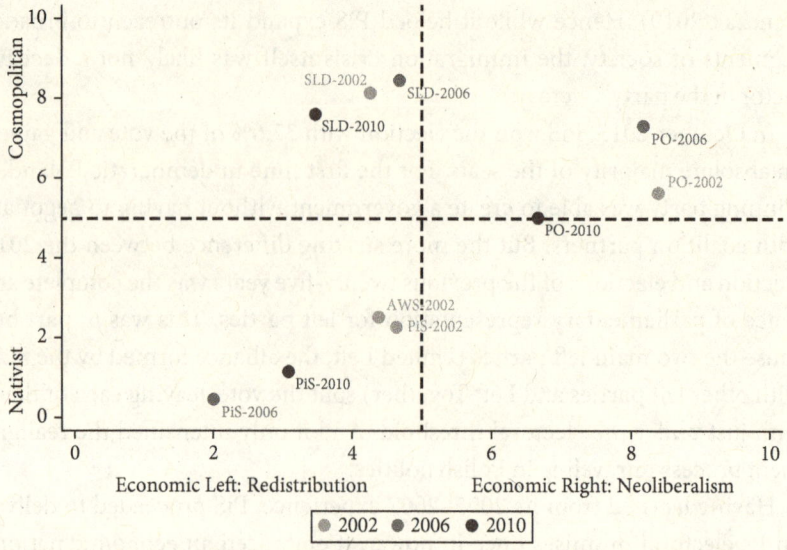

**Figure 4.3** Structure of Party Competition in Poland in 2002, 2006, and 2010 elections. For ease of interpretation, the graph excludes the smaller populist right parties Samooborona, League of Polish Families, and Polish People's Party, which were also in Parliament at the time of the analysis.
*Source*: Chapel Hill Expert Survey.

## Individual-Level Surveys

To illustrate the above dynamic, Figure 4.3 depicts the structure of political competition in Poland using the Chapel Hill Expert Survey on the positions of national political parties in 2002–2010 (Polk et al. 2017) along the two dimensions of political competition: the left-right economic dimension, and the cultural dimension. First, Figure 4.3 demonstrates party policy convergence around the time of EU accession, as shown by the alignment of AWS, SLD, and PiS near the center of the economic policy dimension around 2002. Second, while the SLD still retained its pro-market positions by 2006, PiS adopted more redistributionist positions from 2006 to 2010 (shift to the left in the bottom left quadrant). This movement corresponds to the incorporation of working-class electorates whose preferences are also located in the bottom left quadrant, as per Figure 2.2.

Figure 4.4 maps the dynamics of class-based support in Poland using the Alford Index (the working-class minus the professional-class vote share for a given party) for major Polish parties. I used data from the Comparative Study

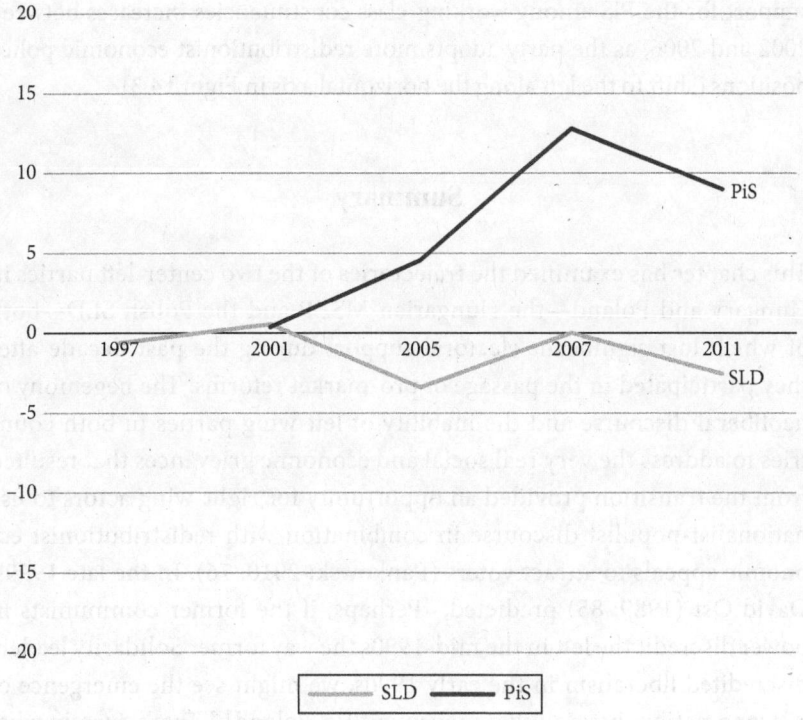

**Figure 4.4** The Index (% party vote among the working class) – (% party vote among the professional class) for the left SLD and the populist right PiS.
*Source:* Comparative Study of the Electoral System.

of the Electoral System (CSES) data set, which was available for the following years: 1997, 2001, 2005, 2007, and 2011. The CSES data set allows for classifying respondents as working-class based on their occupational status (e.g., "main occupation: worker"). The variable, recorded as a dummy, takes a value of "1" for all of the physical work/labor–related occupations and "0" for other occupations. Party choice is coded based on the variable "vote choice—party list—first mention," which reports the respondent's vote choice for the party list.

Comparing[28] party positions in Figure 4.3 with the dynamic of class-based support in Figure 4.4, one notices a pattern of change in line with the aforementioned dynamic. As the SLD shifts further to the right along the economic policy dimension between 2002 and 2006 (Figure 4.3), its support among working-class electorates significantly decreases (Figure 4.4). Accordingly,

---

[28] CSES data availability limited the analysis to the period between 1997 and 2011.

support for the PiS among working-class constituencies increases between 2002 and 2006, as the party adopts more redistributionist economic policy positions (shift to the left along the horizontal axis in Figure 4.3).

## Summary

This chapter has examined the trajectories of the two center-left parties in Hungary and Poland—the Hungarian MSZP and the Polish SLD—both of which lost significant electoral support during the past decade after they participated in the passage of pro-market reforms. The hegemony of neoliberal discourse and the inability of left-wing parties in both countries to address the very real social and economic grievances that resulted from the transition provided an opportunity for right-wing actors to use nationalist-populist discourse in combination with redistributionist economic appeals to attract voters (Pankowski 2010: 76). In the late 1990s, David Ost (1989: 85) predicted, "Perhaps, if the former communists in power discredit the left in the mid-1990s the way former Solidarity leaders discredited liberalism in the early 1990s, we might see the emergence of a strong nationalist populist movement [in Poland]." That's exactly what happened in both countries. Since the left did not seek the votes of the socially excluded, the populist right did it instead. Subsequently, in Hungary and Poland populist right parties capitalized on antireform sentiments and lured away sizable shares of working-class voters, which dealigned from the left.

This chapter has demonstrated that in Hungary the adoption of pro-market economic policies by the ex-communist MSZP party in 1996 and during 2006 and 2009 opened up an opportunity for populist parties to challenge it with a more redistributionist economic agenda and to appeal to reform losers. This launched the process of political realignment, which led to working-class voters becoming the main constituency of the populist right. Following Hungary's accession to the EU, populist right parties were less inhibited in their criticism of neoliberalism. Subsequently, they incorporated many former MSZP supporters who abandoned the party after it had introduced vastly unpopular austerity policies during the late 2000s. I traced this complex dynamic across individual-level data in Hungary by showing how, over time, the support by Hungary's working-class became less associated with the center-left MSZP and increasingly associated with the populist right parties Fidesz and Jobbik.

The Polish case demonstrates dynamics similar to the Hungarian case. The implementation of pro-market reforms by the ex-communist left SLD party between 1993 and 1997, and again in 2003, led to the gradual decline of working-class support. This provided Polish populist right parties with a prime opportunity to attract Poles frustrated with the losses resulting from the economic transition by using a combination of nativist and redistributionist economic appeals. Eventually, this led to the increasing incorporation of working-class voters by the PiS. The analysis of this case study was complemented with individual-level data that confirmed that over time support of the Polish working-class constituencies became increasingly associated with the PiS and negatively associated with the ex-communist left SLD.

Notably, as the cases of Hungary and Poland have demonstrated, the major decline in left parties' approval in both instances followed the introduction of unpopular neoliberal reforms involving severe budget cuts. Subsequently these trends were further exacerbated by corruption and other scandals. In this sense, while other factors further deepened the electoral breakdown of reformist parties, the major blow was delivered specifically by the implementation of the unpopular reforms.

Additionally, the chapter has shown that in both instances the electoral success of the populist right preceded the unraveling of the 2015 immigration crisis in part thanks to its successful incorporation of the leftist economic platform and large swaths of former left parties' electorates. In the Hungarian case the rise of Fidesz and Jobbik took place in 2010 following the demise of the MSZP. In the Polish case, PiS presidential candidate Duda won the presidential elections in May 2015 when the refugee inflow was still fairly low. While in both instances the immigration crisis gave these parties an additional boost, the major realignment of supporters between the left and right parties unraveled prior to the 2015 immigration crisis.

Importantly, the results (Figures 4.2 and 4.4) demonstrate that in both Hungary and Poland the differences in the voting of blue-collar workers versus professionals, while significant, are not as pronounced (around 10 to 12 percentage points). This finding suggests that while working-class voters have shown a greater propensity to support populist right parties over reformist left parties, one cannot talk of populist right parties as strictly working class. This conclusion is generally consistent with the catch-all nature of these parties: they tend to compete for various electorates, while, as this book argues, incorporating larger swaths of working-class supporters previously dealigned from left parties. Another implication of this finding is that beyond the watering down of the left's economic profile, other factors should have contributed to the populist right's skyrocketing success across the region (see the book's conclusion for further discussion).

# 5
# When Left Stays Left, Right Stays Small

The previous chapter demonstrated that when ex-communist left parties embraced painful pro-market reforms and ignored the interests of economically vulnerable electorates, they ignited the realignment process in their respective party systems. Subsequently, populist right parties incorporated large chunks of the electorates that previously supported left-wing parties. This chapter examines the opposite phenomenon: two countries where leftist parties remained more faithful to their traditional economic positions and thus retained the support of their traditional constituencies over the analyzed period.

In contrast to their pragmatic and reform-minded Polish and Hungarian counterparts, Communist Party elites in Czechoslovakia were more orthodox and traditional due to the legacy of the post–Prague Spring normalization (Williams 1997). As a result, communist successor parties in both the Czech Republic and Slovakia took a more orthodox stance on political and economic transitions. This might be one reason why in both countries major leftist parties remained generally faithful to their traditional economic positions throughout the analyzed period.[1]

The legacy of tripartism in both the Czech Republic and Slovakia is another possible reason why left parties may have remained loyal to the interests of working-class electorates. Tripartism, a partnership between the government, employer associations, and labor organizations regulating individual and collective labor relations between employers and employees, was originally introduced during the late Czechoslovak period. After the breakup of Czechoslovakia, the separate tripartite bodies in both countries evolved primarily as consultative mechanisms bringing together the unions and the government (Myant, Slocock, and Smith 2000: 736).

[1] But while in the Slovak case there were discussions and seminars organized by the Institute for Marxism-Leninism, where those with nonconforming opinions were invited, general normalization was harsher in the Czech case. This explains the more orthodox orientation of the Czech Communist Party.

*When Left Moves Right.* Maria Snegovaya, Oxford University Press. © Oxford University Press 2024. DOI: 10.1093/oso/9780197699027.003.0006

The left's faithfulness to its traditional platform and base, in turn, helps explain the limited electoral success of populist right parties until the 2015 refugee crisis unraveled. This chapter begins with the case of the Czech Republic. It starts with the Czech KSČM, a left party that preserved traditional leftist economic policy positions and succeeded in promoting policies favorable to workers. Such policies helped to keep Czech working-class voters on the left side of the political spectrum, and left fewer disgruntled constituents for the populist right to mobilize politically. As a result, there were fewer political opportunities for populist right parties in the Czech Republic than there were for right-wing parties in Hungary and Poland. This chapter also examines the case of Slovakia, where one left party, the Party of the Democratic Left (Strana demokratickej ľavice, SDĽ), took part in neoliberal economic reforms during EU accession, while the other, Smer, adopted a more redistributionist left platform. This chapter shows that the SDĽ lost its supporters and disappeared, while Smer-SD (Smer absorbed the SDĽ in 2005) was able to attract working-class voters and limit the share of the electorate available for mobilization by the populist right Slovak National Party (Slovenská národná strana, SNS). This strategy helped Smer-SD win several elections from 2006 until 2016.

For comparative purposes, to match the time period analyzed in Chapter 4, this chapter primarily focuses on the posttransition period preceding the 2015 European refugee crisis. Using quantitative survey evidence, I demonstrate that in both the Czech Republic and Slovakia left-wing parties maintained their programmatic commitments to redistributionist pro-labor policies. This loyalty to working-class constituencies ensured lasting support from those groups and resulted in the preservation of more traditional party alignments throughout the analyzed period.

## Czech Republic

KSČM was the direct heir to the Communist Party of Czechoslovakia, which ruled the country between 1948 until 1989. Unlike in Hungary, where the 1956 revolution resulted in victory for a pro-reformist communist wing, in Czechoslovakia the 1968 revolution, known as the Prague Spring, resulted in the party purging its reformist wing from the apparatus. The cadres who remained in the party were rigid, ossified, and resistant to programmatic change (Stolarik 2016).

Hence, unlike many other parties in the region, KSČM did not embark on democratic reforms during the democratization period. Instead, its posttransition image continued to project remnants of its past (Hanley 2001). The party leadership even opted to keep the label "communist" in the party—unlike the majority of ex-communist parties, which chose to change their names to "social democratic" (Lach et al. 2010). KSČM has, ultimately, remained one of "the least social democratized and least organizationally like other European left parties" (Ishiyama 2006: 24).

Several factors explain KSČM's ability to survive in a relatively unchanged state. One factor is that the party preserved the majority of its membership throughout the transition, while other ex-communist parties preserved very little. By the early 1990s, elites who had retained many of their very rigid and anti-reform-oriented cadres and had little experience negotiating with society, were leading KSČM (Grzymala-Busse 2002b: 55). Meanwhile, its reform wing was still relatively weak from the 1968 purge. Another factor is that, given its own post-1968 legacy, KSČM was concerned that taking on a social democratic identity would disrupt its existing support base without bringing new constituents. Yet another is that KSČM's inability to move closer to the political center was also a consequence of a boycott from the mainstream parties, which tried to punish KSČM for its communist past while avoiding forming coalitions and alliances with it. This contributed to the preservation of KSČM's antiestablishment and ideologically conservative platform. In the long run, this pariah status proved to be quite beneficial electorally. Because KSČM had not participated in the government, it could claim outsider status by projecting the image of a uniquely "clean" party in an otherwise corrupt political system (Lach et al. 2010: 369).[2]

Over the years, KSČM adopted a platform reminiscent of those used by populist right parties in other countries: protectionist on the economic dimension, Euroskeptic and nationalist on the sociocultural dimension (Kopecký 2006; Havlík 2014). Its platform portrayed its constituency in broad populist terms as "working people" (*lidé práce*) and "social groups who derive their living from the results of honest work, in either the past or the present, and from deserved social benefits . . . industrial and agricultural workers . . . farmers in transformed co-operatives . . . and other employees,

[2] In more recent years KSČM has more actively collaborated with established parties, which helps explain its subsequent drop in support. After the 2012 regional elections, the party started a ruling coalition with the ČSSD in ten regions. It has also provided parliamentary support to Andrej Babiš's second cabinet (Brabec 2019). See also note 3.

small businesspeople, the self-employed and socially weak and threatened groups such as young people, pensioners and women" (Hanley 2001: 108). The party contrasted these "good people" with the exploitative forces of capitalism that existentially threatened and pushed them out "to the margins of society and offer[ed] no real chance of change" (Hanley 2001: 108). KSČM (2009) portrayed European integration as "capitalist" and "neoliberal," undermining the living conditions of citizens and not devoting sufficient attention to social issues. It promised to help the "working people" by creating new jobs, increasing social protection, fighting unemployment, and improving conditions for young, disabled, and elderly people.

On the sociocultural dimension, KSČM opposed Czech accession into "the US- and Germany-dominated" NATO and was critical of the European integration process. In particular, it criticized the Lisbon Treaty,[3] calling it a threat to Czech state sovereignty that led to the exploitation of Czech interests by multinational capitalist forces (see KSČM 2009; Kopecký and Mudde 2002: 307).

In other words, KSČM's Party Manifesto combined redistributionist and nationalist appeals (Lach et al. 2010: 376; KSČM 2006, 2010, 2013).[4] These policy stances made KSČM largely a protest party able to preserve relatively orthodox positions on economic issues and to attract the support of working-class electorates, reform losers, and those dissatisfied with the status quo (Stegmaier and Vlachova 2009). Between 1989 and 2012, KSČM consistently gained 10% to 20% of the vote in parliamentary elections. While KSČM sought to represent a broader electorate of "working people," its support was skewed more toward older and retired voters, residents of rural areas and small towns, police and army employees, and localities with historic traditions of communist voting (Hanley 2001; Hanley and House 2004). Studies conducted in the mid-2010s found that support for KSČM strongly correlated to being from regions with high levels of unemployment and crime, as well as being dissatisfied with the functioning of democracy and distrusting official institutions (Lach et al. 2010; Linek 2008; Stegmaier and Vlachova 2009: 808–810).[5]

---

[3] Lisbon Treaty is a set of treaties forming the EU constitutional basis.

[4] KSČM's platform remained fairly socially liberal on gender equality and LGBTQ issues, which distinguished it from typical populist right party platforms.

[5] In the 1990s it was popular among commentators to assume that KSČM would perish in isolation after its voters died off. This argument was supported by empirical data showing that KSČM voters tended to be older than the Czech population in general. Yet until 2017 the party's electoral share proved remarkably stable over time (Linek 2008). In 2013, it ended up winning its second-highest share of the vote ever (Stolarik 2016).

Another Czech left party, the Czech Social Democratic Party (Česká strana sociálně demokratická, ČSSD), included many dissidents pushed out of the Communist Party after the Prague Spring. Early on, ČSSD leadership also included trade unionists who saw the party as a vehicle to provide a new voice for the labor movement (Sil 2017: 433). While some ČSSD members supported the ideas of the Third Way, the party tended to lean toward more traditional leftist economic policies. Unlike their Polish and Hungarian counterparts, the Czech social democrats differed from the right primarily on the socioeconomic dimension (Doyle and Fidrmuc 2003; Hlousek and Kopecek 2008: 24–25; Bakke and Sitter 2021). From the start, ČSSD's platform emphasized a mixed economy, a strong welfare state, progressive taxation, and European integration. For example, the party's 1992 program committed to the support of free education, free healthcare, and a pension system without the responsibility of individual pension contributions (Cabada 2010: 85–87).

In 1992, the right-wing alliance between the Civic Democratic Party (Občanská demokratická strana, ODS), led by Václav Klaus, and the Christian Democratic Party gained the majority of votes; it launched a privatization program and the process toward European integration. This contributed to the formation of the socioeconomic cleavage in the Czech Republic (Kitschelt et al. 1999: 226–231, 244–260; Hlousek and Kopecek 2008: 10). The main policy issues concerning this division included wealth redistribution, state regulation, and public welfare (Linek 2015: 4). Once the right-wing government started to cut welfare provisions, ČSSD and KSČM successfully attacked those reforms, portraying themselves as the defenders of welfare, labor-protective legislation, and pensioners (Kraus 2003). ČSSD (led by Miloš Zeman since 1993) strove to build a noncommunist left alternative to the hegemony of the right ODS (Kopeček and Pšeja 2008). It criticized the specific form of transformation chosen by the right-wing government and exploited KSČM's orthodox-communist background to position itself as the only acceptable party for voters dissatisfied with the outcomes of economic transition.[6]

---

[6] In 1994 Zeman refused to implement the Third Way–style "pragmatic shift" to the center of the political spectrum offered by his consultant Oto Novotný and intended to help the party appeal to the middle class (Kopeček and Pšeja 2008).

## Stability of Alignments

Throughout the analyzed period, the division between left and right on the economic dimension became the main cleavage in Czech politics (Hlousek and Kopecek 2008: 10), and its effects on Czech party alignment have remained stable or increased slightly over time (Smith and Matějů 2011; Linek and Lyons 2013). KSČM and ČSSD criticized numerous aspects of the pro-market reforms chosen by the right-wing government and advocated for increased social protections. These divisions corresponded to class-based choices, separating left-wing parties (the traditional left KSČM and the center-left ČSSD) from the liberal and right-wing parties (ODS, Christian Democratic Party (Křesťanskodemokraticka strana, KDS), Občanská demokratická aliance (ODA), TOP09). Already in late 1993 reform losers started to flock to ČSSD (Doyle and Fidrmuc 2003). In the 1996 election Matějů and Řeháková (1997: 530) discovered the formation of class-based voting with working classes moving toward the left-wing parties more than other economically active groups. By then ČSSD, which started as a fairly marginal party in the elections of 1990 and 1992, nearly caught up with ODS in the 1996 election and eventually surpassed it in 1998 (Doyle and Fidrmuc 2003:12).[7]

Class-based voting remained stable in the Czech Republic for almost two decades. Linek (2015) demonstrated a strong and consistent association between belonging to a specific social group and the corresponding right/left party choice between 1990 and 2013. Right-wing parties received more support among entrepreneurs and professionals, and less support among manual workers and retired people. By contrast, throughout this period support for the left parties ČSSD and KSČM was the strongest among working-class supporters and retired individuals (Strmiska 2002; Snegovaya 2018b).

The existence of a viable left alternative ensured the preservation of the more traditional positioning of parties along the left-right economic scale and curtailed the growth of populist right-wing parties in the Czech Republic. This became quite visible in the 1998 election, when the re-formist government of right-wing parties (ODS, ODA, and Christian and Democratic Union – Czechoslovak People's Party (Křesťanská a demokratická

---

[7] According to Libor Rouček (in discussion with the author, July 2022), who at the time was a spokesman for the Zeman government, the ČSSD benefited from having come to power not at the onset of reforms but later, in 1998, when the major bulk of reforms were already implemented by previous right-wing coalition.

unie—Československá strana lidová (KDU-ČSL)) in Parliament faced opposition from more redistribution-oriented parties: two left-wing parties (ČSSD and KSČM) and the right-wing Republican Party of Czechoslovakia (SPR-RSČ). Founded in 1989, SPR-RSČ made it to the Czech Parliament in 1996 with 8% of the vote. A significant part of SPR-RSČ's identity was formed by the populist appeal of accusing the "governmental garniture" of "stealing the revolution" or "stealing national property" and presenting itself as a defender of the interests of "common men" (Havlík and Pinková 2021: 12, 114). This rhetoric helped the party attract significant shares of votes from economically vulnerable groups, including workers, employees without tertiary education, the unemployed, and residents from the regions with high levels of unemployment. Almost one in eight manual workers voted for the Republicans in 1996, and this group comprised about one-third of SPR-RSČ voters in total. About two-thirds of the party's voters have completed only elementary school or attended a trade program which did not grant diplomas (Havlík and Pinková 2021: 119).

However, in the 1998 election ČSSD and KSČM were able to successfully incorporate significant shares of SPR-RSČ supporters into their electorates by presenting themselves as more electorally viable left-wing alternatives (Kreidl et al. 2000: 87). The incorporation of significant shares of SPR-RSČ supporters was possible due to a programmatic similarity between SPR-RSČ and left-wing party platforms. Kreidl et al. (2000: 80) estimate that two-thirds of SPR-RSČ voters named left-wing parties as their second choice in 1998. ČSSD was the most popular, with 37%, and KSČM the next most popular, with 19.1%. As left-wing parties incorporated substantive shares of former SPR-RSČ supporters, the SPR-RSČ failed to get into the 1998 Parliament and remained on the margins of the Czech political system.

Similarly, the existence of a viable left alternative helped counterbalance the ČSSD's pro-market shift. It would not take long for KSČM to attract voters who previously supported ČSSD, which campaigned on pledges to build an extensive welfare state and increase wages in 1998, but walked back on these promises once in power. After entering Parliament, ČSSD reached an agreement (the so-called Opposition Agreement) with the second largest center-right party, ODS, in hopes of limiting the influence of small parties and to facilitate government formation. The Opposition Agreement resulted in policy convergence between center-left and center-right parties. In an effort to ensure EU accession, the new government formulated and carried out an extensive program of reforms and legislative acts to speed up the full adjustment of the Czech Republic in anticipation of the 2003–2004 entry date

(Kopecký and Mudde 2002). The ruling coalition continued the privatization of state companies, eschewed social reforms, and in 2001 attempted fiscal consolidation. As a result of this pro-market move, KSČM was able to lure away a significant percentage of former ČSSD voters. It presented itself as the protest alternative and criticized European integration (Kopeček and Pšeja 2008). In the 2002 election, KSČM won 18.5% of the vote—improving its 1998 election outcome by 7.5 percentage points. In the same election, it also gained more than 200,000 votes and seventeen additional seats. Meanwhile, ČSSD lost more than 400,000 votes, winning only 30.2% of the total share (Stegmaier and Vlachova 2009).[8]

Yet again in the mid-2000s, the existence of KSČM as a viable left-wing alternative helped preserve traditional party alignments. In the midst of the ČSSD's centrist shift, in 2003 the populist right Czech Workers' Party (DSSS) emerged, attempting to steal voters who had grown frustrated with ČSSD policies. DSSS was founded in 2002 by Tomáš Vandas, who was the former treasurer of SPR-RSČ. The DSSS adopted a KSČM-like redistributionist platform catering specifically to working-class voters. However, it consistently failed to mobilize enough support to make it to Parliament (Vachudova 2008a; Mareš 2011).

Throughout the 2000s, both KSČM and ČSSD collaborated with Czech unions, such as the Bohemian-Moravian Confederation of Trade Unions (ČMKOS), and often voted together on issues relevant to Czech labor. This created a more pro-labor climate than in Hungary or Poland (Ost 1998; Orenstein 2000; Sil 2017). A convergence in positions of labor and left-wing parties was sustained through direct policy consultations with trade unions, ČSSD's strong links to ČMKOS, whose members constituted a sizable portion of its electorate, as well as frequent movement of key leaders between ČMKOS and ČSSD. For example, Milan Štěch, the ČMKOS chairman in 2002–2010, served as a ČSSD senator and became president of the Senate in 2008. Similarly, Jaroslav Zavadil, chairman of ČMKOS in 2010–2013, was elected on the ČSSD ticket to the Czech Chamber of Deputies. In the 2006 election the analysis of party manifestos by ČMKOS concluded that on key issues of relevance to workers—including wage policy, employment law, and collective bargaining—the union's preferences aligned closer with

---

[8] In this sense, the role of the KSČM is similar to that of the left party die Linke in Germany, which for a while was able to capture a sizable share of the vote in Germany's postcommunist East, where grievances related to the injustices of the transformation period constituted one of its bread-and-butter issues (Kim 2017; Hilmar 2022).

the stances of ČSSD and KSČM than those of any other party in the Czech Republic (Myant 2010: 27; Sil 2017: 433). According to Jana Maláčová (in discussion with the author, July 2022), who was the minister of labor and social affairs in the Czech Republic in 2018–2021, the main social policy achievements by the Czech left were the valorization of pensions, an increase in the minimum wage, general improvement in working conditions, family support, protection of the public health system, and prevention of neoliberal pension reform in 2011.[9]

The pro-labor orientation of left-wing parties proved favorable to Czech labor during debates over the Labor Code. During the ČSSD-led government of 2002–2006 the ČSSD and KSČM jointly worked on revisions to the Labor Code and other pieces of legislation in coordination with ČMKOS (Hlousek and Kopecek 2008: 24–26). When after the 2006 election a new right-wing coalition attempted additional revisions to the just amended Labor Code, organized labor and the left-wing parties quickly joined forces to ensure the preservation of worker-friendly provisions in the Code (Sil 2017: 434).

Overall, the presence of viable left-wing alternatives throughout the 1990s and 2000s helped push more pro-labor and redistributionist policies, strengthened Czech workers' support for the left, and preserved party alignments more consistent with traditional left/right divides throughout the analyzed time period. Jiri Pehe (in discussion with the author, July 2022), formerly an advisor to President Václav Havel, agrees that was one of the main reasons behind the stability of political alignments for a period after 1989: "The right parties, such as Civic Democratic Party of Václav Klaus, were promoting conservative ideas and economic neoliberalism, while the left was embracing policies more consistent with traditional left positions."[10] Empirical studies have shown that the presence of the communist and social democratic parties in the system has limited the opportunities available for populist parties for a while. For example, Voda and Havlík (2021) have demonstrated that the presence of KSČM and ČSSD until the mid-2010s inhibited populist parties from utilizing the issues of rising unemployment and distrust, as these conditions were already successfully used by the left parties.

[9] Jana Malacová was the minister of labor and social affairs in the Czech Republic in the Babiš government 2018–2021. Between March 2019 and December 2021 she was also deputy chairperson of the ČSSD.
[10] Jiri Pehe was the director of the political cabinet in the office of President Havel in 1997–1999 and continued serving as his external political advisor until the end of Havel's term in 2003.

Thus, the limited success of the Czech populist right was conditioned by the setting of the party system in general, and the strategies of left parties in particular. This cleavage structure helped stabilize the system, with the right dominated by the ODS and the left by ČSSD.

## Individual-Level Surveys

Between 1998 and 2010 the Czech electoral competition was characterized by the classic left-right model of political competition, with two main parties on the right (ODS) and on the left (ČSSD) rotating in power. Since the elections of 1996, the ODS and the ČSSD together regularly received over half of the votes, with a maximum of 67.07% in 2006 (Maškarinec 2019). The economic-redistributive divides during that time sustained the existing major political cleavage: voters in the top 10th percentile of income in the Czech Republic consistently voted more for the right than voters in the bottom 90th percentile of income. The opposite was true for ČSSD-KSČM (Lindner et al. 2020). Traditional left-wing parties had their party support bases in peripheral and socioeconomically disadvantageous regions (Lysek, Pánek, and Lebeda 2021).

To illustrate the stability of the Czech cleavages, Figure 5.1 depicts the structure of political competition in the Czech Republic using the Chapel Hill data set on the positions of national political parties in 2002–2010 along the economic and sociocultural dimensions of political competition. Figure 5.1 shows that throughout the analyzed period KSČM consistently occupied the bottom-left quadrant. with some variation along the sociocultural (vertical) dimension. This position corresponds to the preferences of working-class electorates per Figure 2.2. At the same time, the positions of the ČSSD are also pro-redistribution-oriented throughout the analyzed period.

To demonstrate the dynamic of class-based support in the Czech Republic, Figure 5.2 plots the Alford Index (the working-class minus the professional-class vote share for a given party) for Czech left-wing parties. The data from the CSES data set are used for this purpose, available in the Czech case for the following years: 1996, 2002, 2006, 2010, and 2013.

Figure 5.2 illustrates a dynamic consistent with the above argument. Working-class status is positively associated with votes for Czech left parties over time, as both KSČM and ČSSD occupy fairly redistributive economic positions corresponding to the preferences of working-class electorates. This finding is in line with this book's theoretical expectations: the preservation

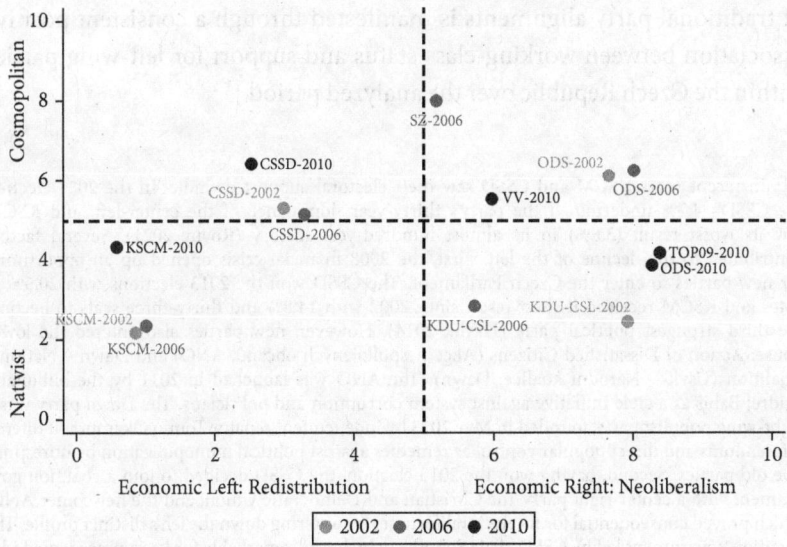

**Figure 5.1** Structure of Party Competition in the Czech Republic in the 2002, 2006, and 2010 elections.

*Source*: Chapel Hill Expert Survey.

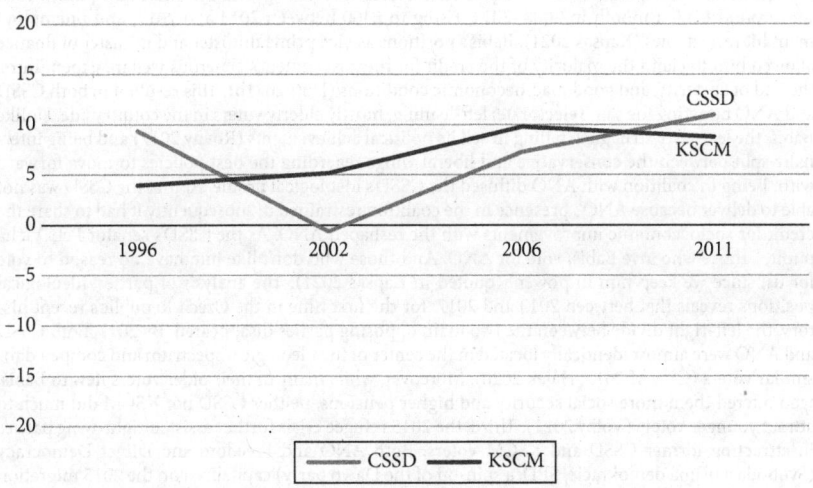

**Figure 5.2** The Index (% party vote among working class) – (% party vote among professional class) for the left ČSSD and KSČM.

*Source*: Comparative Study of the Electoral System.

of traditional party alignments is manifested through a consistent positive association between working-class status and support for left-wing parties within the Czech Republic over the analyzed period.[11]

[11] In recent years KSČM and ČSSD saw their electoral support dwindle. In the 2021 election the ČSSD's 4.7% undermined the party's thirty-year dominance of the center-left, and KSČM saw its worst result (3.6%) in its almost hundred-year history (Rovny 2021). Several factors contributed to the decline of the left. First, the 2008 financial crisis opened up an opportunity for new parties to enter the Czech Parliament. The ČSSD won the 2013 elections with 20.5% of votes and KSČM received its best result since 2002 with 14.8% and thirty-three seats to become the third strongest political party (Havlík 2014). However, new parties also entered the lower house: Action of Dissatisfied Citizens (Akce nespokojených občanů, ANO) and Dawn – National Coalition (Úsvit – Národní koalice, Dawn). The ANO was launched in 2011 by the billionaire Andrej Babiš as a civic initiative against system corruption and politicians. The Dawn party was a right-wing populist party, founded in May 2013 by independent senator Tomio Okamura. It offered referendums and direct popular control as remedies against political monopolization by unresponsive old parties. Second, having won the 2013 election, the ČSSD decided to join a coalition government with a center-right party, the Christian and Democratic Union, and the newcomer ANO, which proved consequential for its electoral fortunes by watering down the left's distinct profile. The coalition government led by ČSSD chair Sobotka, which was remarkable for its unprecedented ideological diversity, appointed Babiš as its first deputy prime minister and finance minister. At that time ANO held a broadly center-right agenda with pro-market positions on the economy and neutral positions on sociocultural issues (Hanley and Vachudova 2018) and attracted most of its support from voters on the right side of the spectrum (Prokešová 2016). However, since 2015 ANO has adopted a much more left-leaning economic agenda in government, while borrowing some ideas from the ČSSD platform. The government took measures to help those hit hardest by the financial crisis, such as lower-paid workers and pensioners. Salaries went up with the minimum wage, which was around €300 a month in 2008–2014, rising to €400 between 2014 and 2017, and unemployment hit record lows (Kapsas 2021). Babiš's positions as vice prime minister and minister of finance allowed him to claim the majority of the credit for the government's generous welfare expenditure, the end of austerity, and good macroeconomic conditions (Hutt 2021b). This resulted in both ČSSD and ANO targeting the same electorate: left-leaning, mostly elderly voters in the countryside. Unlike Babiš, the left party struggled, failing to sell its political achievements (Rovny 2017) and being internally split between the conservative and liberal wings regarding the best policies to move forward with. Being in coalition with ANO diffused the ČSSD's ideological profile. At first the ČSSD was not able to deliver because ANO's presence in the coalition restrained it; subsequently it had to share the credit for socioeconomic improvements with the reshaped ANO. As the ČSSD's senator Petr Vícha put it, "Those who love Babiš, vote for ANO. And those who don't like him have no reason to vote for us, since we keep him in power" (quoted in Kapsas 2021). The analysis of parties' ideological positions reveals that between 2013 and 2017, for the first time in the Czech Republic's recent history, the left-right divide between the two main opposing parties disappeared. By 2017, both ČSSD and ANO were almost identically located in the center of the ideological spectrum and competed for similar voters (CVVM 2017; Hájek 2020). Moreover, while many of their older voters flew to Babiš, who offered them more social security and higher pensions, neither ČSSD nor KSČM did much to attract younger voters (Volby 2021). Third, the 2015 refugee crisis further assisted right-wing parties in attracting former ČSSD and KSČM voters. Both ANO and Freedom and Direct Democracy (Svoboda a přímá demokracie, SPD, a spin-off of the Dawn party) capitalized on the 2015 migration crisis that they portrayed as a security threat to the country. Babiš repeatedly accused international institutions, like the EU, of their inability to resolve the crisis and argued for migration policy to be retained strictly in national hands (Strapáčová and Hloušek 2018). The SPD held the strongest anti-immigrant views, describing immigrants in xenophobic terms as "uneducated and nonworking individuals abusing the social system" who threatened to take away local jobs (Strapáčová and Hloušek 2018: 19; Kim 2017). The ČSSD and KSČM used a much more moderate language on the refugee crisis. As the 2017 election approached, the ČSSD tried to take tougher stances on migration (Mortkowitz 2017; Wondreys 2021), but it was too late. The 2017 election showed a dramatic shift of voters, with ANO attracting chunks of former electorates of the social democrats and, to a lesser

## Slovakia

Following the dissolution of Czechoslovakia in 1992, the People's Party–Movement for a Democratic Slovakia (Ľudová strana–Hnutie za demokratické Slovensko, HZDS) ruled the country until 1998 (with a short break in 1994). The HZDS, led by Vladimír Mečiar, featured many former Communist Party members. Throughout this period, Slovakia's political system was considered nondemocratic and the economy remained largely unreformed (Potucek and Radicova 1997). Analysts have found it difficult to locate HZDS on the left-right spectrum. Most classify it as a right-wing conservative-leaning party, despite its rather unclear political program and ideological identity (Haughton 2001: 748).

The second-largest party in the Slovak political system at the time was the formerly communist Party of the Democratic Left (Strana Demokratickej Lavice, SDĽ). The SDĽ was formed in 1990 out of the remnants of the Communist Party of Slovakia. As a rump of disaffected hardline politicians left to form a new Communist Party of Slovakia (Komunistická strana Slovenska, KSS) in 1991 under the leadership of the young reformists from the Institute of Marxism-Leninism in Bratislava, Peter Weiss and Pavol

extent, KSČM. The party's rise was achieved predominantly at the expense of decreasing support for both leftist parties, which each lost more than half of their voters: the ČSSD vote fell to 7.3%, and KSČM to 7.8%. Polls have demonstrated that up to 40% of former ČSSD voters switched to ANO, which also attracted many former communist voters (ČTK 2018; Horký 2021). Spatial analysis of the 2017 elections shows high support for ANO and Dawn/SPD in traditionally leftist strongholds, such as northwestern Bohemia and northern and northeastern Moravia (Maškarinec 2019; Lysek, Pánek, and Lebeda 2021; Suchánek and Hasman 2022). Despite having suffered dramatic losses, the ČSSD again joined the minority government of Babiš (but this time as a junior partner). This continued to erode the party's distinct profile. KSČM also received a lot of criticism from its core supporters for agreeing in 2018 to informally back Babiš's minority government (Hutt 2021b). As Libor Rouček (in discussion with the author, July 2022) points out, "The communists had presented for one hundred years their ideology as a fight against capitalists, especially big capitalists.... And at the end, one hundred years later, they supported the biggest capitalist in the country. Lenin must be turning around in his grave!" Presenting social policy achievements as a consequence of Babiš's personal interventions helped ANO siphon off even more voters from the left-wing parties (Hutt 2021a), while the left-wing parties have been unable to distance themselves from the "Babiš question" and to present a clear vision of the leftist policies that they would want to implement (Kapsas 2021). In the 2021 election both the ČSSD and KSČM recorded their worst ever results and failed to make it to the lower chamber for the first time since the dissolution of Czechoslovakia in 1993. Overall, while stability of the Czech party system throughout the 1990s and 2000s was to a large extent conditioned by left parties' ability to incorporate support for their traditional electorates using redistributive appeals, it was undermined by the ČSSD's and KSČM's decision to support a coalition with ANO, which watered down these parties' distinct profile. (This is consistent with literature on parties' brand dilution, e.g., Nissan and Carter 2005; Lupu 2014, 2016; Bagashka, Bodea, and Han 2022; Lynch 2019.) The immigration crisis, which increased the salience of the sociocultural issues, further benefited the right parties while eroding the left. By combining nativist positions with increasingly redistributive pledges, the right-wing ANO and SPD have been able to incorporate significant chunks of former left parties' electorates.

Kanis, the SDĽ distanced itself from the hardline Czech communists. The party adopted a social democratic path rebranding itself as the Party of the Democratic Left (Žiak 1996; Haughton and Rybář 2004). Many SDĽ members, hoping to see the party modulate from a former communist party into a Western European–style social democratic party, maintained active contact with the Socialist International (an organization SDĽ aspired to join) (Haughton 2002: 1321). The party professed its allegiance to the "model of European society implemented in the West" and its support for "political orientations manifested in the Socialist International" (Handl and Leška 2014: 112). Its platform, which most closely resembled a Western European social democratic party, stressed pragmatism, commitment to democracy, equality of opportunity, and social justice market reform. Throughout the 1990s the SDĽ avoided joining the government of the HZDS (Deegan-Krause 2006).

During the early 1990s, public opinion polls in Slovakia showed a sizable preference for redistribution and state regulation of the economy, a legacy of the communist regime, with the majority of the population (75–90%) supporting guaranteed jobs and housing for each family, state regulation of prices (Butora and Butorova 1993: 725). Given societal preferences, throughout this period the HZDS and the SDĽ programs had strong similarities. HZDS emphasized the "social aspect" of the market (Haughton 2004; Williams 2000: 4–8) and played the nationalist card, claiming that privatization primarily benefited foreign interests while destroying vital Slovak industries in the process (Mahr and Nagle 1995: 405). The leftist and rightist elements in the HZDS program combined with a dose of national protectionism allowed it to sustain a fairly mixed support base. HZDS drew voter support from across the social spectrum, but—largely due to its reluctance to launch in-depth reforms—was more successful in attracting votes from the group of reform losers (the unemployed, the retired, and blue-collar and agricultural workers) than reform winners (private entrepreneurs, white-collar workers, university-educated people) (Haughton 2001: 760).

As in the Czech case, Slovakia maintained its tripartite institutions throughout this period (Ost 2000: 103). Under the Mečiar government, negotiations "approached the form of a distinct mode of governance, at least in relation to industrial relations and public policies" (Myant, Slocock, and Smith 2000: 733). The Mečiar government actively sought unions' opinions on the legislation it was considering and was able to compromise with them on a number of crucial issues concerning labor laws, the incorporation of fundamental international conventions, and wage development (Bohle and Greskovits 2010: 354).

SDĽ emphasized solidarity, social justice, and the promotion of the health and economic well-being of working people. It called for privatization with as few social losses as possible. While SDĽ also attracted social groups reluctant to accept the economic transition (Hlousek and Kopecek 2008: 1549), the social groups skeptical about marketization and nostalgic for the communist era generally tended to support HZDS rather than SDĽ (Bútorová and Bútora 1993: 32; Evans and Whitefield 1998: 131; Haughton 2004: 183). The ability of HZDS to capture the support of a large percentage of groups most severely affected by economic transition, which would normally be expected to lean toward a party with a social democratic orientation, limited the growth of SDĽ's support base (Mahr and Nagle 1995: 405).

The absence of reforms delayed the formation of socioeconomic cleavages in Slovakia (Deegan-Krause 2006; O'Dwyer 2006). The real change in the Slovak political system came in the late 1990s. Throughout most of that decade, HZDS resisted any preparation for reforms necessary for European integration. Brigita Schmögnerová (in discussion with the author, June 2022), who became the SDĽ finance minister in the reformist government, explains that Slovakia was facing multiple economic problems: a wave of bankruptcies, very low domestic capital, and total lack of foreign capital; the results were persistent high unemployment, regional disparities, deterioration of the social situation, and macroeconomic instability.[12] Subsequently, Slovakia was not included in the 1997 Luxembourg group of EU candidates. In light of the EU's rejection of Slovakia's accession, many segments of civil society mobilized to bring reformist parties to power. Following the 1998 parliamentary election, despite HZDS winning a majority of votes yet again, pro-reform-oriented right-wing parties in alliance with ideologically diverse parties managed to create a broad pro-European coalition and to form a government (Haughton 2004: 186). SDĽ chose to join the coalition by presenting itself as a party of "technocrats and advocates of reform" in their newly formed cabinet (Vachudova 2008a: 391). Joining the EU thus provided the "focal point for cooperation" by giving an extra incentive to the anti-Mečiar

---

[12] Brigita Schmögnerová was the minister of finance in Slovakia from 1998 to 2002 under Prime Minister Mikuláš Dzurinda.

forces to coalesce and keeping the ideologically broad-based 1998–2002 government together (Vachudova 2005: 178).

Helped by the IMF and the World Bank, the new government, led by Prime Minister Mikuláš Dzurinda (1998–2002), implemented a series of public-sector reforms and wide-scale economic restructuring (Laursen and Sasin 2004). As a result, by the 2002 elections Slovakia had successfully asserted its fundamental commitments to markets and democracy (Vachudova 2005) and in 2004 was finally granted EU membership. While these policies attracted a lot of foreign investment, stabilized the economy, and launched structural reforms, they also, at least in the short run, restricted growth, increased unemployment, and fed public discontent, creating a strong opposition movement from the country's unions (CRS Report for Congress 2002). Dzurinda's government dismissed the unions as reform partners (O'Dwyer and Kovalcík 2007), which ended a tripartite bargaining system that had de facto existed in Slovakia since 1989. The radical and comprehensive public-sector reforms helped the country meet its Maastricht criteria, paving a way toward early Eurozone entry (Greskovits 2008: 286).

As the reforms were put in place, the ex-communist SDĽ found itself in the ambiguous position of being a left-wing party in a largely center-right government (Henderson 2002). The party's decision to take the finance portfolio during the reform years and therefore to become the public face of a painful economic restructuring decreased its overall popularity and exacerbated tensions within the party (Haughton 2004: 188). The most controversial case involved Finance Minister Schmögnerová, who was responsible for mar-ketization policies in the 1998–2002 government and was highly criticized for her reform-oriented austerity measures. When launching her economic package in May 1999, Schmögnerová argued that, like a surgeon who wants to save his patient "it is sometimes necessary to use a scalpel" (quoted in Leško 2000: 183). But voters disagreed: the socioeconomic difficulties, such as spiraling unemployment, that followed the reforms placed a heavy burden on the SDĽ, as its core constituencies were becoming dissatisfied with the party (Ishiyama and Bozóki 2001).

The SDĽ's participation in government and Schmögnerová's position as finance minister deepened internal tensions between the party's so-called modernizers and traditionalists. The traditionalists, who included the two successive leaders of SDĽ, Jozef Migaš and Pavol Koncoš, preferred more statist policies and criticized Schmögnerová for having advocated Third Way policies, comparing her to the Hungarian reformer Bokros or the Polish reformer Balzerowicz (Handl and Leška 2014: 114). The modernizers, who grouped around Weiss and Schmögnerová, wanted the party to become a mainstream social democratic party and were prepared to make the sacrifices needed to join NATO, OECD, and especially the EU (Haughton 2003: 79). As Schmögnerová explains in her July 2022 interview with me:

> Slovakia was in urgent need of macroeconomic stabilization to reduce the government's borrowing costs, to improve its country rating, and to attract foreign investors. Modernists within the SDĽ thus argued that modern leftism does not mean running budget deficits, increasing government debt, or looking for short-term solutions. Rather, they argued in favor of a social market economy with a strong social state that would aim at reducing social inequalities, provide social services of general interest, and favor social dialogue. SDĽ played a decisive role in breaking the deadlock in negotiations towards the EU and OECD. A major part of the chapters that needed to be closed before joining the EU could be approved were under the responsibility of the SDĽ ministers (finance, social affairs, and agriculture). As a result, Slovakia became an OECD member in 2000 and an EU member in 2004. However, the measures adopted to stabilize the economy had short-term negative consequences and were harmful to SDĽ's popularity.

In early 2002, in response to dissatisfaction with government policy, Koncoš (who was an elected leader in November 2001) called for Schmögnerová's dismissal. Despite Prime Minister Dzurinda's public defense of Schmögnerová, she ended up resigning from the government in February 2002, leading many representatives of the modernizers' group to leave the party and form the Social Democratic Alternative (Haughton 2003: 80). Internal divisions on the party's positioning vis-à-vis government policy were further exacerbated by several corruption scandals, which contributed to the dramatic decline in SDĽ support. Eventually, SDĽ lost the 2002 election by gaining only 1.4% of the vote and subsequently ended up merging with its splinter party, Smer-SD, in January 2005.[13]

The SDĽ's vote slump in the 2002 election contributed to gains for several parties. First, the hardline KSS gained parliamentary representation. While the KSS had failed to make any electoral breakthroughs in 1992, 1994,

---

[13] The Social Democratic Alternative was also unable to cross the 5% threshold in the 2002 elections.

or 1998, it won 6.3% of the vote in 2002. In its electoral campaign the KSS emphasized the poor macroeconomic conditions in Slovakia, such as the decline in industrial production and GDP, and growing unemployment, and offered a package of "first aid for Slovakia" and to defend Slovak interests in the face of globalization and European integration (Korba 2002: 37). Using this platform, the KSS benefited from more traditional SDĽ voters, who, fearing that their votes would be wasted following the SDĽ's implosion, switched to the KSS (Haughton 2003: 81; Haughton and Rybář 2004). By some estimates, about 13.8% of those who voted for the SDĽ in the 1998 elections shifted to the KSS in 2002 (Haughton 2003: 69).

Second, Smer (Smer–Sociálna Demokracia, Smer-SD since 2005, after it absorbed the SDĽ) had emerged back in 1999 as a breakaway from the SDĽ. It was founded by Robert Fico, the most popular SDĽ member at that time. The party's name (*smer* means "direction" in Slovak) sought to distinguish it from existing political camps of Slovak politics (Fico 2000; Haughton 2014). Until the 2002 election Fico's appeal was originally ideologically vague and even temporarily played with the language of the Third Way.[14]

However, the 2002 elections again brought to power a center-right coalition, which continued pro-market reforms until 2006. As the second Dzurinda government embarked on even harsher neoliberal reforms than before, Fico foresaw a unique opportunity to campaign against market reforms led by the center-right ruling coalition and to appeal to electorates dissatisfied with reforms, and as a result quickly transformed his party into one of the most popular in Slovakia. Among other factors, the disintegration of SDĽ allowed Fico to project his party as an alternative to the neoliberal policies of the Dzurinda government (Haughton and Rybář 2008; Haughton 2014). His party campaigned on a traditional left platform, criticizing Slovak center-right governments for ignoring Slovakia's growing disparities while catering to multinational corporations and financial interests. For example, in 2004 in alliance with trade unions and the radical right Slovak National Party (Slovenská národná strana, SNS), Smer, protesting reforms, called for a referendum on early parliamentary elections (Greskovits 2008: 287). Smer offered a protectionist solution, emphasizing the need to return to the basic principles of solidarity and state involvement in the economy. It offered to introduce changes in the labor code and pension and taxation systems and

---

[14] The party took part in the 2002 elections under the name of Smer–Tretia Cesta (Smer–the Third Way).

to increase public spending (Rybář 2006). This profile helped Smer attract traditional left voters and keep traditional left issues like poverty and social justice at the forefront of constituents' minds. In particular, it brought the "largest single group" of vote switches from SDĽ to Smer between 1998 and 2002 (Rybář and Deegan-Krause 2008: 514). By some polls, of those who voted for SDĽ in 1998, about a quarter (25.3%) voted for Smer in 2002 (Haughton 2003: 69).

Since 2002, socioeconomic themes had largely shaped political alignments (Rybář 2006). The center-right government was heavily criticized by opposition parties, especially by Smer. Rybář illustrated the importance of socioeconomic themes throughout this period on two expert surveys carried out in 2004 and 2006. The 2004 survey revealed that two economic issues—redistribution and a state-run versus a market economy—were the most prominent in Slovak politics, followed by nationalism and democracy (Rohrschneider and Whitefield 2004). In the 2006 expert survey, two economic issues (state versus market and social welfare) were estimated as being the most important on the political scene, followed by nationalism and social order (Rybář 2006).

## Stability of Alignments

Throughout this period, the Smer-SD kept attacking the reformist right parties, accusing them of having brought poverty to Slovakia (Henderson 2006: 6). The party portrayed the ruling right-wing government as neoliberal (a term with negative connotations in the Slovak context). In its platform, Smer-SD combined redistributionist economic policies with some nationalistic overtones and presented itself as the defender of Slovak national and state interests promoting "solidarity, justice and equality of opportunity." For example, while opposing the flat tax, Smer promised to lower taxes on basic goods (such as food and medicine) and to introduce progressive taxation for persons with "exceptionally high incomes" and for natural monopolies (Malová 2017: 10). This approach proved successful, helping Smer-SD win the 2006 election with 29.1% of the vote.

Smer's program echoed that of the populist right SNS, which combined a nationalist stance with a left-leaning economic program, including elements of state interventionism, paternalism, and redistribution. The party's 2006 electoral program, "We Are Slovaks. A Slovak Government for Slovaks," discussed at great length what it considered to be the overall threat brought about by the processes of globalization and Europeanization. The SNS manifesto portrayed globalization as a process that created easily malleable cosmopolitan citizens who lacked a national bond. It also questioned the liberalization, commercialization, and de-Christianization of Europe (Černoch et al. 2011: 187). About a fifth (22%) of the SNS 2006 electoral program elaborated on these socioeconomic themes (Haughton and Rybář 2008). In 2006, the SNS entered Parliament with 11.8% of the vote.

Smer's platform contributed to a growing representation of reform losers among its electorates. In 2006, Smer, while also popular in large towns and cities outside the major metropolitan centers of Bratislava and Kosice, took over from HZDS as the dominant force in the countryside (Krivý 2006: 171–172). SNS similarly saw a transfer of its supporters from cities to rural environments and small towns (Gyárfášová and Krivý 2007: 93–94). Differences were also pronounced with regard to income and education levels, with Smer, SNS, and HZDS constituencies being more strongly represented among those with lower levels of education and among poorer rural groups. Smer also did better among low-skilled workers and the unemployed, but less well among the professional and entrepreneurial classes (Bútorová and Gyárfášová 2006: 136–138; Stanley 2011).

Having won the 2006 election, Smer-SD formed a ruling coalition with SNS and HZDS. Gyárfásová and Krivý (2007: 85) demonstrated that supporters of Smer, HZDS, and SNS felt more negatively about the reforms and leaned more toward supporting economic interventionism than voters from other parties (Stanley 2011).[15] Consistent with these preferences, once in power Smer continued to attack neoliberalism, while introducing some pro-redistribution policies. The main redistributive efforts focused on such visible gestures of government largesse as the abolition of doctors' fees and the provision of additional payments to pensioners and new parents (Deegan-Krause and Haughton 2012). The government also suspended further privatization efforts and attempted to limit private ownership of public utilities, pensions, and healthcare insurers (Gould 2009; Malová 2017: 10). But Smer never really reintroduced progressive taxation and only added some minor changes to Dzurinda's flat tax, such as exempting some basic

[15] Governing alongside the nationalists got Smer in trouble. The Party of European Socialists saw it as infringing on its fundamental values, and as a result, it suspended Smer's membership for several years, arguing that "Slovakia needs social democracy, but not at the cost of compromising with extreme nationalism and xenophobia" (Havlík and Hloušek 2021: 120).

goods and services from value-added tax and raising the nontaxable income level for Slovakia's poorest (Gould 2009; Deegan-Krause and Haughton 2012).[16]

These efforts proved popular and helped Smer-SD gradually capture the vote of poorer, older, less educated, and more-rural social groups in subsequent years. In addition, a clearer socioeconomic profile allowed Smer to incorporate some voters in 2010 who had previously supported SNS (Henderson 2012; Haughton and Deegan-Krause 2016). According to some postelection surveys, in 2010, when SNS lost more than half of its electorate, those voters largely went on to support Smer (Gyarfasova 2013). The main reason for switching was that voters attributed more economic and social competence to Smer-SD. Besides strong competence on economic and social issues, Smer-SD's ability to project "nationalism lite" also felt more acceptable to mainstream voters (Gyarfasova 2013: 10). According to Deegan-Krause and Haughton (2012), the gains made on the nationalist vote between 2006 and 2010 helped consolidate Fico's power and gain future success.

Smer-SD would go on to win four subsequent elections, in 2006, 2010, 2012, and 2016.

The Slovak example suggests that the destinies of left parties are not entirely set in stone. In fact, successful rebranding toward more left-leaning economic positions is possible under the right set of circumstances (such as dealignment of sizable shares of voters from other parties). In Slovakia, Smer-SD was able to seize this political opportunity, reject SDL''s pro-market legacy, challenge the reform-oriented right-wing governments from a redistributionist economic agenda, and successfully attract the support of economically vulnerable constituencies.

## Individual-Level Surveys

To illustrate the above dynamic, Figure 5.3 depicts the structure of political competition in Slovakia using the Chapel Hill data set on the positions of national political parties in 2002–2010 along the economic and sociocultural dimensions of political competition. Figure 5.3 shows that throughout the analyzed period Smer-SD increasingly adopts more redistributionist

[16] In 2009 Slovakia also joined the Eurozone. During Fico's second term (2012–2016) the unified flat tax was dismantled.

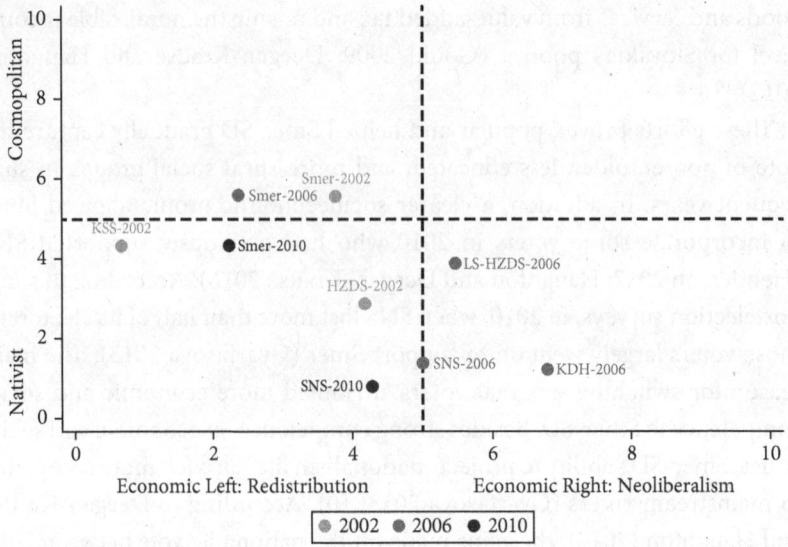

**Figure 5.3** Structure of Party Competition in Slovakia in the 2002, 2006, and 2010 elections.

Source: Chapel Hill Expert Survey.

positions (a shift to the left along the horizontal economic dimension in 2002–2010), as well as more nationalistic positions (as it moves to the bottom-left quadrant between 2006 and 2010). This position corresponds to the preferences of working-class electorates per Figure 2.2.

By contrast, throughout this period SNS remains relatively centrist on the economic dimension, with locations closer to the center of the horizontal axis.

To demonstrate the dynamic of class-based support for Smer-SD and SNS in Slovakia, ESS data available for Slovakia for the years 2002, 2006, 2008, and 2012 were used in the analysis.[17] The party variable was coded based on the answer respondents gave to the ESS question "Which party did you vote for in the last election?" The occupational status was coded based on the International Standard Classification of Occupations (codes ISCO-88 and ISCO-08).

Figure 5.4 maps the dynamic of class voting for Smer-SD and SNS in Slovakia. Between 2006 and 2008 the populist right SNS captured significant

---

[17] CSES data are not available for Slovakia over the period of interest.

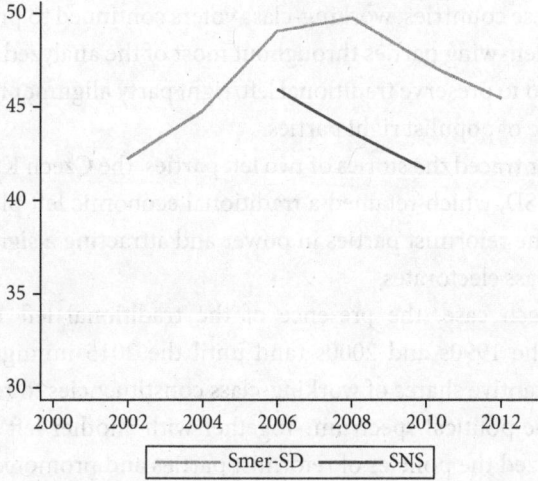

**Figure 5.4**  Alford Index (% party vote among working class) for% party vote among professional class) for the left SMER-SD and the populist right SNS. Data on SDĽ are not available in the ESS data set.
*Source*: European Social Survey.

shares of the working-class electorates. In the 2012, SNS failed to meet the 5% electoral threshold and lost parliamentary representation.

Combining the evidence presented in Figures 5.3 and 5.4, one notices that the representation of workers (as opposed to professionals) in the Smer-SD vote also increased dramatically between the years 2002 and 2006, as Smer-SD adopted a leftist, antireform agenda, attacking the reformist right-wing coalition, and grew in popularity (a move to the left along the economic policy dimension in Figure 5.4). By contrast, adopting more nationalist positions does not help Smer-SD very much in terms of attracting working-class support (its relative representation in Figure 5.4 decreases between the years 2006 and 2010 as Smer-SD moves to the bottom left quadrant after adopting more nationalist positions).

## Summary

This chapter focused on the experiences of two Visegrád countries—the Czech Republic and Slovakia—where major leftist parties remained more faithful to their redistributionist economic platforms. Unlike Hungary and

Poland, in these countries, working-class voters continued to predominantly affiliate with left-wing parties throughout most of the analyzed period. This, in turn, served to preserve traditional left/right party alignments as well as to curtail the rise of populist right parties.

The chapter traced the stories of two left parties, the Czech KSČM and the Slovak Smer-SD, which retained a traditional economic left platform while challenging the reformist parties in power and attracting a significant share of working-class electorates.

In the Czech case, the presence of the traditional left KSČM party throughout the 1990s and 2000s (and until the 2015 immigration crisis) allowed substantive shares of working-class constituencies to remain on the left side of the political spectrum. Together with another left party, ČSSD, KSČM criticized the policies of reformist parties and promoted a pro-labor agenda. This limited the size of working-class constituencies available for mobilization to the Czech populist right, demonstrated by the example of the populist right-wing party SPR-RSČ, whose attempts to attract working-class support eventually failed, as significant shares of those groups were incorporated by left-wing parties. These findings are complemented with an individual-level analysis that illustrates that working-class status has been positively and consistently associated with support for left parties in the Czech Republic throughout the review period.

In addition, this chapter traced the trajectories of two Slovak parties—the ex-communist SDĽ and its splinter, Smer-SD. The trajectory of the ex-communist SDĽ was reminiscent of the cases of the Hungarian and Polish center-left parties. SDĽ adopted a pro-market platform and took part in a reformist coalition of right-wing parties. Subsequently the party lost the support of its core constituencies and suffered from an electoral collapse. By contrast, Smer-SD, a breakaway faction from SDĽ headed by Robert Fico, sensed the political opening on the left created by SDĽ's pro-market shift and was successful in attracting many former SDĽ voters by combining moderate nationalism with redistributionist pledges.

The Czech and Slovak left experiences provide a comparison with the cases of reformist left parties in Hungary and Poland. The adoption of more leftist economic platforms helped the Czech and Slovak left preserve more pro-labor and redistributionist policies, strengthened workers' support for left parties, and preserved party alignments more consistent with traditional left/right divides throughout the analyzed time period (before the 2015 refugee crisis). By contrast, their Hungarian and Polish counterparts, having embraced pro-market reforms, failed to maintain the support of working-class constituencies. Unpopular neoliberal reforms implemented by reformist left parties dealigned their electorates and opened up more political space for populist right parties. These conclusions confirm my theoretical expectations.

This chapter relied on case-study approaches to trace this dynamic. However, case studies also pose limitations when used alone. In particular, given the small number of cases used, it is difficult to control for more than a few factors that can impact the relationship between variables of interest. To compensate for these limitations, the next chapter uses a survey experiment for a more systematic identification of a causal mechanism.

# 6

# Decisions on the Ground

## The Experimental Case for a Left-Right Shift

Previous chapters used cross-country and case-study evidence to analyze how the adoption of pro-market positions by left parties made economically vulnerable electorates more likely to support populist right parties.

But while those chapters have found confirmation that the decline in left parties' support is associated with their pro-market economic policies, we cannot know for sure whether these effects were not ultimately due to the influence of other factors. Case studies presented in Chapters 4 and 5 traced the impact of a single variable on outcomes of interest. However, they cannot match unknown confounders and cannot control for more than a few factors given the small number of cases (Tarrow 2010). After all, there is substantive literature that has postulated that other mechanisms besides left parties' pro-market shift explain the realignment processes in the postcommunist context (see Introduction). The cross-country analysis that provided evidence that postcommunist working-class groups are less prone to back pro-market left parties (presented in Chapter 3) also cannot prove causation. Left parties might have adopted more pro-market stances to attract other groups after they had already lost the support of working-class electorates (which might have abandoned them for reasons other than their pro-market platforms).

This problem is further exacerbated when trying to trace left support among specific constituencies. First, other reasons might explain working-class electorates' switch to the right side of the political spectrum. Voters may be primarily driven to vote for populist parties due to their positions on the sociocultural dimension (Kitschelt et al. 1999). In addition, it is hard to know what specific reasoning and party image motivate voters when they cast votes for a specific party. For example, some studies have shown that voters do not always adjust their perceptions of parties' positions in response to shifts in parties' policy statements during election campaigns (Adams, Ezrow, and Somer-Topcu 2011; Fernandez-Vazquez and Somer-Topcu 2019) or that they adjust such perceptions only on specific issues (Somer-Topcu, Tavits,

*When Left Moves Right.* Maria Snegovaya, Oxford University Press. © Oxford University Press 2024.
DOI: 10.1093/oso/9780197699027.003.0007

and Baumann 2020). In other words, when relying on case studies or cross-country analysis alone there is no definite way to know why voters select one party over the other.

To be more confident about this book's argument and to establish causal links between parties' platforms and voter support, we need to directly test whether the embrace of more pro-market positions by left parties affects their support among specific electorates, and how that relates to the populist right vote. Experimental approaches are a better fit for these purposes. By randomly assigning subjects to treatment and control groups, experimental designs make both groups probabilistically equal on all variables other than the experimental one. Survey experiments allow scholars a far greater degree of control over exogenous variation and thereby minimize the impact of timing. This allows us to better identify causality in relationships fraught with endogeneity (Morton and Williams 2010; Gerber and Green 2012; Lupu 2016).

In order to test the effect of left parties' pro-market positions on party choices, I ran a set of experiments in Hungary in March 2018 (ahead of the April 2018 parliamentary election). Hungary is a useful case to investigate these questions. First, as Chapter 4 demonstrated, the dynamic of realignment between left and right parties in Hungary unraveled in line with this book's expectations. Second, Hungary features several populist right parties whose positions on economic and sociocultural dimensions are useful for the purposes of my experiment. Third, Hungary also features a left party, which could be credibly assigned different positions on the economic dimension. While Hungarian voters had some prior beliefs about left party brands, previous left party platform shifts should have made those beliefs potentially more pliable (Lupu 2016). Specifically, in the 2018 election, the left MSZP attempted to move away from its pro-market policies during the 1990s and 2010s and adopted a highly redistributionist platform. For the purposes of the experiment, this attempted rebranding of the left party provided an opportunity to present to respondents both positions (pro-market and redistributionist) of the MSZP as fairly credible alternatives (since these were close to the positions the MSZP adopted in real life).

## Survey Experiment 1

In Hungary at the time of my analysis, there were two major populist right parties represented in Parliament: the conservative Fidesz party and the radical right Jobbik party (Rooduijn et al. 2019). Since the MSZP and Fidesz have historically alternated in power (see Chapter 4 for a detailed description), Fidesz may be a natural choice for voters frustrated with the MSZP policies regardless of its platform, which might inflate the estimates. To avoid this problem my experimental design assigned Fidesz a neutral platform; this allowed respondents to refocus their attention on Jobbik, which was assigned a protectionist policy stance (in line with its existing electoral platform).

Could Jobbik still be described as a right-wing populist party in 2018? In 2015, to attract a new electorate the party underwent some rebranding, deradicalized its rhetoric, and removed anti-Semitism, racism, and calls for revisionism from its public statements (Biró Nagy and Boros 2016; Stojarová 2018; Karl 2019). With regard to this experiment, one possible concern has to do with the fact that Jobbik's self-rebranding as a more centrist party since 2014 (as opposed to its previous, more radical stance) may have made this party a more acceptable voting option for some of the respondents, and hence the models may have overestimated the effects of the treatment (Byrne 2017).

Yet there are solid reasons to describe Jobbik as a populist right party at the time of the 2018 election. The "mainstreaming" the party underwent was not atypical for other populist right parties across Europe (Akkerman, de Lange, and Rooduijn 2016; Herman and Muldoon 2018). In recent years many populist right parties, most famously the French Front National (Stockemer and Barisione 2017), have sought to broaden their appeal, in part by expunging anti-Semitic and xenophobic attributes (Mondon 2017). Despite their deradicalization, in most instances the rebranding was superficial—it did not lead to a fundamental change in platforms (Akkerman, de Lange, and Rooduijn 2016; Pytlas 2018) but aimed to improve the reputation of populist parties among the mainstream (Akkerman, de Lange, and Rooduijn 2016). Indeed, this was the case for Jobbik as well. Following its rebranding, the party refrained from fundamentally altering its composition and did not distance itself from radical politicians, such as Sándor Pözse, who cofounded Jobbik's paramilitary wing Magyar Gárda (Héjj 2017; Schultheis 2018). In the 2018 electoral campaign, the party also preserved many of its nativist and antiestablishment overtones while increasing its reliance on populism (Borbáth and Gessler 2021; Hyttinen 2022). In fact, ahead of the 2018 elections Jobbik actively relied on nativist appeals when targeting its core electorate (Borbáth and Gessler 2021). The 2019 CHES continued to classify Jobbik as belonging to the radical right party family (Jolly et al., forthcoming). Hence, it is safe to count the 2018 Jobbik as a populist right party for the purposes of this experiment.

In the 2018 parliamentary elections, the left party (the MSZP), in an effort to recover from its previous electoral losses, adopted a program with the central slogan "Let the rich pay!," which put a strong emphasis on redistribution. The party's platform, titled "Let's do justice!," was primarily devoted to redistributionist pledges, such as that Hungarian wages would reach the EU average and no one would earn less than 100,000 forints; that low- and medium-income earners would receive tax refunds; that pensions would be indexed; that low-earning pensioners would receive pension supplements; that the cost of utilities would radically decrease; that family allowances would be increased; and that higher taxes on the rich would be mandated (MSZP 2018; Adam 2017a). This attempted rebranding along with the legacy of MSZP's pro-market policies provided an opportunity to present to respondents both positions of the left (neoliberal and redistributionist) as fairly credible alternatives. Among other pledges, ahead of the 2018 parliamentary elections the MSZP offered to implement a guaranteed basic income for all (Adam 2017b).[1] This campaign pledge was used in the experimental setup.

## Design

The research was carried out on a nationally representative sample of the Hungarian adult population between eighteen and sixty-four years old. The subjects were randomly recruited from a representative sample of Hungary's population by the professional polling company Solid Data. Respondents were told that the experiment would study the frequency of their exposure to various political news and were debriefed at the end of the survey. Like similar experiments conducted by Brader and Tucker (2008) and Lupu (2014, 2016) treatments provided respondents with information about each party's platforms.

---

[1] The issue was adopted by MSZP from the Párbeszéd party, with which it formed an electoral alliance in the spring of 2018.

For the purposes of the experiment, I split the sample into two groups of equal size (504 respondents per group). Both groups were shown different combinations of fabricated excerpts purportedly from an article in a Hungarian newspaper. The excerpts contained information about party platforms in the upcoming parliamentary election. The information was compiled using parties' electoral platforms and programs. Four Hungarian native speakers were consulted to discuss the specific formulations of the treatments. They examined the treatments sentence by sentence to make sure they accurately reflected the political realities in Hungary. Whenever a sentence was in dispute, they deliberated until they reached an agreement.

To strengthen the treatment and simplify the content, the respondents were shown the same information about the three Hungarian parties in different combinations. First, they were shown the information about Fidesz and MSZP platforms; second, they were shown the information regarding the platforms of Fidesz and Jobbik; and third, they were shown the information on the policy positions of all three parties together. The experiment was sequenced this way in order to provide the respondents sufficient time to process the data, to ensure compliance, and to allow respondents to maintain a steady focus on the information being presented. The only difference across the two treatments was the information on the platform adopted by the MSZP in the upcoming election. In the first treatment, the MSZP embraced a pro-market policy, while in the second treatment it adopted redistributionist policy positions. The positions of both Fidesz (neutral policy stance) and Jobbik remained constant across these two treatments.

The pro-market treatment contained the following information:

> Please read the following newspaper abstract: "As the political parties prepare for the April 2018 parliamentary election, they are revising their political platforms and strategies.
>
> Fidesz, the ruling party, will preserve its current policy focus as part of its electoral strategy.
>
> MSZP **will push for policies of economic openness and seek to satisfy international investors in order to further integrate the Hungarian economy into global markets.**
>
> Jobbik in the meantime will maintain its focus on the protection of the Hungarian economy and propose to limit the presence of multinational

companies because, as it claims, multinational companies stifle the development of Hungarian-owned enterprises."[2]

The redistributionist treatment contained the following information:

> Please read the following newspaper abstract: "As the political parties prepare for the April 2018 parliamentary election, they are revising their political platforms and strategies.
> Fidesz, the ruling party, will preserve its current policy focus as part of its electoral strategy.
> MSZP **has decided to focus on improving living standards and will campaign for the introduction of a guaranteed basic income for all citizens.**
> Jobbik, in the meantime, will maintain its focus on the protection of the Hungarian economy and propose to limit the presence of multinational companies because, as it claims, multinational companies stifle the development of Hungarian-owned enterprises."

## Results

Appendix VIII provides the summary statistics for the two treatment groups. As Table A.9 suggests, the data in both samples appear to be balanced by basic demographic characteristics. The differences in gender, age, and education are not statistically significant across both groups.

Following the treatment exposure, respondents in each group were asked a question designed to evaluate the likelihood that they would vote for Jobbik in the upcoming parliamentary elections. Given the controversial reputation of populist right parties like Jobbik, I was aware of the possibility that respondents would not openly declare their preference. To counter this,

---

[2] One possible criticism of such experimental framing has to do with the fact that emphasizing "international investors" with regard to MSZP may indirectly prompt respondents on the sociocultural dimension (nationalist vs. international axis). To control for the possible impact of a cultural frame, I ran an additional smaller experiment reformulating the treatment in the following way:

> MSZP will push for policies of economic openness in order to further integrate the Hungarian economy into global markets.

In this alternative specification the results echoed the findings of the main experiment (estimations available upon request).

I used a 4-point Likert-type scale question, offering continuum response categories that are better suited than binary options to measure attitudinal changes (Croasmun and Ostrom 2011). A higher number on the scale indicated a stronger likelihood of voting for Jobbik.

How likely it is that you will vote for Jobbik (the Movement for a Better Hungary) party in the upcoming parliamentary election?
- Not likely
- Probably not likely
- Probably likely
- Very likely

Table A.10 in Appendix IX presents the results of this analysis. Age, squared age, and gender were included as controls to account for possible confounding factors. For a robustness check, an ordinal probit model was provided as well. Results in columns (1) and (3) confirm that the treatment had a statistically significant effect. In the group shown treatments where the left party had pro-market (as compared to redistributive) stances, support for the populist right Jobbik increased significantly overall: an increase of about 0.15 points on a scale that ranges from 1 to 4, roughly a 5% change. The size of the effect is robust to alternative specifications of the model.

For ease of interpretation, Figure 6.1 plots the findings of the OLS regression (Model 1 in Table A.10) graphically. The outcomes are regressed on the binary treatment variable, with the dots representing the estimated magnitude of the effect of pro-market MSZP positions compared with redistributionist MSZP positions on support for Jobbik and the "whiskers" spanning the 90% confidence interval. The faint line plots the OLS regression coefficient; the dark line plots the coefficient of the ordinal probit regression.

These results are in line with the hypothesis. The respondents in the group that received treatments with pro-market MSZP positions were more likely to vote for the Jobbik party compared to the group that received treatments with redistributionist MSZP positions. At a 5% level, the effects are statistically significant.

Next, I included in the analysis the interaction between the treatment and the respondents' occupational status. Respondents were categorized into socioeconomic categories based on their professional status according to the

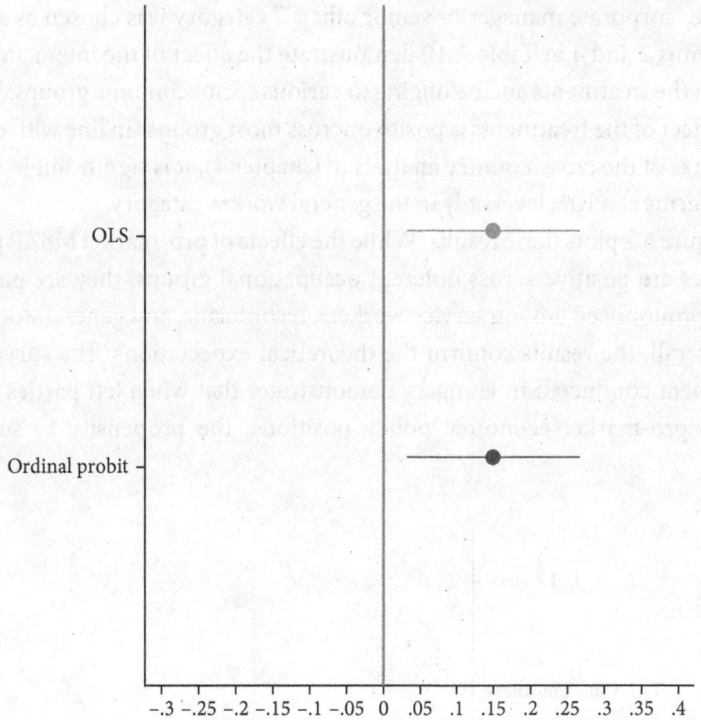

**Figure 6.1** Effects on the Group Receiving the Treatment with Pro-market MSZP Economic Policy Positions Compared with the Group That Received the Treatment with Redistributionist Policy Positions of the MSZP. OLS (faint line) and ordinal probit (dark line) regression coefficients, 90% confidence interval. Robust standard errors.

standard Hungarian occupational schema, which is similar to the Oesch classification (Oesch 2006a, b):

- Corporate manager or senior official
- Professional (scientist, mathematician, computer scientist, architect, engineer, life science and health professional, teacher, legal professional, social scientist, writer, artist, religious professional)
- Technician or associate professional
- Small business owner (< 25 employees)
- Clerk
- Service or sales worker (including artisan or commercial worker)
- General worker (including agricultural or fishery worker, foreman, machine operator)

The "corporate manager or senior official" category was chosen as a base. Columns 2 and 4 in Table A.10 demonstrate the effect of the interaction between the treatments and belonging to various socioeconomic groups. While the effect of the treatments is positive across most groups (in line with earlier findings of the cross-country analysis in Chapter 4), it is significant in statistical terms at a 10% level only in the general worker category.

Figure 6.2 plots these results. While the effects of pro-market MSZP policy stances are positive across different occupational groups, they are particularly pronounced among service workers, technicians, and general workers.

Overall, the results confirm the theoretical expectations. The survey experiment conducted in Hungary demonstrates that when left parties adopt more pro-market economic policy positions, the propensity to support

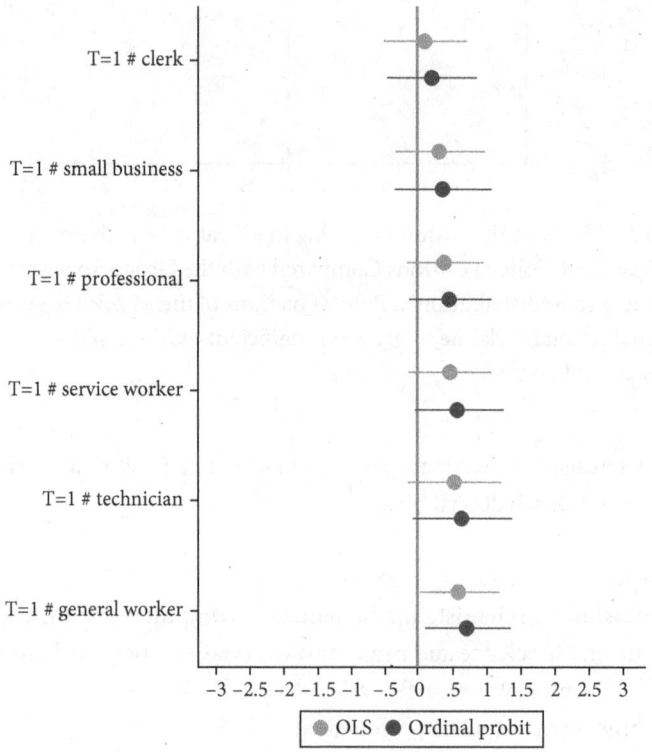

**Figure 6.2** Effects on the Group Receiving Treatment with Pro-market MSZP Economic Policy Positions Compared with the Group That Received the Treatment with Redistributionist Policy Positions of the MSZP. OLS coefficients (faint lines), ordinal probit coefficients dark lines), 90% confidence interval. Robust standard errors.

populist parties significantly increases among the population at large. These effects are especially pronounced among working-class respondents.

Importantly, these results are conditional on the populist right party's economic appeals. In this specification, the Jobbik party was assigned more protectionist stances on the economic dimension. As the next section demonstrates, in an alternative specification of the survey experiment, the anti-immigrant appeals of the Jobbik party alone were not enough to cause respondents to shift their support to the populist right.

## Survey Experiment 2

Survey Experiment 1 demonstrated that when left parties adopt pro-market positions, support for populist right parties increases as long as the populist right parties adopt protectionist economic positions. However, a popular counterargument states that populist right parties primarily compete for voters with other parties along the sociocultural dimension (Kriesi 2008: 13; Norris and Inglehart 2019; see also the discussion on the relative importance of the economic and the sociocultural dimension in this book's Introduction). If the latter assumption is correct, then one should expect that when left parties adopt pro-market positions, support for the populist right parties increases as long as they adopt more radical positions across the sociocultural dimension. To account for this possibility, Survey Experiment 2 uses a design almost identical to that in Survey Experiment 1, except that Jobbik's economic stances are replaced with anti-immigrant policy stances.

The rest of this chapter looks at the results of this alternative survey experiment. If the key competition between left-wing and right-wing parties occurs along the economic policy scale, as this book argues, one should not see an increase in Jobbik support in the current specification of the experimental survey. By contrast, if the cultural positions of the populist right matter primarily when it comes to competition with left parties, then support for Jobbik should increase when the left party adopts more pro-market policies.

## Design

This online survey was carried out on a nationally representative sample of the Hungarian adult population eighteen to sixty-four years old and split into two groups of equal size (500 respondents per group). Similarly to the first survey experiment, both groups were shown different combinations of fabricated excerpts from a Hungarian newspaper, which contained information about party platforms. The treatment with a pro-market policy stance of MSZP contained the following information:

> Please read the following newspaper abstract: "As the political parties prepare for the April 2018 parliamentary election, they are revising their political platforms and strategies.
> Fidesz, the ruling party, will preserve its current policy focus as part of its electoral strategy.
> MSZP **will push for policies of economic openness and seek to satisfy international investors in order to further integrate the Hungarian economy into global markets.**
> Jobbik's **leadership will return to the party's radical roots and, leaving other issues aside, focus primarily on the need to limit the inflow of migrants into Hungary."**

The redistributionist treatment contained the following information:

> Please read the following newspaper abstract: "As the political parties prepare for the April 2018 parliamentary election, they are revising their political platforms and strategies.
> Fidesz, the ruling party, will preserve its current policy focus as part of its electoral strategy.
> MSZP **has decided to focus on improving living standards and will campaign for the introduction of a guaranteed basic income for all citizens.**
> Jobbik's **leadership will return to the party's radical roots and, leaving other issues aside, focus primarily on the need to limit the inflow of migrants into Hungary."**

## Results

Appendix X provides the summary statistics for the two treatment groups. Based on Table A.11, the data in both samples appear to be balanced by basic demographic characteristics.

Following the treatment exposure, respondents in each group were asked a question designed to evaluate the likelihood that they would vote for Jobbik in the upcoming parliamentary elections. Table A.12 in Appendix XI reports the results of the main analysis. Age, squared age, and gender were included as controls to account for possible confounding factors. Results in columns 1 and 3 demonstrate that the treatment does not have a statistically significant effect on support for the Jobbik party when Jobbik adopts more radical positions on the sociocultural axis.

For ease of interpretation, Figure 6.3 reports the findings of the OLS and probit regression graphically. The blue line plots the OLS regression coefficient; the red line plots the coefficient of the ordinal probit regression. As

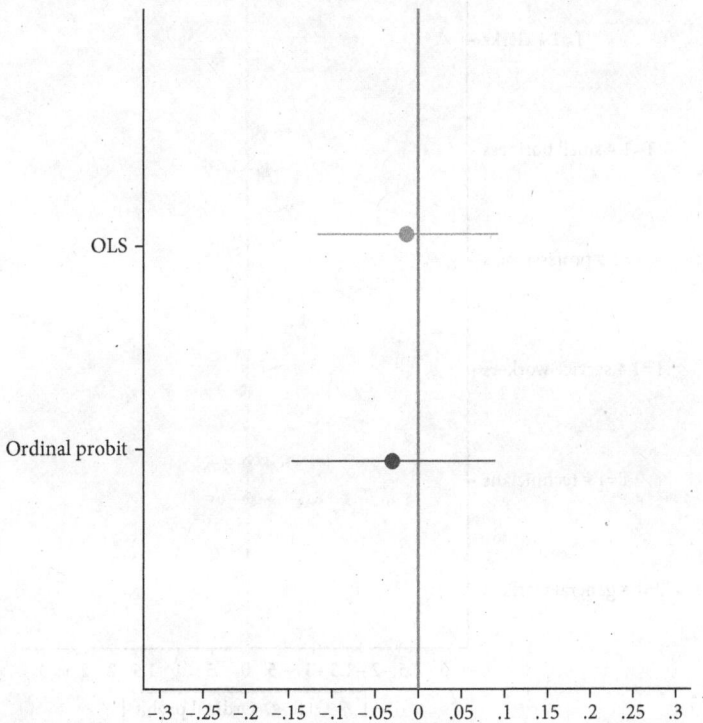

**Figure 6.3** Effects on the Group Receiving the Treatment with Pro-market MSZP Economic Policy Positions Compared with the Group That Received the Treatment with Redistributionist Policy Positions of the MSZP. OLS (faint line) and ordinal probit (dark line) regression coefficients, 90% confidence interval. Robust standard errors.

the graph illustrates, the treatment does not have a significant effect on respondents' propensity to support Jobbik.

Next, the interaction between treatment exposure and respondents' occupational status was added to the analysis. Columns 2 and 4 in Table A.12 in Appendix XI demonstrate the effect of the interaction between treatment and belonging to different socioeconomic groups. Figure 6.4 plots the interaction coefficients between the exposure to treatment and different occupational categories. The effects of the treatment vary only slightly in terms of its direction across the occupational groups, and none is statistically significant.

Overall, the results suggest that exposing respondents to Jobbik's anti-immigration platform while showing them the treatment with pro-market

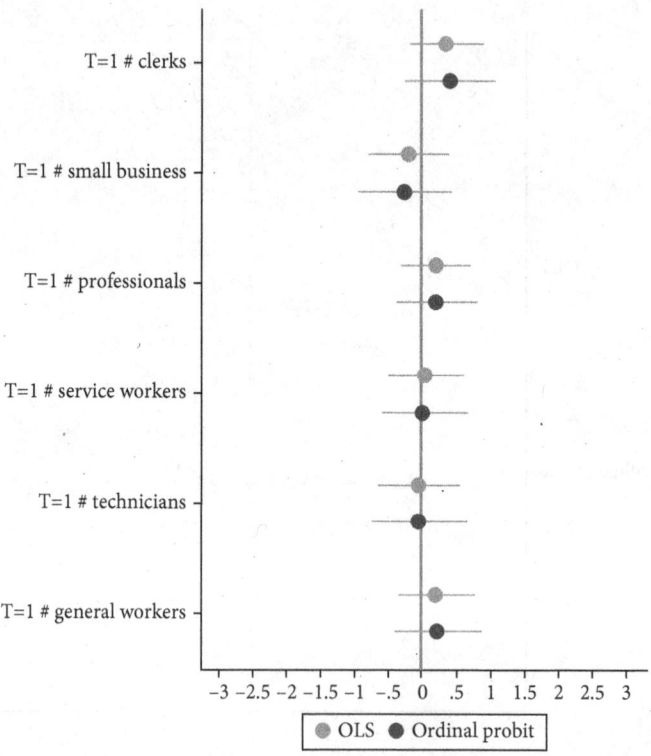

**Figure 6.4** Effects on the Group Receiving the Treatment with Pro-market MSZP Economic Policy Positions Compared with the Group That Received the Treatment with Redistributionist Policy Positions of the MSZP. OLS regression (faint lines), ordinal probit (dark lines), 90% confidence interval. Robust standard errors.

MSZP positions does not have a significant impact on respondents' inclination to vote for the populist right.

These null findings are consistent with the main theoretical argument of this book—that competition between left-wing and populist right parties occurs primarily along the economic policy dimension. Therefore, populist right parties fail to attract the former constituencies of left parties when competing across the sociocultural dimension alone. It is only after populist right parties adopt protectionist economic platforms (and left-wing parties adopt pro-market ones) that populist right parties are able to increase their electoral shares and lure away the left's former constituencies. Hence, party competition along the socioeconomic dimension seems to play a more important role within this context.

## Summary

This chapter has discussed the results of two experimental surveys conducted in Hungary in the time leading up to the 2018 parliamentary election. These surveys tested how the left's adoption of pro-market policies may affect the likelihood that voters will support the populist right. In the first experiment, some respondents were told that a left party embraced pro-market policies (as opposed to pro-redistributionist policies in the control group). After exposure to this treatment, respondents showed a greater likelihood to support the populist right in the next election, when its platforms offered greater social protection. The effects were particularly pronounced among the more economically vulnerable respondents in working-class occupations. The findings from the first experiment supported the results of the cross-country analysis provided in Chapter 3 and the general argument of this book: in countries with more pro-market left parties, working-class electorates are more likely to back populist right-wing parties that adopt redistributionist economic policies.

As the second experiment demonstrated, in treatments where populist right parties did not adopt redistributionist economic platforms, but only anti-immigrant, nativist appeals, respondents did not shift their support to the populist right. This suggests that the use of cultural appeals alone is not enough to attract supporters to the populist right, even when the left has shifted to a pro-market platform. In order to attract new supporters, the populist right must adopt protectionist economic stances.

While the results overall confirm these original expectations, the inter-action effect between working-class status and the propensity to support Jobbik is only significant at a 10% level, and the magnitude of the discovered effect remains relatively low (about 5% change in the range of the variables' scale). One reason for the small magnitude of the effect is that internet-based experiments commonly underestimate treatment effects, which tend to be larger using alternative methods (Krantz and Dalai 2000). Another reason is that, due to methodological considerations, in my experimental setting I diverted respondents' attention from Fidesz, which historically has been a more natural alternative than Jobbik for voters frustrated with the MSZP policies. This setup therefore underestimates the effects of the left's pro-market rebranding. Also, as mentioned in Chapter 1, the dynamic discussed in this book tends to unravel over longer periods of time. There is a lag in voters updating their perceptions of party positions, and party re-alignment takes even longer. In both Western and postcommunist Europe, these processes usually take several electoral rounds (Karreth, Polk, and Allen 2013). By contrast, the above experiments assumed that respondents would immediately update their perceptions of party platforms and that those changes would instantly translate into party preferences. Therefore, the findings of these experiments can only remotely approximate the real dy-namics of party realignment.

Moreover, like all survey experiments, my treatments abstract from the real world. This leads to a limited external validity of the results obtained through such an approach. Experimental surveys allow us to establish a certain level of control over situations by randomly assigning respondents to conditions and ruling out the effects of extraneous variables. But this can backfire by creating circumstances in which respondents feel removed from the information presented because it does not relate to their daily experiences. However, the design of my experimental survey helps address some concerns regarding external validity. First, the experiment's findings were backed by additional evidence through case studies and cross-country analysis presented in earlier chapters. Second, the study was run on a rep-resentative sample taken from a cross-section of Hungarian society, which increases the generalizability of the findings (Siedler and Sonnenberg 2010). Third, the treatments were designed to reflect the realities of Hungary's po-litical context leading up to the 2018 parliamentary elections. During this period, the left MSZP had started to return to an increasingly redistribu-tionist agenda—it offered to introduce a universal income to all Hungarian citizens—shifting away from the pro-market policies it had adopted during the 1990s and 2010s. At the same time, Hungary's populist right Jobbik party mixed nationalist positions with redistributionist stances on economy. Therefore, the treatment contained information that was in line with the political developments in Hungary at that time.

Overall, the results presented in this chapter fall in line with the main theoretical argument: competition between left-wing and populist right parties takes place primarily along the economic policy dimension. Populist right parties fail to attract the left's former constituencies on the cultural dimension alone. To attract these constituencies they have to adopt protectionist positions on the economic policy scale. These findings explain why many populist right parties that have been successful over the past decade tended to add redistributionist economic positions to their nativist stances (Allen 2015; Bustikova and Kitschelt 2009; Bustikova 2018; see also the book's Introduction).

# Conclusion

Over the past two decades, postcommunist countries have witnessed a shift in the electoral fortunes of their political parties: previously successful center-left parties suffered dramatic electoral defeats and often disappeared from the political scene, while populist right parties soared in popularity and came to power. Scholars have often provided region-specific idiosyncratic explanations for this phenomenon. In particular, they tended to assume that these post-transition party systems are simply different, that is, that they are highly fluid and unstable in part because they are not aligned by class or programmatic cleavages (Rovny 2015).

However, as this book has argued, these accounts alone cannot explain the observed cross-regional parallels. These trends are not limited to Western or Eastern Europe, or even to Europe at all (Berman and Snegovaya 2019; Roberts 2013; Binev 2022b). This book aimed to demonstrate the generalizability of the experiences that underpin many seemingly idiosyncratic patterns of party competition in a postcommunist context. Many of the party systems dynamics in postcommunist Europe are not a regional anomaly determined by the idiosyncrasies of postcommunist transitions. Instead, as previous chapters have shown, the basic ingredients for stable alignments were present in the postcommunist region. It is left parties' failures to align programmatically that contributed to the volatility of party systems in general, and to the success of populist right parties in particular—much like the patterns of neoliberal dealignment in Western Europe opened the door to new types of populist contenders (on the left in Southern Europe and on the right in Northern Europe).[1] In spite of the region-wide nature of this phenomenon, until this book there has not been sufficient attention devoted to the important correspondence between these trends across Europe. This concluding chapter further explores this comparison.

---

[1] These trends are also closely paralleled in Latin America, where neoliberal dealignment opened the door for the rise of populist challengers on the left (Roberts 2013, 2017a, 2017b; Binev 2022a, 2022b).

*When Left Moves Right.* Maria Snegovaya, Oxford University Press. © Oxford University Press 2024.
DOI: 10.1093/oso/9780197699027.003.0008

While highlighting generalizable cross-regional patterns, however, this book does not claim that postcommunist systems lack region-specific factors that played a role in these trends. Instead, I aimed to demonstrate that the dynamic of postcommunist party systems is best explained with a combination of generalizable cross-regional patterns that were aggravated by factors specific to a postcommunist context. This conclusion complements my analysis by exploring ways in which regional idiosyncrasy in Eastern Europe has reinforced these trends. It discusses the role of region-specific factors, such as EU conditionality, the instability of the novel postcommunist systems and more culturally conservative orientations of postcommunist electorates, as well as the larger size of working-class electorates in the region.

In addition, the conclusion focuses on the implications of the book's key argument. Specifically, I discuss whether the collapse of left parties is ultimately that important for the stability of corresponding party systems as long as other parties fill in the space they vacated. I conclude by offering ways for center-left parties to recover support of working-class electorates in the future and curtail the dangerous consequences of the populist right swing.

## Eastern Europe Is Not Unique . . .

Question: "Is there any policy of Labour's that you would not be prepared to abandon if you thought it would gain votes?"
Peter Mandelson, a British Labour Party politician and one of several key people responsible for its rebranding as New Labour: "No."
—Conversation at the Political Studies Association
Conference, Durham, 1990, cited in Temple (2000: 304)

This book has postulated that the effects of the pro-market shift by center-left parties in the postcommunist region have direct parallels to Western Europe. This argument was tested on various levels of analysis: cross-country observational data, case studies, and individual-level experimental surveys. The mixed-methods approach allowed me to draw on the strengths of both qualitative and quantitative methods.

Specifically, this book has postulated three distinct steps in which this process unraveled in both regions.

First, across both regions the process was launched by the rebranding of left parties. Chapter 1 discussed how, in postwar Europe, Western European left parties successfully built their support by politicizing primarily economic issues, offering redistributive policies, and relying to a large extent on the industrial working class. However, by the end of the century these parties were stretched ideologically as doubts about the long-term viability of interventionist policies, exacerbated by globalization and financialization, undermined the egalitarian achievements of the postwar era (Meyerson 2020). As a result, during the 1990s many of these parties in Western European countries changed their platforms to embrace more pro-market positions, a move that has become known as the Third Way (Bonoli and Powell 2004). Indeed, originally, this "catch-all" approach allowed left-wing parties to expand their voter bases by incorporating more middle-class supporters while retaining their traditional working-class electorates. As result, these left parties successfully won several elections.

The rebranded ex-communist left parties followed a very similar pattern. In fact, eager to dissociate themselves from the tarnished communist legacy and signal the embrace of "Europeanization," ex-communist left parties were all too happy to adopt neoliberal platforms. Eastern European left parties often implemented even deeper pro-market reforms than parties on the right side of the political spectrum (Tavits and Letki 2009; Dandashly and Verdun 2018). This strategy originally helped the ex-communist left to expand their electorates. Chapter 2 has shown that while rebranding helped gain support of pro-reform groups, in early elections the ex-communist left offering more social protections against painful economic shocks also captured larger swaths of working-class electorates. In this sense, early on the catch-all strategy appeared to work quite well for the ex-communist left, just as it did for its Western counterparts.

Second, however, in both regions the Third Way policies eventually proved to be incapable of reconciling these newly adopted platforms with the domestic demands of their traditional constituents (Allen 2009). The success of Western European social democratic parties in the postwar era relied on the assertion that the democratic state could temper the market's dangerous consequences. Having abandoned this view, left parties were poorly positioned to capture the resentment that followed the weakening of the postwar social democratic order and its fallout (Berman and Snegovaya 2019: 9). As a result, the Third Way reforms typically led to the dealignment of left parties' core voters, primarily blue-collar and lower-level white-collar electorates (Arndt 2013: 282). While in the 1970s working-class electorates voted for Western European social democratic parties more than average and represented a large share of their electorates, since the 1990s working-class association with Western European left parties has consistently weakened (Meyerson 2020). Eventually, working classes became much less distinctive in their support for center-left parties and constituted a smaller share of these parties' votes compared to other social groups (Rennwald 2020).

The watering down of their economic profile in both regions tended to de-align left traditional supporters. These effects were particularly pronounced among economically vulnerable occupational groups (such as working-class electorates) due to their more redistribution-oriented preferences (see Chapter 2). This pattern was even more pronounced in the postcommunist context because the ex-communist left often pushed for harsher reforms, partly due to pressure coming from international institutions, such as the EU and also because postcommunist electorates generally tended to be more sensitive to welfare cuts. The book provided empirical evidence to back up this argument. In particular, the cross-country analysis presented in Chapter 3 demonstrated that in a postcommunist context pro-market positions adopted by ex-communist left parties are associated with a lower propensity of respondents to support them. In Chapters 4 and 5 the analysis of Hungarian, Polish, and Slovak cases showed that the major decline in left parties' approval in all instances occurred after they had introduced unpopular reforms involving severe budget cuts.

The dealignment of traditional left electorates took time to unravel. In Western Europe, the left's core supporters were initially willing to accept their pro-market shift as a means for short-term success even if a move to the center was not in their true interests (Karreth, Polk, and Allen 2013; Polk and Karreth 2020). It was only after left parties maintained this new position that they went on to lose voters in elections that took place more than one electoral cycle after moderation (Horn 2021). In Eastern Europe, this dynamic was further delayed by the timing of EU accession. Postcommunist societies and parties tended to coalesce around the necessity of joining the EU. Before accession, parties critical of reforms had limited electoral success, and even if they were successful, once in power they had to continue on the reform track. As Chapter 1 argued, it was not until after EU accession was guaranteed that other (often right-wing) parties relied on populist appeals to sweep up economically vulnerable voters who had been abandoned by the left's pro-market shift.

Third, with leftist parties no longer able to capture the support of economically vulnerable groups, in both regions an opportunity emerged on the opposite side of the political spectrum. Populist right parties tended to add more leftist economic positions (particularly in the aftermath of the 2008 crisis) to their traditionally nativist stances on the sociocultural dimension. These parties offered protection for the economically vulnerable social groups from the instability of world markets (Szanyi 2016; Miszerak and Rohac 2017; Toplišek 2020). They mixed economically redistributionist positions with nativist stances by arguing that welfare spending should be limited to the native population. They portrayed ethnic minorities as "a drain on state coffers" and "ordinary people" as the main victims of such policies (Brubaker 2020; de Cleen 2017), suggesting that a reduction in immigration would free up funds for more deserving welfare recipients (Adorf 2018: 30). This platform strongly resonated with working-class electorates, whose preferences have historically been more redistributionist and anti-immigration-oriented than those of average citizens in European democracies (Rennwald 2020: 71–85, see also Chapter 2). Indeed, as the studies cited in Chapter 1 have shown, more redistributive platforms of populist right parties correspond to their higher support from working-class electorates.

The cases of Britain, Germany, and Sweden discussed in Chapter 1 suggest that populist right parties tended to succeed electorally after partly incorporating working-class groups dealigned from social democratic parties. Similarly, Chapters 2, 3, and 4 provided evidence that the populist right in postcommunist Europe gained a substantive electoral advantage by incorporating large swaths of the electorates that formerly aligned with reformist left parties. Thus Chapter 3 showed, using a cross-country data set, that in postcommunist countries with a pro-market left, working-class groups have a higher propensity to support populist right-wing parties. The findings from the experimental survey presented in Chapter 6 also supported this conclusion: an experiment in Hungary demonstrated that when left parties embraced more pro-market positions, working-class electorates were more likely to back populist right-wing parties that adopted more left-leaning economic agendas.

To sum up, across both regions the fortunes of reformist left and populist right parties appear to be interconnected. This analysis lends credence to the position that political differences between the European West and European East are not categorical. By uniting the study of postcommunist transitions to the theoretical arguments that have emerged in the broader comparative politics literature on party politics and comparative political economy, the book has demonstrated that across both regions left rebranding was detrimental for their electoral fortunes. At the onset of the transition, postcommunist party systems had preconditions for the creation of stable party alignments consistent with postwar Western Europe, with left-wing parties appealing to economically vulnerable electorates on redistributive platforms and right-wing parties offering more pro-market policies. For the reasons discussed in this book, ex-communist parties' failure to align themselves programmatically and anchor themselves in relevant social cleavages was one of the main (but often neglected) factors that contributed to the instability of these party systems and to the rise of populist right parties.

By engaging with the literature on political strategies and the policy choices of ex-communist parties (Hanley 2001; Grzymala-Busse 2002a, 2002b; March and Mudde 2005; Vachudova 2005, 2008a, 2008b; Tavits and Letki 2009), this book has shown that these policy choices fueled the "proletarization" of the Eastern European populist right, echoing the dynamics in Western European countries (Ignazi 2003; Norris 2005; Rydgren 2007; Arzheimer 2013; Evans and Tilley 2012; Ost 2018; Rennwald 2020). While multiple scholars have hypothesized that there is a degree of convergence between Western and postcommunist processes, this was previously undocumented. And while the argument about the long-term impact of the Third Way has been discussed in Western European scholarship, until now few studies had attempted to apply it to the context of postcommunist Europe.

Why is it important to move beyond idiosyncratic explanations for party system dynamics in the postcommunist region? The analysis presented in this book deepens our understanding of party-system trajectories in different contexts: it shows the existence of generalizable cross-regional patterns of party system dynamics across various regions. While I do not deny the existence of significant variance across regions in the extent to which political competition occurs over economic and sociocultural issues, my analysis reveals that by and large, trends in the postcommunist region are comparable to those of Western European party systems (Rovny 2015; Rovny and Polk 2017).

The comparative framework proposed in this book helps highlight the importance of party choices. Despite the multicausal nature of the analyzed phenomena, matching the consequences of concrete economic policy choices by left parties on the supply side with voter behavior on the demand side helps account for the specific timing of left parties' demise in the postcommunist region. Where right-wing parties were in power during the periods of neoliberal adjustment, their reforms generally tended to stabilize party competition and channel societal resistance toward institutionalized leftist parties, which adopted more redistributionist economic positions (Roberts 2013). By contrast, where center-left parties in power implemented structural adjustment policies, they tended to dealign party systems programmatically, which led to these parties' demise and to the surge of populist parties (Hutter and Kriesi 2019: 24). Across both regions, in the electoral cycles following the adoption of neoliberal policies by reformist left parties, new opportunities emerged for right-wing populist parties.

As the following discussion reveals, understanding these cross-regional parallels helps develop more effective policy responses to counter this trend.

## ... But It Is Special

Despite these pronounced parallels, party systems in both regions also exhibit distinct differences.

First, reasons for left parties' programmatic rebranding were somewhat different across both regions. In Western Europe, left parties moved to the center of the economic dimension primarily because of the changing nature of their electorates. The working class, which had comprised the traditional constituencies of left-wing parties all over the region, was shrinking (Rennwald 2020). Industrial jobs moved abroad, and the labor force all over developed Europe reconstituted itself. The share of production workers in the Western European workforce declined from 31% in the 1970s to 16% in the 2010s, while the share of service workers increased from 14% to 20% throughout the same period (Rennwald 2020). With fewer blue-collar workers to make up their voter bases, social democratic parties had to expand their electorates by incorporating broader middle-class groups (Berman and Snegovaya 2019; Mudge 2018). As result, Western European left parties gradually developed an increasingly pro-market agenda. In this sense, for the Third Way left the rebranding was necessitated by the shifting profile of their electorates.

By contrast, the rebranding of postcommunist left parties was a product of other considerations: the desire to reject the association with a tainted communist past (Grzymala-Busse 2002a, 2002b; Tavits and Letki 2009: 556), the need for Western economic assistance, the failure of existing administrative economic systems, pressure from international institutions (Lendvai

2009: 26; Appel and Orenstein 2018: 87), as well as the overall desire to "imitate the West" (Krastev and Holmes 2018). This book paid particular attention to the neoliberal consensus that formed at the time of this rebranding, leaving left ex-communist successor parties few alternatives to adopting neoliberal reforms while simultaneously making them less responsive to their electorates. As a result, they took on pro-market policies faster and adopted them at a more "dramatic rate" (Orenstein 2013a: 375; 2013b), than did their Western counterparts (Tavits and Letki 2009; Appel and Orenstein 2016). Chapter 4, for example, showed how left parties often introduced austerity policies under the pressure of the EU or the IMF despite these policies' unpopularity among many of their supporters. In the long run, this provoked a stronger backlash from constituencies who were particularly hurt by such policies (Orenstein and Bugarič 2019). Many of these groups were subsequently incorporated by the populist right.

Second, in postcommunist regions the challenging experience of economic transition created sharper divisions between reform "winners" and "losers," which only exacerbated the trends outlined above. The communist legacy resulted in enduring mass support for the state-funded provision of social welfare (Pop-Eleches and Tucker 2014; Mason et al. 2000). Indeed, Chapter 2 showed that postcommunist voters are generally in favor of redistributional policies regardless of their individual socioeconomic status. These preferences of the electorates further deepened disenchantment with neoliberalism in the region (Orenstein and Bugarič 2019). Incentivized by EU conditionality, many postcommunist parties continued with episodes of radical neoliberal reform for nearly twenty years (Orenstein and Bugarič 2019: 3). As Chapter 4 illustrated, the adoption of pro-market policies by left-wing parties in this context often meant that the social groups that found themselves on the losing side of these reforms consistently lacked any political representation. These processes contributed to a stronger backlash against neoliberalism and reformist parties.

Somewhat ironically, this backlash took place sooner and went deeper in countries where the political establishment converged more strongly around the neoliberal consensus at the onset of the reforms. In Hungary and Poland, where ex-communist left parties became avowedly social democratic and engaged in reforms in an effort to convincingly signal to the public that they were economically and culturally modern, reform losers were subsequently more fully integrated by emerging nationalist-populist parties and the illiberal right-wing backlash was felt more strongly. By contrast, in the Czech

Republic and Slovakia, where large left-wing parties were reluctant to implement radical austerity reforms, throughout most of the observed period reform-resistant social groups were split across both sides of the political spectrum. This decreased the share of electorates available for populist right mobilization.

Third, in the postcommunist context it was more beneficial for challenger parties to attack reformist left-wing incumbents from the opposite side of the political spectrum. As Chapter 1 discussed, the legacy of communist regimes often forced left parties across the region to stay away from overly statist economic positions to avoid unfavorable policy associations with the former regime (Tavits and Letki 2009: 556; Ost 2018). By contrast, the same legacy gave an advantage to the parties on the opposite side of the political spectrum: there were fewer reservations about right-wing parties adopting redistributionist economic stances. This dynamic was unique to the postcommunist region. In Southern Europe, for example, the legacy of authoritarian right-wing regimes gave an advantage to the rise of populist parties on the left that could challenge reformist right parties from more redistributionist economic positions (Hutter and Kriesi 2019).

Fourth, in the postcommunist context this problem was further exacerbated by the sheer size of these constituencies. As discussed in the Introduction, this book's argument goes beyond working classes and is applicable to broader groups usually described as transition or reform losers (older and less educated, unemployed, or disproportionately exposed to income cuts) (Bornschier 2010a, 2010b; Inglehart and Norris 2016). However, in Eastern Europe working-class groups were particularly important, as they constituted a disproportionally larger portion of the electorates than they did in the West (see Chapter 2). Industrial jobs still dominated the postcommunist workforce given the structure of their economies (and received an additional boost from the relocation of industries from Western to Eastern Europe). Therefore, working classes continued to represent large shares of electorates in Eastern Europe. Chapter 2 showed that in the past two decades production workers accounted for about 30% to 35% of the postcommunist labor force, and the combined share of production workers, service workers, and clerks comprised about 66% of the population. As a result, the dealignment of working-class voters that resulted from the left's rebranding in postcommunist Europe left many more voters open to populist mobilization than it had in Western Europe, thus contributing to a stronger populist swing. Eastern European populist right parties skyrocketed in size, which led to their electoral domination in countries like Hungary and Poland. By contrast, populist parties in Western Europe had a relatively smaller share of voters to mobilize.

Fifth, and perhaps most important, is the fact that young democracies in Eastern Europe are substantially less institutionalized, more volatile, and more vulnerable than the established Western European democracies (Tavits 2005, 2013; Powell and Tucker 2014; Gherghina 2014). Postcommunist parties tend to have lower levels of popular party identification and lack stable partisan identities (Kopecký 2006). In particular, unlike Western social democrats who were around for almost a hundred years (Berman 2006), ex-communist left parties were never particularly anchored in their polities. While voters tended to punish rebranded leftist parties in both contexts, weaker party attachments of postcommunist electorates (Rose and Mshler 1998; Gherghina 2014) contributed to more dramatic voter swings between different parties to reward or to punish party behavior (Gherghina 2014; Bértoa 2014).[2] In this context, the pro-market shift of ex-communist left parties led to a stronger outflow of their former supporters. Once their profiles were watered down, these parties did not have much to keep their voters attached. Thus, the shift had a stronger impact on their electoral success, as compared to left parties in Western European countries. In turn, the lack of institutionalization of the party systems provided populist parties greater latitude in mobilizing support (Kriesi 2016; Sitter 2002).

Sixth, the quantitative evidence presented in Chapters 3 and 4 suggests that while the shifts of the working-class vote are clear and in line with the book's claims, the aggregate differences are too small to fully account for the rise of the populist right or the decline of the left. This suggests that other factors also played an important role in explaining the unprecedented success of the populist right across the region. Among them, in the context of poorly institutionalized postcommunist systems, populists' own strategies proved particularly consequential (Sitter 2002; Enyedi 2005; Kriesi 2016). In postcommunist Europe, populists combined economically protectionist positions with nationalist frames of a looming demise of "national identity" brought about by societal modernization and facilitated by external forces and internal opposition (Pytlas 2015, 2018). They presented the diverse

---

[2] For example, in the first generations of postcommunist elections, voters disaffected with the status quo frequently experimented with one set of incumbents after another, punishing all of the incumbents subsequently and opting for untried mainstream party alternatives (Pop-Eleches 2010; Sikk 2012).

array of alleged threats to an imagined homogeneous nation-state coming from ethnic (especially in the aftermath of the 2015 refugee crisis) or sexual minorities, Western or left-liberal values, and their societal supporters (Gidron and Bonikowski 2013; Kenny 2017). Populists' ability to capitalize on these issues was reinforced by voters' more culturally conservative orientations in the region where the recent experience of political and economic transition came to be associated with the destruction of traditional social structures (Pirro 2015; Pytlas 2015, 2018; Minkenberg 2017a; Snegovaya 2022a). They further exploited the existence of contested national borders (such as national diasporas in neighboring countries), the unassimilated legacy of World War II and the communist regimes, and "more deep-seated vulnerabilities" (Haughton 2014: 80; Hutter and Kriesi 2019).

A combination of these factors helps explain why in response to the decay of left parties in the postcommunist region the rightward populist drift was much more pronounced. The patterns common to both regions were exacerbated in the postcommunist context by region-specific factors. As result, the right populist drift was much stronger in Eastern Europe. While in recent years many European countries (Italy, Austria, the Netherlands, Sweden, Britain, France, and Germany) have seen right-wing populist parties become increasingly competitive in key elections, only in Poland and Hungary have these parties been able to win elections and form governments for several consecutive terms (Grzymala-Busse 2019b). An analytical approach that reconciles case specificity with a need for general analytical frames stemming from the cross-regional parallels in party-system dynamics is best positioned to explain this phenomenon (Rovny 2015).

## The Importance of Party Choices

This book makes several important contributions to the field.

First, it reveals that party choices matter far more than had been suspected. Scholarship on the populist right often postulated that the rise of populism is very much a demand-driven phenomenon based on the individual-level preferences of these parties' electorates (Norris and Inglehart 2019; Halikiopoulou 2019: 36). Yet, as discussed in the Introduction, the demand-side explanations alone are not sufficient to explain the electoral success of populist parties. Bringing together both the supply side (specific choices by left and populist right parties) and the demand side (voters' responses to these choices) allows us to more convincingly explain how left parties' pro-market policies provided right-wing populists with an opportunity to capture the resulting discontent, particularly among economically vulnerable electorates. This approach better accounts for the variation in the electoral fortunes of center-left and populist right parties across various countries, as well as specific timing of the left demise and the rise of right-wing populist parties.

Second, these findings challenge the conventional arguments that the constituencies of ex-communist parties remained loyal in spite of these parties' programmatic turnarounds (Fidrmuc 2000; Grzymala-Busse 2002a, 2002b; Kostelecký 2002; van Biezen 2003; Curry 2003; Morlang 2003; Tavits and Letki 2009). Instead, pro-market reforms implemented by left parties often went unnoticed due to the programmatic convergence of mainstream parties before EU accession, making it seem as though voters had remained loyal to left parties despite their programmatic turnaround. It was primarily after EU accession that other (often conservative and radical right) parties used populist appeals to sweep up economically vulnerable voters who had been abandoned by the left's pro-market shift. This shows that postcommunist voters are consistent and tend to support parties that best represent their interests.

Third, the relative importance of competition along the economic versus the sociocultural axis in support for the populist right remains an unresolved question within the current literature. A significant portion of the scholarship on this topic has emphasized the role of the sociocultural dimension in the popularity of populist right parties. Such studies have stressed that the populist right's success arose from a backlash against diversity and inclusiveness or (specifically for the postcommunist context) against "Westernization" (Spies 2013; Golder 2016; Norris and Inglehart 2019; Krastev and Holmes 2018). While this book did not reject the importance of such accounts, it aimed to demonstrate that the populist phenomenon needs to be understood in combination with leftist parties' policy choices on the economic dimension: As the empirical evidence presented in Chapters 3 and 6 has shown, these parties' positioning on the sociocultural dimension alone cannot fully account for the dealignment of left electorates and their incorporation by populist right parties. The pro-market rebranding of the ex-communist left has enabled the populist right to unite culturally conservative and redistribution-oriented electorates in their support bases. Chapter 4 has shown the continuous relevance of the economic policy dimension for postcommunist populist parties like Fidesz, Jobbik, and PiS. To appeal to their newly found support bases, these parties conflated nationalist with economic frames, portaying the "ordinary people" as the prime victims of a multicultural society, living in poor areas with high immigration rates or "Roma crime," and the prime sufferers of the social injustices of the transition period (de Cleen 2017: 11; Hilmar 2022; Waterbury 2020). They adopted economic nationalist policies offering to bolster and protect national economies against the volatility and unpredictability of world markets, as well as the influence of the international institutions (Johnson and Barnes 2015; Mikecz 2019; Bohle and Greskovits 2019). This significantly expanded the support bases of populist right parties.

Fourth, the scholarship on party system dynamics in postcommunist Europe remains mostly qualitative. By contrast, this book offered methodologically rigorous and innovative ways to account for the electoral dynamics there by using various forms of analysis and types of evidence to support the theoretical argument. In addition to my cross-country and individual survey analysis, I introduced an experimental survey framework that helps empirically identify the causal mechanisms underlying the popularity of populist right parties.

## When Right Is Left

Once social democratic parties rebrand, it opens up opportunities for different parties to move to the lower left quadrant in the two-dimensional space of party competition to attract more votes. There are different trajectories for parties to get there. While PiS and Fidesz started with cultural conservatism, only later adding redistributionist positions, the Czech KSČM was on the left economically from the start but subsequently adopted nativist positions; Smer-SD also started with more statist economic positions and subsequently periodically added "nationalism lite" (Figure 5.3) to its platform. This begs the question: Should one care which particular *kind* of party occupies the space, a left party or a populist right party, as long as they offer similar platforms and incorporate similar electorates? The comparative framework introduced in this book helps answer this question. Western European comparisons help highlight the essential role of social democratic left parties in the stability of liberal democracy.

While a breakdown of established parties often leaves in its wake fragmented and ideologically vacuous party systems (Lupu 2016), it is particularly alarming when those that break down are social democratic parties. After all, social democrats were an integral part of why postwar Western Europe "was able—for the first time in its history—to combine economic growth, well-functioning democracy, and social stability" (Berman 2016: 72). During the economic collapse and social chaos of the interwar period, in the search for stability, community, and social protection, European voters were often drawn to extremist movements. Polanyi (1944) famously argued that fascist movements could be understood as a form of social resistance to the imposition of a global market society, in which labor, land, and money all had to be simultaneously converted into commodities regardless of associated social costs. This is because those movements and parties offered a (much needed) vision of society in which states control markets and fight the atomization, dislocation, and other discords brought about by capitalism. Thus, for many voters, fascism and national socialism represented real solutions to the contradictions and problems of market society (Berman 2006, 2016). Alas, the cure ended up being much worse than the disease.

In the aftermath of the Second World War, the emergence of social democracy was a search for an alternative remedy by Western European societies to create a vision of "a world in which the market's reach and excesses could be controlled and people's longing for social solidarity could be satisfied—without the sacrifice of democracy and the trampling of freedom that fascism and Nazism brought in their wake" (Berman 2006: 5). And that cure ended up working. For several decades social democratic parties were able to achieve just that: bringing working classes and other economically vulnerable groups toward the political center and support for democracy, and away from the extremes where these electorates often found themselves in interwar Europe.

Conversely, the decay of center-left parties risks the reemergence of opposite trends. Populist right parties respond to frustrations and economic fears of working classes and other groups that see themselves as losing out by offering protection against the deleterious effects of globalization and economic transformation. However, populist right parties pair redistributionist positions on the economic dimension with polarizing frames on the sociocultural dimension. They politicize national, ethnic, religious, or cultural identity issues, blaming the misfortunes of their supporters on groups (both inside and outside) that allegedly pose a threat to the popular will; they thus spread hostility to various "outsiders," sexual and ethnic minorities, and other groups (Rodrik 2018, 2021). Hence, populist right parties tend to create serious risks for democratic stability. Müller (2014), for example, argues that these illiberal elements of right-wing populism are direct threats to democracy; such parties often disregard the rights of those they do not include in the broad definition of "the people," for example, ethnic or sectarian minorities, and undermine the checks on government power that they claim stifle the "will of the people." Taking advantage of the unpopularity of neoliberal economic policies, many right-wing populist parties intentionally conflate neoliberalism with liberal democracy. They argue against "liberalism" as such and claim that moving away from neoliberal economic policies necessitates dismantling liberal democracy (Vachudova 2020). Such tendencies are indeed pronounced in postcommunist countries where such parties came to power and used their appeals to legitimize an assault on democratic norms and institutions to reduce the power of the so-called enemies of the people (Cianetti, Dawson, and Hanley 2018; Grzymala-Busse 2019c; Bochsler and Juon 2020; Vachudova 2020).

Even when populist right parties are not in power, they still risk deepening social polarization and fragmentation. Left parties—even when they move to the lower left quadrant—tend to adopt lighter positions on the sociocultural dimension, as they primarily compete on the economic dimension. Left parties' competition along the economic dimension presupposes a certain degree of structured and long-term interactions of the parties in a given system (Hernández and Kriesi 2016). This contrasts with the hard nativism of the populist right that is more dangerous to minority rights and to the stability of corresponding polities (Kalb 2009, 2018; Kalb and Halmai 2011; Ost 2000, 2006; Scheiring 2020b). When party competition shifts to the sociocultural dimension, the politicization of identity may lead to social fragmentation (Fukuyama 2020). It is much harder to find common ground for the groups that disagree about identity issues than for those that disagree on economic issues.

Unlike Western social democrats, postcommunist left parties like Smer-SD and KSČM are prone to using national and populist appeals (Malová 2017). But even then, they tend to be less polarizing. Moreover, their presence offers viable left alternative splitting electorates who combine nativist and redistributionist preferences across both sides of the political spectrum. This helps curtail the mobilization potential of extremist parties. By contrast, in the absence of a political tool to appeal to their class-based political identity, larger shares of electorates with nativist and redistributionist preferences risk getting incorporated by extremist parties contributing to their rise.

This explains why the decay of left parties creates particularly serious risks for stability and democracy in corresponding party systems.

## Winning Back the Working Class?

In light of these considerations, understanding ways for left parties to regain enough support from their traditional electorates is of particular importance (Thorsen 2021). In the past decades a series of bad policy choices often made the European left look like "dead men walking, losing momentum, enthusiasm, and the ability to weather difficulties" (Berman 2006: 217). Their electoral defeats launched a scholarly debate about the ability for center-left parties to come back to power.

The solutions that have been proposed commonly emphasized adopting a more restrictive immigration agenda to reclaim those electorates (Mudde 2002). However, this book's findings do not support this conclusion. Historically, center-left parties of Western and postcommunist Europe have been more liberal on socioeconomic issues. Using a redistributive agenda, they attracted voters who are more redistribution-oriented but took a variety of stances on sociocultural issues, from postmaterialism to social traditionalism. In recent years, as their pro-market orientations increased, the share of higher social classes (upper middle classes and sociocultural professionals) in the left's electorates, the group with postmaterialist cultural preferences, has grown larger as well. Therefore, if they were to take more conservative positions on the sociocultural dimension, left parties would risk splitting their existing voters on cultural issues and lose their middle-class supporters to parties with more moderate stances on immigration (primarily to green parties) (Berman and Snegovaya 2019). At the same time, the left's ability to reattract working-class electorates from populist right parties would still be questionable, since the populist right overall has an advantage over the left and more credibility among lower-income groups on sociocultural issues. Overall, the potential risks from adopting more restrictive immigration agendas run high, while the advantages are not clear. To be successful, left parties would need to offer policies that unite various class categories.

An alternative recommendation is for left parties to move back to their traditional leftist positions on the economy, on which there is more agreement among the diverse segments of the left's (potential) electoral base (Rennwald 2020: 97). This is particularly relevant in the postcommunist context, where (as Chapter 2 shows) the working class and economically vulnerable still constitute a substantive (up to two-thirds) share of electorates. For example, Ost (2018: 124) suggests that in Poland left parties should take more redistributionist economic positions to stop the spread of the populist right while acknowledging that it would be particularly hard to do so in a regional context where the radical left is still associated with communist dictatorships.

Recently in Western Europe such an approach worked for the Portuguese Socialist Party, which had adopted Third Way rebranding in the past (Lobo and Magalhães 2004). In 2015 a socialist government came to power, supported by the communists and two small left-wing parties. Austerity policies introduced by the previous center-right government created incentives for these parties to enter an alliance despite significant disagreements on other issues (Ferreira and Fonseca 2018; Jalali, Moniz, and Silva 2020). When this "quasi-coalition government" (Fernandes 2016) was formed, few commentators believed it would survive more than six months (Goes 2019). Yet the coalition defied these expectations. In preceding years Portugal saw unemployment and poverty increase and young people leave the country in high numbers. Claiming to put "an end to the sacrifices" imposed by the right-wing government (Ferreira and Fonseca 2018: 142), the left coalition reversed some of the previous government's austerity measures that directly affected pockets of the working classes and the most vulnerable, including cutbacks in social security payments, wages, and pensions (Goes 2019; Berman and Snegovaya 2019). The success of these policies allowed the party to win several consecutive electoral terms.

A similar strategy was attempted in the United Kingdom. Jeremy Corbyn reoriented the Labour Party toward a more traditional leftist economic platform and emphasized the need to fight austerity, while scaling down emphasis on issues that were controversial with voters, such as Britain's relationship with the EU (Rennwald 2020: 99). This strategy succeeded as long as Brexit was not at the center of the electoral campaign. In 2017, Labour received 40% of the vote share, its highest level since the 2001 general election. However, in the 2019 election, when Brexit dominated the electoral campaign, Labour suffered a strong electoral defeat, receiving its weakest electoral outcome since 1935. This is a good illustration of the fact that such approaches do not guarantee eventual electoral success. And it begs the question: Under which conditions are left-wing parties able to recuperate some of their traditional electorates by offering distinctive and convincing left-leaning economic policies that correspond to the preferences of economically vulnerable groups? Some of this book's key findings address this.

First, in Chapter 1 it was shown that the pro-market shift of left parties was at least in part driven by EU conditionality, which required them to cut down their welfare spending and reform labor markets. The EU-imposed constraints may also limit the capacity of these parties to adopt more leftist economic stances in the future. The EU has powers and duties to enforce budgetary austerity, which constrains the spending policies of its member states (Greer, Jarman, and Baeten 2016) and therefore decreases the ability of parties in power to implement more redistributionist policies. In recent years there are some promising signs that the mood in Brussels is changing. In particular, several members of the European Commission (2017) started talking about the need to focus on the social dimension of the EU, which might create more leeway for social democrats (Goes 2019).

Second, the realignment of electorates tends to occur when a political opening—a large social group available for political mobilization—is present in a given party system. Once the left party rebrands economically and large swaths of its former electorates get incorporated by the populist right, it becomes much harder for left parties, whether old or new, to win back working-class electorates. That is because by then the space vacated by the left is occupied by populist right parties. This suggests that pro-market left parties willing to rebrand themselves in order to reattract economically vulnerable electorates may be limited in their abilities to do so now that sizable shares of these groups have already aligned with populist right parties. This is important to keep in mind when considering any future rebranding by center-left parties. In the future, new political openings allowing left parties to regain some working-class constituencies will most likely emerge when right-wing populist parties switch their economic platforms, for instance by adopting austerity. Roberts (2013), for example, shows that when Latin American populist parties played a major role in the implementation of market reforms, this opened the door for a dealignment of party systems much in line with the logic of this book.

While this discussion suggests that none of the proposed solutions guarantees a clear win for center-left parties, one conclusion is certain: left parties should recover their distinctive and convincing economic profile. This profile would involve taking more protectionist and redistributionist stances on the economic dimension as well as undergoing a political revitalization in order to be able to offer their prospective supporters a compelling vision to vote for. The main problem is one of intellectual imagination: social democratic parties will have to figure out ways to make their commitment to European integration compatible with their ideological goals of catering to the needs of economically vulnerable groups.

# Factor Analysis for Chapter 2

**Table A.1** Factor Analysis for the Economic Preference Axis

| | Variable | Factor 1 |
|---|---|---|
| 1. | Standard of living for the unemployed, government responsibility | 0.7835 |
| 2. | Standard of living for the old, government responsibility | 0.7663 |
| 3. | Job for everyone, government responsibility | 0.8289 |
| 4. | Government should reduce differences in income levels | 0.5260 |

**Table A.2** Factor Analysis for the Sociocultural Preference Axis

| | Variable | Factor 1 |
|---|---|---|
| 1. | Country's cultural life undermined or enriched by immigrants | 0.7542 |
| 2. | Immigrants make country worse or better place to live | 0.7407 |
| 3. | Allow few/many immigrants of same race/ethnic group as majority | 0.7958 |
| 4. | Allow few/many immigrants of different race/ethnic group from majority | 0.8701 |
| 5. | Allow few/many immigrants from poorer countries outside Europe | 0.8303 |

# Cross-Country Analysis: Left Vote vs. Other Parties—Probit Model (Basic)

Table A.3 Class-Based Structure of Left Parties Vote *vs.* Other Parties

| | (1) | Margins | (2) | Margins | (3) | Margins | (4) | Margins |
|---|---|---|---|---|---|---|---|---|
| Self-employed professionals and large employers | -0.328*** | -0.098*** | -0.323*** | -0.093*** | -0.328*** | -0.098*** | -0.323*** | -0.093*** |
| | (0.068) | (0.019) | (0.067) | (0.019) | (0.068) | (0.019) | (0.067) | (0.019) |
| Sociocultural (semi-)professionals | -0.035 | -0.011 | -0.037 | -0.012 | -0.035 | -0.011 | -0.037 | -0.012 |
| | (0.031) | (0.010) | (0.031) | (0.010) | (0.031) | (0.010) | (0.031) | (0.010) |
| Small business owners | -0.297*** | -0.089*** | -0.303*** | -0.092*** | -0.297*** | -0.089*** | -0.303*** | -0.092*** |
| | (0.035) | (0.010) | (0.035) | (0.010) | (0.035) | (0.010) | (0.035) | (0.010) |
| Technical (semi-)professionals | -0.136*** | -0.043*** | -0.135*** | -0.043*** | -0.136*** | -0.043*** | -0.135*** | -0.043*** |
| | (0.037) | (0.011) | (0.037) | (0.011) | (0.037) | (0.011) | (0.037) | (0.011) |
| Clerks | 0.029 | 0.009 | 0.027 | 0.007 | 0.029 | 0.009 | 0.027 | 0.007 |
| | (0.033) | (0.011) | (0.033) | (0.011) | (0.033) | (0.011) | (0.033) | (0.011) |
| Service workers | -0.012 | -0.004 | -0.010 | -0.006 | -0.012 | -0.004 | -0.010 | -0.006 |
| | (0.029) | (0.009) | (0.029) | (0.009) | (0.029) | (0.009) | (0.029) | (0.009) |
| Production workers | -0.027 | -0.009 | -0.025 | -0.011 | -0.027 | -0.009 | -0.025 | -0.011 |
| | (0.027) | (0.009) | (0.027) | (0.009) | (0.027) | (0.009) | (0.027) | (0.009) |
| Economic policy position | -0.274*** | -0.086*** | -0.212*** | -0.087*** | -0.274*** | -0.086*** | -0.212*** | -0.087*** |
| | (0.020) | (0.006) | (0.028) | (0.006) | (0.020) | (0.006) | (0.028) | (0.006) |
| **Self-employed professionals# Economic policy position** | | | -0.024 | -0.020 | | | 0.124* | -0.024 |
| | | | (0.019) | (0.019) | | | (0.070) | (0.019) |
| Sociocultural (semi-)professionals# Economic policy position | | | -0.068*** | -0.062*** | | | 0.001 | -0.068*** |
| | | | (0.010) | (0.010) | | | (0.032) | (0.010) |

| | (1) | (2) | (3) | (4) | (5) | (6) | (7) | (8) |
|---|---|---|---|---|---|---|---|---|
| Small business owners# Economic policy position | | | -0.059*** | -0.055*** | | | -0.002 | -0.059*** |
| | | | (0.009) | (0.010) | | | (0.036) | (0.009) |
| Technical (semi-)professionals# Economic policy position | | | -0.065*** | -0.060*** | | | -0.002 | -0.065*** |
| | | | (0.011) | (0.012) | | | (0.039) | (0.011) |
| Clerks# Economic policy position | | | -0.089*** | **-0.083*** | | | **-0.059*** | -0.089*** |
| | | | (0.010) | **(0.011)** | | | **(0.033)** | (0.010) |
| Service workers# Economic policy position | | | -0.102*** | **-0.096*** | | | **-0.105*** | -0.102*** |
| | | | (0.008) | **(0.009)** | | | **(0.028)** | (0.008) |
| Production workers# Economic policy position | | | -0.107*** | **-0.102*** | | | **-0.124*** | -0.107*** |
| | | | (0.007) | **(0.008)** | | | **(0.025)** | (0.007) |
| Sociocultural policy position | | | | | -0.003 | -0.001 | 0.004 | 0.001 |
| | | | | | (0.032) | (0.010) | (0.032) | (0.010) |
| Gender | 0.008 | 0.003 | 0.009 | 0.003 | 0.008 | 0.003 | 0.009 | 0.003 |
| | (0.016) | (0.005) | (0.016) | (0.005) | (0.016) | (0.005) | (0.016) | (0.005) |
| Age | 0.012*** | 0.002*** | 0.011*** | 0.002*** | 0.012*** | 0.002*** | 0.011*** | 0.002*** |
| | (0.003) | (0.000) | (0.003) | (0.000) | (0.003) | (0.000) | (0.003) | (0.000) |
| Age squared | -0.000 | | -0.000 | | -0.000 | | -0.000 | |
| | (0.000) | | (0.000) | | (0.000) | | (0.000) | |
| Lower secondary education | 0.079* | 0.024* | 0.083* | 0.026* | 0.079* | 0.024* | 0.083* | 0.026* |
| | (0.047) | (0.014) | (0.047) | (0.014) | (0.047) | (0.014) | (0.047) | (0.014) |
| Upper secondary education completed | 0.111** | 0.034** | 0.108** | 0.033** | 0.111** | 0.034** | 0.108** | 0.033** |
| | (0.047) | (0.014) | (0.047) | (0.014) | (0.047) | (0.014) | (0.047) | (0.014) |

(continued)

**Table A.3** Continued

| | (1) | Margins | (2) | Margins | (3) | Margins | (4) | Margins |
|---|---|---|---|---|---|---|---|---|
| Postsecondary nontertiary education | 0.148** | 0.046** | 0.141** | 0.044** | 0.148** | 0.046** | 0.141** | 0.044** |
| | (0.059) | (0.018) | (0.059) | (0.018) | (0.059) | (0.018) | (0.059) | (0.018) |
| Tertiary education | 0.100** | 0.031** | 0.092* | 0.028* | 0.100** | 0.031** | 0.092* | 0.028* |
| | (0.051) | (0.015) | (0.051) | (0.015) | (0.051) | (0.015) | (0.051) | (0.015) |
| Retired | 0.053** | 0.017** | 0.053** | 0.017** | 0.053** | 0.017** | 0.053** | 0.017** |
| | (0.025) | (0.008) | (0.026) | (0.008) | (0.025) | (0.008) | (0.026) | (0.008) |
| Unemployed | −0.029 | −0.009 | −0.032 | −0.010 | −0.029 | −0.009 | −0.032 | −0.010 |
| | (0.038) | (0.012) | (0.038) | (0.012) | (0.038) | (0.012) | (0.038) | (0.012) |
| Czech Republic | 0.132*** | 0.043*** | 0.145*** | 0.047*** | 0.136*** | 0.044*** | 0.139*** | 0.045*** |
| | (0.029) | (0.009) | (0.029) | (0.009) | (0.050) | (0.016) | (0.050) | (0.016) |
| Estonia | −0.269*** | −0.078*** | −0.256*** | −0.074*** | −0.264*** | −0.077*** | −0.265*** | −0.077*** |
| | (0.037) | (0.011) | (0.038) | (0.011) | (0.076) | (0.023) | (0.076) | (0.023) |
| Hungary | 0.627*** | 0.223*** | 0.651*** | 0.231*** | 0.632*** | 0.224*** | 0.642*** | 0.228*** |
| | (0.056) | (0.019) | (0.056) | (0.019) | (0.084) | (0.027) | (0.084) | (0.027) |
| Lithuania | 0.400*** | 0.138*** | 0.411*** | 0.141*** | 0.403*** | 0.139*** | 0.406*** | 0.140*** |
| | (0.053) | (0.018) | (0.053) | (0.018) | (0.064) | (0.021) | (0.064) | (0.021) |
| Latvia | −1.337*** | −0.246*** | −1.348*** | −0.244*** | −1.337*** | −0.245*** | −1.349*** | −0.246*** |
| | (0.074) | (0.008) | (0.074) | (0.008) | (0.074) | (0.015) | (0.074) | (0.015) |
| Poland | −0.619*** | −0.158*** | −0.619*** | −0.156*** | −0.610*** | −0.155*** | −0.633*** | −0.160*** |
| | (0.040) | (0.010) | (0.040) | (0.010) | (0.110) | (0.028) | (0.111) | (0.028) |

| | | | | | | | | |
|---|---|---|---|---|---|---|---|---|
| Romania | -0.256*** | -0.075*** | -0.263*** | -0.076*** | -0.256*** | -0.075*** | -0.263*** | -0.077*** |
| | (0.053) | (0.014) | (0.053) | (0.014) | (0.054) | (0.015) | (0.054) | (0.015) |
| Slovenia | -0.014 | -0.004 | -0.008 | -0.003 | -0.009 | -0.003 | -0.017 | -0.005 |
| | (0.035) | (0.011) | (0.035) | (0.011) | (0.075) | (0.024) | (0.075) | (0.024) |
| Slovakia | 0.366*** | 0.126*** | 0.374*** | 0.128*** | 0.370*** | 0.127*** | 0.368*** | 0.126*** |
| | (0.028) | (0.009) | (0.028) | (0.009) | (0.053) | (0.016) | (0.053) | (0.016) |
| 2008 | 0.024 | 0.008 | 0.023 | 0.008 | 0.024 | 0.008 | 0.023 | 0.008 |
| | (0.022) | (0.007) | (0.022) | (0.007) | (0.022) | (0.007) | (0.022) | (0.007) |
| 2010 | -0.279*** | -0.088*** | -0.280*** | -0.088*** | -0.278*** | -0.088*** | -0.280*** | -0.088*** |
| | (0.026) | (0.008) | (0.026) | (0.008) | (0.026) | (0.008) | (0.026) | (0.008) |
| 2012 | -0.156*** | -0.051*** | -0.155*** | -0.050*** | -0.155*** | -0.050*** | -0.156*** | -0.051*** |
| | (0.026) | (0.008) | (0.026) | (0.008) | (0.026) | (0.008) | (0.026) | (0.008) |
| 2014 | -0.455*** | -0.136*** | -0.455*** | -0.136*** | -0.454*** | -0.136*** | -0.456*** | -0.137*** |
| | (0.035) | (0.010) | (0.035) | (0.010) | (0.036) | (0.010) | (0.036) | (0.010) |
| Constant | -1.021*** | | -1.025*** | | -1.025*** | | -1.018*** | |
| | (0.090) | | (0.090) | | (0.104) | | (0.104) | |
| Observations | 39,448 | 39,448 | 39,448 | 39,448 | 39,448 | 39,448 | 39,448 | 39,448 |
| r2_p | 0.0883 | | 0.0897 | | 0.0883 | | 0.0897 | |

*Note:* All models include controls for gender, age, age squared, and education. Table reports effects of probit regressions and marginal effects. Robust standard errors in parentheses. * $p < 0.1$, ** $p < 0.05$, *** $p < 0.01$.

# Cross-Country Analysis: Left Vote vs. Other Parties—Probit Model (Controlling for Religiosity and Immigration)

**Table A.4** Class-Based Structure of Left Parties Vote vs. Other Parties

|  | (1) | (2) | (3) | (4) |
|---|---|---|---|---|
| Self-employed professionals and large employers | −0.312*** | −0.307*** | −0.312*** | −0.307*** |
|  | (0.069) | (0.068) | (0.069) | (0.068) |
| Small business owners | −0.284*** | −0.290*** | −0.284*** | −0.290*** |
|  | (0.036) | (0.037) | (0.036) | (0.037) |
| Technical (semi-)professionals | −0.158*** | −0.156*** | −0.157*** | −0.155*** |
|  | (0.039) | (0.039) | (0.039) | (0.039) |
| Production workers | −0.008 | −0.003 | −0.007 | −0.003 |
|  | (0.028) | (0.029) | (0.028) | (0.029) |
| Clerks | 0.032 | 0.032 | 0.032 | 0.031 |
|  | (0.034) | (0.035) | (0.034) | (0.035) |
| Sociocultural (semi-)professionals | −0.020 | −0.019 | −0.020 | −0.019 |
|  | (0.032) | (0.032) | (0.032) | (0.032) |
| Service workers | −0.005 | −0.001 | −0.006 | −0.001 |
|  | (0.030) | (0.030) | (0.030) | (0.030) |
| **Economic policy position** | −0.263*** | −0.202*** | −0.262*** | −0.201*** |
|  | (0.020) | (0.029) | (0.020) | (0.029) |
| Self-employed professionals# Economic policy position |  | 0.116 |  | 0.115 |
|  |  | (0.072) |  | (0.072) |
| Small business owners# Economic policy position |  | −0.011 |  | −0.012 |
|  |  | (0.037) |  | (0.037) |
| Technical (semi-)professionals# Economic policy position |  | −0.000 |  | −0.001 |
|  |  | (0.041) |  | (0.041) |

(*continued*)

## Table A.4 Continued

| | (1) | (2) | (3) | (4) |
|---|---|---|---|---|
| Production workers# Economic policy position | | −0.115*** (0.027) | | −0.116*** (0.027) |
| Clerks# Economic policy position | | −0.057* (0.034) | | −0.058* (0.034) |
| Sociocultural (semi-)professionals# Economic policy position | | −0.015 (0.033) | | −0.016 (0.033) |
| Service workers# Economic policy position | | −0.102*** (0.029) | | −0.103*** (0.029) |
| Gender | −0.044** (0.017) | −0.043** (0.017) | −0.044** (0.017) | −0.043** (0.017) |
| Age | 0.011*** (0.003) | 0.011*** (0.003) | 0.011*** (0.003) | 0.011*** (0.003) |
| Age squared | −0.000 (0.000) | −0.000 (0.000) | −0.000 (0.000) | −0.000 (0.000) |
| Lower secondary education | 0.141** (0.055) | 0.142*** (0.055) | 0.141** (0.055) | 0.142*** (0.055) |
| Upper secondary education completed | 0.137** (0.054) | 0.131** (0.054) | 0.137** (0.054) | 0.131** (0.054) |
| Postsecondary nontertiary education | 0.175*** (0.065) | 0.165** (0.065) | 0.176*** (0.065) | 0.166** (0.065) |
| Tertiary education | 0.118** (0.058) | 0.108* (0.058) | 0.119** (0.058) | 0.108* (0.058) |
| Retired | 0.077*** (0.027) | 0.077*** (0.027) | 0.077*** (0.027) | 0.076*** (0.027) |
| Unemployed | −0.044 (0.040) | −0.046 (0.040) | −0.045 (0.040) | −0.047 (0.040) |
| How religious are you | −0.171*** (0.009) | −0.170*** (0.009) | −0.172*** (0.009) | −0.171*** (0.009) |
| Culture undermined (0) or enriched (10) by immigrants | 0.015* (0.008) | 0.013 (0.008) | 0.015* (0.008) | 0.013 (0.008) |
| Czech Republic | 0.059* (0.032) | 0.067** (0.032) | 0.026 (0.054) | 0.028 (0.054) |
| Estonia | −0.311*** (0.039) | −0.301*** (0.039) | −0.366*** (0.081) | −0.365*** (0.081) |

Table A.4 Continued

|  | (1) | (2) | (3) | (4) |
|---|---|---|---|---|
| Hungary | 0.615*** | 0.633*** | 0.563*** | 0.572*** |
|  | (0.058) | (0.058) | (0.089) | (0.089) |
| Lithuania | 0.497*** | 0.504*** | 0.467*** | 0.469*** |
|  | (0.055) | (0.055) | (0.068) | (0.068) |
| Latvia | −1.296*** | −1.311*** | −1.300*** | −1.315*** |
|  | (0.078) | (0.078) | (0.078) | (0.078) |
| Poland | −0.513*** | −0.515*** | −0.597*** | −0.614*** |
|  | (0.042) | (0.042) | (0.116) | (0.117) |
| Romania | −0.151** | −0.158*** | −0.156*** | −0.163*** |
|  | (0.059) | (0.059) | (0.059) | (0.059) |
| Slovenia | 0.006 | 0.008 | −0.049 | −0.056 |
|  | (0.037) | (0.037) | (0.079) | (0.080) |
| Slovakia | 0.489*** | 0.493*** | 0.452*** | 0.450*** |
|  | (0.030) | (0.030) | (0.056) | (0.056) |
| 2008 | 0.036 | 0.036 | 0.037 | 0.037 |
|  | (0.023) | (0.023) | (0.023) | (0.023) |
| 2010 | −0.270*** | −0.272*** | −0.273*** | −0.276*** |
|  | (0.027) | (0.027) | (0.027) | (0.027) |
| 2012 | −0.151*** | −0.151*** | −0.155*** | −0.155*** |
|  | (0.027) | (0.027) | (0.028) | (0.028) |
| 2014 | −0.437*** | −0.438*** | −0.446*** | −0.448*** |
|  | (0.037) | (0.037) | (0.038) | (0.038) |
| Sociocultural policy position |  |  | 0.026 | 0.031 |
|  |  |  | (0.034) | (0.034) |
| Constant | −1.072*** | −1.070*** | −1.031*** | −1.021*** |
|  | (0.097) | (0.097) | (0.111) | (0.111) |
| Observations | 36,341 | 36,341 | 36,341 | 36,341 |
| r2_p | 0.0976 | 0.0987 | 0.0976 | 0.0987 |

*Note*: Table reports effects of probit regressions. All models include controls for gender, age, age squared, education, religiosity, and immigration attitudes. * $p < 0.1$, ** $p < 0.05$, *** $p < 0.01$.

# Cross-Country Analysis: Left Vote vs. Other Parties—Probit Model (Controlling for Presence of a Radical Right Party)

**Table A.5** Class-Based Structure of Left Parties Vote vs. Other Parties, Controlling for Presence of a Radical Right Party

|  | (1) | (2) | (3) | (4) |
|---|---|---|---|---|
| Self-employed professionals and large employers | −0.329*** | −0.324*** | −0.329*** | −0.324*** |
|  | (0.068) | (0.067) | (0.068) | (0.067) |
| Small business owners | −0.297*** | −0.303*** | −0.297*** | −0.303*** |
|  | (0.035) | (0.035) | (0.035) | (0.035) |
| Technical (semi-)professionals | −0.137*** | −0.136*** | −0.137*** | −0.136*** |
|  | (0.037) | (0.037) | (0.037) | (0.037) |
| Production workers | −0.027 | −0.025 | −0.027 | −0.025 |
|  | (0.027) | (0.027) | (0.027) | (0.027) |
| Clerks | 0.028 | 0.026 | 0.028 | 0.026 |
|  | (0.033) | (0.033) | (0.033) | (0.033) |
| Sociocultural (semi-)professionals | −0.036 | −0.038 | −0.036 | −0.038 |
|  | (0.031) | (0.031) | (0.031) | (0.031) |
| Service workers | −0.013 | −0.010 | −0.013 | −0.010 |
|  | (0.029) | (0.029) | (0.029) | (0.029) |
| Economic policy position | −0.258*** | −0.194*** | −0.258*** | −0.194*** |
|  | (0.023) | (0.030) | (0.023) | (0.030) |
| Self-employed professionals# Economic policy position |  | 0.123* |  | 0.123* |
|  |  | (0.070) |  | (0.070) |
| Small business owners# Economic policy position |  | −0.003 |  | −0.003 |
|  |  | (0.036) |  | (0.036) |
| Technical (semi-)professionals# Economic policy position |  | −0.002 |  | −0.002 |
|  |  | (0.039) |  | (0.039) |

(*continued*)

**Table A.5** Continued

|  | (1) | (2) | (3) | (4) |
|---|---|---|---|---|
| Production workers# Economic policy position |  | −0.125*** |  | −0.125*** |
|  |  | (0.026) |  | (0.026) |
| Clerks# Economic policy position |  | −0.060* |  | −0.060* |
|  |  | (0.033) |  | (0.033) |
| Sociocultural (semi-)professionals# Economic policy position |  | −0.000 |  | −0.000 |
|  |  | (0.032) |  | (0.032) |
| Service workers# Economic policy position |  | −0.106*** |  | −0.105*** |
|  |  | (0.028) |  | (0.028) |
| Gender | 0.008 | 0.009 | 0.008 | 0.009 |
|  | (0.016) | (0.016) | (0.016) | (0.016) |
| Age | 0.012*** | 0.011*** | 0.012*** | 0.011*** |
|  | (0.003) | (0.003) | (0.003) | (0.003) |
| Age squared | −0.000 | −0.000 | −0.000 | −0.000 |
|  | (0.000) | (0.000) | (0.000) | (0.000) |
| Lower secondary education | 0.079* | 0.083* | 0.079* | 0.083* |
|  | (0.047) | (0.047) | (0.047) | (0.047) |
| Upper secondary education completed | 0.111** | 0.109** | 0.111** | 0.109** |
|  | (0.047) | (0.047) | (0.047) | (0.047) |
| Postsecondary nontertiary education | 0.148** | 0.141** | 0.148** | 0.141** |
|  | (0.059) | (0.059) | (0.059) | (0.059) |
| Tertiary education | 0.100** | 0.092* | 0.100** | 0.092* |
|  | (0.051) | (0.051) | (0.051) | (0.051) |
| Retired | 0.053** | 0.052** | 0.053** | 0.052** |
|  | (0.025) | (0.026) | (0.025) | (0.026) |
| Unemployed | −0.029 | −0.032 | −0.029 | −0.032 |
|  | (0.038) | (0.038) | (0.038) | (0.038) |
| Presence of a radical right party | −0.043 | −0.046 | −0.044 | −0.046 |
|  | (0.033) | (0.033) | (0.034) | (0.034) |
| Czech Republic | 0.089** | 0.099** | 0.101* | 0.103* |
|  | (0.044) | (0.044) | (0.057) | (0.057) |
| Estonia | −0.302*** | −0.291*** | −0.282*** | −0.284*** |
|  | (0.046) | (0.046) | (0.077) | (0.078) |
| Hungary | 0.559*** | 0.578*** | 0.577*** | 0.585*** |
|  | (0.074) | (0.074) | (0.092) | (0.093) |

**Table A.5** Continued

|  | (1) | (2) | (3) | (4) |
|---|---|---|---|---|
| Lithuania | 0.319*** | 0.324*** | 0.327*** | 0.327*** |
|  | (0.082) | (0.082) | (0.086) | (0.086) |
| Latvia | −1.360*** | −1.372*** | −1.359*** | −1.372*** |
|  | (0.076) | (0.076) | (0.076) | (0.076) |
| Poland | −0.643*** | −0.644*** | −0.611*** | −0.633*** |
|  | (0.043) | (0.043) | (0.110) | (0.110) |
| Romania | −0.248*** | −0.253*** | −0.245*** | −0.252*** |
|  | (0.054) | (0.054) | (0.054) | (0.054) |
| Slovenia | −0.029 | −0.024 | −0.008 | −0.017 |
|  | (0.036) | (0.037) | (0.075) | (0.075) |
| Slovakia | 0.354*** | 0.361*** | 0.368*** | 0.366*** |
|  | (0.029) | (0.029) | (0.053) | (0.053) |
| 2008 | 0.025 | 0.024 | 0.024 | 0.024 |
|  | (0.022) | (0.022) | (0.022) | (0.022) |
| 2010 | −0.274*** | −0.275*** | −0.272*** | −0.274*** |
|  | (0.026) | (0.026) | (0.026) | (0.027) |
| 2012 | −0.152*** | −0.151*** | −0.150*** | −0.150*** |
|  | (0.026) | (0.026) | (0.027) | (0.027) |
| 2014 | −0.418*** | −0.416*** | −0.413*** | −0.414*** |
|  | (0.046) | (0.046) | (0.048) | (0.048) |
| Sociocultural policy position |  |  | −0.010 | −0.004 |
|  |  |  | (0.033) | (0.033) |
| Constant | −0.969*** | −0.969*** | −0.983*** | −0.974*** |
|  | (0.099) | (0.098) | (0.109) | (0.109) |
| Observations | 39,448 | 39,448 | 39,448 | 39,448 |
| r2_p | 0.0883 | 0.0897 | 0.0883 | 0.0897 |

*Note*: Table reports effects of probit regressions. All models include controls for gender, age, age squared, and education. * $p < 0.1$, ** $p < 0.05$, *** $p < 0.01$.

# Cross-Country Analysis: Left Vote vs. Other Parties—Multilevel Model

**Table A.6** Class-Based Structure of Left Parties Vote vs. Other Parties

| | (1) | (2) | (3) | (4) |
|---|---|---|---|---|
| Self-employed professionals and large employers | −0.324*** | −0.263*** | −0.324*** | −0.318*** |
| | (0.087) | (0.063) | (0.087) | (0.079) |
| Small business owners | −0.301*** | −0.292*** | −0.301*** | −0.307*** |
| | (0.072) | (0.032) | (0.072) | (0.074) |
| Technical (semi-)professionals | −0.128*** | −0.100*** | −0.128*** | −0.126*** |
| | (0.031) | (0.033) | (0.031) | (0.030) |
| Production workers | −0.019 | −0.016 | −0.019 | −0.017 |
| | (0.079) | (0.025) | (0.079) | (0.075) |
| Clerks | 0.034 | 0.034 | 0.034 | 0.032* |
| | (0.022) | (0.030) | (0.022) | (0.019) |
| Sociocultural (semi-)professionals | −0.038 | −0.039 | −0.038 | −0.040 |
| | (0.040) | (0.028) | (0.040) | (0.040) |
| Service workers | −0.010 | −0.005 | −0.010 | −0.007 |
| | (0.052) | (0.026) | (0.052) | (0.051) |
| **Economic policy position** | **−0.264***** | **−0.210***** | **−0.262***** | **−0.196**** |
| | (0.057) | (0.081) | (0.059) | (0.083) |
| **Self-employed professionals# Economic policy position** | | 0.049 | | 0.104* |
| | | (0.066) | | (0.062) |
| Small business owners# Economic policy position | | −0.012 | | −0.008 |
| | | (0.032) | | (0.059) |
| Technical (semi-)professionals# Economic policy position | | −0.011 | | −0.010 |
| | | (0.034) | | (0.034) |
| **Production workers# Economic policy position** | | **−0.126***** | | **−0.125**** |
| | | (0.023) | | (0.062) |

(*continued*)

**Table A.6** Continued

| | (1) | (2) | (3) | (4) |
|---|---|---|---|---|
| **Clerks# Economic policy position** | | −0.047 | | −0.064*** |
| | | (0.029) | | (0.024) |
| Sociocultural (semi-)professionals# Economic policy position | | −0.018 | | 0.001 |
| | | (0.029) | | (0.032) |
| **Service workers# Economic policy position** | | −0.101*** | | −0.113** |
| | | (0.024) | | (0.046) |
| Gender | 0.009 | 0.000 | 0.009 | 0.010 |
| | (0.026) | (0.015) | (0.026) | (0.026) |
| Age | 0.011 | 0.012*** | 0.011 | 0.011 |
| | (0.008) | (0.003) | (0.008) | (0.008) |
| Age squared | −0.000 | −0.000 | −0.000 | −0.000 |
| | (0.000) | (0.000) | (0.000) | (0.000) |
| Lower secondary education | 0.091 | 0.055 | 0.091 | 0.095 |
| | (0.066) | (0.041) | (0.066) | (0.060) |
| Upper secondary education completed | 0.144* | 0.094** | 0.144* | 0.142* |
| | (0.087) | (0.041) | (0.087) | (0.074) |
| Postsecondary nontertiary education | 0.157 | 0.061 | 0.157 | 0.151 |
| | (0.110) | (0.051) | (0.110) | (0.098) |
| Tertiary education | 0.128 | 0.062 | 0.128 | 0.120 |
| | (0.110) | (0.045) | (0.110) | (0.099) |
| Retired | 0.047 | 0.040* | 0.047 | 0.046 |
| | (0.052) | (0.023) | (0.052) | (0.052) |
| Unemployed | −0.015 | −0.021 | −0.015 | −0.018 |
| | (0.051) | (0.035) | (0.051) | (0.053) |
| Czech Republic | 0.123 | 0.092 | 0.044 | 0.050 |
| | (0.079) | (0.133) | (0.253) | (0.248) |
| Estonia | −0.311*** | −0.345** | −0.444 | −0.439 |
| | (0.086) | (0.157) | (0.388) | (0.380) |
| Hungary | 0.556*** | 0.561** | 0.434 | 0.450 |
| | (0.160) | (0.241) | (0.402) | (0.400) |
| Lithuania | 0.350** | 0.313 | 0.277 | 0.281 |
| | (0.139) | (0.200) | (0.286) | (0.281) |
| Latvia | −1.352*** | −1.439*** | −1.356*** | −1.369*** |
| | (0.136) | (0.194) | (0.134) | (0.133) |

**Table A.6** Continued

|  | (1) | (2) | (3) | (4) |
|---|---|---|---|---|
| Poland | −0.605*** | −0.632*** | −0.809 | −0.822 |
|  | (0.095) | (0.166) | (0.555) | (0.546) |
| Romania | −0.272*** | −0.352** | −0.280** | −0.287** |
|  | (0.105) | (0.167) | (0.113) | (0.113) |
| Slovenia | −0.051 | −0.084 | −0.190 | −0.192 |
|  | (0.052) | (0.144) | (0.375) | (0.368) |
| Slovakia | 0.347*** | 0.298** | 0.260 | 0.263 |
|  | (0.023) | (0.128) | (0.224) | (0.220) |
| 2008 | 0.078 | 0.073 | 0.078 | 0.077 |
|  | (0.232) | (0.095) | (0.232) | (0.233) |
| 2010 | −0.202 | −0.194* | −0.213 | −0.215 |
|  | (0.244) | (0.103) | (0.230) | (0.229) |
| 2012 | −0.112 | −0.085 | −0.123 | −0.124 |
|  | (0.162) | (0.103) | (0.147) | (0.148) |
| 2014 | −0.406* | −0.388*** | −0.423** | −0.423** |
|  | (0.227) | (0.140) | (0.206) | (0.206) |
| Sociocultural policy position |  |  | 0.065 | 0.069 |
|  |  |  | (0.158) | (0.158) |
| Constant | −1.088*** | −1.002*** | −0.984*** | −0.980*** |
|  | (0.231) | (0.143) | (0.244) | (0.225) |
| var(_cons[country]) | 0.000 | 0.000 | 0.000 | 0.000 |
|  | (0.000) | (0.000) | (0.000) | (0.000) |
| var(_cons[country>essround]) | 0.036** | 0.031*** | 0.036** | 0.036** |
|  | (0.017) | (0.008) | (0.017) | (0.017) |
| Observations | 39,448 | 41,294 | 39,448 | 39,448 |
| Number of groups | 10 | 10 | 10 | 10 |

*Note*: Table reports effects of multilevel probit regressions. All models include controls for gender, age, age squared, and education. Robust standard errors in parentheses. * $p < 0.1$, ** $p < 0.05$, *** $p < 0.01$.

# Cross-Country Analysis: Right vs. Left Vote—Probit Model

**Table A.7** Class-Based Structure of Right (Conservative and Radical Right) Parties Vote vs. Left Parties

| | (1) Conservative | Margins | (2) Radical Right | Margins |
|---|---|---|---|---|
| Self-employed professionals and large employers | 0.394*** | 0.129*** | −0.019 | −0.002 |
| | (0.075) | (0.025) | (0.174) | (0.027) |
| Sociocultural (semi-)professionals | 0.024 | 0.009 | 0.164** | 0.027** |
| | (0.036) | (0.013) | (0.064) | (0.011) |
| Small business owners | 0.244*** | 0.088*** | 0.496*** | 0.096*** |
| | (0.041) | (0.014) | (0.066) | (0.012) |
| Technical (semi-)professionals | 0.156*** | 0.056*** | 0.153** | 0.028** |
| | (0.042) | (0.015) | (0.074) | (0.013) |
| Clerks | −0.050 | −0.014 | 0.136* | 0.027** |
| | (0.038) | (0.014) | (0.069) | (0.011) |
| Service workers | −0.057* | −0.011 | 0.211*** | 0.044*** |
| | (0.034) | (0.012) | (0.058) | (0.010) |
| Production workers | −0.083*** | −0.018 | 0.289*** | 0.056*** |
| | (0.032) | (0.012) | (0.054) | (0.009) |
| **Economic policy position** | 0.148*** | 0.089*** | 0.460*** | 0.100*** |
| | (0.031) | (0.008) | (0.063) | (0.008) |
| **Self-employed professionals# Economic policy position** | −0.133* | 0.005 | **0.048** | 0.083*** |
| | (0.081) | (0.026) | (0.190) | (0.028) |
| Sociocultural (semi-)professionals# Economic policy position | 0.008 | 0.056*** | −0.070 | 0.072*** |
| | (0.037) | (0.012) | (0.072) | (0.012) |

(*continued*)

**Table A.7** Continued

| | (1)<br>Conservative | Margins | (2)<br>Radical<br>Right | Margins |
|---|---|---|---|---|
| Small business owners#<br>Economic policy position | 0.032 | 0.062*** | 0.066 | 0.113*** |
| | (0.041) | (0.013) | (0.070) | (0.012) |
| Technical<br>(semi-)professionals#<br>Economic policy position | 0.007 | 0.055*** | 0.049 | 0.091*** |
| | (0.045) | (0.015) | (0.082) | (0.013) |
| **Clerks# Economic policy<br>position** | **0.070*** | **0.079*** | **0.097** | **0.098*** |
| | (0.037) | (0.012) | (0.070) | (0.010) |
| **Service workers#<br>Economic policy position** | **0.168*** | **0.112*** | **0.169*** | **0.115*** |
| | (0.032) | (0.010) | (0.058) | (0.009) |
| **Production workers#<br>Economic policy position** | **0.207*** | **0.125*** | **0.124**** | **0.112*** |
| | (0.029) | (0.009) | (0.055) | (0.009) |
| Gender | −0.048** | −0.017** | 0.146*** | 0.027*** |
| | (0.019) | (0.007) | (0.030) | (0.006) |
| Age | −0.016*** | −0.003*** | −0.019*** | −0.001*** |
| | (0.003) | (0.000) | (0.005) | (0.000) |
| Age squared | 0.000** | | 0.000** | |
| | (0.000) | | (0.000) | |
| Lower secondary education | −0.038 | −0.014 | 0.211** | 0.035*** |
| | (0.057) | (0.020) | (0.082) | (0.013) |
| Upper secondary education<br>completed | 0.008 | 0.003 | 0.331*** | 0.057*** |
| | (0.056) | (0.020) | (0.082) | (0.013) |
| Postsecondary nontertiary<br>education | −0.070 | −0.025 | 0.268** | 0.045** |
| | (0.071) | (0.025) | (0.122) | (0.021) |
| Tertiary education | 0.050 | 0.018 | 0.231** | 0.039** |
| | (0.061) | (0.022) | (0.093) | (0.015) |
| Retired | −0.043 | −0.015 | −0.081* | −0.015* |
| | (0.030) | (0.011) | (0.047) | (0.009) |
| Unemployed | −0.024 | −0.009 | −0.086 | −0.016 |
| | (0.043) | (0.015) | (0.067) | (0.012) |
| Czech Republic | −0.062* | −0.022* | −1.645*** | −0.315*** |
| | (0.033) | (0.012) | (0.085) | (0.015) |
| Estonia | −0.422*** | −0.155*** | −1.283*** | −0.279*** |
| | (0.050) | (0.018) | (0.137) | (0.022) |

Table A.7 Continued

| | (1)<br>Conservative | Margins | (2)<br>Radical<br>Right | Margins |
|---|---|---|---|---|
| Hungary | −0.259*** | −0.095*** | −1.735*** | −0.322*** |
| | (0.061) | (0.022) | (0.116) | (0.019) |
| Lithuania | −0.590*** | −0.216*** | −2.758*** | −0.358*** |
| | (0.062) | (0.021) | (0.220) | (0.018) |
| Latvia | 1.430*** | 0.352*** | 1.601*** | 0.471*** |
| | (0.085) | (0.012) | (0.129) | (0.026) |
| Poland | 0.650*** | 0.208*** | 1.087*** | 0.343*** |
| | (0.045) | (0.015) | (0.074) | (0.027) |
| Romania | | | −0.240** | −0.070** |
| | | | (0.121) | (0.034) |
| Slovenia | 0.054 | 0.020 | −0.741*** | −0.191*** |
| | (0.040) | (0.014) | (0.075) | (0.018) |
| Slovakia | −0.315*** | −0.116*** | −0.531*** | −0.145*** |
| | (0.031) | (0.011) | (0.055) | (0.015) |
| 2008 | 0.029 | 0.010 | −0.103*** | −0.019*** |
| | (0.025) | (0.009) | (0.035) | (0.006) |
| 2010 | 0.513*** | 0.180*** | −0.019 | −0.003 |
| | (0.029) | (0.010) | (0.050) | (0.009) |
| 2012 | 0.388*** | 0.138*** | −0.271*** | −0.047*** |
| | (0.029) | (0.010) | (0.047) | (0.008) |
| 2014 | 0.453*** | 0.160*** | 1.241*** | 0.294*** |
| | (0.041) | (0.014) | (0.085) | (0.020) |
| Constant | 0.608*** | | −0.376** | |
| | (0.104) | | (0.162) | |
| Observations | 26,596 | 26,596 | 16,041 | 16,041 |
| r2_p | 0.0957 | | 0.410 | |

*Note*: Table reports effects of probit regressions. All models include controls for gender, age, age squared, and education. * $p < 0.1$, ** $p < 0.05$, *** $p < 0.01$.

# Cross-Country Analysis: Right vs. Left Vote—Multilevel Model

**Table A.8** Class-Based Structure of Right Parties Vote vs. Left Parties Conditional on Left Parties' Positions on Economic Policy

|  | (1)<br>Conservative | (2)<br>Radical Right |
|---|---|---|
| Self-employed professionals and large employers | 0.392*** | −0.022 |
|  | (0.085) | (0.166) |
| Small business owners | 0.234*** | 0.475*** |
|  | (0.074) | (0.120) |
| Technical (semi-)professionals | 0.136*** | 0.155* |
|  | (0.015) | (0.086) |
| Production workers | −0.103 | 0.263*** |
|  | (0.079) | (0.076) |
| Clerks | −0.069** | 0.111 |
|  | (0.028) | (0.076) |
| Sociocultural (semi-)professionals | 0.015 | 0.163* |
|  | (0.026) | (0.084) |
| Service workers | −0.076 | 0.209*** |
|  | (0.052) | (0.074) |
| **Economic policy position** | **0.159** | **0.577***** |
|  | (0.142) | (0.186) |
| **Self-employed professionals# Economic policy position** | −0.125 | 0.107 |
|  | (0.078) | (0.150) |
| Small business owners# Economic policy position | 0.039 | 0.084 |
|  | (0.048) | (0.085) |
| Technical (semi-)professionals# Economic policy position | 0.000 | 0.077 |
|  | (0.028) | (0.089) |

*(continued)*

## Table A.8 Continued

|  | (1) Conservative | (2) Radical Right |
|---|---|---|
| **Production workers# Economic policy position** | **0.199\*\*\*** | **0.171\*\*** |
|  | (0.045) | (0.073) |
| **Clerks# Economic policy position** | **0.064\*\*** | **0.119\*\*** |
|  | (0.026) | (0.048) |
| Sociocultural (semi-)professionals# Economic policy position | −0.009 | −0.037 |
|  | (0.021) | (0.064) |
| **Service workers# Economic policy position** | **0.170\*\*\*** | **0.207\*\*\*** |
|  | (0.036) | (0.057) |
| Gender | −0.054\* | 0.152 |
|  | (0.029) | (0.124) |
| Age | −0.015\* | −0.020\*\*\* |
|  | (0.008) | (0.004) |
| Age squared | 0.000 | 0.000\* |
|  | (0.000) | (0.000) |
| Lower secondary education | −0.054 | 0.200 |
|  | (0.152) | (0.171) |
| Upper secondary education completed | −0.023 | 0.245 |
|  | (0.220) | (0.247) |
| Postsecondary nontertiary education | −0.043 | 0.196 |
|  | (0.242) | (0.349) |
| Tertiary education | 0.021 | 0.145 |
|  | (0.259) | (0.308) |
| Retired | −0.041 | −0.088 |
|  | (0.070) | (0.091) |
| Unemployed | −0.051 | −0.095 |
|  | (0.041) | (0.115) |
| Czech Republic | −0.058 | −2.121\*\*\* |
|  | (0.117) | (0.371) |
| Estonia | −0.336\*\* | −1.472\*\*\* |
|  | (0.171) | (0.391) |
| Hungary | −0.221 | −2.086\*\*\* |
|  | (0.364) | (0.558) |
| Lithuania | −0.508\* | −2.592\*\*\* |

## Table A.8 Continued

|  | (1) Conservative | (2) Radical Right |
|---|---|---|
|  | (0.285) | (0.533) |
| Latvia | 1.495*** | 1.970*** |
|  | (0.250) | (0.277) |
| Poland | 0.677*** | 0.875*** |
|  | (0.194) | (0.337) |
| Romania |  | 0.001 |
|  |  | (0.161) |
| Slovenia | 0.110 | −0.684*** |
|  | (0.111) | (0.165) |
| Slovakia | −0.222*** | −0.630*** |
|  | (0.032) | (0.067) |
| 2008 | 0.046 | −0.181 |
|  | (0.293) | (0.149) |
| 2010 | 0.473 | 0.025 |
|  | (0.355) | (0.311) |
| 2012 | 0.359 | −0.241 |
|  | (0.300) | (0.332) |
| 2014 | 0.491 | 1.277* |
|  | (0.335) | (0.720) |
| var(_cons[country]) | 0.000 | 0.000 |
|  | (0.000) | (0.000) |
| var(_cons[country>essround]) | 0.071** | 0.198*** |
|  | (0.035) | (0.074) |
| Constant | 0.577 | −0.233 |
|  | (0.362) | (0.372) |
| Observations | 26,596 | 16,041 |
| Number of groups | 9 | 10 |

Note: Table reports effects of multilevel models. All models include controls for gender, age, age squared, and education. * $p < 0.1$, ** $p < 0.05$, *** $p < 0.01$.

# Survey Experiment 1: Descriptive Statistics

**Table A.9** Descriptive Statistics for Survey Experiment 1

| Variable | Treatment 1 Mean (se) | Treatment 2 Mean (se) | N |
|---|---|---|---|
| Gender 1—man, 0—woman | 0.4941 (0.50) | 0.4921 (0.50) | 504 |
| Age 18–64 y.o. | 41.4564 (13.32) | 41.1786 (13.50) | 504 |
| Education | | | |
| 1—Less than high school | 0.3710 (0.48) | 0.3810 (0.49) | 504 |
| 2—High school | 0.2818 (0.02) | 0.2897 (0.02) | |
| 3—Some college, no degree | 0.0655 (0.25) | 0.0575 (0.23) | |
| 4—Bachelor's degree | 0.2302 (0.42) | 0.2401 (0.43) | |
| 5—Master's degree | 0.0278 (0.17) | 0.0298 (0.17) | |
| 6—Doctoral degree | 0.0139 (0.12) | 0.0119 (0.11) | |

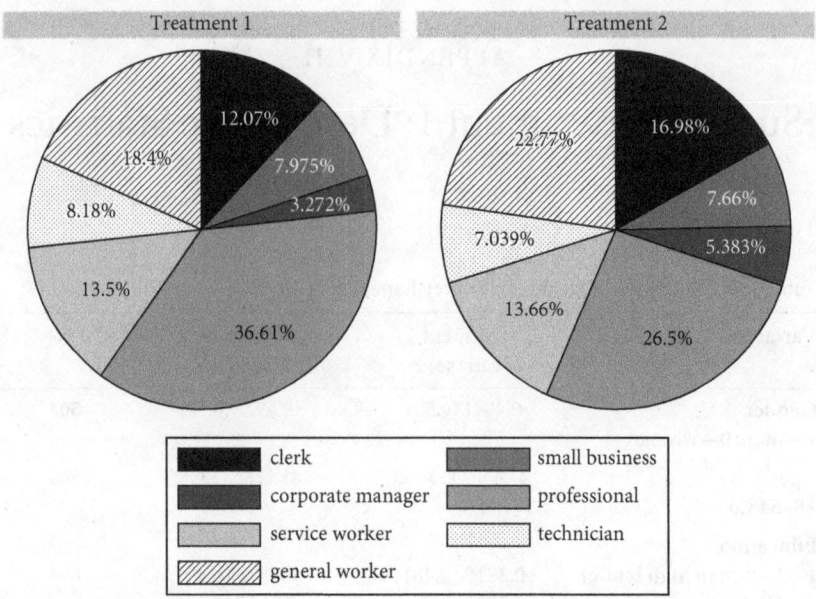

**Figure A.1** Experiment 1: Distribution of Occupational Status Categories by Treatment Group 1 and Treatment Group 2

# Survey Experiment 1: Propensity of Voting for Jobbik

**Table A.10** Effects of Treatment on Respondents' Party Choice: "How Likely Is It That You Will Vote for Jobbik (the Movement for a Better Hungary) Party?"

|  | (1)<br>OLS | (2)<br>OLS | (3)<br>Ordinal<br>Probit | (4)<br>Ordinal<br>Probit |
|---|---|---|---|---|
| T | 0.150** | −0.278 | 0.150** | −0.375 |
|  | (0.066) | (0.314) | (0.071) | (0.342) |
| Clerk |  | −0.003 |  | −0.038 |
|  |  | (0.289) |  | (0.301) |
| Small business |  | −0.112 |  | −0.121 |
|  |  | (0.296) |  | (0.306) |
| Professional |  | −0.182 |  | −0.218 |
|  |  | (0.256) |  | (0.266) |
| Service worker |  | −0.320 |  | −0.392 |
|  |  | (0.289) |  | (0.305) |
| Technician |  | −0.210 |  | −0.251 |
|  |  | (0.310) |  | (0.322) |
| General worker |  | −0.286 |  | −0.358 |
|  |  | (0.282) |  | (0.296) |
|  |  |  |  |  |
| T # clerk |  | 0.103 |  | 0.211 |
|  |  | (0.363) |  | (0.394) |
| T # small business |  | 0.322 |  | 0.364 |
|  |  | (0.396) |  | (0.424) |
| T # professional |  | 0.394 |  | 0.470 |
|  |  | (0.335) |  | (0.365) |
| T # service worker |  | 0.468 |  | 0.591 |
|  |  | (0.366) |  | (0.398) |

(continued)

**Table A.10** Continued

|  | (1) OLS | (2) OLS | (3) Ordinal Probit | (4) Ordinal Probit |
|---|---|---|---|---|
| T # technician |  | 0.534 |  | 0.643 |
|  |  | (0.416) |  | (0.439) |
| **T # general worker** |  | **0.599*** |  | **0.729*** |
|  |  | (0.351) |  | (0.380) |
| Male | 0.231*** | 0.232*** | 0.256*** | 0.266*** |
|  | (0.067) | (0.070) | (0.071) | (0.075) |
| Age | −0.026 | −0.009*** | −0.020 | −0.009*** |
|  | (0.017) | (0.003) | (0.018) | (0.003) |
| Age squared | 0.000 | 0.000 | 0.000 | −0.000 |
|  | (0.000) | (0.000) | (0.000) | (0.000) |
| Less than high school diploma | 0.603*** | 0.863*** | 0.945** | 1.504*** |
|  | (0.233) | (0.145) | (0.473) | (0.531) |
| High school diploma | 0.613*** | 0.876*** | 0.965** | 1.522*** |
|  | (0.236) | (0.136) | (0.474) | (0.529) |
| Some college, no degree | 0.524** | 0.781*** | 0.862* | 1.414*** |
|  | (0.261) | (0.178) | (0.489) | (0.543) |
| Bachelor degree | 0.432* | 0.679*** | 0.777 | 1.320** |
|  | (0.233) | (0.132) | (0.473) | (0.529) |
| Master's degree | 0.353 | 0.590*** | 0.696 | 1.227** |
|  | (0.289) | (0.221) | (0.514) | (0.569) |
| Constant | 1.959*** | 1.530*** |  |  |
|  | (0.420) | (0.304) |  |  |
| Observations | 1,008 | 972 | 1,008 | 972 |
| R-squared | 0.051 | 0.051 |  |  |
| Pseudi R-squared |  |  | 0.021 | 0.023 |

*Note*: The group with pro-market economic policy positions of the MSZP compared with the group with redistributionist positions of the MSZP. OLS and Ordinal Probit regressions with controls. Robust standard errors. * $p < 0.1$, ** $p < 0.05$, *** $p < 0.01$.

# Survey Experiment 2: Descriptive Statistics

Table A.11 Descriptive Statistics for Survey Experiment 1

| Variable | Treatment 2 Mean (se) | Treatment 1 Mean (se) | N |
|---|---|---|---|
| Gender 1—man, 0—woman | 0.493 (0.50) | 0.495 (0.50) | 500 |
| Age 18–64 y.o. | 41.173 (13.30) | 41.341 (13.60) | 500 |
| Education | | | |
| 1—"Less than high school" | 0.3777 (0.49) | 0.3723 (0.48) | |
| 2—"High school" | 0.2903 (0.45) | 0.2871 (0.45) | |
| 3—"Some college, no degree" | 0.0596 (0.24) | 0.0634 (0.24) | 500 |
| 4—"Bachelor's degree" | 0.2266 (0.42) | 0.2317 (0.42) | |
| 5—"Master's degree" | 0.0378 (0.19) | 0.0337 (0.18) | |
| 6—"Doctoral degree" | 0.0080 (0.09) | 0.0120 (0.11) | |

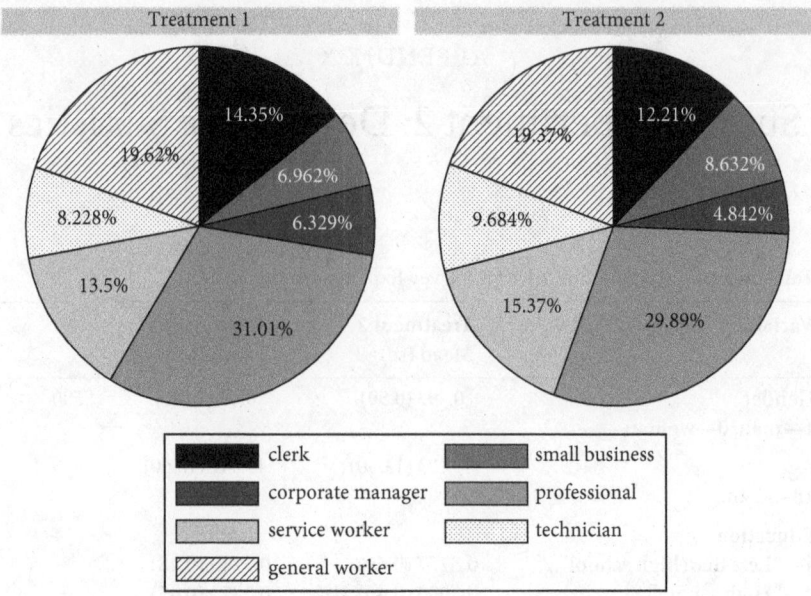

**Figure A.2** Experiment 2: Distribution of Occupational Status Categories by Treatment Group 1 and Treatment Group 2

# Survey Experiment 2: Propensity of Voting for Jobbik

Table A.12 Effects of Treatment on Respondents' Party Choice: "How Likely Is It That You Will Vote for Jobbik (the Movement for a Better Hungary) Party?"

| | (1)<br>OLS | (2)<br>OLS | (3)<br>Ordinal<br>Probit | (4)<br>Ordinal<br>Probit |
|---|---|---|---|---|
| T | −0.012 | −0.159 | −0.029 | −0.178 |
| | (0.064) | (0.276) | (0.072) | (0.330) |
| clerks | | −0.170 | | −0.179 |
| | | (0.220) | | (0.264) |
| small business | | 0.124 | | 0.157 |
| | | (0.254) | | (0.285) |
| professionals | | −0.081 | | −0.073 |
| | | (0.207) | | (0.247) |
| service workers | | −0.008 | | 0.040 |
| | | (0.236) | | (0.267) |
| technicians | | 0.029 | | 0.029 |
| | | (0.266) | | (0.299) |
| general workers | | 0.024 | | 0.018 |
| | | (0.239) | | (0.271) |
| T # clerks | | 0.366 | | 0.417 |
| | | (0.323) | | (0.384) |
| T # small business | | −0.190 | | −0.244 |
| | | (0.344) | | (0.404) |
| T # professionals | | 0.211 | | 0.219 |
| | | (0.298) | | (0.358) |
| T # service workers | | 0.068 | | 0.024 |
| | | (0.326) | | (0.379) |

(continued)

## Table A.12 Continued

| | (1)<br>OLS | (2)<br>OLS | (3)<br>Ordinal<br>Probit | (4)<br>Ordinal<br>Probit |
|---|---|---|---|---|
| T # technicians | | −0.033 | | −0.030 |
| | | (0.357) | | (0.414) |
| T # general workers | | 0.225 | | 0.236 |
| | | (0.327) | | (0.376) |
| male | 0.141** | 0.156** | 0.154** | 0.176** |
| | (0.064) | (0.067) | (0.072) | (0.076) |
| age | −0.014 | −0.028 | −0.014 | −0.030 |
| | (0.017) | (0.019) | (0.018) | (0.021) |
| age squared | −0.000 | 0.000 | −0.000 | 0.000 |
| | (0.000) | (0.000) | (0.000) | (0.000) |
| less than high school diploma | 0.317 | 0.268 | 0.372 | 0.329 |
| | (0.254) | (0.264) | (0.340) | (0.348) |
| high school diploma | 0.163 | 0.181 | 0.201 | 0.221 |
| | (0.256) | (0.260) | (0.342) | (0.345) |
| some college, no degree | 0.281 | 0.266 | 0.317 | 0.304 |
| | (0.285) | (0.291) | (0.369) | (0.373) |
| bachelor's degree | −0.034 | −0.040 | −0.008 | −0.015 |
| | (0.254) | (0.258) | (0.343) | (0.345) |
| master's degree | −0.033 | −0.035 | −0.036 | −0.038 |
| | (0.287) | (0.289) | (0.387) | (0.387) |
| Constant | 2.196*** | 2.538*** | | |
| | (0.413) | (0.501) | | |
| Observations | 1,008 | 949 | 1,008 | 949 |
| R-squared | 0.062 | 0.075 | | |
| Pseudo R-squared | | | 0.0251 | 0.0303 |

*Note*: The group with pro-market economic policy positions of the MSZP compared with the group with redistributionist positions of the MSZP. OLS and ordinal probit regressions with controls. Robust standard errors. * $p < 0.1$, ** $p < 0.05$, *** $p < 0.01$.

# Elite Interviews

Most of the elite interviews were conducted in person during my research trips to Hungary, Poland, the Czech Republic, and Slovakia. Some of the later interviews were conducted over phone and Zoom. Political elites were selected on the basis of their participation in government throughout the time periods of interest in this book. They included individuals in formal political positions and external political consultants. The average duration of the interviews was forty to sixty minutes.

These interviews aimed to flesh out the motivations behind specific policy choices of corresponding governments, cabinets, and parties. The information collected during the interviews was corroborated either in subsequent interviews with other political actors or through secondary source materials (such as scholarly and journalistic works as well as policymakers' memoirs). The interviews relied on a general conceptual framework developed in advance to ensure that they focus on specific topics. The list of the interviewed subjects follows:

**Ara-Kovács, Attila** is a Hungarian politician, philosopher, and journalist and a member of the European Parliament from the Democratic Coalition Party. January 2015.

**Aslund, Anders** has served as an advisor on economic policy for Central and Eastern Europe governments. He was also an informal advisor to Leszek Balcerowicz and Jacek Rostowski, who served as minister of finance in 2007–2013 and deputy prime minister of Poland in 2013. June 2022.

**Balcerowicz, Leszek** is a Polish economist and policymaker. He served as chairman of the National Bank of Poland (2001–2007) and twice as deputy prime minister of Poland (1989–1991, 1997–2001). In 1989, he became minister of finance in Tadeusz Mazowiecki's first noncommunist government and led the free-market economic reforms. June 2016.

**Boris, János** is a managing director of Hungary's right-leaning think-tank Freedom and Reform Institute. January 2015.

**Bozoki, Andras** was a participant in the Hungarian Roundtable Talks and subsequently a spokesman for Fidesz in 1990. In 2003–2004 he was a political advisor to MSZP's prime minister Péter Medgyessy. From February 2005 to June 2006, he was a minister of culture in the first Gyurcsány government. May 2022.

**Demeš, Pavol** was the minister of international relations of the Slovak Republic in 1991–1992. In 1993–1996, he managed the Foreign Policy Department of the Office of the President of the Slovak Republic, and was also an advisor to President Michal Kováč. March 2015.

**Gúr, Nándor** is a Hungarian politician, a member of the National Assembly from the Hungarian Socialist Party from 2002 to 2018. He was the executive responsible for vocational training and employment policy in the Chamber of Commerce and Industry of Borsod-Abaúj-Zemplén County from 1999 until he became a member of Parliament in 2002. September 2016.

**Gyöngyösi, Márton** was a member of the National Assembly from Hungary's Jobbik party from 2010 to 2019. In 2010–2018 he has served as the vice chair of the Foreign Committee of the Hungarian National Assembly. He was the leader of Jobbik's parliamentary group from 2018 to 2019. August 2016.

**Hann, Endre** was one of the founders and early participants in the work of the Free Initiatives Network and the SZDSZ in Poland. January 2015.

**Kolodko, Grzegorz** was a vice president of the Council of Ministers and Poland's minister of finance in 1994–1997 and 2002–2003, and the creator of the socioeconomic development programs Strategy for Poland, Package 2000, and the Program for Repairing the Finances of the Republic of Poland. June 2022.

**Magyar, Balint** was a founder of the SZDSZ (1988), a member of the Hungarian Parliament (1990–2010), and the minister of education under MSZP governments (1996–1998, 2002–2006). April 2022.

**Malacová, Jana** is a member of the ČSSD. She was the minister of labor and social affairs in the Czech Republic in the government led by Andrej Babiš in 2018–2021. Between March 2019 and December 2021 she was also deputy chairperson of the ČSSD. July 2022.

**Mizsei, Kálmán** worked as an advisor to the governor of the National Bank of Hungary in 1990–1992. He was also Viktor Orbán's economic advisor in formal and informal capacities in 1990–1994. January 2015 and July 2022.

**Pehe, Jiri** was the director of the political cabinet in the office of Czech president Václav Havel in 1997–1999 and continued serving as Havel's external political advisor until the end of Havel's term in 2003. August 2016 and June 2022.

**Piatkowski, Marcin** served as an advisor to Poland's deputy prime minister and minister of finance Grzegorz W. Kolodko in 2002–2003, contributing to the fiscal reform program. June 2022.

**Refozs, Lajos** is a Hungarian sociologist and politician. He was a member of the MSZP between 1991 and 1994, participated in the National Assembly in 1994 and 2010, and again from May 2018 to the present. September 2016.

**Rouček, Libor** is a Czech politician and member of the European Parliament with the ČSSD. In 1998–2002 he was a spokesman for the government of Miloš Zeman; before that, in 1998, he was the spokesperson of the ČSSD. July 2022.

**Schmögnerová, Brigita** was a member of Slovakia's SDĽ party and a minister of finance of Slovakia from 1998 to 2002 under Prime Minister Mikuláš Dzurinda. June 2022.

**Severa, Borek** is a country representative of the Friedrich Naumann Foundation in the Czech Republic since 1991. His work includes strategy and communication consulting as well as political marketing. August 2016.

**Siwiec, Marek** was a member of the SLD; from 1991 to 1997 he was a member of the Polish Sejm from the Kalisz district. In 1993–1996 he was a member of the Parliamentary Assembly of the Council of Europe. From 1996 to 2004 he was a national security advisor at the Chancellery of the president of Poland, Aleksander Kwaśniewski. June 2022.

**Šramko, Ivan** served as the governor of the National Bank of Slovakia from January 2005 to January 2010 (during the Eurozone entry). March 2015.

**Such, Gyorgy** is a Hungarian economist and journalist; he was a president of Magyar Rádió between 2006 and 2010. January 2015.

**Szabo, David J.** is the international director of the Hungarian conservative political think-tank Szazadveg Foundation. September 2016.

# References

Abedi, Amir. 2004. *Anti-Political Establishment Parties: A Comparative Analysis*. London: Routledge.

Abou-Chadi, T., and M. Wagner. 2020. "Electoral Fortunes of Social Democratic Parties: Do Second Dimension Positions Matter?" *Journal of European Public Policy* 27:2.

Adam, Christopher. 2017a. "Let the Rich Pay! A New Left-Wing Populism in Hungary?" *Hungarian Free Press*, March 16. https://hungarianfreepress.com/2017/03/16/let-the-rich-pay-a-new-left-wing-populism-in-hungary/.

Adam, Christopher. 2017b. "Socialist Candidate for Prime Minister Sees Higher Taxes for the Wealthy and Corporations." *Hungarian Free Press*, February 28. https://hungarianfreepress.com/2017/02/28/socialist-candidate-for-prime-minister-sees-higher-taxes-for-the-wealthy-and-corporations/.

Adams, J., L. Ezrow, and Z. Somer-Topcu. 2011. "Is Anybody Listening? Evidence That Voters Do Not Respond to European Parties' Policy Statements during Elections." *American Journal of Political Science* 55:370–382.

Adams, J., and Z. Somer-Topcu. 2009. "Moderate Now, Win Votes Later: The Electoral Consequences of Parties' Policy Shifts in Twenty-Five Postwar Democracies." *Journal of Politics* 71:678–692.

Adorf, Philipp. 2018. "A New Blue-Collar Force: The Alternative for Germany and the Working Class." *German Politics and Society* 36(4):29–49.

Afonso, Alexandre. 2015. "Choosing Whom to Betray: Populist Right-Wing Parties, Welfare State Reforms and the Trade-off between Office and Votes." *European Political Science Review* 7(2):271–292.

Afonso, Alexandre, and Line Rennwald. 2018. "Social Class and the Changing Welfare State Agenda of Radical Right Parties in Europe." In *Welfare Democracies and Party Politics: Explaining Electoral Dynamics in Times of Changing Welfare Capitalism*, edited by Philip Manow, Bruno Palier, and Hanna Schwander, 171–194. Oxford: Oxford University Press.

Agerberg, Mattias. 2017. "Failed Expectations: Quality of Government and Support for Populist Parties in Europe." *European Journal of Political Research* 56(3):578–600.

Agerberg, Mattias. 2019. "The Lesser Evil? Corruption Voting and the Importance of Clean Alternatives." *Comparative Political Studies* 52(2):253–287.

Ágh, Attila. 1995. "Partial Consolidation of the East-Central European Parties: The Case of the Hungarian Socialist Party." *Party Politics* 1(4):491–514.

Ahrens, Achim, and Joachim Zweynert. 2012. "Conditionality or Specificity? Bulgaria and Romania's Economic Transition Performance in Comparative Perspective." *Post-Communist Economies* 24(2):291–307.

Akkerman, T., S. de Lange, and M. Rooduijn, eds. 2016. *Radical Right-Wing Populist Parties in Western Europe: Into the Mainstream?* New York: Routledge.

Albertazzi, D., and D. McDonnell. 2015. *Populists in Power*. New York: Routledge.

Alesina, A., and N. Fuchs-Schündeln. 2007. "Goodbye Lenin (or Not?): The Effect of Communism on People's Preferences." *American Economic Review* 97(4):1507–1528.

Allen, Trevor J. 2015. "All in the Party Family? Comparing Far Right Voters in Western and Post-Communist Europe." *Party Politics* 23(3):274–285.

Amable, Bruno. 2011. "Morals and Politics in the Ideology of Neo-Liberalism." *Socio-Economic Review* 9:3–30.

Amable, B., and S. Palombarini. 2017. "The Emergence of an Anti-bourgeois Bloc in France." In *Growth, Crisis, Democracy*, edited by Bruno Amable and Hideko Magara, 16–45. New York: Routledge.

Andersson, Jenny. 2013. "Between Growth and Security: Swedish Social Democracy from a Strong Society to a Third Way." In *Between Growth and Security*, edited by John Callaghan, Steven Fielding, and Steve Ludlam, 1–160. Manchester: Manchester University Press.

Andersson J., and K. Östberg. 2020. "The Swedish Social Democrats, Reform Socialism and the State after the Golden Era." In *European Socialists and the State in the Twentieth and Twenty-First Centuries*, edited by M. Fulla and M. Lazar, 323–343. Palgrave Studies in the History of Social Movements. Cham, Switzerland: Palgrave Macmillan.

Andorka, Rudolf. 1999. *A Society Transformed: Hungary in Time-Space Perspective.* Budapest: Central European University Press.

Andreev, Svetlozar A. 2008. "The Unbearable Lightness of EU Membership: Post-Accession Challenges Facing Bulgaria and Romania." In *New Perspectives for the EU Team Presidencies: New Members, New Candidates and New Neighbours*, edited by Attila Ágh and Judit Kis-Varga, 161–183. Budapest: Kossuth Kiadó Zt.

Angelucci, D., and D. Vittori. 2021. "Look Where You're Going: The Cultural and Economic Explanations of Class Voting Decline." *West European Politics* 46(1):1–26.

Appel, Hilary, and Mitchell A. Orenstein. 2016. "Why Did Neoliberalism Triumph and Endure in the Post-Communist World?" *Comparative Politics* 48(3):313–331.

Appel, Hilary, and Mitchell A. Orenstein. 2018. *From Triumph to Crisis: Neoliberal Economic Reform in Postcommunist Countries.* Cambridge: Cambridge University Press.

Arndt, Christoph. 2013. *The Electoral Consequences of Third Way Welfare State Reforms.* Amsterdam: Amsterdam University Press.

Art, David. 2011. *Inside the Radical Right: The Development of Anti-Immigrant Parties in Western Europe.* Cambridge: Cambridge University Press.

Arzheimer, Kai. 2009. "Contextual Factors and the Extreme Right Vote in Western Europe, 1980–2002." *American Journal of Political Science* 53(2):259–275.

Arzheimer, Kai. 2013. "Working Class Parties 2.0? Competition between Centre Left and Extreme Right Parties." In *Class Politics and the Radical Right*, edited by Jens Rydren, 75–90. London: Routledge.

Arzheimer, K., and C. Berning. 2019. "How the Alternative for Germany (AfD) and Their Voters Veered to the Radical Right, 2013–2017." *Electoral Studies* 60:1–10.

Arzheimer, K., and E. Carter. 2006. "Political Opportunity Structures and Right-Wing Extremist Party Success." *European Journal of Political Research* 45(3):419–443.

Ausserladscheider, Valentina. 2019. "Beyond Economic Insecurity and Cultural Backlash: Economic Nationalism and the Rise of the Far Right." *Sociology Compass* 13(4):e12670.

Autor, David, David Dorn, Gordon Hanson, and Kaveh Majlesi. 2016. "Importing Political Polarization? The Electoral Consequences of Rising Trade Exposure." NBER Working Paper No. 22637, Cambridge, MA.

Avdagic, Sabina. 2005. "State–Labor Relations in East-Central Europe: Explaining Variations in Union Effectiveness." *Socio-Economic Review* 3:25–53.

Awan, A. G. 2015. "Analysis of the Impact of 2008 Financial Crisis on the Economic, Political and Health Systems and Societies of Advanced Countries." *Global Journal of Management and Social Sciences* 1(1):1–16.

Azmanova, Albena. 2004. "The Mobilisation of the European Left in the Early 21st Century." *European Journal of Sociology/Archives Européennes de Sociologie* 45(2):273–306.

Bagashka, T., C. Bodea, and S. M. Han. 2022. "Populism's Rise in Post-Communist Countries: Breaking Electoral Promises and Incumbent Left Parties' Vote Losses." *European Journal of Political Research* 61:134–153. http://doi.org/10.1111/1475-6765.12444.

Bagashka, T., and R. W. Stone. 2013. "Risky Signals: The Political Costs of Exchange Rate Policy in Post-Communist Countries." *International Studies Quarterly* 57(3):519–531.

Bagenholm, Andreas. 2013a. "The Electoral Fate and Policy Impact of 'Anti-Corruption Parties' in Central and Eastern Europe." *Human Affairs* 23(2):174–195.

Bagenholm, Andreas. 2013b. "Throwing the Rascals Out? The Electoral Effects of Corruption Allegations and Corruption Scandals in Europe 1981–2011." *Crime, Law and Social Change* 60(5):595–609.

Bailey, David J. 2009. "The Transition to 'New' Social Democracy: The Role of Capitalism, Representation and (Hampered) Contestation." *British Journal of Politics & International Relations* 11(4):593–612.

Bain, S., and R. Prince. 1972. "Who Is a White Collar Employee?" *British Journal of Industrial Relations* 10:325–339.

Baiocchi, Gianpaolo. 2019. "The Problem Is Not Populism, but the Failure of Liberal Democracy: Comments on Schmitter's Essay." *Sociologica* 13(2):3–5.

Bakke, Elisabeth, and Nick Sitter. 2005. "Patterns of Stability: Party Competition and Strategy in Central Europe since 1989." *Party Politics* 11(2):243–263.

Bakke, E., and N. Sitter. 2021. "Each Unhappy in Its Own Way? The Rise and Fall of Social Democracy in the Visegrád Countries since 1989." In *Social Democracy in the 21st Century (Comparative Social Research, Vol. 35)*, edited by N. Brandal, Ø. Bratberg, and D. E. Thorsen, 37–68. Bingley: Emerald Publishing Limited.

Bale, T., C. Green-Pedersen, A. Krouwel, K. R. Luther, and N. Sitter. 2010. "If You Can't Beat Them, Join Them? Explaining Social Democratic Responses to the Challenge from the Populist Radical Right in Western Europe." *Political Studies* 58(3):410–426.

Bale, T., D. Hough, and S. Van Kessel. 2012. "In or Out of Proportion? Labour and Social Democratic Parties' Responses to the Radical Right." In *Class Politics and the Radical Right*, edited by J. Rydgren, 91–106. New York: Routledge.

Bandau, Frank. 2022. "What Explains the Electoral Crisis of Social Democracy? A Systematic Review of the Literature." *Government and Opposition* 58(1):1–23.

Bánkuti, M., G. Halmai, and K. L. Scheppele. 2012. "Hungary's Illiberal Turn: Disabling the Constitution." *Journal of Democracy* 23(3):138–146.

Bartels, Larry M. 2014. "Ideology and Retrospection in Electoral Responses to the Great Recession." In *Mass Politics in Tough Times: Opinions, Votes, and Protest in the Great Recession*, edited by N. Bermeo and B. Bartels, 1–39. Oxford: Oxford University Press.

Bartels, Larry M. 2017. "The 'Wave' of Right-Wing Populist Sentiment Is a Myth." *Monkey Cage* (political science blog), *Washington Post*, June 21. cage/wp/2017/06/21/the-wave-of-right-wing-populist-sentiment-is-a-myth/.

Bartha, E., and A. Tóth. 2017. "What Lies Beneath the Appeal of the Radical Right to Elite Skilled Workers? The Impact of Deeply Ingrained Nationalism and Perceptions of Multiple Exploitations 1." In *The Rise of Populist Nationalism: Social Resentments and Capturing the Constitution in Hungary*, edited by Margit Feischmidt and Balázs Majtényi, 247–268. Budapest: Central European University Press, 2019.

Bartolini, S., and P. Mair. 1990. "Policy Competition, Spatial Distance and Electoral Instability." *West European Politics* 13(4):1–16.

Batory, Agnes. 2002. *The Political Context of EU Accession in Hungary*. London: Royal Institute of International Affairs.

Batory, Agnes. 2008. "Euroscepticism in the Hungarian Party System: Voices from the Wilderness." In *Opposing Europe? The Comparative Party Poitics of Euroscepticism*, edited by P. Taggart and A. Szczerbiak, 263–276. Oxford: Oxford University Press.

Batory, Agnes. 2009. "The European Parliament Election in Hungary, June 7 2009: European Parties Elections and Referendums." Election Briefing No 25, Network EP. http://www.sussex.ac.uk/sei/documents/epernep2009hungary.pdf.

Batory, Agnes. (2010). "Europe and the Hungarian Parliamentary Elections of April 2010, European Parties Elections and Referendums." Election Briefing No 51, Network EP. https://www.sussex.ac.uk/webteam/gateway/file.php?name=epern-election-briefing-no-51.pdf&site=266.

BBC. 2006. "Europe | Excerpts: Hungarian 'Lies' Speech." BBC News, September 19. http://news.bbc.co.uk/2/hi/europe/5359546.stm.

Beblavý, Miroslav. 2014. "Why Is 'New' Europe More Neoliberal? Pension Privatization and Flat Tax in the Postcommunist EU Member States." *Eastern European Economics* 52(1):55–78.

Becker, Jens. 2010. "The Rise of Right-Wing Populism in Hungary." *SEER: Journal for Labour and Social Affairs in Eastern Europe* 13(1):29–40.

Becker, Sascha O., Thiemo Fetzer, and Dennis Novy. 2016. "Who Voted for Brexit? A Comprehensive District-Level Analysis." Warwick University WP N. 305. https://academic.oup.com/economicpolicy/article/32/92/601/4459491.

Belfrage, C., and M. Ryner. 2009. "Renegotiating the Swedish Social Democratic Settlement: From Pension Fund Socialism to Neoliberalization." *Politics & Society* 37(2):257–287.

Bellucci, Paolo. 2014. "The Political Consequences of Blame Attribution for the Economic Crisis in the 2013 Italian National Election." *Journal of Elections, Public Opinion and Parties* 24:243–263.

Benedetto, G., S. Hix, and N. Mastrorocco. 2020. "The Rise and Fall of Social Democracy, 1918–2017." *American Political Science Review* 114(3):928–939.

Bennhold, Katrin. 2018. "Workers of Germany, Unite: The New Siren Call of the Far Right." *New York Times*, February 5. https://www.nytimes.com/2018/02/05/world/eur ope/afd-unions-social-democrats.html.

Benoit, Kenneth. 2001. "Evaluating Hungary's Mixed-Member Electoral System." In *Mixed-Member Electoral Systems: The Best of Both Worlds*, edited by Matthew Soberg Shugart and Martin P. Wattenberg, 477–493. Oxford: Oxford University Press.

Benoit, K., and A. Baturo. 2005. *National Party Competition and Support for European Integration*. September 8, 2005– September 10, 2005. Budapest: ECPR General Conference.

Benoit, Kenneth, and Michael Laver. 2008. *Party Policy in Modern Democracies*. London: Routledge, 2006.

Benoit, K., and J. W. Schiemann. 2001. "Institutional Choice in New Democracies: Bargaining over Hungary's 1989 Electoral Law." *Journal of Theoretical Politics* 13(2):153–182.

Bergmann, Eirikur. 2017. "Sweden: Far Right Sentiments Simmering underneath the Model Democratic Welfare Society." In *Nordic Nationalism and Right-Wing Populist Politics,* edited by Bergmann, Eirikur, 159–183. London: Palgrave Macmillan.

Berman, Sheri. 1998. *The Social Democratic Moment: Ideas and Politics in the Making of Interwar Europe.* Cambridge, MA: Harvard University Press.

Berman, Sheri. 2006. *The Primacy of Politics: Social Democracy and the Making of Europe's Twentieth Century.* New York: Cambridge University Press.

Berman, Sheri. 2010. "What Happened to the European Left?" *Dissent* 57:3.

Berman, Sheri. 2016. "The Specter Haunting Europe: The Lost Left." *Journal of Democracy* 27(4):69–76.

Berman, Sheri. 2019a. "Populism Is a Symptom Rather Than a Cause: Democratic Disconnect, the Decline of the Center-Left, and the Rise of Populism in Western Europe." *Polity* 51(4):654–667.

Berman, Sheri. 2019b. "Racially Divisive Parties Have More Voters Now, but Voters Aren't Becoming More Racist. What Explains This?" *Monkey Cage* (political science blog), *Washington Post,* December 2.

Berman, S., and H. Kundnani. 2021. "The Cost of Convergence." *Journal of Democracy* 32(1):22–36.

Berman, S., and M. Snegovaya. 2019. "Populism and the Decline of Social Democracy." *Journal of Democracy* 30(3):5–19.

Bernaciak, Magdalena. 2017. "Coming Full Circle? Contestation, Social Dialogue and Trade Union Politics in Poland." In *Rough Waters: European Trade Unions in a Time of Crises,* edited by H. Dribbusch, S. Lehndorff, and T. Schulten, 151–172. Brussels: ETUI aisbl.

Berning, Carl C. 2017. "Alternative Für Deutschland (Afd)—Germany's New Radical Right-Wing Populist Party." *ifo DICE Report* 15(4):16–19.

Bertelsmann Stiftung. 2010. "BTI 2010 Poland Country Report (Bertelsmann Stiftung's Transformation Index (BTI) 2016)." Gütersloh. www.bti-project.org.

Bértoa, Fernando Casal, 2014. "Party Systems and Cleavage Structures Revisited: A Sociological Explanation of Party System Institutionalization in East Central Europe." *Party Politics* 20(1):16–36.

Betz, Hans-Georg. 1994. *Radical Right-Wing Populism in Western Europe.* New York: St. Martin's Press.

Betz, Hans-Georg. 2002. "Conditions Favoring the Success and Failure of Radical Right-Wing Populist Parties in Contemporary Democracies." In *Democracies and the Populist Challenge,* edited by Y. Mény and Y. Surel, 197–213. New York: Palgrave.

Betz, Hans-Georg. 2018. "The Radical Right and Populism." In *The Oxford Handbook of the Radical Right,* edited by Rydgren, Jens, 86–104. New York: Oxford University Press.

Binev, Binio S. 2022a. "Post-Communist Junctures, the Left, and Illiberalism: Theory with Evidence from Central and Eastern Europe." *Comparative Political Studies* 56(4):00104140221109432.

Binev, Binio S. 2022b. "The Social Bases of Populist Domination: Market Reforms and Popular Reactions in Latin America and Post-Communist Europe." *Government and Opposition* 1–24. https://www.cambridge.org/core/journals/government-and-opp osition/article/abs/social-bases-of-populist-domination-market-reforms-and-popu lar-reactions-in-latin-america-and-postcommunist-europe/C2A1EA49F94B0C1B0 0CC9169410975AF.

Biró Nagy, A., and T. Boros. 2016. *Jobbik Going Mainstream: Strategy Shift of the Far Right in Hungary*. Budapest: Policy Solutions.

Biró-Nagy, A., and Dániel Róna. 2012. "Freefall: Political Agenda Explanations for the Hungarian Socialist Party's Loss of Popularity between 2006–2010." Working Papers in Political Science, Budapest: Institute for Political Science, MTA Centre for Social Sciences.

Biró-Nagy, A. B., and Dániel Róna. 2013. "Rational Radicalism: Jobbik's Road to the Hungarian Parliament." In *Alternative Politics? The Rise of New Parties in Central Europe*, edited by Grigorij Meseznikov, Olga Gyárfásova, and Zora Butorova, 149–184. Bratislava: Institute for Public Affairs.

Blair, Tony. 1997. Introduction to *Because Britain Deserves Better*. London: Labour Party.

Bluhm, Katharina, and Mihai Varga. 2019. "Conservative Developmental Statism in East Central Europe and Russia." *New Political Economy* 25(4):1–18.

Blyth, M. 2003. "Globalization and the Limits of Democratic Choice: Social Democracy and the Rise of Political Cartelization." *Internationale Politik und Gesellschaft* 3:60–82.

Blyth, M. 2013. *Austerity: The History of a Dangerous Idea*. Oxford: Oxford University Press.

Bochsler, D., and A. Juon. 2020. "Authoritarian Footprints in Central and Eastern Europe." *East European Politics* 36(2):167–187.

Bocskor, Ákos. 2018. "Anti-immigration Discourses in Hungary during the 'Crisis' Year: The Orbán Government's 'National Consultation' Campaign of 2015." *Sociology* 52(3):551–568.

Boda, Z., and G. Scheiring. 2006. "Water Privatisation in the Context of Transition." In *Beyond the Market: The Future of Public Services (Public Services Yearbook 2005)*. Amsterdam: Transnational Institute.

Bodea, Cristina. 2010. "The Political Economy of Fixed Exchange Rate Regimes: The Experience of Post-Communist Countries." *European Journal of Political Economy* 26(2):248–264.

Bodea, C., T. Bagashka, and S. M. Han. 2019. "Are Parties Punished for Breaking Electoral Promises? Market Oriented Reforms and the Left in Post-Communist Countries." *Market Oriented Reforms and the Left in Post-Communist Countries*, March 27. https://papers.ssrn.com/sol3/papers.cfm?abstract_id=3361134.

Bohle, Dorothee, and Greskovits, Bela. 2004. *Capital, Labor, and the Prospects of the European Social Model in the East. CES Central & Eastern Europe Working Paper, no. 58, 2004*. [Working Paper]. http://aei.pitt.edu/9275/.

Bohle, Dorothee, and Béla Greskovits. 2007. "Neoliberalism, Embedded Neoliberalism, and Neocorporatism: Paths towards Transnational Capitalism in Central-Eastern Europe." *West European Politics* 30(3):443–466.

Bohle, Dorothee, and Béla Greskovits. 2009. "East-Central Europe's Quandary." *Journal of Democracy* 20(4):50–63.

Bohle, D., and B. Greskovits. 2010. "Slovakia and Hungary: Successful and Failed Euro Entry without Social Pacts." *After the Euro and Enlargement: Social Pacts in the EU, Brussels: ETUI*, 345–369. https://www.etui.org/sites/default/files/017%20Book%20Social%20Pacts%202010_0.pdf#page=345.

Bohle, D., and Béla Greskovits. 2012. *Capitalist Diversity on Europe's Periphery*. New York: Cornell University Press.

Bohle, D., and B. Greskovits. 2019. "Politicising Embedded Neoliberalism: Continuity and Change in Hungary's Development Model." *West European Politics* 42(5):1069–1093.

Bojar, A., B. Bremer, H. Kriesi, and C. Wang. 2022. "The Effect of Austerity Packages on Government Popularity during the Great Recession." *British Journal of Political Science* 52(1):181–199.

Bonikowski, B., D. Halikiopoulou, E. Kaufmann, and M. Rooduijn. 2019. "Populism and Nationalism in a Comparative Perspective: A Scholarly Exchange." *Nations and Nationalism* 25(1):58–81.

Bönker, Frank. 2006. *The Political Economy of Fiscal Reform in Central-Eastern Europe: Hungary, Poland, and the Czech Republic from 1989 to EU Accession.* Cheltenham: Edward Elgar.

Bonoli, G., and M. Powell, eds. 2004. *Social Democratic Party Policies in Contemporary Europe.* London: Routledge.

Borbáth, E., and T. Gessler. 2021. "How Do Populist Radical Right Parties Differentiate Their Appeal? Evidence from the Media Strategy of the Hungarian Jobbik Party." *Government and Opposition* 58(1):1–22.

Bornschier, Simon. 2009. "Cleavage Politics in Old and New Democracies." *Living Reviews in Democracy* 1–13. https://www.zora.uzh.ch/id/eprint/26412/.

Bornschier, Simon. 2010a. *Cleavage Politics and the Populist Right: The New Cultural Conflict in Western Europe.* Philadelphia, PA: Temple University Press.

Bornschier, Simon. 2010b. "The New Cultural Divide and the Two-Dimensional Political Space in Western Europe." *West European Politics* 33(3):419–444. doi:10.1080/01402381003654387.

Bornschier, Simon. 2018. "Globalization, Cleavages, and the Radical Right." In *The Oxford Handbook of the Radical Right*, edited by Jens Rydgren, 212–238. New York: Oxford University Press.

Bornschier, Simon, and Hanspeter Kriesi. 2012. "The Populist Right, the Working Class, and the Changing Face of Class Politics." In *Class Politics and the Radical Right*, edited by Jens Rydgren, 11–29. Abingdon: Routledge.

Boros-Kazai, András. 2005. "Hungary." In *Eastern Europe: An Introduction to the People, Lands and Culture*, edited by Richard Frucht, 329–410. Santa Barbara, CA: ABC-CLIO.

Bozóki, Andras. 1997. "The Ideology of Modernization and the Policy of Materialism: The Day After for the Socialists." *Journal of Communist Studies and Transition Politics* 13(3):56–102.

Bozoki, Andras, and John T. Ishiyama, eds. 2002. *The Communist Successor Parties of Central and Eastern Europe.* Armonk, NY: M. E. Sharpe.

Brabec, Dušan. 2019. "Who Votes with Whom: Co-voting Network of the Lower House of Czech Parliament after the 2017 Elections." *Politologický časopis/Czech Journal of Political Science* 26(3):145–163.

Brader, T., and J. Tucker. 2008. "Pathways to Partisanship: Evidence from Russia." *Post-Soviet Affairs* 24(3): 263–300.

Bremer, Björn. 2018. "The Missing Left? Economic Crisis and the Programmatic Response of Social Democratic Parties in Europe." *Party Politics* 24(1):23–38.

Bremer, Björn, and S. McDaniel. 2020. "The Ideational Foundations of Social Democratic Austerity in the Context of the Great Recession." *Socio-Economic Review* 18(2):439–463.

Bremer, B., and L. Rennwald. 2022. "Who Still Likes Social Democracy? The Support Base of Social Democratic Parties Reconsidered." *Party Politics* 29(4):741–754.

Brubaker, Rogers. 2020. "Populism and Nationalism." *Nations and Nationalism* 26(1):44–66.

Bruszt, László. 1995. "The Antall Government, the Labor Unions, and the Employers' Associations." In *Lawful Revolution in Hungary, 1989–94,* edited by Béla Király and András Bozóki, 369–394. New York: Columbia University Press.

Bruszt, László. 2002. "Making Markets and Eastern Enlargement: Diverging Convergence?" *West European Politics* 25(2, April):121–140.

Bruszt, László. 2006. "Making Capitalism Compatible with Democracy: Tentative Reflections from the East." In *The Diversity of Democracy: A Tribute to Philippe C. Schmitter,* edited by C. Crouch and W. Streeck, 149–175. Northampton, MA: Edward Elgar.

Bugarič, Bojan. 2016. "Neoliberalism, Post-communism, and the Law." *Annual Review of Law and Social Science* 12:313–329.

Bugarič, Bojan. 2019. "Central Europe's Descent into Autocracy: A Constitutional Analysis of Authoritarian Populism." *International Journal of Constitutional Law* 17(2):597–616.

Buras, Piotr. 2005. "Polish Social Democracy, Policy Transfer and Programmatic Change." *Journal of Communist Studies and Transition Politics* 21(1):84–104.

Buras, Piotr. 2014. "Polish Social Democracy, Policy Transfer and Programmatic Change." In *Learning from the West?* 84–104. Routledge.

Bürgisser, R., and T. Kurer. 2021. "Insider-Outsider Representation and Social Democratic Labor Market Policy." *Socio-Economic Review* 19(3):1065–1094.

Bustikova, Lenka. 2014. "Revenge of the Radical Right." *Comparative Political Studies* 47(12):1738–1765.

Bustikova, Lenka. 2018. "The Radical Right in Eastern Europe." In *The Oxford Handbook of the Radical Right,* edited by Jens Rydgren, 565–581. New York: Oxford University Press.

Bustikova, L., and P. Guasti. 2017. "The Illiberal Turn or Swerve in Central Europe?" *Politics and Governance* 5(4):166–176.

Buštíková, L., and P. Guasti. 2019. "The State as a Firm: Understanding the Autocratic Roots of Technocratic Populism." *East European Politics and Societies* 33(2):302–330.

Bustikova, L., and H. Kitschelt. 2009. "The Radical Right in Post-Communist Europe: Comparative Perspectives on Legacies and Party Competition." *Communist and Post-Communist Studies* 42(4):459–483.

Butora, M., and Z. Butorova. 1993. "Slovakia: The Identity Challenges of the Newly Born State." *Social Research* 60(4):705–736.

Bútorová, Z., and O. Gyárfášová. 2006. "Trendy vo verejnej mienke a volebnom správaní." In *Slovenské voľby '06: Výsledky, príčiny, súvislosti,* edited by G. Mesežnikov, O. Gyárfášová, and M. Kollar, 111–142. Bratislava: Institute for Public Affairs.

Byrne, Andrew. 2017. "Hungary's Far-Right Jobbik Party Tries to Soften Image." *Financial Times,* March 5. https://www.ft.com/content/43137b62-ff25-11e6-96f8-3700c 5664d30.

Cabada, Ladislav. 2010. "Traditional, Third Way or a Different Path? The Czech Social Democrat Party in 2010." *Politics in Central Europe* 6(1):83–89.

Caiani, M., and P. Graziano. 2019. "Understanding Varieties of Populism in Times of Crises." *West European Politics* 42(6):1141–1158.

Cameron, A. Colin, Jonah B. Gelbach, and Douglas L Miller. 2008. "Bootstrap-Based Improvements for Inference with Clustered Errors." *Review of Economics and Statistics* 90(3):414–427.

Carter, Elisabeth. 2005. *The Extreme Right in Western Europe: Success or Failure?* Manchester: Manchester University Press.

Castel, Robert. 2003. *From Manual Workers to Wage Laborers: Transformation of the Social Question*. New Brunswick, NJ: Transaction.

Cavallaro, Matteo, David Flacher, and Massimo Angelo Zanetti. 2018. "Radical Right Parties and European Economic Integration: Evidence from the Seventh European Parliament." *European Union Politics* 19(2):321–343.

CBOS. 2004. "Current Problems and Events." Report No. POCBOS2004-0417. Warsaw: Centrum Badania Opinii Spolecznej.

Celiński, A. 1999. "Nie wykłócajmy sie, z historia." *Trybuna*, November 20–21.

Cernat, Lucien. 2002. "Institutions and Economic Growth: Which Model of Capitalism for Central and Eastern Europe?" *Journal for Institutional Innovation, Development, and Transition* 6(1):18–34.

Cernat, Lucien. 2006. *Europeanization, Varieties of Capitalism, and Economic Performance in Central and Eastern Europe*. Houndmills: Palgrave.

Černoch, Filip, Jan Husák, Ondrej Schütz, and Michal Vít. 2011. *Political Parties and Nationalism in Visegrad Countries*. Monography Series 46. Brno: Masarykova Univerzita, Mezinárodní Politologický Ustav.

Cerny, Philip G. 2008. "Embedding Neoliberalism: The Evolution of a Hegemonic Paradigm." *Journal of International Trade and Diplomacy* 2(1):1–46.

Chicowski, Rachel A. 2000. "Western Dreams, Eastern Realities: Support for the European Union in Central and Eastern Europe." *Comparative Political Studies* 33:1243–1278.

Cianetti, L., J. Dawson, and S. Hanley. 2018. "Rethinking 'Democratic Backsliding' in Central and Eastern Europe: Looking beyond Hungary and Poland." *East European Politics* 34(3):243–256.

Ciobanu, Monica. 2009. "Reconstructing the Role of the Working Class in Communist and Postcommunist Romania." *International Journal of Politics, Culture, and Society IJPS* 22(3):315–335.

Clark, Terry Nichols. 2003. "The Breakdown of Class Politics." *American Sociologist* 34(1):17–32.

Clasen, Jochen. 2005. *Reforming European Welfare States: Germany and the United Kingdom Compared*. Oxford: Oxford University Press.

Clasen, J., and D. Clegg. 2004. "Does the Third Way Work? The Left and Labour Market Policy Reform in Britain, France, and Germany." In *Welfare State Change: Towards a Third Way*, edited by J. Lewis and R. Surender, 89–110. New York: Oxford University Press.

Coffey, Eva. 2013. "Pain Tolerance: Economic Voting in the Czech Republic." *Electoral Studies* 32(3):432–437.

Colantone, Italo, and Piero Stanig. 2016. "Global Competition and Brexit." Working Paper No. 2016-44, Bocconi University.

Colantone, I., and P. Stanig. 2018. "The Trade Origins of Economic Nationalism: Import Competition and Voting Behavior in Western Europe." *American Journal of Political Science* 62(4):936–953.

Collier, D., H. E. Brady, and J. Seawright. 2010. "Outdated Views of Qualitative Methods: Time to Move On." *Political Analysis* 18(4):506–513.

Connolly, Richard. 2012. "The Determinants of the Economic Crisis in Post-Socialist Europe." *Europe-Asia Studies* 64(1):35–67.

Cook, L., and M. A. Orenstein. 1999. "The Return of the Left and Its Impact on the Welfare State in Poland, Hungary, and Russia." In *Left Parties and Social Policy in Postcommunist Europe*, edited by L. Cook, M. A. Orenstein, and M. Rueschemeyer, 47–108. Boulder, CO: Westview.

Croasmun, J. T., and L. Ostrom. 2011. "Using Likert-Type Scales in the Social Sciences." *Journal of Adult Education* 40(1):19–22.

CRS Report for Congress. 2002. "Slovakia: 2002 Elections." https://www.everycrsreport. com/files/20021107_RS21265_e9dff002229ceae054f0294248b42f2e770722cb.pdf.

Csaba, László. 2013. "Growth, Crisis Management and EU: The Hungarian Trilemma." *SüdEuropa Mitteilungen* 53(3–4):154–169.

Csizmadia, Lidia. 2008. "The Transition Economy of Hungary between 1990 and 2004." M.Sc. diss., University of Aarhus. http://pure.au.dk/portal/files/2620/Csizmadia-The sis.pdf.

ČTK. 2018. "Průzkum: Babiš znovu posiluje, ČSSD se nachází na hranici zvolení." *E15*, May 6. https://www.e15.cz/domaci/pruzkum-babis-znovu-posiluje-ČSSD-se-nach azi-na-hranici-zvoleni-1346454.

Cukierman, A., and M. Tommasi. 1998. "When Does It Take a Nixon to Go to China?" *American Economic Review* 88(1):180–197.

Culpepper, Pepper D. 2005. "Single Country Studies and Comparative Politics." *Politics & Society*, no. 60(Spring):2–5.

Curry, Jane Leftwich. 2003. "Poland's Ex-Communists: From Pariahs to Establishment Party." In *The Left Transformed: Post-Communist Societies*, edited by Jane Leftwich Curry and Joan Barth Urban, 19–60. New York: Rowman and Littlefield.

Cusack, T., T. Iversen, and P. Rehm. 2006. "Risks at Work: The Demand and Supply Sides of Government Redistribution." *Oxford Review of Economic Policy* 22(3):365–389.

CVVM. 2017. *Naše společnost 2017—leden*. Version 1.0. Prague: Sociologický ústav Akademie věd ČR. nesstar.soc.cas.cz.

Dal Bó, E., F. Finan, O. Folke, T. Persson, and J. Rickne 2018. "Economic Losers and Political Winners: Sweden's Radical Right." Unpublished manuscript, Department of Political Science, UC Berkeley.

Dalton, Russell J. 2002. *Citizen Politics: Public Opinion and Political Parties in Advanced Industrial Democracies*. 3rd edition. New York: Chatham House.

Dandashly, A., and A. Verdun. 2009. "A Road with Multiple Lanes: The Journeys of the Czech Republic, Poland and Slovenia towards Euro Adoption." In *Eleventh Biennial International EUSA Conference*, Los Angeles.

Dandashly, A., and A. Verdun. 2018. "Euro Adoption in the Czech Republic, Hungary and Poland: Laggards by Default and Laggards by Choice." *Comparative European Politics* 16(3):385–412.

Decker, Frank. 2016. "The 'Alternative for Germany': Factors behind Its Emergence and Profile of a New Right-Wing Populist Party." *German Politics and Society* 34(2):1–16.

De Cleen, Benjamin. 2017. "Populism and Nationalism." In *The Oxford Handbook of Populism*, edited by P. O. Espejo, C. Kaltwasser, P. Ostiguy, and P. Taggart, 342–362. New York: Oxford University Press.

Deegan-Krause, Kevin. 2006. "New Dimensions of Political Cleavage." In *Oxford Handbook of Political Science*, edited by R. Dalton and H.-D. Klingemann, 538–556 Oxford: Oxford University Press.

Deegan-Krause, K., and T. Haughton. 2012. "2012 Parliamentary Elections in Slovakia: The Building Blocks of Success." *Pozorblog*, March 12. http://www.pozorb log.com/2012/03/2012-parliamentary-elections-in-slovakiathe-building-blocs-of-success/.

de Jonge, Léonie. 2021. *The Success and Failure of Right-Wing Populist Parties in the Benelux Countries*. Abingdon: Routledge.

de Koster, W., P. Achterberg, and J. van der Waal. 2013. "The New Right and the Welfare State: The Electoral Relevance of Welfare Chauvinism and Welfare Populism in the Netherlands." *International Political Science Review* 34(1):3–20.

de Lange, Sarah L. 2007. "A New Winning Formula?" *Party Politics* 13(4):411–435.

Derks, Anton. 2006. "Populism and the Ambivalence of Egalitarism: How Do the Underprivileged Reconcile a Right-Wing Party Preference with Their Socio-economic Attitudes?" *World Political Science* Review 2, Article 1.

De Vries, C. E., and S. B. Hobolt. 2020. *Political Entrepreneurs: The Rise of Political Research*. Princeton University Press.

Diamant, J., and K. J. Starr. 2018. "Western Europeans Vary in Their Nationalist, Anti-immigrant and Anti-religious Minority attitudes." FactTank, Pew Research Center, June 19. https://www.pewresearch.org/fact-tank/2018/06/19/western-europeans-vary-in-their-nationalist-anti-immigrant-and-anti-religious-minority-attitudes/?utm _source=Pew+Research+Center&utm_campaign=be1a9b7135-Global_2018_07_ 02&utm_medium=email&utm_term=0_3e953b9b70-be1a9b7135-400431161.

Dingsdale, A., and Z. Kovacs. 1996. "A Return to Socialism: The Hungarian General Election of 1994." *Geography* 81(3):267–272.

Domański, Henryk. 2000. "Death of Classes in Poland? Electoral Voting and Class Membership in 1991–1997." *Polish Sociological Review* 2(130):151–178.

Doolan, K., and D. Cepić. 2022. "Introduction to the Special Issue on Class Dynamics from Socialism to Post-Socialism." *Communist and Post-Communist Studies* 55(2):1–10.

Dostal, Jörg Michael. 2017. "The Crisis of German Social Democracy Revisited." *Political Quarterly* 88(2):230–240.

Downes, J. F., and M. Loveless. 2018. "Centre Right and Radical Right Party Competition in Europe: Strategic Emphasis on Immigration, Anti-incumbency, and Economic crisis." *Electoral Studies* 54:148–158.

Downs, Anthony. 1957a. *An Economic Theory of Democracy*. New York: Addison Wesley.

Downs, Anthony. 1957b. "An Economic Theory of Political Action in a Democracy." *Journal of Political Economy* 65(2):135–150.

Doyle, O., and J. Fidrmuc. 2003. "Evolution of Voting Intentions during Post-communist Transition: Czech Republic 1990–98." *Political Economy of Transition and Development: Institutions, Politics and Policies*, 139–164.

*The Economist*. 2016. "Rose Thou Art Sick." April 2. https://www.economist.com/briefing/ 2016/04/02/rose-thou-art-sick.

Edwards, Erica. E. 2008. "Products of Their Past? Cleavages and Intra-Party Dissent over European Integration." IHS Political Science Series Paper No. 118, February, Vienna.

Eickhoff, Matthias. 2008. "'Ungarische Kapriolen' Blätter für deutsche und internationale Politik." *Blätter für deutsche und internationale Politik* 4:24–27.

Eiermann, M., Y. Mounk, and L. Gultchin. 2017. "European Populism: Trends, Threats and Future Prospects." Report 29, Tony Blair Institute for Global Change, London.

Ekiert, G., J. Kubik, M. A. Vachudova, F. Schimmelfennig, and Ulrich Sedelmeier, eds. 2005. *Democracy in the Postcommunist World: An Unending Quest? The Europeanization of Central and Eastern Europe*. Ithaca, NY: Cornell University Press.

Eley, Geoff. 2002. *Forging Democracy: The History of the Left in Europe, 1850–2000*. New York: Oxford University Press.

Engler, S. 2020. "'Fighting Corruption' or 'Fighting the Corrupt Elite'? Politicizing Corruption within and beyond the Populist Divide." *Democratization* 27(4): 643–661.

Engler, Fabian, and Reimut Zohlnhöfer. 2019. "Left Parties, Voter Preferences, and Economic Policy-Making in Europe." *Journal of European Public Policy* 26(11):1620–1638.

Engler, Sarah, Bartek Pytlas, and Kevin Deegan-Krause. 2019. "Assessing the Diversity of Anti-establishment and Populist Politics in Central and Eastern Europe." *West European Politics* 42(6):1310–1336.

Enyedi, Zsolt. 2005. "The Role of Agency in Cleavage Formation." *European Journal of Political Research* 44:697–720.

Enyedi, Z., and D. Róna. 2018. "Governmental and Oppositional Populism: Competition and Division of Labor." In *Absorbing the Blow*, edited by S. Wolinetz and A. Zaslove, 251–272.Colchester: ECPR Press.

Epstein, R. A. 2008. "The Social Context in Conditionality: Internationalizing Finance in Postcommunist Europe." *Journal of European Public Policy* 15(6):880–898.

Erikson, Robert, and John Goldthorpe. 1992. *The Constant Flux: A Study of Class Mobility in Industrial Societies*. Oxford: Clarendon Press.

Erikson, R., J. H. Goldthorpe, and L. Portocarero. 1979. "Intergenerational Class Mobility in Three Western European Societies: England, France and Sweden." *British Journal of Sociology* 30(4):415–441.

Erikson, Robert, Michael MacKuen, and James Stimson. 2002. *The Macro Polity*. Cambridge: Cambridge University Press.

Esarey, Justin, and Andrew Menger. 2018. "Practical and Effective Approaches to Dealing with Clustered Data." *Political Science Research and Methods* 7(3):1–19.

European Commission. 2017. "Reflection Paper on the Social Dimension of Europe." https://ec.europa.eu/info/publications/reflection-paper-social-dimension-europe_en.

Evans, Geoffrey. 1992. "Testing the Validity of the Goldthorpe Class Schema." *European Sociological Review* 8:211–232.

Evans, Geoffrey. 1997. "Class Inequality and the Formation of Political Interests in Eastern Europe." *European Journal of Sociology* 38(2):207–234.

Evans, Geoffrey. 2000. "The Continued Significance of Class Voting." *Annual Review of Political Science* 3(1):401–417.

Evans, Geoffrey. 2006. "The Social Bases of Political Divisions in Post-Communist Eastern Europe." *Annual Review of Sociology* 32:245–270.

Evans, Geoffrey. 2017. "Social Class and Voting." In *The Sage Handbook of Electoral Behaviour*, edited by K. Arzheimer, J. Evans, and M. S. Lewis-Beck, 177–198. London: Sage.

Evans, G., and N. D. De Graaf. 2013. *Political Choice Matters: Explaining the Strength of Class and Religious Cleavages in Cross-National Perspective*. Oxford: Oxford University Press.

Evans, G., Anthony Heath, and Clive Payne. 1995. "Class and Party Revisited: A New Model for Estimating Changes in Levels of Class Voting." *British Elections and Parties Yearbook* 5(1):157–174.

Evans, G., and J. Mellon. 2016. "Working Class Votes and Conservative Losses: Solving the UKIP Puzzle." *Parliamentary Affairs* 69(2):464–479.

Evans, G., and Colin Mills. 1999. "Are There Classes in PostCommunist Societies? A New Approach to Identifying Class Structure." *Sociology* 33:23–46.

Evans, Geoffrey, and J. Tilley. 2012. "How Parties Shape Class Politics: Explaining the Decline of the Class Basis of Party Support." *British Journal of Political Science* 42(1):137–161.

Evans, Geoffrey, and J. Tilley. 2017. *The New Politics of Class: The Political Exclusion of the British Working Class*. New York: Oxford University Press.

Evans, Geoffrey, and Stephen Whitefield. 1995. "Social and Ideological Cleavage Formation in Post-Communist Hungary." *Europe-Asia Studies* 47(7):1177–1204.

Evans, Geoffrey, and Stephen Whitefield. 1998. "The Structuring of Political Cleavages in Post-Communist Societies: The Case of the Czech Republic and Slovakia." *Political Studies* 46(1):115–139.

Evans, Geoffrey, and Stephen Whitefield. 2000. "Explaining the Formation of Electoral Cleavages in Post-Communist Democracies." In *Elections in Central and Eastern Europe: The First Wave*, edited by H.-D. Klingemann, E. Mochmann, and K. Newton, 36–68. Berlin: Edition Sigma.

Evans, Geoffrey, and Stephen Whitefield. 2001. "The Dynamics of Cleavage Formation in Conditions of Economic Transformation: Comparing Cleavages in Russia, Ukraine and Lithuania." Paper presented at the Annual Meeting of the American Political Science Association, San Francisco.

Evans, Geoffrey, and Stephen Whitefield. 2006. "Explaining the Emergence and Persistence of Class Voting for Presidential Candidates in Post-Soviet Russia, 1993–2001." *Political Research Quarterly* 59(1):23–34.

Eyal, G., I. Szelényi, and E. R. Townsley. 1998. *Making Capitalism without Capitalists: Class Formation and Elite Struggles in Post-communist Central Europe*. Verso.

Fabry, Adam. 2019. *The Political Economy of Hungary. From State Capitalism to Authoritarian Neoliberalism*. Cham, Switzerland: Palgrave.

Feischmidt, Margit, and Kristóf Szombati. 2017. "Understanding the Rise of the Far Right from a Local Perspective: Structural and Cultural Conditions of Ethno-Traditionalist Inclusion and Racial Exclusion in Rural Hungary." *Identities* 24(3):313–331.

Fenger, Menno. 2018. "The Social Policy Agendas of Populist Radical Right Parties in Comparative Perspective." *Journal of International and Comparative Social Policy* 34(3):188–209.

Fernandes, J. 2016. "The 2015 Portuguese General Election." *West European Politics* 39(4):890–900.

Fernandez-Vazquez, P., and Z. Somer-Topcu. 2019. "The Informational Role of Party Leader Changes on Voter Perceptions of Party Positions." *British Journal of Political Science* 49(3):977–996.

Ferreira, M. J., and P. Fonseca. 2018. "The Portuguese Left against Austerity Policies." In *Crisis, Austerity, and Transformation: How Disciplinary Neoliberalism Is Changing Portugal*, edited by I. David, 133–156. London: Lexington Books.

Fico, R. 2000. "Rationale for a New Political Party." In *Slovakia after Communism and Mečiarism*, edited by K. Williams, 21–24. London: SSEES Occasional Papers.

Fidrmuc, Jan. 2000. "Economics of Voting in Post-Communist Countries." *Electoral Studies* 19(2–3):199–217.

Fomina, J., and J. Kucharczyk. 2016. "The Specter Haunting Europe: Populism and Protest in Poland." *Journal of Democracy* 27(4):58–68.

Ford, R., and M. J. Goodwin. 2010. "Angry White Men: Individual and Contextual Predictors of Support for the British National Party." *Political Studies* 58(1):1–25.

Ford, R., and M. J. Goodwin. 2014a. *Revolt on the Right: Explaining Support for the Radical Right in Britain*. Abingdon: Routledge.

Ford, R., and M. J. Goodwin. 2014b. "Understanding UKIP: Identity, Social Change and the Left Behind." *Political Quarterly* 85(3):277–284.

Fowler, Brigid. 2004. "Concentrated Orange: Fidesz and the Remaking of the Hungarian Centre-Right, 1994–2002." *Journal of Communist Studies and Transition Politics* 20(3, September):80–113.

Franz, C., M. Fratzscher, and A. S. Kritikos. 2018. "German Right-Wing Party AfD Finds More Support in Rural Areas with Aging Populations." *DIW Weekly Report* 8(7–8):69–79.

Franzmann, Simon, and Dennis C. Spies. 2011. A Two-Dimensional Approach to the Political Opportunity Structure of Extreme Right Parties in Western Europe. *West European Politics* 34(5):1044–1069.

Freudenberg, Christoph, Tamás Berki, and Ádám Reiff. 2016. "A Long-Term Evaluation of Recent Hungarian Pension Reforms." Magyar Nemzeti Bank Working Papers 2016/2, Budapest.

Fukuyama, Francis. 2020. "30 Years of World Politics: What Has Changed?" *Journal of Democracy* 31(1):11–21.

Funke, M., and C. Trebesch. 2017. "Financial Crises and the Populist Right." *ifo DICE Report* 15(4):6–9.

Ganev, Venelin I. 2017. " 'Neoliberalism Is Fascism and Should Be Criminalized': Bulgarian Populism as Left-wing Radicalism." *Slavic Review* 76(S1):S9–S18.

Gardawski, J., and G. Meardi. 2008. "Explaining Failures and Chances of Polish 'Social Pacts.' " Report. Industrial Relations Research Unit, Warwick Business School.

Gardawski, J., and G. Meardi. 2010. "Keep Trying? Polish Failures and Half-Successes in Social Pacting." *Warsaw Forum of Economic Sociology* 1(1):69–90.

Gardawski, J., and T. Zukowski. 1992. *Robotnicy 1991*. Warsaw: Friedrich Ebert Foundation.

Gardawski, J., and T. Zukowski. 1994. *Robotnicy 1993*. Warsaw: Friedrich Ebert Foundation.

Gerber, A. S., and D. P. Green. 2012. *Field Experiments: Design, Analysis, and Interpretation*. New York: W. W. Norton.

Gerring, John. 2007. *Case Study Research: Principles and Practices*. New York: Cambridge University Press.

Gest, Justin. 2016. "The White Working-Class Minority: A Counter-Narrative." *Politics, Groups, and Identities* 4(1):126–143.

Gherghina, Sergiu. 2014. *Party Organization and Electoral Volatility in Central and Eastern Europe: Enhancing Voter Loyalty*. Abingdon: Routledge.

Gibson, J., and A. Cielecka. 1995. "Economic Influences on the Political Support for Market Reform in Post-Communist Transitions: Some Evidence from the 1993 Polish Parliamentary Elections." *Europe-Asia Studies* 47(5):765–785.

Giddens, Anthony. 1998. *The Third Way: The Renewal of Social Democracy*. London: Polity Press.

Gidron, Noam, and Bart Bonikowski. 2013. "Varieties of Populism: Literature Review and Research Agenda." Working Paper Series No. 13-0004, Weatherhead Center for International Affairs, Harvard University. https://ssrn.com/abstract=2459387.

Gijsberts, M., and P. Nieuwbeerta. 2000. "Class Cleavages in Party Preferences in the New Democracies in Eastern Europe: A Comparison with Western Democracies." *European Societies* 2:397–430.

Gill, S. 2003. "A Neo-Gramscian Approach to European Integration." In *A Ruined Fortress? Neo-liberal Hegemony and Transformation Europe*, edited by M. Ryner and A. Cafruny, 47–70. New York: Rowman & Littlefield.

Gingrich, J., and S. Häusermann. 2015. "The Decline of the Working Class Vote, the Reconfiguration of the Welfare Support Coalition and Consequences for the Welfare State." *Journal of European Social Policy* 25(1):50–75.

Glyn, Andrew, ed. 2001. *Social Democracy in Neoliberal Times: The Left and Economic Policy since 1980.* Oxford: Oxford University Press.

Goes, Eunice. 2019. "Portuguese Left Tests the Limits of European Social Democracy." *Hard Times* 103(1):55–64.

Golder, Matt. 2003. "Electoral Institutions, Unemployment and Extreme Right Parties." *British Journal of Political Science* 33:525–534.

Golder, Matt. 2016. "Far Right Parties in Europe." *Annual Review of Political Science* 19:477–497.

Goodwin, Matthew, and Robert Ford. 2014. "How Labour Is Failing to Grasp UKIP's Appeal to Angry White Voters." *The Guardian*, June 24. https://www.theguardian.com/commentisfree/2014/jun/24/labour-ukip-appeal-to-angry-white-voters.

Goraus-Tańska, Karolina. 2017. "The Family 500+: Battling Child Poverty in Poland." World Bank: Eurasian Perspectives. http://blogs.worldbank.org/europeandcentrala sia/family-500-battling-child-poverty-poland.

Gougou, F., and N. Mayer. 2013. "The Class Basis of Extreme Right Voting in France: Generational Replacement and the Rise of New Cultural Issues (1984–2007)." In *Class Politics and the Radical Right*, edited by J. Rydgren, 156–172. Abingdon: Routledge.

Gould, John A. 2009. "Slovakia's Neoliberal Churn: The Political Economy of the Fico Government, 2006–2008." Working Papers Series 1, Institute of European Studies and International Relations, Bratislava.

Grabbe, H. 2006. *The EU's Transformative Power: Europeanization through Conditionality in Central and Eastern Europe.* New York: Palgrave Macmillan.

Greer, S. L., H. Jarman, and R. Baeten. 2016. "The New Political Economy of Health Care in the European Union: The Impact of Fiscal Governance." *International Journal of Health Services* 46(2):262–282.

Greskovits, B. 2000. "Hungary's Post-Communist Development in Comparative Perspective." In *Liberalization and Its Consequences: A Comparative Perspective on Latin America and Eastern Europe*, edited by W. Baer and J. L. Love, 126–149. Cheltenham: Edward Elgar.

Greskovits, Béla. 2007. "Economic Woes and Political Disaffection." *Journal of Democracy* 18(4):40–46.

Greskovits, Béla. 2008. "Hungary and Slovakia: Compliance and Its Discontents." *The Euro at 10: Europeanization, Power, and Convergence* 10 (September):274–291.

Greskovits, Béla. 2020. "Rebuilding the Hungarian Right through Conquering Civil Society: The Civic Circles Movement." *East European Politics* 36(2):247–266.

Grittersova, J., I. H. Indridason, C. Gregory, and R. Crespo. 2016. "Austerity and Niche Parties: The Electoral Consequences of Fiscal Reforms." *Electoral Studies* 42:276–289.

Gromadzki, J., K. Sałach, and M. Brzezinski. 2022. "When Populists Deliver on Their Promises: The Electoral Effects of a Large Cash Transfer Program in Poland." IBS Working Paper 02/2022, Instytut Badan Strukturalnych, Warszawa.

Grzymała-Busse, Anna. 2002a. "The Programmatic Turnaround of Communist Successor Parties in East Central Europe." *Communist and Post-Communist Studies* 35(1):51–66 .

Grzymala-Busse, Anna. 2002b. *Redeeming the Communist Past: The Regeneration of Communist Parties in East Central Europe.* Cambridge: Cambridge University Press.

Grzymala-Busse, Anna. 2017. "Global Populisms." *Slavic Review* 76(1):1.

Grzymala-Busse, Anna. 2019a. "Conclusion: The Global Forces of Populism." *Polity* 51(4):718–723.

Grzymala-Busse, Anna. 2019b. "Hoist on Their Own Petards? The Reinvention and Collapse of Authoritarian Successor Parties." *Party Politics* 25(4):569–582.

Grzymala-Busse, Anna. 2019c. "How Populists Rule: The Consequences for Democratic Governance." *Polity* 51(4):707–717.

Grzymala-Busse, Anna. 2019d. "The Failure of Europe's Mainstream Parties." *Journal of Democracy* 30(4):35–47.

Grzymala-Busse, Anna, and Abby Innes. 2003. "Great Expectations: The EU and Domestic Political Competition in East Central Europe." *East European Politics and Societies* 17(1):64–73.

*The Guardian.* 2015. "Andrzej Duda Victory in Polish Presidential Election Signals Shift to Right." May 25. https://www.theguardian.com/world/2015/may/25/andrzej-duda-victory-polish-presidential-election?CMP=share_btn_tw.

Gubernat, R., and H. Rammelt. 2012. "Austerity: The Trigger for Waves of Contention in Romania." *Journal of Community Positive Practices* 2:256–265.

Guiso, L., H. Herrera, M. Morelli, and T. Sonno. 2017. *Demand and Supply of Populism.* London: Centre for Economic Policy Research.

Gyarfasova, Olga. 2013. "Metamorphosis of Radical Right in Slovakia." Paper presented at ECPR Bordeaux. https://ecpr.eu/filestore/paperproposal/169d2ade-7048-4d73-83d2-d7e1288d2a09.pdf.

Gyárfášová, O., and V. Krivý. 2007. "Electoral Behaviour—Persistent Volatility or Clear Signs of Consolidation? The Case of Slovakia." In *Parliamentary Elections and Party Landscape in the Visegrád Group Countries*, edited by V. Hloušek, R. Chytilek, 79–106. Brno: Democracy and Culture Studies Centre.

Győri, Gábor. 2015. "Hungarian Politics in 2014." Policy Solution Research Papers, Friedrich Ebert Stiftung Foundation, Bonn.

Hainmueller, J., and M. J. Hiscox. 2007. "Educated Preferences: Explaining Attitudes toward Immigration in Europe." *International Organization* 61(2):399–442.

Hájek, Lukáš. 2020. "Dynamic Roll Call Analysis of Parties' Ideological Positions in the Czech Republic." *Journal of Legislative Studies* 26(1):133–157.

Halikiopoulou, Daphne. 2019. "Right-Wing Populism as a Nationalist Vision of Legitimating Collective Choice: A Supply-Side Perspective." *International Spectator* 54(2):35–49.

Hall, Stuart. 2003 "New Labour's Double-Shuffle." *Soundings* 24:10–24.

Halmai, Gábor. 2011. "(Dis)possessed by the Spectre of Socialism: Nationalist Mobilization in 'Transitional' Hungary." In *Headlines of Nation, Subtexts of Class: Working Class Populism and the Return of the Repressed in Neoliberal Europe*, edited by D. Kalb and G. Halmai, 113–141. New York: Berghahn Books.

Handl, V., and V. Leška. 2014. "Between Emulation and Adjustment: External Influences on Programmatic Change in the Slovak SDL." In *Learning from the West? Policy Transfer and Programmatic Change in the Communist Successor Parties of East Central Europe*, edited by Hough, Dan, William E. Paterson, and Sloam James, 105–122. Routledge: London and New York.

Hanley, S. 2001. "Toward Breakthrough or Breakdown? The Consolidation of KSČM as a NeoCommunist Successor Party in the Czech Republic." *Journal of Communist Studies and Transition Politics* 17(3):96–116.

Hanley, S. 2004. "Getting the Right Right: Redefining the Centre-Right in Postcommunist Europe." *Journal of Communist Studies and Transition Politics* 20(3):9–27.

Hanley, S. 2008. "Embracing Europe, Opposing EU-rope? Party-Based Euroscepticism in the Czech Republic. In *Opposing Europe? The Comparative Party Politics of Euroscepticism*. Vol. 1: *Case Studies and Country Surveys*, edited by A. Szczerbiak and P. Taggart, 243–262. Oxford: Oxford University Press on Demand.

Hanley, S., and S. House. 2004. "Breaking Through or Breaking Apart? The Communist Party of Bohemia and Moravia in Czech Politics Since 1998." In *CREES Annual Conference, Cumberland Lodge, Windsor Great Park*, 11–13. London.

Hanley, Seán, and Allan Sikk. 2016. "Economy, Corruption or Floating Voters? Explaining the Breakthroughs of Anti-Establishment Reform Parties in Eastern Europe." *Party Politics* 22(4):522–553.

Hanley, S., and Milada Anna Vachudova. 2018. "Understanding the Illiberal Turn: Democratic Backsliding in the Czech Republic." *East European Politics* 34(3):276–296.

Hansen, Michael A., and Jonathan Olsen. 2019. "Flesh of the Same Flesh: A Study of Voters for the Alternative for Germany (AfD) in the 2017 Federal Election." *German Politics* 28(1):1–19.

Hantrais, L., and S. Mangen. 1998. *Cross-national Research Methods in the Social Sciences: Method and Management of Cross-National Social Research*. London: Pinter.

Harteveld, Eelco. 2016. "Winning the 'Losers' but Losing the 'Winners'? The Electoral Consequences of the Radical Right Moving to the Economic Left." *Electoral Studies* 44:225–234.

Haughton, Tim. 2001. "HZDS: The Ideology, Organization and Support Base of Slovakia's Most Successful Party." *Europe-Asia Studies* 53(5):745–769.

Haughton, Tim. 2002. "Vladimír Meciar and His Role in the 1994–1998 Slovak Coalition Government." *Europe-Asia Studies* 54(8):1319–1338.

Haughton, Tim. 2003. "'We'll Finish What We've Started': The 2002 Slovak Parliamentary Elections." *Journal of Communist Studies and Transition Politics* 19(4):65–90.

Haughton, Tim. 2004. "Explaining the Limited Success of the Communist-Successor Left in Slovakia: The Case of the Party of the Democratic Left (SDL')." *Party Politics* 10(March):177–191.

Haughton, Tim. 2007. "When Does the EU Make a Difference? Conditionality and the Accession Process in Central and Eastern Europe." *Political Studies Review* 5(2):233–246.

Haughton, Tim. 2014. "Exit, Choice and Legacy: Explaining the Patterns of Party Politics in Post-communist Slovakia." *East European Politics* 30(2):210–229.

Haughton, T., and Kevin Deegan-Krause. 2016. "Slovakia Will Probably Reelect Its Center-Left Government. Here's Why That Party Has Held On." *Monkey Cage* (political science blog). *Washington Post,* February 25. https://www.washingtonpost.com/news/monkey-cage/wp/2016/02/25/slovakia-will-probably-reelect-its-center-left-governm ent-heres-why-that-party-has-held-on/?noredirect=on&utm_term=.8f8a295171f4.

Haughton, T., and K. Deegan-Krause. 2020. *The New Party Challenge: Changing Cycles of Party Birth and Death in Central Europe and Beyond*. Oxford: Oxford University Press.

Haughton, Tim, and Marek Rybář. 2004. "The Communist Party of Slovakia: Electoral Performance, Parliamentary Experience and Policy Choice." *Sociológia* 36(6):545–559.

Haughton, Tim, and Marek Rybář. 2008. "A Change of Direction: The 2006 Parliamentary Elections and Party Politics in Slovakia." *Journal of Communist Studies and Transition Politics* 24(2):232–255.

Haughton, T., M. Rybář, and K. Deegan-Krause. 2021. "Corruption, Campaigning, and Novelty: The 2020 Parliamentary Elections and the Evolving Patterns of Party Politics in Slovakia." *East European Politics and Societies* 36(3):728–752.

Häusermann, Silja. 2018. "Welfare State Research and Comparative Political Economy." *Oxford Research Encyclopedia of Politics*. https://doi.org/10.1093/acrefore/9780190228 637.013.654.

Häusermann, S., and H. Kriesi. 2015. "What Do Voters Want? Dimensions and Configurations in Individual-Level Preferences and Party Choice." In *Politics of Advanced Capitalism*, edited by P. Beramendi, S. Häusermann, H. Kitschelt, and H. Kriesi, 202–230. New York: Cambridge University Press.

Hausner, Jerzy. 2007. *Pętle rozwoju: O polityce gospodarczej lat 2001–2005*. Warszawa: Wydawnictwo Naukowe "Scholar."

Havlik, Peter. 2001. "EU Enlargement: Economic Impacts on Austria, the Czech Republic, Hungary, Poland, Slovakia and Slovenia." WIIW Research Report No. 280, Vienna.

Havlík, V. 2014. "The 2013 Parliamentary Election in the Czech Republic." *Evropská volební studia* 9:43–49.

Havlík, V., and V. Hloušek. 2017. *Europeanised Defiance—Czech Euroscepticism since 2004*. Berlin: Verlag Barbara Budrich.

Havlík, V., and V. Hloušek. 2021. "Differential Illiberalism: Classifying Illiberal Trends in Central European Party Politics." In *Illiberal Trends and Anti-EU Politics in East Central Europe*, edited by Lisa H. Anders and A. Lorenz, 111–136. Cham, Switzerland: Palgrave Macmillan.

Havlík, Vlastimil, and Aneta Pinková. 2021. *Populist Political Parties in East-Central Europe*. Brno: Masaryk University Press.

Hazans, Mihail. 2011. "Informal Workers across Europe: Evidence from 30 Countries." IZA Discussion Paper 5871, Institute for the Study of Labor, Bonn.

Heath, A. F., R. M. Jowell, and J. K. Curtice. 2001. *The Rise of New Labour: Party Policies and Voter Choices*. Oxford: Oxford University Press.

Heinisch, R. 2003. "Success in Opposition—Failure in Government: Explaining the Performance of Right-Wing Populist Parties in Public Office." *West European Politics* 26(3):91–130.

Heins, Elke, and Caroline de la Porte. 2015. "The Sovereign Debt Crisis, the EU and Welfare State Reform." *Comparative European Politics* 13:1–7.

Héjj, Dominik. 2017. "The Rebranding of Jobbik." *New Eastern Europe* 6(29):83–90.

Henderson, Karen. 2002. *Slovakia: The Escape from Invisibility*. London: Routledge.

Henderson, Karen. 2006. "Election Briefing #26: Europe and the Slovak Parliamentary Election of June 2006." European Parties Election and Referendums Network. https://www.sussex.ac.uk/webteam/gateway/file.php?name=epern-election-briefing-no-26.pdf&site=266.

Henderson, Karen. 2012. "Election Briefing #69: Europe and the Slovak Parliamentary Election of June 2012." European Parties Election and Referendums Network. https://www.sussex.ac.uk/webteam/gateway/file.php?name=epernslovakia2012. pdf&site=266.

Hendrick, J. 2002. "ISKO: Stata Module to Recode 4-Digit ISCO-88 Occupational Codes." Statistical Software Components S425802, Boston College Department of Economics.

Herbut R. 2002. *Teoria i praktyka funkcjonowania partii politycznych*. Wrocław: Wydawnictwo Uniwersytetu Wrocławskiego.

Herman, L. E., and J. Muldoon, eds. 2018. *Trumping the Mainstream: The Conquest of Democratic Politics by the Populist Radical Right*. Routledge.

Hernández, E., and H. Kriesi 2016. "The Electoral Consequences of the Financial and Economic Crisis in Europe." *European Journal of Political Research* 55:203–224.

Hilmar, Till. 2022. "Restoring Economic Pride? How Right-Wing Populists Moralize Economic Change." *Journal of Contemporary European Studies* 31(2):1–15.

Hirst, Paul. 1999. "Has Globalisation Killed Social Democracy?" *Political Quarterly* 70(1):84–96.

Hlousek, Vit, and Lubomir Kopecek. 2008. "Cleavages in Contemporary Czech and Slovak Politics: Between Persistence and Change." *East European Politics and Societies* 22:518–552.

Hloušek, V., and L. Kopeček. 2016. *Origin, Ideology and Transformation of Political Parties: East-Central and Western Europe Compared*. Abingdon: Routledge.

Holland, David. 2007. "Who Dug the Grave of the Polish Left?" *Debatte: Journal of Contemporary Central and Eastern Europe* 15(2):257–269.

Hooghe, L., and G. Marks. 2009. "A Postfunctionalist Theory of European Integration: From Permissive Consensus to Constraining Dissensus." *British Journal of Political Science* 39(1):1–23.

Hooghe, L., J. J. Huo, and G. Marks. 2007. "Does Occupation Shape Attitudes on Europe? Benchmarking Validity and Parsimony." *Acta Politica* 42(2):329–351.

Hopkin, J., and M. Blyth. 2019. "The Global Economics of European Populism: Growth Regimes and Party System Change in Europe." *Government and Opposition: An International Journal of Comparative Politics* 54:193–225.

Hopkin, J., and M. Blyth. 2020. Global Trumpism: Understanding Anti-system Politics in Western Democracies." In *The Emergence of Illiberalism*, edited by B. Vormann and M. Weinman, 101–123. New York: Routledge.

Horký, Petr. 2021. "The Czech Left on the Ropes." *Respekt*, June 11. https://www.respekt.cz/respekt-in-english/the-czech-left-on-the-ropes.

Horn, Alexander. 2021. "The Asymmetric Long-Term Electoral Consequences of Unpopular Reforms: Why Retrenchment Really Is a Losing Game for Left Parties." *Journal of European Public Policy* 28(9):1494–1517.

Hugrée, Cédric, Etienne Penissat, and Alexis Spire. 2020. "Is There a European Working Class? Social Domination and National Relegations in Europe." *Social Sciences Review* 11:96–113. https://hal.archives-ouvertes.fr/hal-02904025/document.

Hunter, R. J., and L. V. Ryan. 1998. *From Autarchy to Market: Polish Economics and Politics 1945–1995*. Westport, CT: Praeger.

Hutt, David. 2021a. "Czech Election: Are the Czech Social Democrats Locked in a Death Spiral? *Euronews*, October 8. https://www.euronews.com/2021/10/07/are-the-czech-social-democrats-locked-in-a-death-spiral.

Hutt, David. 2021b. "Why the Czechs Have Finally Turned Their Back on Communism?" *Euronews*, October 12. https://www.euronews.com/my-europe/2021/10/11/why-the-czechs-have-finally-turned-their-back-on-communism.

Hutter, S., and H. Kriesi, eds. 2019. *European Party Politics in Times of Crisis*. Cambridge: Cambridge University Press.

Hyttinen, Anniina. 2022. "Deradicalisation of Jobbik and Its Consequences—A Visual Ethnographic Analysis of the Symbolic and Ritual Change of a Hungarian Radical Right Party." *European Journal of Cultural and Political Sociology* 9(22):423–450.

Ignazi, Piero. 2003. *Extreme Right Parties in Western Europe.* New York: Oxford University Press.

Inglehart, Ronald. 1977. *The Silent Revolution: Changing Values and Political Style among Western Publics.* Princeton, NJ: Princeton University Press.

Inglehart, R., and P. Norris. 2016. "Trump, Brexit and the Rise of Populism: Economic Have-Nots and Cultural Backlash. HKS Working Paper 16-026. Harvard University, Cambridge, MA.

Inglehart, R., and P. Norris. 2017. "Trump and the Populist Authoritarian Parties: The Silent Revolution in Reverse." *Perspectives on Politics* 15(2):443–454.

Innes, Abby. 2002. "Party Competition in Postcommunist Europe: The Great Electoral Lottery." *Comparative Politics* 35(1):85–104.

Innes, Abby. 2014. "The Political Economy of State Capture in Central Europe." *JCMS: Journal of Common Market Studies* 52(1):88–104.

Innes, Abby. 2017. "Draining the Swamp: Understanding the Crisis in Mainstream Politics as a Crisis of the State." *Slavic Review* 76(1):S30–S38.

Ishiyama, J. T. 1995. "Communist Parties in Transition: Structures, Leaders, and Processes of Democratization in Eastern Europe." *Comparative Politics* 27(2):147–166.

Ishiyama, J. T. 1997. "The Sickle or the Rose? Previous Regime Types and the Evolution of the Ex-communist Parties in Postcommunist Politics." *Comparative Political Studies* 30(3):299–330.

Ishiyama, J. T. 2006. "Europeanization and the Communist Successor Parties in Post-Communist Politics. *Politics and Policy* 34(1): 3–29.

Ishiyama, J., and A. Bozóki. 2001. "Adaptation and Change: Characterizing the Survival Strategies of the Communist Successor Parties." *Journal of Communist Studies and Transition Politics* 17(3):32–51.

Ivaldi, Gilles. 2013. "A New Radical Right Economic Agenda? The Transformation of the Front National in France." *Workshop on Radical Right-Wing Populists and the Economy,* 1–24. Groningen.

Ivarsflaten, Elisabeth. 2008. "What Unites Right-Wing Populists in Western Europe? Re-examining Grievance Mobilization Models in Seven Successful Cases." *Comparative Political Studies* 41(1):3–23.

Iversen, T., and D. Soskice. 2001. "An Asset Theory of Social Policy Preferences." *American Political Science Review* 95:875–893.

Jackson, John E., Jacek Klich, and Krystyna Poznanska, eds. 2005. *The Political Economy of Poland's Transition: New Firms and Reform Governments.* New York: Cambridge University Press.

Jalali, C., J. Moniz, and P. Silva. 2020. "In the Shadow of the 'Government of the Left': The 2019 Legislative Elections in Portugal." *South European Society and Politics* 25(2):229–255.

Jańczak, Jaroslaw. 2019. "Why Do Poles Oppose Immigrats? The Polish Political Elite's (Anti-)Immigration Rhetoric." In *National Rhetorics in the Syrian Immigration Crisis: Victims, Frauds, and Floods,* edited by C. Rountree and J. Tilli, 125–152. East Lansing, MI: MSU Press.

Jansen, G., G. Evans, and N. D. De Graaf. 2013. "Class Voting and Left-Right Party Positions: A Comparative Study of 15 Western Democracies, 1960–2005." *Social Science Research* 42(2):376–400.

Jasiewicz, Krzysztof. 1992. "Problems of Postcommunism: From Solidarity to Fragmentation." *Journal of Democracy* 3(2):55–69.

Jasiewicz, Krzysztof. 2009. "'The Past Is Never Dead': Identity, Class, and Voting Behavior in Contemporary Poland." *East European Politics and Societies* 23(4):491–508.

Jaskiernia, Jerry. 2019. "Authoritarian Tendencies in the Polish Political System." In *New Authoritarianism*, edited by Jerzy J. Wiatr, 152–268. Berlin and Toronto: Barbara Budrich Publishers Opladen, Berlin and Toronto.

Jensen, J. Bradford, Dennis P. Quinn, and Stephen Weymouth. 2016. "Winners and Losers in International Trade: The Effects on U.S. Presidential Voting." NBER Working Paper No. 21899, Cambridge, MA.

Jobbik Magyarországért Mozgalom. 2010. "Radikális változás: A Jobbik országgyűlési választási programja a nemzeti önrendelkezésért és a társadalmi igazságosságért." Budapest. https://docplayer.hu/158036-Radikalis-valtozas-a-jobbik-orszaggyulesi-valasztasi-programja-a-nemzeti-onrendelkezesert-es-a-tarsadalmi-igazsagossag ert.html.

Johns, Luke. 2013. "Evaluating Research Methods of Comparative Politics." *E-International Relations Students*, May 13. http://www.e-ir.info/2013/05/09/evaluating-research-methods-of-comparative-politics.

Johnson, J. 2008. "The Remains of Conditionality: The Faltering Enlargement of the Euro Zone." *Journal of European Public Policy* 15(6):826–841.

Johnson, J., and A. Barnes. 2015. "Financial Nationalism and Its International Enablers: The Hungarian Experience." *Review of International Political Economy* 22(3):535–569.

Jolly, Seth, Ryan Bakker, Liesbet Hooghe, Gary Marks, Jonathan Polk, Jan Rovny, Marco Steenbergen, and Milada Anna Vachudova. Forthcoming. "Chapel Hill Expert Survey Trend File, 1999–2019." *Electoral Studies* 75.

Judis, J. B. 2016. *The Populist Explosion: How the Great Recession Transformed American and European Politics*. New York: Columbia Global Reports.

Jylhä, K. M., J. Rydgren, and P. Strimling. 2019. "Radical Right-Wing Voters from Right and Left: Comparing Sweden Democrat Voters Who Previously Voted for the Conservative Party or the Social Democratic Party." *Scandinavian Political Studies* 42(3–4):220–244.

Kalb, Don. 2009. "Conversations with a Polish Populist: Tracing Hidden Histories of Globalization, Class, and Dispossession in Postsocialism (and Beyond)." *American Ethnologist* 36:207–223.

Kalb, Don. 2018. "Upscaling Illiberalism: Class, Contradiction, and the Rise and Rise of the Populist Right in Post-Socialist Central Europe." *Fudan Journal of the Humanities and Social Sciences* 11(3):303–321.

Kalb, Don, and Gabor Halmai, eds. 2011. *Headlines of Nation, Subtexts of Class: Working Class Populism and the Return of the Repressed in Neoliberal Europe*. Oxford: Berghahn Books.

Kaminski, P., and P. Rozbicka. 2016. "Political Parties and Trade Unions in the Post-Communist Poland: Class Politics That Have Never a Chance to Happen." *Polish Political Science Yearbook* 45:191.

Kando, Thomas M. 2001. "Demographic and Public Health Trends in Hungary in the First Post-Communist Decade." *Society and Economy in Central and Eastern Europe* 23(1–2):7–27.

Kapsas, Andre. 2021. "The Czech Left Is Being Punished for Its Disastrous Record in Government." *Jacobinmag*, October 8. https://jacobinmag.com/2021/10/czech-republic-andrej-babis-social-democrats-communists-ano-election.

Karácsony, G., and D. Róna. 2010. A Jobbik titka: A szélsőjobb magyarországi megerősödésének lehetséges okairól." *Politikatudományi Szemle* 19(1):31–63.

Karácsony, Gergely, and Daniel Róna. 2011. "The Secret of Jobbik: Reasons behind the Rise of the Hungarian Radical Right." In "Democratic Institutionalism." Special issue of *Journal of East European and Asian Studies* 2(1):61–92.

Karl, P. 2019. "Creating a New Normal: The Mainstreaming of Far-Right Ideas through Online and Offline Action in Hungary." In *Post-digital Cultures of the Far Right: Online Actions and Offline Consequences in Europe and the US*, edited by M. Fielitz and N. Thurston, 67–78. Bielefeld: Transcript.

Karreth, J., J. T. Polk, and C. S. Allen. 2013. "Catchall or Catch and Release? The Electoral Consequences of Social Democratic Parties' March to the Middle in Western Europe." *Comparative Political Studies* 46(7):791–822.

Kelley, Judith G. 2006. *Ethnic Politics in Europe: The Power of Norms and Incentives*. Princeton, NJ: Princeton University Press.

Keman, Hans. 2011. "Third Ways and Social Democracy: The Right Way to Go?" *British Journal of Political Science* 41(3):671–680.

Kenny, Paul D. 2017. *Populism and Patronage: Why Populists Win Elections in India, Asia, and Beyond*. Oxford: Oxford University Press.

Kiblitskaya, Marina. 2000. "'Once We Were Kings': Male Experiences of Loss of Status at Work in Post-Communist Russia." In *Gender, State and Society in Soviet and Post-Soviet Russia*, edited by S. Ashwin, 90–103. London: Routledge.

Kideckel, David. 2004. "Miners and Wives in Romania's Jiu Valley: Perspectives on Postsocialist Class, Gender, and Social Change." *Identities* 11:39–63.

Kim, Dae Soon. 2016. "The Rise of European Right Radicalism: The Case of Jobbik." *Communist and Post-Communist Studies* 49(4):345–357.

Kim, Seongcheol. 2017. "Between Milieu and Vacuum." *Politologický časopis: Czech Journal of Political Science* 24(3):302–329.

Kim, Seongcheol. 2021. "Because the Homeland Cannot Be in Opposition: Analysing the Discourses of Fidesz and Law and Justice (PiS) from Opposition to Power." *East European Politics* 37(2):332–351.

King, Lawrence, and Aleksandra Sznajder. 2006. "The State-Led Transition to Liberal Capitalism: Neoliberal, Organizational, World Systems, and Social Structural Explanations of Poland's Economic Success." *American Journal of Sociology* 112(3, November):751–801.

Kirchheimer, Otto. 1966. "The Transformation of Western European Party Systems." In *Political Parties and Political Development*, edited by Joseph Lapalombara and Myron Weiner, 177–200. Princeton, NJ: Princeton University Press.

Kite, Melissa. 2006. "BNP Case 'a Wake-Up Call to Labour.'" *Daily Telegraph*, November 12. http://www.telegraph.co.uk/news/uknews/1533905/BNP-case-a-wake-up-call-to-Labour.html.

Kitschelt, Herbert. 1992. "The Formation of Party Systems in East Central Europe." *Politics & Society* 20(1):7–50.

Kitschelt, Herbert. 1994. *The Transformation of European Social Democracy*, Cambridge: Cambridge University Press.

Kitschelt, Herbert P. 1995a. "Formation of Party Cleavages in Post-Communist Democracies: Theoretical Propositions." *Party Politics* 1:447–472.

Kitschelt, Herbert P. 1995b. *The Radical Right in Western Europe: A Comparative Analysis.* Ann Arbor: University of Michigan Press.

Kitschelt, Herbert P. 2007. "Growth and Persistence of the Radical Right in Postindustrial Democracies: Advances and Challenges in Comparative Research." *West European Politics* 30(5):1176–1206.

Kitschelt, Herbert P. 2013. "Social Class and the Radical Right: Conceptualizing Political Preference Formation and Partisan Choice." In *Class Politics and the Radical Right*, edited by Jens Rydgren, 224–251. London: Routledge.

Kitschelt, Herbert, Zdenka Mansfeldova, Radowslaw Markowski, and Gabor Toka. 1999. *Post-Communist Party Systems. Competition, Representation, and Inter-Party Cooperation.* Cambridge: Cambridge University Press.

Kitschelt, Herbert, and Anthony J. McGann. 1997. *The Radical Right in Western Europe: A Comparative Analysis.* Ann Arbor: University of Michigan Press.

Kitschelt, H., and P. Rehm. 2014. "Occupations as a Site of Political Preference Formation." *Comparative Political Studies* 47(12):1670–1706.

Knutsen, O. P. 2006. *Class Voting in Western Europe: A Comparative Longitudinal Study.* Lanham, MD: Lexington Books.

Knutsen, O. P. (2013). "Social Structure, Social Coalitions and Party Choice in Hungary." *Communist and Post-Communist Studies* 46(1):25–38.

Kolodko, Grzegorz W. and Grzegorz W. Kolodko, and Domenico Mario Nuti. *The Polish Alternative: Old Myths, Hard Facts and New Strategies in the Successful Transformation of the Polish Economy.* https://ssrn.com/abstract=170889 or http://dx.doi.org/10.2139/ssrn.170889.

Kopeček, L., and P. Pšeja. 2008. "Czech Social Democracy and Its 'Cohabitation' with the Communist Party: The Story of a Neglected Affair." *Communist and Post-Communist Studies* 41(3):317–338.

Kopecký, Petr. 2006. "Political Parties and the State in Postcommunist Europe: The Nature of Symbiosis." *Journal of Communist Studies and Transition Politics* 22(3):251–273.

Korba, M. 2002. "Zahraničná, bezpečnostná a obranná politika." *Votby2002: Analýza volebných programov politických strán a hnutí (Bratislava: IVO, 2002)*, 35–58.

Korkut, Umut. 2007. "The 2006 Hungarian Election: Economic Competitiveness versus Social Solidarity." *Parliamentary Affairs* 60(4):675–690.

Korkut, U., and A. Buzogány. 2015. "Successful Transplants, Reform Governments, and Health Care Policy Reform in Slovakia and Hungary." In *Discursive Governance in Politics, Policy, and the Public Sphere*, edited by U. Korkut, K. Mahendran, G. Bucken-Knapp, and R. H. Cox, 47–61. New York: Palgrave Macmillan.

Kornai, János. 1992. *The Socialist System: The Political Economy of Communism.* Princeton, NJ: Princeton University Press.

Kostadinova, Tatiana. 2009. "Abstain or Rebel: Corruption Perceptions and Voting in East European Elections." *Politics & Policy* 37(4):691–714.

Kostelecký, Tomáš. 2002. *Political Parties after Communism: Developments in East-Central Europe.* Baltimore, MD: Johns Hopkins University Press.

Kovács, András. 2012. "Antisemitic Prejudice and Political Antisemitism in Present-Day Hungary." *Journal for the Study of Antisemitism* 4(2):443–467.

Kovář, Jan. 2022. "Politicisation of Immigration in Central and Eastern Europe: Evidence from Plenary Debates in Two Countries." *Problems of Post-Communism*, 1–12.

Köves, András. 1995. "After the Bokros Package: What Next?" *Acta Oeconomica* 37(3–4):249–265.

Kramer, Mark. 1995. "Polish Workers and the Post-communist Transition, 1989–1993." *Communist and Post-Communist Studies* 28(1):71–114.

Krantz, J. H., and R. Dalai. 2000. "Validity of Web-Based Psychological Research." In *Psychological Experiments on the Internet,* edited by M. H.Birnbaum, 35–60. San Diego, CA: Academic Press.

Krastev, Ivan. 2007. "Is East-Central Europe Backsliding? The Strange Death of the Liberal Consensus." *Journal of Democracy* 18(4):56–64.

Krastev, Ivan. 2018. "Eastern Europe's Illiberal Revolution." *Foreign Affairs,* April 16. https://www.foreignaffairs.com/articles/hungary/2018-04-16/eastern-europes-illibe ral-revolution.

Krastev, Ivan, and Stephen Holmes. 2018. "Explaining Eastern Europe: Imitation and Its Discontents." *Journal of Democracy* 29(3):117–128.

Kraus, Michael. 2003. "The Czech Republic's First Decade." *Journal of Democracy* 14(2):50–64.

Kreidl, M., K. Vlachová, M. Halova, and P. Rakušanová. 2000. "Rise and Decline of Right-Wing Extremism in the Czech Republic in the 1990s." *Czech Sociological Review* 8(1):69–91.

Krekó, P., and Attila Juhász. 2017. *The Hungarian Far Right: Social Demand, Political Supply, and International Context*. Stuttgart: Ibidem Press.

Krekó, Peter, and Gregor Mayer. 2015. *Transforming Hungary—Together? An Analysis of the Fidesz-Jobbik Relationship*. London and New York: Routledge.

Kriesi, Hanspeter. 1999. "Movements of the Left, Movements of the Right: Putting the Mobilization of Two New Types of Social Movement into Political Context." In *Continuity and Change in Contemporary Capitalism,* edited by H. Kitschelt, P. Lange, G. Marks and J. D. Stephens, 398–423. Cambridge: Cambridge University Press.

Kriesi, Hanspeter. 2008. "Political Mobilisation, Political Participation and the Power of the Vote." *West European Politics* 31(1–2):147–168.

Kriesi, Hanspeter. 2016. "The Politicization of European Integration." *Journal of Common Market Studies* 54:32–47.

Kriesi, H., E. Grande, M. Dolezal, M. Helbling, D. Höglinger, S. Hutter, and B. Wüest. 2012. *Political Conflict in Western Europe*. New York: Cambridge University Press.

Kriesi, H., E. Grande, R. Lachat, M. Dolezal, S. Bornschier, and T. Frey. 2006. "Globalization and the Transformation of the National Political Space: Six European Countries Compared." *European Journal of Political Research* 45(6):921–956.

Kriesi, H., E. Grande, R. Lachat, M. Dolezal, S. Bornschier, and T. Frey. 2008. *West European Politics in the Age of Globalization*. Cambridge: Cambridge University Press.

Krivý, V. 2006. "Parlamentné voľby 2006: Staré a nové vzorce rozdelení voličských hlasov." In *Slovenské voľby '06: Výsledky, príciny, súvislosti,* edited by G. Mesežnikov, O. Gyárfášová, and M. Kollar, 143–206. Bratislava: Institute for Public Affairs.

KSČM. 2006. "Volební program Komunistické strany Čech a Moravy na období 2006–2010: Volební program KSČM pro volby do 2006–2010." (Election Program of the Communist Party of Bohemia and Moravia for the Period 2006–2010). http://www.KSČM.cz/article.asp?thema=3783&item=35527.

KSČM. 2009. "Statement on the Ratification of the Lisbon Treaty by the Czech National Parliament." February 18. http://www.KSČM.cz.

KSČM. 2010. "Volebníprogram Komunistické strany Cech a Moravyna obdobi 2010–2013" (Election Program of the Communist Party of Bohemia and Moravia for the Period 2010–2013). http://www.KSČM.cz/index.asp?thema=2680&category=, staženo.

KSČM. 2013. "Volebníprogram Komunistické strany Cech a Moravyna obdobi 2013–2017" (Election Program of the Communist Party of Bohemia and Moravia for the Period 2013–2017). http://old.KSČM.cz/uvodni-stranka/nas-program/volebni-program.

Kubicek, Paul. 1999. "Organized Labor in Postcommunist States: Will the Western Sun Set on It, Too?" *Comparative Politics* 32(1):83–102.

Kuhnle, Stein. 2000. *Survival of the European Welfare State*. London: Routledge.

Kurlantzick, Joshua. 2016. *State Capitalism: How the Return of Statism Is Transforming the World*. New York: Oxford University Press.

Lach, Jiří, James T. La Plant, Jim Peterson, and David Hill. 2010. "The Party Isn't Over: An Analysis of the Communist Party in the Czech Republic." *Journal of Communist Studies and Transition Politics* 26(3):363–388.

Ladányi, J., and I. Szelényi. 2006. *Patterns of Exclusion: Constructing Gypsy Ethnicity and the Making of an Underclass in Transitional Societies of Europe*. New York: Columbia University Press.

Laursen, Thomas, and Marcin Sasin. 2004. "World Bank EU8 Quarterly Economic Report (English)." Washington, DC: World Bank Group. http://documents.worldbank.org/curated/en/626861468771053419/World-Bank-EU8-quarterly-economic-report.

Lehndorff, Steffen. 2014. *Divisive Integration. The Triumph of Failed Ideas in Europe— Revisited*. Brussels: ETUI.

Lendvai, Noemi. 2009. "Variety of Post-communist Welfare: Europeanisation and Emerging Welfare Regimes in the New EU Member States." Unpublished manuscript.

Lengyel, L. 2011. "The Last Peaceful Days?" *Russia in Global Affairs* 9(3):21–32.

Levitz, P., and G. Pop-Eleches. 2010. "Why No Backsliding? The European Union's Impact on Democracy and Governance before and after Accession." *Comparative Political Studies* 43(4):457–485.

Leško, M. 2000. *Masky a tváre novej elity: Čítanie o dvanástich politikoch z piatich vládnych strán*. Bratislava: Inštitút pre verejné otázky.

Lewis, Flora. 1990. "Triumph's Challenge." *New York Times*, May 29. https://www.nytimes.com/1990/05/29/opinion/foreign-affairs-triumph-s-challenge.html?smid=tw-share.

Lewis, Paul. 2002. *Political Parties in Post-communist Eastern Europe*. London: Routledge.

Lewis, P., S. Clarke, C. Barr, J. Holder, and N. Kommenda. 2018. "Revealed: One in Four Europeans Vote Populist." *The Guardian*, November 20. https://www.theguardian.com/world/ng-interactive/2018/nov/20/revealed-one-in-four-europeans-vote-populist.

Linden, Marcel van der. 2018. "Workers and the Radical Right." *International Labor and Working-Class History* 93(Spring): 74–78.

Attila Lindner, Filip Novokmet, Thomas Piketty, and Tomasz Zawisza. 2020. *Political conflict, social inequality and electoral cleavages in Central-Eastern Europe, 1990-2018*. World Inequality Lab WP 2020/25: 1-52.

Linek, L. 2008. "Kdy vymřou voliči KSČM? K věkové struktuře elektorátu KSČM." *Politologický časopis: Czech Journal of Political Science* 15(4):318–336.

Linek, L. 2015. "Class, Religion, and Generations: Cleavage Voting and the Mediating Role of Party Identification in the Czech Republic, 1990–2013." Paper presented at

ECPR Joint Sessions of Workshops, Warsaw, March 29–April 4. https://ecpr.eu/Filest ore/PaperProposal/1047884d-ea32-4367-857d-346bbf32b72a.pdf.

Linek, L., and P. Lyons. 2013. "Dočasná stabilita? Volební podpora politických stran v České republice v letech 1990–2010." *Sociologické nakladatelství* 17(2):786–788.

Lipset, Seymour M., and Stein Rokkan, eds. 1967. *Party Systems and Voter Alignments.* New York: Free Press.

Lobo, M. C., and P. C. Magalhães. 2004. "The Portuguese Socialists and the Third Way." In *Social Democratic Party Policies in Contemporary Europe,* edited by G. Bonoli and M. Powell, 101–119. London: Routledge.

Loxbo, K., J. Hinnfors, M. Hagevi, S. Blombäck, and M. Demker. 2021. "The Decline of Western European Social Democracy: Exploring the Transformed Link between Welfare State Generosity and the Electoral Strength of Social Democratic Parties, 1975–2014." *Party Politics* 27(3):430–441.

Lubbers, M., M. Gijsberts, and P. Scheepers. 2002. "Extreme Right-wing Voting in Western Europe." *European Journal of Political Research* 41(3):345–378.

Lupton, R., J. Hills, K. Stewart, and P. Vizard. 2013. "Labour's Social Policy Record: Policy, Spending and Outcomes 1997–2010." Research Report 1, LSE Center for the Analysis of Social Exclusion, Social Policy in a Cold Climate Project, London.

Lupu, Noam. 2014. "Brand Dilution and the Breakdown of Political Parties in Latin America." *World Politics* 66(4):561–602.

Lupu, Noam. 2016. *Party Brands in Crisis: Partisanship, Brand Dilution, and the Breakdown of Political Parties in Latin America.* New York: Cambridge University Press.

Lust, Aleksander. 2016. "The Blue Awakening? The Rise of the Far Right in Estonia." Paper presented at American Political Science Association, Philadelphia, PA.

Lütz, Susanne, and Matthias Kranke. 2014. "The European Rescue of the Washington Consensus? EU and IMF Lending to Central and Eastern European Countries." *Review of International Political Economy* 21(2):310–338.

Lynch, Julia. 2019. "Populism, Partisan Convergence, and Mobilization in Western Europe." *Polity* 51(4):668–677.

Lysek, J., J. Pánek, and T. Lebeda. 2021. "Who Are the Voters and Where Are They? Using Spatial Statistics to Analyse Voting Patterns in the Parliamentary Elections of the Czech Republic." *Journal of Maps* 17(1):33–38.

Magalhaes, P. C. 2014. "The Elections of the Great Recession in Portugal: Performance Voting under a Blurred Responsibility for the Economy." *Journal of Elections, Public Opinion* 24:180–202.

Mahr, A., and J. Nagle. 1995. "Resurrection of the Successor Parties and Democratization in East-Central Europe." *Communist and Post-Communist Studies* 28(4):393–409.

Malka, A., Y. Lelkes, and C. Soto. 2019. "Are Cultural and Economic Conservatism Positively Correlated? A Large-Scale Cross-National Test." *British Journal of Political Science* 49(3):1045–1069.

Malová, Darina. 2017. "Strengthening Social Democracy in the Visegrad Countries. Limits and Challenges Faced by Smer-SD." *Bratislava: Friedrich Ebert Stiftung*: 5–18. https://library.fes.de/pdf-files/bueros/prag/13217.pdf.

Malová, D., and B. Dolný. 2016. "Economy and Democracy in Slovakia during the Crisis: From a Laggard to the EU Core." *Problems of Post-Communism* 63(5–6):300–312.

Malová, D., E. Láštic, and M. Rybář. 2005. *Slovensko ako nový členský štát Európskej únie: Výzva z periférie?* Bratislava: Friedrich Ebert Stiftung.

Mann, Michael. 1995. "Sources of Variation in Working-Class Movements in Twentieth-Century Europe." *New Left Review* 212:14–54.

Manwaring, R., and J. Holloway. 2022. "A New Wave of Social Democracy? Policy Change across the Social Democratic Party Family, 1970s–2010s." *Government and Opposition: An International Journal of Comparative Politics* 57:84–107.

Manwaring, R., and P. Kennedy, eds. 2017. *Why the Left Loses: The Decline of the Centre-Left in Comparative Perspective*. Policy Press.

March, L., and C. Mudde. 2005. "What's Left of the Radical Left? The European Radical Left after 1989: Decline and Mutation." *Comparative European Politics* 3(1):23–49.

Mareš, M. 2011. "Konsolidace levice ve stranickém systému České republiky." *Politologický časopis: Czech Journal of Political Science* 18(2):133–159.

Margalit, Yotam. 2013. "Explaining Social Policy Preferences: Evidence from the Great Recession." *American Political Science Review* 107(1):80–103.

Markowski, R. 2006. "The Polish Elections of 2005: Pure Chaos or a Restructuring of the Party System?" *West European Politics* 29(4):814–832.

Markowski, Radoslaw. 2016. "The Polish Parliamentary Election of 2015: A Free and Fair Election That Results in Unfair Political Consequences." *West European Politics* 39(6):1311–1322.

Marks, G. 1997. "A Third Lens: Comparing European Integration and State Building." In *European Integration in Social and Historical Perspective: 1850 to the Present*, edited by Jytte Klausen and Louise A. Tilly. New York: Rowman & Littlefield.

Marks, G., L. Hooghe, M. Nelson, and E. Edwards. 2006. "Party Competition and European Integration in the East and West: Different Structure, Same Causality." *Comparative Political Studies* 39(2):155–175.

Markus, Gyorgy G. 1999. "Cleavages and Parties in Hungary after 1989." In *Cleavages, Parties, and Voters*, edited by Kay Lawson, Andrea Rommele, and Georgi Karasimeonov, 141–158. Westport, CT: Praeger.

Marsh, M., and S. Mikhaylov. 2012. "Economic Voting in a Crisis: The Irish Election of 2011." *Electoral Studies* 31:478–484.

Marx, P., and G. Schumacher. 2018. "Do Poor Citizens Vote for Redistribution, against Immigration or against the Establishment? A Conjoint Experiment in Denmark." *Scandinavian Political Studies* 41(3):263–282.

Maškarinec, Pavel. 2019. "The Rise of New Populist Political Parties in Czech Parliamentary Elections between 2010 and 2017: The Geography of Party Replacement." *Eurasian Geography and Economics* 60(5):511–547.

Mason, D. S., J. R. Kluegel, L. Khakhulina, P. Matějů, A. Orkeny, A. Stoyanov, and B. Wegener. 2000. *Marketing Democracy: Changing Public Opinion about Politics, the Market, and Social Inequality in Central and Eastern Europe*. Lanham, MD: Rowman & Littlefield.

Matějů, P., and B. Řeháková. 1997. "Turning Left or Class Realignment? Analysis of the Changing Relationship between Class and Party in the Czech Republic, 1992–96." *East European Politics and Societies* 11(3):501–542.

Mateju, P., B. Rehakova, and G. Evans. 1999. "The Politics of Interests and Class Realignment in the Czech Republic, 1992–1996." In *The End of Class Politics*, edited by G. Evans, 231–253. New York: Oxford University Press.

Mayda, Anna Maria. 2006. "Who Is against Immigration? A Cross-Country Investigation of Individual Attitudes toward Immigrants." *Review of Economics and Statistics* 88(3):510–530.

McGann, A. J., and Herbert Kitschelt. 2005. "The Radical Right in the Alps: Evolution of Support for the Swiss SVP and Austrian FPO." *Party Politics* 11(2):147–171.

McKenna, Amy, ed. 2013. *Estonia, Latvia, Lithuania, and Poland. The Britannica Guide to Countries of the European Union Series*. New York: Britannica Educational Publishing, Rosen Publishing Group.

McLaren, L. (2005). Identity, interests and attitudes to European integration. Springer.

McManus, Ian P. 2019. "The Re-emergence of Partisan Effects on Social Spending after the Global Financial Crisis." *JCMS: Journal of Common Market Studies* 57(6):1274–1291.

McManus, Ian P. 2022. *The Re-politicization of the Welfare State after the Global Financial Crisis*. Ann Arbor: University of Michigan Press.

Melios, Georgios. 2020. "Europe in Crisis: Political Trust, Corruption and Austerity." Institute for Global Prosperity. https://www.ucl.ac.uk/bartlett/igp/sites/bartlett/files/europe_in_crisis.pdf.

Meyerson, Harold. 2020. "All Unhappy Social Democratic Parties Are Alike: They've Lost the White Working Class." *New Labor Forum* 29(2):11–14.

Mikecz, Robert. 2019. "The Cornerstone of Economic Nationalism: National Self-Image." *Fudan Journal of the Humanities and Social Sciences* 12:587–608.

Milanovic, Branko. 1993. "Social Costs of Transition to Capitalism: Poland, 1990–1993." Policy Research Working Paper Series No. 871, World Bank, Washington, D.C., August.

Milliman, J., and M. Glinow. 1998. "Research and Publishing Issues in Large Scale Cross-National Studies." *Journal of Managerial Psychology* 13(3–4):137–142.

Minkenberg, M. 2017. *The Radical Right in Eastern Europe. Democracy under Siege?* New York: Palgrave Macmillan.

Miszerak, M., and D. Rohac. 2017. "Poland's Rush to Banking Sector Socialism." *Financial Times*, June 30. https://www.ft.com/content/f7283548-5cd1-11e7-b553-e2df1b0c3220.

Moene, K. O., and M. Wallerstein. 2001 "Inequality, Social Insurance, and Redistribution." *American Political Science Review* 95:859–874.

Mondon, Aurelien. 2017. "Limiting Democratic Horizons to a Nationalist Reaction: Populism, the Radical Right and the Working Class." *Javnost: The Public* 24(4):355–374.

Moravcsik, A., and M. A. Vachudova. 2003. "National Interests, State Power, and EU Enlargement." *East European Politics and Societies* 17(1):42–57.

Morlang, Diana. 2003. "Hungary: Socialists Building Capitalism." In *The Left Transformed in Post-Communist Societies*, edited by Jane Leftwich Curry and Littlefield, 61–98. Lanham, MD: Rowan & Littlefield.

Mortkowitz, Siegfried. 2017. "Czech Center Left Realigns with 'Pork-and-Cabbage' Voters." *Politico*, September 11. https://www.politico.eu/article/czech-election-2017-ČSSD-center-left-realigns-with-pork-and-cabbage-voters/.

Morton, R., and K. Williams. 2010. *From Nature to the Lab: The Methodology of Experimental Political Science and the Study of Causality*. New York: Cambridge University Press.

Moschonas, Gerassimos. 2002. *In the Name of Social Democracy—The Great Transformation: 1945 to the Present*. London: Verso.

Moschonas, G. 2011. "Historical Decline or Change of Scale." In *What's Left of the Left: Democrats and Social Democrats in Challenging Times*, edited by J. Cronin, G. Ross, and J. Shoch, 50–85. London: Duke University Press.

Mouffe, Chantal. 2005. *On the Political: Thinking in Action*. London: Routledge.

Mouffe, Chantal. 2019. *For a Left Populism*. London: Verso.

MSZP. 2018. "Tegyünk igazságot! MSZP választási program 2018." https://mszp.hu/page/download?ct=doc&cid=218&dt=atch&did=478.

MTIE. 2013. "Orban: Hungary Stands on Its Own Feet." *MTI EcoNews*, June 22.

Mudde, Cas. 2000. "Extreme Right Parties in Eastern Europe." *Patterns of Prejudice* 34:5–27.

Mudde, Cas. 2002. *The Ideology of the Extreme Right*. Manchester: Manchester University Press.

Mudde, Cas. 2004. "The Populist Zeitgeist." *Government and Opposition* 39(4):542–563.

Mudde, Cas. 2007. *Populist Radical Right Parties in Europe*. Cambridge: Cambridge University Press.

Mudde, Cas. 2016. *Populist Radical Right Parties in Europe Today. Transformations of Populism in Europe and the Americas: History and Recent Tendencies*. London: Bloomsbury Academic.

Mudge, S. L. 2018. *Leftism Reinvented: Western Parties from Socialism to Neoliberalism*. Cambridge, MA: Harvard University Press.

Müller, J. W. 2014. "The People Must Be Extracted from within the People." *Constellations* 21(4):483–493.

Myant, Martin. 2010. "Trade Unions in the Czech Republic." Report 115 of the European Trade Union Institute, Brussels.

Myant, Martin, and Jan Drahokoupil. 2012. "International Integration, Varieties of Capitalism and Resilience to Crisis in Transition Economies." *Europe-Asia Studies* 64(1):1–33.

Myant, M., J. Drahokoupil, and I. Lesay. 2013. "The Political Economy of Crisis Management in East-Central European Countries." *Europe-Asia Studies* 65(3):383–410.

Myant, M., B. Slocock, and S. Smith. 2000. "Tripartism in the Czech and Slovak Republics." *Europe-Asia Studies* 52(4):723–739.

Nachtwey, Oliver. 2013. "Market Social Democracy: The Transformation of the SPD up to 2007." *German Politics* 22:235–252.

Navracsics, Tibor. 1997. "A Missing Debate? Hungary and the European Union." Working Paper 1997/21, Brighton: SEI.

Nikolenyi, Csaba. 2004. "Strategic Co-ordination in the 2002 Hungarian Election." *Europe-Asia Studies* 56(7):1041–1058.

Nissan, E., and G. Carter. 2005. "Decomposition of Regional Metropolitan and Nonmetropolitan Income Inequality." *Journal of Economics and Finance* 29(1):73–84.

Norris, Pippa. 2005. *Radical Right: Voters and Parties in the Electoral Market*. Cambridge: Cambridge University Press.

Norris, P., and R. Inglehart. 2019. *Cultural Backlash: Trump, Brexit, and Authoritarian Populism*. Cambridge: Cambridge University Press.

O'Dwyer, Conor. 2006. *Runaway State-Building: Patronage Politics and Democratic Development*. Baltimore, MD: Johns Hopkins University Press.

O'Dwyer, C., and D. Kovalčík. 2007. "And the Last Shall Be First: Party System Institutionalization and Second-Generation Economic Reform in Postcommunist Europe." *Studies in Comparative International Development* 41(4):3–26.

Oesch, Daniel. 2006a. "Coming to Grips with a Changing Class Structure." *International Sociology*, 21(2):263–288.

Oesch, Daniel. 2006b. *Redrawing the Class Map: Stratification and Institutions in Britain, Germany, Sweden and Switzerland*. Basingstoke: Palgrave Macmillan.

Oesch, Daniel. 2008. "Explaining Workers' Support for Right-Wing Populist Parties in Western Europe: Evidence from Austria, Belgium, France, Norway, and Switzerland."

*International Political Science Review/Revue internationale de science politique* 29(3):349–373.

Oesch, Daniel. 2012. "The Class Basis of the Cleavage between the New Left and the Radical Right: An Analysis for Austria, Denmark, Norway and Switzerland." In *Class Politics and the Radical Right*, edited by J. Rydren, 31–51. London: Routledge.

Oesch, D., and L. Rennwald. 2018. "Electoral Competition in Europe's New Tripolar Political Space: Class Voting for the Left, Centre-Right and Radical Right." *European Journal of Political Research* 57(4):783–807.

Offe, Claus, and Pierre Adler. 1991. "Capitalism by Democratic Design? Democratic Theory Facing the Triple Transition in East Central Europe." *Social Research* 58(4):865–892.

O'Grady, Tom. 2019. "Careerists versus Coal-Miners: Welfare Reforms and the Substantive Representation of Social Groups in the British Labour Party." *Comparative Political Studies* 52(4):544–578.

Olsen, Jonathan. 2018. "The Left Party and the AfD: Populist Competitors in Eastern Germany." *German Politics and Society* 36(1):70–83.

Oltay, E. 1994a. "The Former Communists' Election Victory in Hungary." *Radio Free Europe/Radio Liberty* 23:1–6.

Oltay, E. 1994b. "Hungary: Political Fragmentation and Economic Recession." *Radio Free Europe/Radio Liberty* 25:76–80.

Orenstein, M. A. 1998. "A Genealogy of Communist Successor Parties in East Central Europe and the Determinants of Their Success." *East European Politics and Societies* 12(3):472–499.

Orenstein, M. A. 2000. *Out of the Red: Building Capitalism and Democracy in Post-Communist Europe*. Ann Arbor: University of Michigan Press.

Orenstein, M. A. 2008. "Out-liberalizing the EU: Pension Privatization in Central and Eastern Europe." *Journal of European Public Policy* 15(6):899–917.

Orenstein, M. A. 2009. "What Happened in East European (Political) Economies? A Balance Sheet for Neoliberal Reform." *East European Politics and Societies* 23(4):479–490.

Orenstein, M. 2013a. "Reassessing the Neo-liberal Development Model in Central and Eastern Europe." In *Resilient Liberalism in Europe's Political Economy*, edited by V. Schmidt and M. Thatcher, 374–402. Cambridge: Cambridge University Press.

Orenstein, M. 2013b. "Recovering from Transition in Eastern Europe: Neoliberal Reforms in Retrospect." In *Developments in Central and East European Politics 5*, edited by S. White, P. G. Lewis, and J. Batt, 228–240. Durham, NC: Duke University Press.

Orenstein, M. A. 2019. "Poland's Leaders Are the Better Trumps." *Foreign Policy*, August 30. https://foreignpolicy.com/2019/08/30/polands-leaders-are-the-better-trumps/.

Orenstein, M. A., and Bojan Bugarič. 2019. "Economic Causes (and Policies) of Populism in Central and East European Countries." Paper presented at the European Union Studies Association, Denver, May 9–11.

Orenstein, M. A., and Bojan Bugarič. 2020. "Work, Family, Fatherland: The Political Economy of Populism in Central and Eastern Europe." *Journal of European Public Policy* 29(2):1–20.

Oskarson, M. 2005. "Social Structure and Party Choice." In *The European Voter: A Comparative Study of Modern Democracies*, edited by J. Thomassen, 84–105. Oxford: Oxford University Press.

Oskarson, M., and M. Demker. 2013. "Another Kind of Class Voting: The Working-Class Sympathy for Sweden Democrats." In *Class Politics and the Radical Right*, edited by J. Rydgren, 91–106. Abingdon: Routledge.

Oskarson, M., and M. Demker. 2015. "Room for Realignment: The Working-Class Sympathy for Sweden Democrats." *Government and Opposition* 50(4):629–651.

Ost, David. 2010. "The Radical Right in Poland: Rationality of the Irrational." In *Radical Right in Central and Eastern Europe since 1989*, edited by Sabrina P. Ramet, 85–107. University Park: Penn State Press.

Ost, David. 1993. "The Politics of Interest in Post-communist East Europe." *Theory and Society* 22(4):453–485.

Ost, David. 1998. "Can Unions Survive Communism?" *Dissent*, Winter.

Ost, David. 2000. "Illusory Corporatism in Eastern Europe: Neoliberal Tripartism and Postcommunist Class Identities." *Politics & Society* 28(4):503–530.

Ost, David. 2002. "The Weakness of Strong Social Movements: Models of Unionism in the East European Context." *European Journal of Industrial Relations* 8(1):33–51.

Ost, David. 2006. *The Defeat of Solidarity: Anger and Politics in Postcommunist Europe.* Ithaca, NY: Cornell University Press.

Ost, David. 2009. "The End of Postcommunism. Trade Unions in Eastern Europe's Future." *East European Politics and Societies* 23(1):13–33.

Ost, David. 2015a. "Class after Communism: Introduction to the Special Issue." *East European Politics and Societies* 29(3):543–564.

Ost, David. 2015b. "Stuck in the Past and the Future: Class Analysis in Postcommunist Poland." *East European Politics and Societies* 29(3):610–624.

Ost, David. 2018. "Workers and the Radical Right in Poland." *International Labor and Working-Class History* 93:113–124.

Ottaway, David B. 1994. "Socialists Win in Hungary: Analysts Cite 'Nostalgia for Communist Era.'" *Washington Post*, May 9.

Otjes, S., G. Ivaldi, A. R. Jupskås, and O. Mazzoleni. 2018. "It's Not Economic Interventionism, Stupid! Reassessing the Political Economy of Radical Right-Wing Populist Parties." *Swiss Political Science Review* 24(3):270–290.

Owens, L. A., and D. S. Pedulla. 2014. "Material Welfare and Changing Political Preferences: The Case of Support for Redistributive Social Policies." *Social Forces* 92(3):1087–1113.

Padgett, Stephen. 2001. "The German Volkspartei and the Career of the Catch-all Concept." *German Politics* 10(2):51–72.

Pankowski, Rafal. 2010. *The Populist Radical Right in Poland: The Patriots.* Abingdon: Routledge.

Pap, András. 2017. *Democratic Decline in Hungary: Law and Society in an Illiberal Democracy.* London: Routledge.

Paradowska, Janina, Mariusz Janicki, and Radoslaw Markowski. 1993. "Krajobraz po wyborach: Mapa mandatow." *Polityka*, October 2, 14–15.

Patocka, M., and M. Dubiel. 2017. "Minimum Hourly Wage for Service Providers in Poland. *Global Workplace Insider*, June 28. https://www.globalworkplaceinsider.com/2017/07/minimum-hourly-wage-for-service-providers-in-poland/.

Pechova, Andrea. 2012. "Legitimising Discourses in the Framework of European Integration: The Politics of Euro Adoption in the Czech Republic and Slovakia." *Review of International Political Economy* 19(5):779–807.

Phelan, Craig. 2007. *Trade Union Revitalisation: Trends and Prospects in 34 Countries.* 18th edition. Oxford: Peter Lang.

Phillips, Leigh. 2010. "A Far-Right for the Facebook Generation: The Rise and Rise of Jobbik." *EU Observer,* April 19. https://euobserver.com/political/29866.

Pienkos, D. E. 2003. "Consensus and Division over Poland's Entry into the European Union." *East European Quarterly* 37(4):461.

Piętka K. 2007 "Social Protection in Poland." Background paper prepared for the EU8 Social Inclusion Study, Centre for Social and Economic Research, Warsaw.

Piketty, Thomas. 2014. *Capital in the Twenty-first Century.* Cambridge, MA: Havard Press University.

Piotrowski, M. A., and A. R. Rachwald. 2001. "Poland: Returning to Europe." In *Enlarging NATO: The National Debates,* edited by G. Mattox and A. Rachwald, 111–128. Boulder, CO: Lynne Rienner.

Pirro, Andrea. 2015. *The Populist Radical Right in Central and Eastern Europe: Ideology, Impact, and Electoral Performance.* Abingdon: Routledge.

PiS. 2006. "Solidarne państwo, solidarnych obywateli: 365 Dni Realizacji Programu." http://old.pis.org.pl/download.php?g=mmedia&f=365_dni_realizacji_programu_soli darnego_panstwa.pdf.

Poguntke, Thomas. 2002. *Parties without Firm Social Roots? Party Organisational Linkage.* Keele European Parties Research Unit.

Polacko, Matthew. 2022. "The Rightward Shift and Electoral Decline of Social Democratic Parties under Increasing Inequality." *West European Politics* 45(4):665–692.

Polanyi, Karl. 1944. *The Great Transformation: The Political and Economic Origins of Our Time.* New York: Farrar & Rinehart.

Polk, A., and Johannes Karreth. 2020. "After the Third Way: Voter Responses to Social Democratic Ideological Moderation." Unpublished manuscript.

Polk, Jonathan, Jan Rovny, Ryan Bakker, Erica Edwards, Liesbet Hooghe, Seth Jolly, Jelle Koedam, Filip Kostelka, Gary Marks, Gijs Schumacher, Marco Steenbergen, Milada Vachudova, and Marko Zilovic. 2017. "Explaining the Salience of Anti-Elitism and Reducing Political Corruption for Political Parties in Europe with the 2014 Chapel Hill Expert Survey Data." *Research & Politics* 4(1):1–9.

Polskie Radio. 2015. "Beata Szydło: PiS Wypełni Postulaty Solidarności." http://www. polskieradio.pl/5/3/Artykul/1497260,Beata-Szydlo-PiS-wypelni-postulaty-Solid arnosci.

Pop-Eleches, Grigore. 2010. "Throwing Out the Bums: Protest Voting and Unorthodox Parties after Communism." *World Politics* 62(2):221–260.

Pop-Eleches, Grigore, and Joshua A. Tucker. 2010. "After the Party: Legacies and Left-Right Distinctions in Post-Communist Countries." Paper prepared for presentation at the 2010 Annual Meeting of the American Political Science Association, Washington, D.C., September 2–5.

Pop-Eleches, Grigore, and J. A. Tucker. 2014. "Communist Socialization and Post-Communist Economic and Political Attitudes." *Electoral Studies* 33:77–89.

Pop-Eleches, Grigore, and J. A. Tucker. 2017. *Communism's Shadow: Historical Legacies and Contemporary Political Attitudes.* Princeton, NJ: Princeton University Press.

Potucek, M., and I. Radicova. 1997. "Splitting the Welfare State: The Czech and Slovak Cases." *Social Research* 64(4):1549–1587.

Powell, Eleanor Neff, and Joshua A. Tucker. 2014. "Revisiting Electoral Volatility in Post-Communist Countries: New Data, New Results, and New Approaches." *British Journal of Political Science* 44:123–147.

Pridham, Geoffrey. 2005. *Designing Democracy: EU Enlargement and Regime Change in Post-communist Europe*. New York: Palgrave Macmillan.

Prokešová, Alžbeta. 2016. *Explaining Electoral Success of Anti-Establishment Parties: The Case of ANO 2011*. Brno[cit. August 17, 2023]. Diplomová práce. Masarykova univerzita, Fakulta sociálních studií. Vedoucí práce doc. Mgr. et Mgr. Vlastimil Havlík, Ph.D.

Prokop, Jakub. 2015. "Plany nowego rządu Beaty Szydło a oczekiwania związkowców: Są różnice." *pulsHR*, November 19. http://www.pulshr.pl/zwiazki-zawodowe/planynow ego-rzadu-beaty-szydlo-a-oczekiwania-zwiazkowcow-sa-roznice,29782.html.

Przeworski, A., and J. D. Sprague. 1986. *Paper Stones: A History of Electoral Socialism*. Chicago: University of Chicago Press.

Pytlas, Bartek. 2015. *Radical Right Parties in Central and Eastern Europe: Mainstream Party Competition and Electoral Fortune*. Abingdon: Routledge.

Pytlas, Bartek. 2020. "From Mainstream to Power: The Law and Justice Party in Poland." In *Aufstand der Außenseiter: Die Herausforderung der europäischen Politik durch den neuen Populismus*, edited by F. Decker, B. Henningsen, M. Lewandowsky, and P. Adorf, 401–414. Baden-Baden: Nomos.

Pytlas, Bartek., Lise Esther Herman, and James Muldoon. 2018. "Populist Radical Right Mainstreaming and Challenges to Democracy in an Enlarged Europe." *Trumping the Mainstream: The Conquest of Democratic Politics by the Populist Radical Right*, Oxon: Routledge.

Racz, Barnabas. 1993. "The Socialist-Left Opposition in Post-communist Hungary." *Europe-Asia Studies* 45(4):647–670.

Racz, Barnabas. 2000. "The Hungarian Socialists in Opposition: Stagnation or Renaissance." *Europe-Asia Studies* 52(2):319–347.

Rae, Gavin. 2017. "Non-Voting and Support for Left Parties in Poland." *Transform Europe!* https://www.transform-network.net/el/anazitisi/overview/article/yearbook-2017/ non-voting-and-support-for-left-parties-in-poland/.

Rehm, Philipp. 2009. "Risks and Redistribution: An Individual-Level Analysis." *Comparative Political Studies* 42(7):855–881.

Rennwald, Line. 2020. *Social Democratic Parties and the Working Class: New Voting Patterns*. Cham, Switzerland: Springer Nature, Palgrave Macmillan.

Rennwald, L., and Geoffrey Evans. 2014. "When Supply Creates Demand: Social Democratic Party Strategies and the Evolution of Class Voting." *West European Politics* 37:5.

Reuters. 2010. "Hungary Seeks to Curb Court Power over State Finances." *Reuters News*, October 26. https://www.reuters.com/article/hungary-pensions-association/upd ate-2-hungary-seeks-to-curb-court-power-over-state-finances-idUSLDE69P1M52 0101026.

Riker, William H. 1986. *The Art of Political Manipulation*. Vol. 587. New Haven, CT: Yale University Press.

Roberts, K. M. 2013. "Market Reform, Programmatic (De)alignment, and Party System Stability in Latin America." *Comparative Political Studies* 46(11):1422–1452.

Roberts, K. M. 2015. "Populism, Political Mobilizations, and Crises of Political Representation." In *The Promise and Perils of Populism: Global Perspectives*, edited by C. de la Torre, 140–158. Lexington: University Press of Kentucky.

Roberts, K. M. 2017a. "Party Politics in Hard Times: Comparative Perspectives on the European and Latin American Economic Crises." *European Journal of Political Research* 56(2):218–233.

Roberts, K. M. 2017b. "State of the Field: Party Politics in Hard Times: Comparative Perspectives on the European and Latin American Economic Crises. *European Journal of Political Research* 56(2):218–233.

Roberts, K. M. 2017c. "Varieties of Capitalism and Subtypes of Populism: The Structural Foundations of Political Divergence in Northern and Southern Europe." Lunch Seminar Series Paper, SNS, Florence, November 17.

Roberts, Kenneth M. 2019a. "Bipolar Disorders: Varieties of Capitalism and Populist Out-Flanking on the Left and Right." *Polity* 51:641–653.

Roberts, K. M. 2019b. "Crises of Representation and Populist Challenges to Liberal Democracy." *Chinese Political Science Review* 4(2):188–199.

Robertson, Graeme B. 2004. "Leading Labor: Unions, Politics, and Protest in New Democracies." *Comparative Politics* 36(3):253–272.

Robinson, Anthony. 1997. "Socialism of Left and Right." *Financial Times Supplement on Poland,* March 26.

Rodrik, Dani. 2018. "Populism and the Economics of Globalization." *Journal of International Business Policy* 1:12–33.

Rodrik, Dani. 2021. "Why Does Globalization Fuel Populism? Economics, Culture, and the Rise of Right-Wing Populism." *Annual Review of Economics* 13:133–170.

Roháč, Dalibor. 2013. "What Are the Lessons from Post-Communist Transitions?" *Economic Affairs* 33:65–77.

Rohrschneider, Robert, and Stephen Whitefield. 2004. "Support for Foreign Ownership in Eastern Europe: Economic Interests, Ideological Commitments and International Context." *Comparative Political Studies* 37(3):313–339.

Rohrschneider, R., and S. Whitefield. 2009. "Understanding Cleavages in Party Systems: Issue Position and Issue Salience in 13 Post-communist Democracies." *Comparative Political Studies* 42(2):280–313.

Rooduijn, Matthijs. 2015. "The Rise of the Populist Radical Right in Western Europe." *European View* 14(1):3–11.

Rooduijn, M., S. Van Kessel, C. Froio, A. Pirro, S. De Lange, D. Halikiopoulou, P. Lewis, C. Mudde, and P. Taggart. 2019. "The PopuList: An Overview of Populist, Far Right, Far Left and Eurosceptic Parties in Europe." www.popu-list.org.

Rose, R., and W. Mishler. 1998. "Negative and Positive Party Identification in Post-communist Countries." *Electoral Studies* 17(2):217–234.

Rosenau, Pauline Vaillancourt. 2003. *The Competition Paradigm: America's Romance with Conflict, Contest, and Commerce.* Lanham, MD: Rowman & Littlefield.

Ross, Fiona. 2000. "Beyond Left and Right: The New Partisan Politics of Welfare." *Governance* 13(2):155–183.

Röth, L., A. Afonso, and D. C. Spies. 2018. "The Impact of Populist Radical Right Parties on Socio-economic Policies." *European Political Science Review* 10(3):325–350.

Rovny, Jan. 2014. "The Other 'Other': Party Responses to Immigration in Eastern Europe." *Comparative European Politics* 12(6):637–662.

Rovny, Jan. 2015. "Party Competition Structure in Eastern Europe: Aggregate Uniformity versus Idiosyncratic Diversity?" *East European Politics and Societies* 29(1):40–60.

Rovny, Jan. 2018. "What Happened to Europe's Left?" EUROPP—European Politics and Policy at LSE, February 20. https://www.socialeurope.eu/happened-europes-left.

Rovny, Jan. 2021. "Populism Punished: The 2021 Czech Parliamentary Election." *LSE European Politics and Policy (EUROPP) Blog.* https://blogs.lse.ac.uk/europpblog/2021/10/11/populism-punished-the-2021-czech-parliamentary-election/.

Rovny, J., and J. Polk. 2017. "Stepping in the Same River Twice: Stability amidst Change in Eastern European Party Competition." *European Journal of Political Research* 56(1):188–198.

Rovny, J., and J. Polk. 2020. "Still Blurry? Economic Salience, Position and Voting for Radical Right Parties in Western Europe." *European Journal of Political Research* 59(2):248–268.

Rupnik, Jacques. 2007. "Is East-Central Europe Backsliding? From Democracy Fatigue to Populist Backlash." *Journal of Democracy* 18(4):17–25.

Rupnik, Jacques. 2018. "Explaining Eastern Europe: The Crisis of Liberalism." *Journal of Democracy* 29(3):24–38.

Rybář, Marek. 2006. "The 2006 Parliamentary Election and Its Impact on Party Political Scene in Slovakia." Unpublished manuscript. http://ispo.fss.muni.cz/uploads/2downl oad/v4/v4-rybar.pdf.

Rybář, M., and K. Deegan-Krause. 2008. "Slovakia's Communist Successor Parties in Comparative Perspective." *Communist and Post-Communist Studies* 41(4):497–519.

Rydgren, Jens. 2007. "The Sociology of the Radical Right." *Annual Review of Sociology* 33:241–262.

Rydgren, Jens. 2008. "Immigration Sceptics, Xenophobes or Racists? Radical Right-Wing Voting in Six West European Countries." *European Journal of Political Research* 47(6):737–765.

Rydgren, Jens. 2013. *Class Politics and the Radical Right.* London: Routledge.

Ryner, Magnus. 2012. "US Power and the Crisis of Social Democracy in Europe's Second Project of Integration." In *European Regionalism and the Left*, edited by G. Strange and O. Worth, 21–38. Manchester: Manchester University Press.

Saarts, Tonis. 2015. "The 'Third Revolution' and the Formation of Cleavages in Central and Eastern Europe: Some Conceptual and Theoretical Innovations." Paper presented at the ECPR Joint Sessions, Warsaw, March 29–April 4.

Safran, William. 2009. "The Catch-All Party Revisited: Reflections of a Kirchheimer Student." *Party Politics* 15(5):543–554.

Sass, Magdolna, and Gábor Hunya. 2014. "Escaping to the East? Relocation of Business Activities to and from Hungary, 2003–2011." IEHAS Discussion Papers, No. MT-DP-2014/7, ISBN 978-615-5447-16-7, Hungarian Academy of Sciences, Institute of Economics, Centre for Economic and Regional Studies, Budapest. https://www.econs tor.eu/bitstream/10419/108341/1/MTDP1407.pdf.

Scheiring, Gábor. 2020a. "Left Behind in the Hungarian Rustbelt: The Cultural Political Economy of Working-Class Neo-Nationalism." *Sociology* 54(6):1159–1177.

Scheiring, Gábor. 2020b. *The Retreat of Liberal Democracy: Authoritarian Capitalism and the Accumulative State in Hungary.* Cham, Switzerland: Palgrave Macmillan.

Scheiring, G., and K. Szombati. 2020. "From Neoliberal Disembedding to Authoritarian Re-embedding: The Making of Illiberal Hegemony in Hungary." *International Sociology* 35(6):721–738.

Schiemann, John W. 2005. *The Politics of Pact-Making: Hungary's Negotiated Transition to Democracy in Comparative Perspective*. New York: Springer.

Schimmelfennig, F., and U. Sedelmeier, eds. 2005. *The Europeanization of Central and Eastern Europe*. Ithaca, NY: Cornell University Press.

Schmidt-Catran, A. W., and M. Fairbrother. 2016. "The Random Effects in Multilevel Models: Getting Them Wrong and Getting Them Right." *European Sociological Review* 32(1):23–38.

Schultheis, Emily. 2018. "How Hungary's Far-Right Extremists Became Warm and Fuzzy." *Foreign Policy*, blog, April 6. https://foreignpolicy.com/2018/04/06/how-hungarys-far-right-extremists-became-warm-and-fuzzy/.

Schumacher, G., and K. van Kersbergen. 2016. "Do Mainstream Parties Adapt to the Welfare Chauvinism of Populist Parties?" *Party Politics* 22(3):300–312.

Schwander, H., and P. Manow. 2017. "'Modernize and Die'? German Social Democracy and the Electoral Consequences of the Agenda 2010." *Socio-Economic Review* 15:117–134.

Schwartz, S. H. 1999. "A Theory of Cultural Values and Some Implications for Work." *Applied Psychology* 48(1):23–47.

Scoggins, Bermond. 2022. "Identity Politics or Economics? Explaining Voter Support for Hungary's Illiberal FIDESZ." *East European Politics and Societies* 36(1):3–28.

Sedelmeier, Ulrich. 2008. "After Conditionality: Post-accession Compliance with EU Law in East Central Europe." *Journal of European Public Policy* 15(6):806–825.

Sengoku, Manabu. 2018. "2015 Parliamentary Election in Poland: Does the Migrant/Refugee Issue Matter?" *Journal of the Graduate School of Letters* 13:35–47.

Shields, Stuart. 2007. "From Socialist Solidarity to Neo-Populist Neoliberalisation? The Paradoxes of Poland's Post-communist Transition." *Capital & Class* 31(3):159–178.

Shields, Stuart. 2012. "Opposing Neoliberalism? Poland's Renewed Populism and Postcommunist Transition." *Third World Quarterly* 33(2):359–381.

Sides, John, and Jack Citrin. 2007. "European Opinion about Immigration: The Role of Identities, Interests, and Information." *British Journal of Political Science* 37:477–504.

Siedler, Thomas, and Bettina Sonnenberg. 2010. "Experiments, Surveys and the Use of Representative Samples as Reference Data." Working Paper Series of the German Council for Social and Economic Data 146, German Council for Social and Economic Data (RatSWD), Berlin.

Sikk, Allan. 2012. "Newness as a Winning Formula for New Political Parties." *Party Politics* 18(4):465–486.

Sil, Rudra. 2017. "The Battle over Flexibilization in Post-communist Transitions: Labor Politics in Poland and the Czech Republic, 1989–2010." *Journal of Industrial Relations* 59(4):420–443.

Singer, Matthew M. 2013. "The Global Economic Crisis and Domestic Political Agendas." *Electoral Studies* 32(3):404–410.

Sitter, Nick. 2002. "Cleavages, Party Strategy, and Party System Change in Europe, East and West." *Perspectives on European Politics and Society* 3(3):425–451.

Sitter, Nick, and Agnes Batory. 2006. "Europe and the Hungarian Elections of April 2006." Election Briefing 28, Sussex European Institute.

SLD. 1999. "Manifest programowy SLD: Nowy wiek—Nowy Sojusz Lewicy Demokratycznej." Socjaldemokratyczny program dla Polski, Warsaw.

Słomczyński, K. M., and G. Shabad. 1996. "Systemic Transformation and the Salience of Class Structure in East Central Europe." *East European Politics and Societies* 11(1):155–189.

Smilov, D., and I. Krastev. 2008. "The Rise of Populism in Eastern Europe: Policy Paper." In *Populist Politics and Liberal Democracy in Central and Eastern Europe*, edited by Mesežnikov, Grigorij, Oľga Gyárfášová, and Daniel Smilov, 7–13. IVO (IPA) working paper series, Bratislava.

Smith, M. L., and P. Matějů. 2011. "Restratifikace české politiky: Vývoj třídně podmíněného volebního chování v České republice v letech 1992–2010." *Sociologický časopis* 47(1):33–59.

Somer-Topcu, Z., M. Tavits, and M. Baumann. 2020. "Does Party Rhetoric Affect Voter Perceptions of Party Positions?" *Electoral Studies* 65:1–10.

Snegovaya, Maria. 2018a. "The Economic Origins of Populist Support." *The American Interest*, February 22. https://www.the-american-interest.com/2018/02/22/economic-origins-populist-support.

Snegovaya, Maria. 2018b. "Ex-Communist Party Choices and the Electoral Success of the Radical Right in Central and Eastern Europe." Doctoral diss., Columbia University.

Snegovaya, Maria. 2020a. "Different Strokes for Different Folks: Who Votes for Technocratic Parties?" *Politics and Governance* 8(4):556–567.

Snegovaya, Maria. 2020b. "Voice or Exit? Political Corruption and Voting Intentions in Hungary." *Democratization* 27(7):1162–1182.

Snegovaya, Maria. 2022a. "Fellow Travelers or Trojan Horses? Similarities across Pro-Russian Parties' Electorates in Europe." *Party Politics* 28(3):409–418.

Snegovaya, Maria. 2022b. "How Ex-Communist Left Parties Reformed and Lost." *West European Politics* 45(4):716–743.

Sniderman, Paul M., Louk Hagendoorn, and Markus Prior. 2004. "Predisposing Factors and Situational Triggers: Exclusionary Reactions to Immigrant Minorities." *American Political Science Review* 98(1):35–49.

Spies, Dennis. 2013. "Explaining Working-Class Support for Extreme Right Parties: A Party Competition Approach." *Acta Politica* 48:296–325.

Spies, D., and T. Franzmann. 2011. "A Two-Dimensional Approach to the Political Opportunity Structure of Extreme Right Parties in Western Europe." *West European Politics* 34(5):1044–1069.

Standing, Guy. 2014. *A Precariat Charter: From Denizens to Citizens*. London: Bloomsbury Academic.

Stanley, Ben. 2011. "Populism, Nationalism, or National Populism? An Analysis of Slovak Voting Behaviour at the 2010 Parliamentary Election." *Communist and Post-Communist Studies* 44(4):257–270.

Stanley, Ben. 2016. "Confrontation by Default and Confrontation by Design: Strategic and Institutional Responses to Poland's Populist Coalition Government." *Democratization* 23(2):263–282.

Stefanovic, Djordje, and Geoffrey Evans. 2019. "Multiple Winning Formulae? Far Right Voters and Parties in Eastern Europe." *Europe-Asia Studies* 71(9):1443–1473.

Stegmaier, M., and M. S. Lewis-Beck. 2011. "Shocks and Oscillations: The Political Economy of Hungary." *Electoral Studies* 30(3):462–467.

Stegmaier, Mary, and Klára Vlachová. 2009. "The Endurance of the Czech Communist Party." *Politics and Policy* 37(4):799–820.

Stockemer, Daniel. 2017. "The FN Voters under Jean-Marie Le Pen and Marine Le Pen." In *The Front National in France*, 79–91. Cham, Switzerland: Springer.

Stockemer, D., and M. Barisione. 2017. "The 'New' Discourse of the Front National under Marine Le Pen: A Slight Change with a Big Impact." *European Journal of Communication* 32(2):100–115.

Stockemer, Daniel, Daphne Halikiopoulou, and Tim Vlandas. 2020 "'Birds of a Feather'? Assessing the Prevalence of Anti-Immigration Attitudes among the Far-Right Electorate." *Journal of Ethnic and Migration Studies* 47(15):3409–3436.

Stojarová, Vera. 2018. "Populist, Radical and Extremist Political Parties in Visegrad Countries vis à vis the Migration Crisis: In the Name of the People and the Nation in Central Europe." *Open Political Science* 1(1):32–45.

Stolarik, Mark. 2016. *The Czech and Slovak Republics: Twenty Years of Independence, 1993–2013*. Budapest: Central European University Press.

Stone, Randall W. 2002. *Lending Credibility: The International Monetary Fund and the Post-Communist Transition*. Princeton, NJ: Princeton University Szilagyi Press.

Stoyanov, D., and P. Kostadinova. 2021. "Bulgarian Political Parties and European Integration: From Anticommunism to Euroscepticism." *European Politics and Society* 22(2):222–236.

Strapáčová, M., and V. Hloušek. 2018. "Anti-Islamism without Moslems: Cognitive Frames of Czech Antimigrant Politics." *Journal of Nationalism, Memory & Language Politics* 12(1):1–30.

Strmiska, Maxmilián. 2002. "The Communist Party of Bohemia and Moravia: A Post-Communist Socialist or a Neo-Communist Party?" *German Policy Studies/Politik Feldanalyse* 2:220–240.

Strzelecki, Marek, and David McQuaid. 2003. "Poland's Miller Floats Reform after EU Referendum Passes." *Wall Street Journal*, June 10. https://www.wsj.com/articles/SB105 518763139559300.

Suchánek, Jonáš, and Jiří Hasman. 2022. "Nativist with(out) a Cause: A Geographical Analysis of the Populist Radical Right in the 2017 and 2021 Czech Parliamentary Elections." *Territory, Politics, Governance*:1–22. https://www.tandfonline.com/doi/full/10.1080/21622671.2022.2150287.

Svitych, Alexander. 2021. "Voting for Jobbik and the Front National: Nostalgic, Deprived and Status-Frustrated." *European Review of International Studies* 8(1):49–76.

Swank, D., and H.-G. Betz. 2003. "Globalization, the Welfare State and Right-Wing Populism in Western Europe." *Socio-economic Review* 1:215–245.

Szanyi, Miklos. 2016. "The Emergence of Patronage State in Central Europe: The Case of FDI-Related Policies in Hungary." IWE Working Papers 222, Institute for World Economics, Budapest.

Szczerbiak, Aleks. 2002b. "The Political Context of EU Accession in Poland." Briefing Paper, APER, London.

Szczerbiak, Aleks. 2003. "Old and New Divisions in Polish Politics: Polish Parties' Electoral Strategies and Bases of Support." *Europe-Asia Studies* 55(5):729–746.

Szczerbiak, Aleks. 2004. "The Polish Centre-Right's (Last?) Best Hope: The Rise and Fall of Solidarity Electoral Action." *Journal of Communist Studies and Transition Politics* 20(3):55–79.

Szczerbiak, Aleks. 2007. "'Social Poland' Defeats 'Liberal Poland'? The September–October 2005 Polish Parliamentary and Presidential Elections." *Journal of Communist Studies and Transition Politics* 23:203–232.

Szczerbiak, Aleks, and Monika Bil. 2009. "When in Doubt, (Re-)Turn to Domestic Politics? The (Non-)Impact of the EU on Party Politics in Poland." *Journal of Communist Studies and Transition Politics* 25(4):447–467.

Szelenyi, I., E. Fodor, and E. Hanley. 1996. "Left Turn in Postcommunist Politics: Bringing Class Back In?" *East European Politics and Societies* 11(1):190–224.

Szilagyi, Z. 1995. "A Year of Economic Controversy." *Transition* 1(21):62–66.

Szombati, Kristof. 2018. *The Revolt of the Provinces: Anti-Gypsyism and Right-Wing Politics in Hungary*. Oxford: Berghahn.

Szymański, A. 2014. "Faces of Conservatism in Turkey and Poland: The Case of the AKP and PiS." In *Poland and Turkey in Europe—Social, Economic and Political Experiences and Challenges*, edited by Artur Adamczyk and Przemysław Dubel, 37–51. Centre for Europe, Publishing Programme of the Centre for Europe, Warsaw: University of Warsaw.

Taggart, Paul. 1998. "A Touchstone of Dissent: Euroscepticism in Contemporary Western European Party Systems." *European Journal of Political Research* 33(3):363–388.

Talbot, Colin. 2015. "Supply Side Deficiencies in Our Parties, Parliament, and Local Government Each Contribute to Our Democratic Malaise." *Democratic Audit Blog*, February 18. http://eprints.lse.ac.uk/63215/1/democraticaudit.com-Supply%20s ide%20deficiencies%20in%20our%20parties%20parliament%20and%20local%20gov ernment%20each%20contribute%20to%20our%20democr.pdf.

Tamas, Pal. 2011. "The Radical Right in Hungary: A Threat to Democracy." In *Is Europe on the "Right" Path*, edited by N. Langenbacher and B. Schellenberg, 221–241. Berlin: Friedrich-Ebert-Stiftung.

Tarrow, Sidney. 2010. "The Strategy of Paired Comparison: Toward a Theory of Practice." *Comparative Political Studies* 43(2):230–259.

Tavits, Margit. 2005. "The Development of Stable Party Support: Electoral Dynamics in Post-Communist Europe." *American Journal of Political Science* 49(2):283–298.

Tavits, Margit. 2013. *Post-Communist Democracies and Party Organization*. New York: Cambridge University Press.

Tavits, M., and N. Letki. 2009. "When Left Is Right: Party Ideology and Policy in Post-Communist Europe." *American Political Science Review* 103(4):634–647.

Temple, Michael. 2000. "New Labour's Third Way: Pragmatism and Governance." *British Journal of Politics & International Relations* 2(3):302–325.

Thorsen, Dag Einar. 2021. "Introduction: Social Democracy in the 21st Century." In *Social Democracy in the 21st Century*, edited by N. Brandal, Ø. Bratberg, and D. Thorsen, 1–14 Bingley: Emerald.

Tóka, Gábor. 2014. "Constitutional Principles and Electoral Democracy in Hungary." In *Constitution Building in Consolidated Democracies: A New Beginning or Decay of a Political System?*, edited by E. Bos and K. Pocza, 311–328. Baden-Baden: Nomos Verlag.

Toplišek, Alen. 2020. "The Political Economy of Populist Rule in Post-Crisis Europe: Hungary and Poland." *New Political Economy* 25(3):388–403.

Tóth, András. 1994. "Great Expectations—Fading Hopes: Trade Unions and System Change in Hungary." In *Trade Unions and Society in East-Central Europe*, edited by M. Waller and M. Myant, 85–97. London: Frank Cass.

Tóth, András. 2015. "Coming to the End of the Via Dolorosa? The Rise of Selective Economic Nationalism in Hungary." In *Divisive Integration: The Triumph of Failed Ideas in Europe—Revisited*, edited by S. Lehndorff, 233–251. Brussels: ETUI.

Tóth, András, László Neumann, and Hortenzia Hosszú. 2012. "Hungary's Full-Blown Malaise." In *A Triumph of Failed Ideas: European Models of Capitalism in the Crisis*, edited by S. Lehndorff, 137–153. Brussels: ETUI.

Trappmann, V. 2012. "Trade Unions in Poland." Report prepared for the Friedrich Ebert Stiftung, Bonn.

Traub, James. 2016. "The Party That Wants to Make Poland Great Again." *New York Times Magazine*, November 2. https://mobile.nytimes.com/2016/11/06/magazine/the-party-that-wants-to-make-poland-great-again.html.

Tucker, J. A. 2006. *Regional Economic Voting: Russia, Poland, Hungary, Slovakia, and the Czech Republic, 1990–1999*. Cambridge: Cambridge University Press.

Tucker, J. A., A. C. Pacek, and A. J. Berinsky. 2002. "Transitional Winners and Losers: Attitudes toward EU Membership in Post-communist Countries." *American Journal of Political Science* 46(3):557–571.

Vachudova, M. A. 2005. *Europe Undivided: Democracy, Leverage and Integration after Communism*. Oxford: Oxford University Press.

Vachudova, M. A. 2008a. "Center-Right Parties and Political Outcomes in East Central Europe." *Party Politics* 14(4):387–405.

Vachudova, M. A. 2008b. "Tempered by the EU? Political Parties and Party Systems before and after Accession." *Journal of European Public Policy* 15(6):861–879.

Vachudova, M. A. 2011. "Political Parties and Democratic Change in the Western Balkans: When Do External Actors Change Agendas?" In *APSA 2011 Annual Meeting Paper*. https://ssrn.com/abstract=1902039.

Vachudova, M. A. 2019. "From Competition to Polarization in Central Europe: How Populists Change Party Systems and the European Union." *Polity* 51(4):689–706.

Vachudova, M. A., and L. Hooghe. 2009. "Postcommunist Politics in a Magnetic Field: How Transition and EU Accession Structure Party Competition on European Integration." *Comparative European Politics* 7(2):179–212.

Vadlamannati, K. C. 2020. "Welfare Chauvinism? Refugee Flows and Electoral Support for Populist-Right Parties in Industrial Democracies." *Social Science Quarterly* 101(4): 1600–1626.

Van Biezen, Ingrid. 2003. *Political Parties in New Democracies: Party Organization in Southern and East-Central Europe*. New York: Palgrave Macmillan.

Van der Brug, W., and Meinderti Fennema. 2007. "Causes of Voting for the Radical Right." *International Journal of Public Opinion Research* 19(4):474–487.

Van der Brug, W., and J. Van Spanje. 2009. "Immigration, Europe and the 'New' Cultural Dimension." *European Journal of Political Research* 48(3):309–334.

Van der Waal, J., P. Achterberg, and D. Houtman. 2010. "'Some Are More Equal Than Others': Economic Egalitarianism and Welfare Chauvinism in the Netherlands." *Journal of European Social Policy* 20(4):350–363.

Van der Waal, J., and W. de Koster. 2017. "Populism and Support for Protectionism: The Relevance of Opposition to Trade Openness for Leftist and Rightist Populist Voting in the Netherlands." *Political Studies* 66(3):560–576.

Van Deth, Jan W., and Elinor Scarbrough, eds. 1995. *The Impact of Values*. Oxford: Oxford University Press.

Van Heerden, S., S. L. de Lange, W. van der Brug, and M. Fennema. 2014. "The Immigration and Integration Debate in the Netherlands: Discursive and Programmatic Reactions to the Rise of Anti-immigration Parties." *Journal of Ethnic and Migration Studies* 40(1):119–136.

Vanhuysse, Pieter. 2007. "Workers without Power: Agency, Legacies, and Labour Decline in East European Varieties of Capitalism." *Czech Sociological Review* 43(3):495–522.

Vanhuysse, P. 2009. "Power, Order and the Politics of Social Policy in Central and Eastern Europe." In *Post-communist Welfare Pathways,* edited by A. Carami and P. Vanhuysse, 53–70. London: Palgrave Macmillan.

Van Kessel, S. 2015. *Populist Parties in Europe: Agents of Discontent?* New York: Springer.

Van Spanje, J., and W. Van Der Brug. 2007. "The Party as Pariah: The Exclusion of Anti-immigration Parties and Its Effect on Their Ideological Positions." *West European Politics* 30(5):1022–1040.

Varga, Mihai. 2014. "Hungary's 'Anti-Capitalist' Far Right: Jobbik and the Hungarian Guard." *Nationalities Papers* 42(5):791–807.

Vegetti, Federico. 2019. "The Political Nature of Ideological Polarization: The Case of Hungary." *Annals of the American Academy of Political and Social Science* 681(1):78–96.

Vincensini, C. 2015. "Monetary and Fiscal Policy Conflicts in Central Europe: How Credibly Are Macro Policies Characterized in the Phase of Preparation for EMU?" In *Financial Markets and the Banking Sector,* 135–162. Routledge.

Vines, E., and D. Marsh. 2018. "Anti-politics: Beyond Supply-Side versus Demand-Side Explanations." *British Politics* 13(4):433–453.

Visnovitz, P., and E. K. Jenne. 2021. "Populist Argumentation in Foreign Policy: The Case of Hungary under Viktor Orbán, 2010–2020." *Comparative European Politics* 19(6):683–702.

Voda, P., and V. Havlík. 2021. "The Rise of Populists and Decline of Others: Explanation of Changes in Party Support in the Czech Republic." *Problems of Post-Communism* 68(4):279–291.

Volby. 2021. "Senioři rozhodují volby: Přilákat je mají hlavně vyšší důchody a levné." Idnes, October 6. https://www.idnes.cz/volby/volebni-program-seniori-volby.A21100 5_132320_domaci_knn.

Volford, Csilla. 2012. "Jobbik's Portrayal of MSZP (Hungarian Socialist Party)." Research Master's thesis, Queen's University.

Walter, Stefanie. 2017. "Globalization and the Demand-Side of Politics: How Globalization Shapes Labor Market Risk Perceptions and Policy Preferences." *Political Science Research and Methods* 5(1):55–80.

Waterbury, M. A. 2020. "Populist Nationalism and the Challenges of Divided Nationhood: The Politics of Migration, Mobility, and Demography in post-2010 Hungary." *East European Politics and Societies* 34(4):962–983.

Whiteley, P., M. Poletti, P. Webb, and T. Bale. 2019. "Oh Jeremy Corbyn! Why Did Labour Party Membership Soar after the 2015 General Election?" *British Journal of Politics and International Relations* 21(1):80–98.

Wilkin, Peter. 2016. *Hungary's Crisis of Democracy: The Road to Serfdom.* London: Lexington Books.

Williams, Kieran. 1997. *The Prague Spring and Its Aftermath: Czechoslovak Politics 1968– 1970.* Cambridge: Cambridge University Press.

Williams, K. 2000. "Introduction: What Was Meciarism?" In *Slovakia after Communism and Meciarism,* edited by K. Williams, 1–16. London: School of Slavonic and East European Studies Occasional Papers.

Wolchik, Sharon L., and Jane L. Curry. 2008. "Democracy, the Market, and the Return to Europe: From Communism to the European Union and NATO." In *Central and East*

*European Politics: From Communism to Democracy*, edited by Sharon L. Wolchik and Jane L. Curry, 3–32. New York: Rowman & Littlefield.

Wondreys, Jakub. 2021. "The 'Refugee Crisis' and the Transformation of the Far Right and the Political Mainstream: The Extreme Case of the Czech Republic." *East European Politics* 37(4):722–746.

Wurthmann, L. C., S. Marschall, V. Triga, and V. Manavopoulos. 2020. "Many Losers—One Winner? An Examination of Vote Switching to the AfD in the 2017 German Federal Election Using VAA Data." *Party Politics* 27(5):870–882.

Wysocka, Olga. 2009. "Populism in Poland: In/visible Exclusion." Institute for Human Sciences. http://www.iwm.at/publications/5-junior-visiting-fellows-conferences/vol-xxvi/populism-in-poland/.

Žiak, M. 1996. *Slovensko: Od komunizmu kam?* Bratislava: ARCHA.

Ziblatt, Daniel. 1998. "The Adaptation of Post-Communist Parties to Post-Communist East Central Europe: A Comparative Study of the East German and Hungarian Post-Communist Parties." *Communist and Post-Communist Studies* 31(2):119–137.

Zubek, Radoslaw. 2008. "Poland: From Pacesetter to Semi-permanent Outsider." *The Euro at Ten: Europeanization, Power, and Convergence* 10(September): 292–306.

Zumbrunnen, J., and A. Gangl. 2008. "Conflict, Fusion, or Coexistence? The Complexity of Contemporary American Conservatism." *Political Behavior* 30(2):199–221.

# Index

For the benefit of digital users, indexed terms that span two pages (e.g., 52–53) may, on occasion, appear on only one of those pages.

Tables and figures are indicated by *t* and *f* following the page number